Politics, Race, and Schools

Studies in Education/Politics
(Vol. 2)
Garland Reference Library of Social Science
(Vol. 989)

Studies in Education/Politics

Mark B. Ginsburg, Series Editor

The Politics of Educators' Work and Lives
edited by Mark B. Ginsburg

Politics, Race, and Schools
Racial Integration, 1954–1994
by Joseph Watras

Politics, Race, and Schools
Racial Integration, 1954–1994

Joseph Watras

GARLAND PUBLISHING, INC.
New York & London
1997

Library of Congress Cataloging-in-Publication Data

Watras, Joseph.
    Politics, race, and schools : racial integration, 1954–1994 /
Joseph Watras.
        p.   cm. — (Garland reference library of social science ;
vol. 989. Studies in education/politics ; vol. 2)
        Includes bibliographical references and index.
        ISBN 0-8153-1766-2
        1. School integration—Ohio—Dayton—History—Case studies.
2. Politics and education—Ohio—Dayton—History—Case studies.
3. School integration—United States—History.   4. Politics and education—United States—History.   I. Title.   II. Series: Garland reference
library of social science ; v. 989.   III. Series: Garland reference library
of social science. Studies in education/politics ; vol. 2.
    LC214.23.D29W38   1997
    370.19'342—dc20   96-24099
                                                                                    CIP

Cover photograph courtesy of the *Dayton Daily News.*

Printed on acid-free, 250-year-life paper
Manufactured in the United States of America

Contents

Series Editor's Introduction	vii
Introduction	xi

Part I: Federal Courts, School Desegregation, and Religion: The National Context

Chapter One
The Politics of Racial Desegregation — 3

Chapter Two
Private and Religious Schools — 49

Part II: Racial Desegregation in Dayton, Ohio: City Government, Schools, and Churches

Chapter Three
City and School Administration — 79

Chapter Four
Community Control and Racial Integration — 113

Chapter Five
School Board Elections and Racial Integration — 157

Chapter Six
Dayton Goes to Court — 181

Chapter Seven
Racial Desegregation and Dayton's Catholic Schools — 207

Chapter Eight
A Private School Sets a Good Example   241

Part III: Curriculum, Caring, and Social Reform

Chapter Nine
Curriculum Reforms and Racial Desegregation   261

Chapter Ten
The Politics of Caring   291

Chapter Eleven
Schools and Social Reform   321

Index   335

Series Editor's Introduction
Understanding and Struggling

"Take education out of politics!" "Education should not be a political football!" "Keep politics out of the schools!" "Educators should not be political!" These and similar warnings have been sounded at various times in a variety of societies. Such warnings, however, miss (or misconstrue) the point that education *is* political. Not only is education constituted by and constitutive of struggles over the distribution of symbolic and material resources, but education implies and confers structural and ideological power used to control the means of producing, reproducing, consuming, and accumulating symbolic and material resources (see Ginsburg 1995; Ginsburg and Lindsay 1995).

Political struggles about and through education occur in classrooms and nonformal education settings; school and university campuses; education systems; and local, national, and global communities. Different groups of students, educators, parents, business/industry owners, organized labor leaders, government and international organization officials, and other worker-citizens participate (actively or passively) in such political activity. These struggles not only shape educational policy and practice, they also are dialectically related to more general relations of power among social classes, racial/ethnic groups, gender groups, and nations. Thus, the politics of education and the political work accomplished through education are ways in which existing social relations are reproduced, legitimated, challenged, or transformed.

The "Studies in Education/Politics" series is designed to include books that examine how in different historical periods and in various local and national contexts education *is* political. The focus is on what groups are involved in political struggles in, through, and about education; what material and symbolic resources are of concern; how ideological power and structural power are implicated; and what consequences obtain for the people directly involved and for social relations more generally.

The purpose of this series, however, is not only to help educators and other people understand the nexus of education and politics. It is also concerned with facilitating their active involvement in the politics of and through education. Thus, the issue is not whether education should be taken out of politics, nor whether politics should be kept out of schools, nor whether educators should be apolitical. Rather the questions are toward what ends, by what means, and in whose interests should educators and other citizen/workers engage in political work in and about education.

This volume by Joseph Watras, the second book to appear in the Studies in Education/Politics series, makes an important contribution to our understanding of the politics of education, particularly with respect to race and race relations. Watras recounts the history of the struggles over segregating, desegregating, and resegregating schools in Dayton, Ohio. *Politics, Race, and Schools,* like similar studies of Norfolk (White 1992) and Richmond, Virginia (Pratt 1992), offers an in-depth analysis of intergroup (black/white, liberal/conservative, etc.) struggles in one locality in relation to what Wolters (1984) terms "the burden" of the 1954 U.S. Supreme Court decision, *Brown v Board of Education of Topeka, Kansas.* Watras goes beyond providing a sensitive, yet provocative portrayal of a local case study, however. He not only provides an excellent sketch of developments in other cities and nationally, but he also embeds his intriguing story of Dayton within the changing legal, political, ideological, and economic contexts in Dayton, the state of Ohio and the United States. Moreover, Watras' study of Dayton combines the more traditional focus on segregation and integration in public schools with careful attention to (de)segregation efforts in private schools, both religious and nonreligious.

One comes away from reading this volume with a greater understanding and appreciation of the complex political and ethical challenges faced by the citizens of Dayton and others who became (or should have become) involved in the struggle over the racial composition and the "quality" of schools. Such understanding and appreciation—as well as a commitment to become involved in similar struggles—is critically important today (and likely in the future).

As I am crafting this editor's introduction, the battle over segregation, desegregation, and resegregation has erupted again—if there ever was a cease-fire—in a variety of cities around the United States, including Pittsburgh, Pennsylvania, where I am currently working and living. As students in our nation attend increasingly racially segregated schools (Orfield 1993), maneuvering is occurring in all branches of the federal and state governments as well as at the level of local boards of education to unravel the remaining vestiges of policies and programs to promote desegregated education.

In the city of Pittsburgh, for example, a mostly white coalition of parents and local politicians are pushing for a major school redistricting plan that would emphasize "neighborhood schools," curtail busing for purposes of racial desegregation, and increase racial segregation among students. Ironically, perhaps, this plan was initially being pushed through on a fast track by a black member of the school board who had recently been elected as board president. In the context of Supreme Court decisions making it easier to "abort" school desegregation plans, with Congress and state legislators "retreating" on issues of support for racial equality (integration as well as affirmative action), it appeared as though the redistricting plan would be adopted without any real public debate in the spring of 1996 and implemented in September of that year. A statistically disproportionately black coalition—employing the slogan, "(Re)segregation is Not an Option," and with prominent organizational leadership role played by the local chapters of the Urban League and the NAACP—forced the board into a series of relatively well-attended and highly charged public hearings on the redistricting plan. Rallies and marches were held by both groups, and local media brought the issues (neighborhood schools, racial segregation, and quality education) to the broader community. As a consequence, on 30 April the Board approved a "compromise" plan that would phase in more neighborhood schools without reducing racial integration in schools, in part by increasing the number of racially balanced magnet schools and by only gradually reducing the busing after the first year of the plan's implementation in 1996–97 (Lee 1996). The critical reactions to the plan, particularly by the proponents of neighborhood schools, suggests that the controversy is not over, especially as the plan's cost may lead to increasing school taxes.

Regardless of how this situation develops, there was a significant feature of this struggle that relates directly to one of Watras' major conclusions. The initial salvos of those challenging the board's proposed redistricting plan did not highlight a principled commitment to integration or even desegregation. Much of what was said at the initial public hearing focused on how the redistricting plan would disrupt specific schools, programs, and groups of children's lives because of the changes proposed. In a way, both sides of the debate were making a similar argument: Don't move students around. Leave them where they are, with the difference being whether the "where" refers to "in their current schools" or "in their current neighborhoods." By the second public hearing, though, the opponents of the redistricting plan spoke more frequently and explicitly based on a principled commitment to racial integration; the slogan mentioned previously is one indicator of this. The importance of this stance is something that I learned from reading Watras' volume. I think his book will not only help others to understand "politics, race, and schools" in their own communities, but also inspire participation—on all sides of the issues—in shaping the quality and racial composition of "our" children's schools.

Mark B. Ginsburg
University of Pittsburgh

References

Ginsburg, M. (ed.) 1995. *The Politics of Educators' Work and Lives.* New York: Garland.

Ginsburg, M., and Lindsay, B. (eds.) 1995. *The Political Dimension in Teacher Education: Comparative Perspectives on Policy Formation, Socialization and Society.* New York: Falmer.

Lee, C. 1996. "Remap for City Students Passes: $10.7 Million Plan Adds 3 Neighborhood Schools, Cuts Busing Gradually." *Pittsburgh Post-Gazette* (Wednesday, 1 May): 1 and 14.

Orfield, G. 1993. *The Growth of Segregation in American Schools: Changing Patterns of Segregation and Poverty Since 1968.* Alexandria, Va.: National School Boards Association.

Pratt, R. 1992. *The Color of Their Skin: Education and Race in Richmond, Virginia, 1954– 89.* Charlottesville, Va.: University Press of Virginia.

White, F. 1992. *Pride and Prejudice: School Desegregation and Urban Renewal in Norfolk, 1950–1959.* Westport, Conn.: Praeger.

Wolters, R. 1984. *The Burden of Brown: Thirty Years of School Desegregation.* Knoxville, Tenn.: University of Tennessee Press.

Introduction

This book is about the political controversies surrounding the racial desegregation of public and private schools in a Midwestern city during a forty-year period. It is not about racial desegregation itself. That is, in this volume, the reader will examine the ways such people as business leaders, clergy, elected officials, judges, teachers, and school administrators reacted to challenges to patterns of student attendance.

The story is important but complicated. Within the struggles over the educational programs, the reader will find differing conceptions of how teachers should teach, what subject matter is important, and how the school should serve society. These definitions of good schools unfolded in dialectical patterns. Any innovation prompted several people to criticize it and other people to rally to its defense.

Unfortunately, in Dayton, Ohio, and in the rest of the country, the dialectics took strange twists. First, as the innovations and challenges mounted, the participants changed their views about what they wanted. Second, at times, many associations or political parties tried to use education to reinforce or challenge existing arrangements of social classes and racial groups. The parties did this for a variety of reasons. Sometimes the members advocated what they believed was best for the whole society. At other times people used the words of helping and caring to reinforce their own positions or to avenge some past insults.

Since the book is about politics, it is not about many other important things. In this volume, the reader will not find a careful analysis of whether or how desegregation works. Nor will the reader confront an explanation of the types of instruction that teachers should use in a racially desegregated classroom. Nor will the reader find a thoughtful discussion of effective responses school or civic leaders can make to the challenges presented by any educational innovation.

There are two apparent difficulties with the subject. First, Dayton, Ohio, is small, and the controversy in Dayton attracted little national attention. Second, racial desegregation of schools is an unpopular issue. For example, in 1993 the Center for Evaluation and Research for Phi Delta Kappa sent questionnaires to 926 educators asking them to list the top ten issues facing schools. Only thirteen respondents picked racial integration among their ten selections.

Fortunately, these flaws can be strengths. Although Dayton lacks the attractions of larger cities like Chicago or New York, it reflects the national experiences and moods more than those cities do. In preparing advertising campaigns or predicting national elections, strategists often use Dayton and its suburbs as a microcosm of the nation. For example, on 14 September 1992, to predict the issues that would decide the then upcoming national election, *Time* sampled the views of people in Ohio's Montgomery County, in which Dayton lies. The reason Dayton is a bellwether is that its mix of industry, business, military, and agricultural interests reflects those found elsewhere. Further, Dayton lacks the isolationist impulses expressed by people in other similarly sized cities.

Since the city of Dayton has a population of less than two hundred thousand people, it is an ideal research site. The necessary documents are easily available. The major actors are still living and willing to discuss their roles. Most important, the city is large enough to contain diverse groups holding different views. As a result, while Dayton is small enough for one person to understand, it is large enough to reveal patterns of relationships among churches, schools, businesses, and city government.

Although the racial desegregation of Dayton's schools attracted little national attention, government officials called it the most successful up to that time. Similarly, federal evaluators praised Dayton's Model Cities program for encouraging community residents to direct city services. Consequently, a study of Dayton should show politics when things go well. This is as important as knowing what went wrong in places like Boston, Massachusetts. Finally, unlike Boston, Dayton's legal case was important. During the appeals process, the federal courts clarified the relationship between a court of appeals and a federal district court.

The present unpopularity of racial desegregation is also an advantage. Since racial desegregation has lost its emotional appeal, people can use the issue to consider administrative models or curricula patterns. In this regard, Dayton serves as a valuable case study. The struggle in the city illustrates deeper trends in the national experience. That is, the case in Dayton shows how during the civil rights struggle people came to prefer some form of pluralism instead of a unified community.

In 1913, Dayton was one of the first cities in the nation to adopt a model of city and school administration copied from business. This progressive ideal tried to end party politics in the city. It promised that people elected to the city commission and the school board would draft policies to serve the entire community. The civil rights protests in the 1960s showed that the progressive model had failed. People elected to prominent positions ignored the needs of African Americans. Further, many Dayton residents came to reject any effort to bring people together as something that disguised elitism. For example, some African Americans complained that appeals for racial integration masked white people's desire to control. As a result, the efforts to encourage racial integration often exacerbated the distances among groups.

At its base, the problem may have been an intellectual one. In the 1830s, Alexis de Tocqueville found that people in the United States did not want to engage in speculative philosophy. They chose to concern themselves with practical methods of reducing labor and increasing profits. He thought people in a democracy shared this tendency because they wanted to escape the ties of tradition found in aristocratic countries.

Because of the bias against philosophy, people in the United States search for ways to solve social problems rather than to understand them. This works well if the solutions do not create more problems. Unfortunately, people develop sophisticated methods of achieving shallowly examined ends. In Dayton, people thought about how to desegregate schools. They did not think deeply about why different people should live together. Paying little attention to the reasons for racial integration, people developed techniques that proved to be of limited value.

Politics, Human Rights, and the Law

There are many ways people in the United States could enhance the racial integration of their neighborhoods or of their schools. However, in order for people to accept fair housing or metropolitan school consolidation or the reorganization of Catholic schools, they have to recognize the ideals justifying the change. Americans have the techniques to desegregate their society. They do not have a reason to do it.

Ironically, lawyers, religious leaders, elected officials, and school teachers who took part in the racial desegregation controversies saw themselves as social engineers. However, people in these professions concentrated on strategies to cause desegregation. They did not pursue discussions of the justifications for racial desegregation.

Part of the problem was that people could not show that racial integration was important for its own sake. At best, they contended that integration brought with it other benefits. For example, they said that racial integration improved the life chances of minority students. They said that racial integration was the law of the land and they urged people to obey a lawful order. Some people argued that racial desegregation offered school districts opportunities to redesign education to make it better for all children. They contended that racial mixing gave students a chance to learn to work with different types of people. Unfortunately, when people thought that racial integration was good for other things, they could question whether desegregation was the best or easiest way to accomplish the other goals.

To NAACP lawyers, school desegregation was the key to open a wide range of facilities such as airports, golf courses, and restaurants to all people. Until 1954 federal law apparently approved of legally mandated segregation, although two amendments to the U.S. Constitution prohibited laws abridging personal privileges or freedoms.

In 1896, the U.S. Supreme Court decided that the Thirteenth and Fourteenth Amendments to the U.S. Constitution did not require that people of different races live and work together. Instead, they reasoned those amendments required all people to have equal rights before the law and equal opportunities for improvement and progress. The result was the states throughout the South especially demanded racial segregation of public facilities. Soon, it was common to find racially separate neighborhoods, drinking fountains, and wage scales.

In winning the apparent reversal in 1954, the NAACP lawyers did not show that the U.S. Constitution required the races to live together. The lawyers built up an imposing set of precedents that showed separate facilities or treatment could not offer equal opportunities for improvement and progress. As a result, the justices concluded that separate facilities were unequal.

At first, in 1954, some people argued that the U.S. Supreme Court held that black children had a right to an integrated education. Further, the courts gradually expanded a school district's obligations to provide racial integration, but the justices avoided saying that black children had to attend racially desegregated schools. Finally, in 1974, a new set of justices on the U.S. Supreme Court decided that black children only had a right not to be forced into segregated schools. This implied that racial integration might be useful but not essential.

Ironically, the NAACP started something that opposing groups used. For example, white conservatives striving to maintain neighborhood schools and black power advocates saw racially separate buildings as essential for equal rights. Conservatives felt that when children attended schools in their neighborhoods, even though segregated, the teachers and the administration could structure lessons appropriate to their experiences. Black power groups argued that black children had to go to schools staffed and directed by black people. In such settings, black children would see that schools served black people and white people. Ironically, both the conservatives and the black power advocates used the same justifications the NAACP had used to end legally mandated segregation. They claimed segregated schools protected the personal privileges and advanced the values of freedom and personal liberty recognized in the Fourteenth Amendment to the U.S. Constitution.

While the courts and lawyers could not create a reason for different people to live together, religious leaders could have. By 1956 the national organizations of the major religious denominations in the United States had adopted resolutions opposing segregation and citing moral and religious reasons for ending racial discrimination. These documents asserted that racial prejudice contradicts the truth that God created all people and commands every one to love his or her neighbor.

Unfortunately, throughout the 1950s, local ministers did not speak out in favor of school desegregation. Clergy became more vocal during the summer of 1963 as the Reverend Martin Luther King Jr. led nonviolent demonstrations challenging the slow pace of racial desegregation. However, clergy found it difficult to use religious reasons for desegregation. Parishioners who disagreed would refuse contributions or threaten their posts. Consequently, liberal clergy sponsored open discussions about school issues or asked people to comply peacefully with a lawful order. Even the Reverend King had difficulty using the Bible to justify racial integration. Since he spoke to the public, King advocated what he called the gospel of freedom rather than religious faith. During demonstrations, he focused on the technique of nonviolent resistance to raise the dignity of African Americans and combat the misconceptions of discrimination. He asked other clergy to remind their parishioners that their faith proscribed segregation.

Even when churches ran private schools, the clergy could not use biblical truths to require racial integration. For example, U.S. Catholic bishops never called for the racial integration of schools. They did ask that schools not prohibit the enrollment of children of all races. Unfortunately, open enrollment could cause segregation because the Catholic schools mirrored the racial composition of the neighborhoods they served. Consequently, Catholic schools in white suburbs enrolled few African Americans. The enrollment in many Catholic schools in the cities changed dramatically as white students left the neighborhoods. Often, the schools closed or their students became exclusively black children.

Elected officials could not forge an ideal that required racial integration. During campaigns, school board candidates who sympathized with racial desegregation talked about important educational innovations. They found that speeches for social justice antagonized voters, and they hoped their supporters knew where they stood. Even conservative school board candidates who opposed racial integration rarely spoke about race. They talked about costs and the danger of long bus rides for children. Ironically, when conservatives won, they were the beneficiaries and the victims of movements to cut school spending. Using promises of lower school taxes to win their seats, they found it difficult to manage financially strapped school districts.

City commissioners and urban planners could not increase racial integration within the neighborhoods. Officials in the Miami Valley Regional Planning Commission proposed several ingenious methods to disperse low-income housing throughout Montgomery County in Ohio. Although they supported open housing, suburban residents resisted any enticement or requirement to accept a subsidized housing project. As a result, housing patterns remained segregated.

Finally, school teachers did not intrinsically value school desegregation. Teachers' unions grew rapidly during the 1960s and 1970s. However, these unions had loose connections to racial integration. In the South, the unions did not protect black teachers who lost jobs during desegregation. In the North, as many school districts desegregated faculty and students, union leaders complained that the controversy distracted attention from the job of teaching.

When teachers and educational researchers concentrated on teaching, the curriculum proposals they developed did not speak to the good of racial integration. Innovations such as individualized education, special interest or magnet schools, and interethnic sensitivity did not show people why racial integration was necessary. While these curriculum models could advance racial integration, none of them had racial integration as the aim.

Hoping to prepare for real integration, teachers and researchers developed methods of compensatory education to improve the academic performance of low-income students. The federal government and private philanthropies spent millions of dollars to help. The results were disappointing. The projects could not reduce the problems they set out to solve. Students from low-income homes continued to fail in schools, become pregnant, or abuse drugs. More important, these philanthropic endeavors seemed to make integration more remote. They suggested the environment in low-income neighborhoods rendered the children unable to live and work with people from affluent sections.

Thus, lawyers, clergy, elected officials, and teachers tried many strategies to bring about racial desegregation. If the United States remains a racially segregated country, the problem is not that the techniques failed. They all showed promise and could work if people wanted them to work. The techniques have not worked because people do not know why they should value racial integration.

There is no simple explanation for why different people should live and work together. Nor is it easy to describe what the role of public or private schools should be to usher in a racially integrated society. While this study cannot answer these questions, it can show why the answers are necessary. An exploration of the political controversies that occurred as people tried to bring about the racial desegregation of schools offers other rewards. At best, an account of the politics of desegregation will show how people have thought about education and social life. These are important things to learn.

Part I

Federal Courts, School Desegregation, and Religion

The National Context

Chapter One
The Politics of Racial Desegregation

The racial desegregation of schools should have been a controversy about the best way to make one nation out of many peoples. Instead, the issue became the conflict between the authority of the federal government and the principle of local control. The racial desegregation of schools was the cornerstone in a civil rights movement designed to overturn the legal separation of African Americans and whites. After the U.S. Supreme Court made its decision in *Brown v Board of Education* in 1954, lawyers for the NAACP sought to cast the federal government in the role of upholding the U.S. Constitution. On the opposite side, conservatives in southern states saw their "massive resistance" as a means to uphold their legal rights. As a result, racial integration became a legal concern more than a moral or a spiritual one.

At first, the NAACP was indefatigable. In 1955, Thurgood Marshall decided the NAACP would go after resistant school officials in each state one by one: "Those white crackers are going to get tired of having Negro lawyers beating 'em every day in court" (Ashmore 1994, 111).

As Marshall predicted, until 1974, the NAACP won a string of victories that expanded the definition of school desegregation. In the 1950s, southern communities interpreted the U.S. Supreme Court's decision to mean that black children had to have the opportunity to attend white schools. As a result, communities such as Greensboro, North Carolina, adopted open enrollment policies that created token desegregation. Ruling these policies to be inadequate in 1968, the U.S. Supreme Court used *Green v New Kent County* to say there had to be some results. In 1971, in *Swann v Charlotte-Mecklenburg*, the court approved arithmetic ratios to measure racial balance and accepted busing as a means to achieve it. The court turned its attention to northern school districts in 1972 in *Keyes v School District No. 1, Denver, Colorado.* Here, the school district was guilty of de jure segregation even when the state had not had laws requiring racially separate schools.

Through these cases, the NAACP sought to expand the rights black children derived from the due protection clause of the U.S. Constitution. At first, the lawyers sought only to forbid officials from forcing children to attend racially segregated schools. Since the original 1954 decision relied on social science evidence to show the inferiority of segregated education, it implied that black children had a right to an integrated education. Segregated schools appeared to deny black children the freedom to grow and develop fully. The NAACP pushed the courts in this direction. Opponents to school desegregation used quasi-legal principles of state's rights or of local control to justify the continued operation of segregated schools.

Massive Resistance

In 1954, the U.S. Supreme Court asked officials in various states to participate in discussions about the effects of its *Brown* decision. None of the officials from states in the deep South responded. They refused to recognize the order as valid, and they thought that participation in such a debate would imply an obligation to comply. Instead, in states like Georgia, the legislature passed bills making it a felony for any state or local official to spend public monies on an integrated school. In September 1954 the Mississippi legislature passed a state constitutional amendment allowing the legislature to abolish public schools and provide tuition grants to school children to attend private schools. In 1955 the Mississippi legislature made it unlawful for any white person to attend a racially integrated elementary or high school. Politicians in states such as Texas, Tennessee, and North Carolina that bordered the South had less success in passing similar laws (Bartley 1969, 67–81).

Beginning in small towns and rural communities, business people formed citizens councils to resist school integration and to restrict African American suffrage. These groups began to flourish and move into the cities. In February 1956 twelve thousand people attended a rally in Montgomery, Alabama, supporting the council movement. Similar meetings took place in other southern states (Bartley 1969, 82–106).

The southern white elite resisted integration differently. In 1956 one hundred and one U.S. congressional representatives from the states of the former Confederacy signed the "Declaration of Constitutional Principles." Commonly known as the "Manifesto," the document approved of states that resisted forced racial integration by any lawful means and warned against the dangers of judicial encroachment. Originating from South Carolina's Strom Thurmond, the declaration lent respectability and the appearance of legality to "massive resistance" (Bartley 1969, 108–125).

Public figures often described the justification for massive resistance in different ways, but they made the theory into a southern rallying cry. They used the word "interposition" to say that states could nullify orders from the federal government. Interestingly, the test of the doctrine happened in Arkansas. This state had a tradition of moderation in racial matters. No political hopeful campaigned against the *Brown* decision during Arkansas' 1954 primary election (Bartley 1969, 68, 126–149, 251).

Little Rock, Arkansas

In 1954 the Little Rock school board instructed the superintendent to construct a plan to comply with the U.S. Supreme Court. A year later, the board rejected the superintendent's suggestion of integrating the senior high schools. They opted for a more restricted plan with two phases. The first was to open Central High to a few black students in September 1957. The second was to allow a few black students to enter the white junior high schools in 1960. They did not set dates for the integration of the elementary schools. Unfortunately, although Central High School was a prestigious white school, working class people lived in the neighborhood. The elite whites who supported the desegregation program lived on the other side of town served by Hall High School, untouched by the plan. To mute dissent, the school officials continually stressed that this plan was the minimum required by the law. However, class antagonisms added to racial problems (Freyer 1984, 15–18).

In January 1956 the Little Rock school board began registration for the opening of a new but segregated building, Horace Mann

High School. Thirty black students showed up to enroll. When school officials rejected the children's applications, the parents formally appealed to the NAACP for aid. In February 1956 NAACP lawyers sued in U.S. District Court claiming the school board prevented the black children from attending schools near their homes. Lawyers for the school board argued that the board was providing a slow and orderly program of integration. On 28 August 1956, the judge decided not to interfere as long the school board worked in good faith (Freyer 1984, 41–57).

Unfortunately, political events in Arkansas made peaceful desegregation impossible. In 1955, James Johnson used the school desegregation controversy in Hoxie, Arkansas, to become a candidate for governor. Later, in January 1957, Johnson advocated the adoption of a state constitutional amendment threatening state officials who carried out federal laws requiring integration. Fearing that a strong segregationist stance would alienate his allies in East Arkansas, Governor Orval Faubus tried to remain neutral. When segregationists threatened his reelection, Faubus used the concept of interposition to appear moderate and to bolster his popularity among conservatives (Freyer 1984, 41–68).

Legal authorities agreed that the idea of interposition was absurd. Nonetheless, Faubus formed a committee to evaluate Arkansas' responsibility to comply with *Brown II*. The committee endorsed the theory of interposition and listed eighteen factors for pupil assignment, excluding race. Faubus endorsed the committee's recommendations and won the 1956 primary election by a landslide (Freyer 1984, 68–82).

Before the desegregation of Central High School began in September 1957, Faubus tried to stop it. Testifying in state chancery court, he said he had reports of black and white children obtaining guns in preparation for the impending school desegregation. Although Faubus won the injunction in state court, the federal judge directed the school board to go on (Ashmore 1994, 126–130).

Unswayed, on 2 September 1957 Governor Faubus ordered troops from the National Guard to go to the high school. As the black students entered the building, the troops turned them away. Faubus said the schools should continue as they had until the court case ended. To preserve peace, the school board passed a resolution asking black students not to come to Central High for a time (Blossom 1959, 73–84).

On 24 September 1957 U.S. President Dwight Eisenhower ordered a detachment from the 101st Infantry from Fort Campbell, Kentucky, to replace the Arkansas National Guard at Central High School. He acted to prevent interference with the orders of the court. Pictures in the papers showed troops pushing white students toward the school with fixed bayonets pointed inches from their backs. The troops escorted nine black children into the school building. Many students stayed away. Only 1,250 students out of 2,000 enrolled in Central High attended the first few days (Blossom 1959, 116–127).

Within Central High, some white students tried to welcome the black students. A few days before the integration took place, a white student wrote in the school newspaper urging her colleagues to obey the law and maintain public order. The most publicized incident took place during the baccalaureate services at the end of the year when a white student spit in the face of a black student. The police let the white boy walk away, but they arrested two black students who demanded that they stop him (Bates 1962).

In June 1958 the judge granted the Little Rock school board the opportunity to halt the desegregation of Central High. The U.S. Circuit Court of Appeals overruled him, and the U.S. Supreme Court affirmed the appeals court decision. Faubus closed all senior high schools in Little Rock. The school board agreed to lease the public school facilities to the Little Rock Private School Corporation, but the federal courts rejected this plan. Schools supported by state funds could not bar black children from attending. Nonetheless, in October, a private high school opened, and its enrollment grew to about 800 students. In all, the superintendent estimated that 500 children stayed home during the 1958–59 school year (Blossom 1959, 184–187).

The next year proved better. Little Rock schools opened in August 1959 without federal assistance. Local police maintained order (Freyer 1984, 158–163).

By ordering in federal troops, President Eisenhower proved he would enforce court orders. Consequently, during the fall and winter of 1958–59, massive resistance lost its former prominence in southern politics. As a result, a moderate save-the-schools movement in the cities enlisted middle-class supporters. School people and business leaders tried to prevent extremists from closing schools rather than desegregate them (Bartley 1969, 320–337).

Most important, during the controversy in Little Rock, all officials made legal arguments about racial justice. They did not raise questions about morality. As a result, the means, obedience to the law, became more important than the end, racial integration. Furthermore, when people on both sides of the issue looked to the courts for answers, they began to argue about what powers the judges should assume in a democracy. Liberals looked to the justices to engage in broad policy making. Segregationists asked the courts to exercise the least authority possible (Freyer 1984, 172–174).

Although people in Little Rock lost their reputation for moderation, civil rights protests followed a different path in other southern states. The effort to racially integrate the schools in Greensboro, North Carolina illustrates these differences.

Greensboro, North Carolina

North Carolina's governor appointed a biracial advisory committee in 1954 to preserve the public schools. The committee reported that the public would not accept integrated schools. Among its recommendations, the committee suggested that the state board of education give up any authority for assigning students. The hope was that if local school boards assumed all such responsibilities, each would have to appear in court. In the fall Luther Hodges assumed the governor's office. He asked the legislature to enact the committee's recommendations. Hodges suggested that individual communities begin private schools to replace the public ones (Bagwell 1972, 84–88).

In 1955 Governor Hodges made a statewide address asking all citizens to support voluntary segregation. His attorney general announced that his office would help a local board to maintain segregated schools. Because of these statewide pressures, the Greensboro school board decided to maintain a segregated system. On 8 September 1956 a record turnout of voters for a special election adopted two segregationist amendments to the state constitution. The first offered tuition grants to children who wanted to attend segregated private schools. The second permitted local communities to close their public schools (Bagwell 1972, 89–97).

NAACP civil rights lawyers challenged the new pupil assignment plan in four North Carolina communities. State officials decided that some desegregation had to take place if the statutes were to withstand continued litigation. As a result, local boards adopted resolutions that allowed students to choose to go to any school. If a student wanted to attend a segregated public school but none was available, the board extended a tuition grant to attend a private school. On 23 July 1957 the Greensboro board approved the transfers of six black students to two previously all-white schools. School boards in Charlotte and Winston-Salem voted to approve similar requests (Bagwell 1972, 97–104).

The Greensboro community prepared for a peaceful transition. The newspapers were conciliatory. A ministerial alliance asked the community to support the desegregation. School officials visited other cities, such as Louisville, Kentucky, and Baltimore, Maryland, to see what officials in those systems did to ease desegregation. Greensboro school people held workshops on human relations for school personnel. The superintendent urged any school employees who disagreed with the board's decision to remain quiet or leave the system. Finally, to prevent violence, the city assigned extra police to patrol the schools on the opening day. When school opened in September 1957, only 100 to 250 white people stood around the school to taunt the handful of black children that police escorted into the school. Otherwise, the transition was uneventful (Bagwell 1972, 110–119).

As the national mood came to support increased integration, Greensboro business, civic, religious, and educational leaders asked the school board for more than token racial desegregation. In 1963 the Greensboro school board adopted a freedom of choice plan that altered enrollment patterns quickly. In the 1962–63 school year, thirty-five black students enrolled in one previously white school. The next school year, 1963–64, the number of black students in white schools rose to 200 in twelve buildings. By 1964–65 five hundred black students attended sixteen schools in Greensboro (Bagwell 1972, 120–124).

The experiences similar to those in Greensboro happened in most towns or cities that underwent desegregation. However, cities where people resisted loudly and violently dominated the newspapers (U.S. Commission on Civil Rights 1976). As a result, the public image of school desegregation was one where crowds of angry people threatened black children. Despite these pictures, the children were not the most vulnerable group. School desegregation threatened black educators everywhere.

The Plight of Black Teachers

In 1958 the NAACP awarded the Springarn Medal for contributions to racial advancement to the nine African American children who integrated Central High School in Little Rock, Arkansas, and to Daisy Bates, then president of the Arkansas NAACP. The award symbolized that school desegregation was central in the NAACP's strategy to all forms of segregation. Unfortunately, the bulk of trained African Americans in southern communities were school teachers employed by the school districts. Consequently, they had to sit by silently as the cities and states resisted the federal orders. If they did not, they lost their jobs and their careers (Lomax 1962, 124–125).

Segregationists described the NAACP as an organization of intruders from New York City who did not represent the interests of southern African Americans. As a result, the legislatures of several states took direct action to prevent teachers from supporting the NAACP. They abolished teacher tenure and prohibited schools or other state agencies from employing members of the NAACP (Bagwell 1972, 135–143).

Because of such laws, white teachers and administrators replaced African American teachers and administrators as school desegregation advanced in southern states. In some southern districts, the racial desegregation of schools meant the elimination of black principals and the demotion of black teachers. In 1965 Florida had the most such teacher displacements because of the way the state used the National Teacher Examination for promotion or tenure (Commission on Professional Rights 1970, 7).

The use of the National Teachers Exam as a tool of segregation extended back to 1940. Then, the NAACP won a verdict from the

U.S. Court of Appeals that prohibited Virginia schools from paying black teachers less than equally qualified white teachers. This forced school boards to find legitimate ways to distinguish the pay rates. Florida and South Carolina turned to the National Teachers Exam. For example, the Palm Beach County, Florida, schools divided teachers into four salary groups. No blacks were in the highest group, and although 60 percent of the black teachers were in the lowest salary group no whites were there. Despite these segregative effects, federal courts sustained the practices. The tests were objective and graded by machines that could not tell if a paper came from a black or from a white person (Baker 1995).

In 1965 the NAACP contended that the U.S. Department of Health, Education, and Welfare (HEW) should prevent school districts from displacing black teachers during school desegregation. In the resulting publicity, the Office of Education announced that they considered the systematic firing of black teachers a violation of a district's promise of good faith. Less than a week after the Office of Education made its announcement, a small Florida town dismissed all the local black teachers and retained the white teachers. President Lyndon Johnson took the challenge. He directed the U.S. Commissioner of Education to guard against any pattern of teacher dismissal based on race. As a result, HEW required school districts to offer black teachers the first chance to accept new positions. HEW warned school districts that a drop in the number of black teachers would raise questions (Orfield 1969, 106–107).

Ironically, when President Johnson intervened, his home state of Texas had the nation's highest number of instances of black teacher displacements resulting from racial desegregation of schools. Many of these problems continued in East Texas through 1968.

East Texas consists of twenty-five counties lying east of a line drawn from Dallas to Houston. In 1960 it included one quarter of the land and one half of the population of the state. Called the Black Belt of Texas because black people comprised 30 percent of the population, the median income in East Texas was well below the average for the state in 1960 (Commission on Professional Rights 1970, 13–14).

The pattern of teacher displacement in East Texas was simple. During the racial integration of schools, white teachers moved to buildings formerly occupied by blacks, but black teachers never moved to formerly white schools. Some school districts informed the black teachers they lost their jobs because enrollment declined. During desegregation, one superintendent released all black principals, black teachers, black janitors, black bus drivers, and black cafeteria employees without giving any reasons. Some school districts in East Texas transferred black teachers to white schools and assigned them to federally funded programs. The black teachers lost their jobs when those funds disappeared. Other districts assigned black teachers as counselors or special teachers to black students within those buildings (Commission on Professional Rights 1970, 24–28).

The school districts in East Texas dismissed black personnel with impunity for four reasons. First, the contracts for teachers and administrators typically noted employment subject to placement. Second, the state offered no tenure protection. Black teachers complained to the Texas state commissioner of education that summary dismissal violated tenure. The commissioner replied that there was no provision requiring a district to reemploy teachers no matter how satisfactory their work. Third, the local boards refused to create meaningful standards for measuring the qualifications of teachers. For example, one district said the best candidates for teaching were not necessarily those with the most college preparation. Other important qualities included personality, temperament, and cultural characteristics. Such standards allowed uncertified white teachers to replace black teachers with master's degrees. Fourth, the school boards made personnel decisions in private without public consultation. School administrators refused to open any such information to the public (Commission on Professional Rights 1970, 27–44).

The displaced African American teachers and principals did not ask the local professional associations to which they belonged for help. Since white educators from East Texas predominated in those associations, the black teachers thought appeals would have no effect. More surprising, the 15,000 black educators in Texas did not organize into a black occupational caucus to protect their own interests (Commission on Professional Rights 1970, 52).

Although black teachers in East Texas complained to the U.S. Department of Health, Education, and Welfare, nothing happened.

HEW officials noted that they had a team of six people to service complaints from Arkansas, Texas, Louisiana, and Oklahoma. These people could not do more than acknowledge the letters they received (Commission on Professional Rights 1970, 24–28).

The Department of Health, Education, and Welfare

The role of the U.S. Department of Health, Education, and Welfare was uneven. It had enormous power and lost it. HEW's power grew out of the confrontation on the streets of Birmingham, Alabama, in May 1963. Shocked by pictures in newspapers or on television sets of peaceful marchers threatened by dogs, public sentiment turned against segregation. As a result, the U.S. Congress passed and, on 2 July 1964, President Lyndon Johnson signed the Civil Rights Act. This gave federal bureaucrats the power to change entire school districts (Orfield 1969, 33–46).

Title VI of the Civil Rights Act said that no person could suffer discrimination in any program funded by the federal government. Although the U.S. Congress added several amendments to limit this statement, Title VI forbade school districts that maintained segregation from receiving federal funds. More important, the U.S. Office of Education could make the decision to suspend federal funding without going through protracted legal debates (Orfield 1969, 44–46).

In 1965 the U.S. Department of Health, Education, and Welfare promulgated guidelines that called for school districts to prove actual racial integration. Earlier the districts could simply adopt policies offering the possibility of desegregation. HEW strengthened the guidelines in 1966 by requiring specific progress toward desegregation. In 1967 HEW created the Office of Civil Rights. From 1964 until 1970 HEW staff caused 600 administrative proceedings against segregated school districts. They concentrated on rural districts in 1964. HEW focused on faculty desegregation in 1966. By 1968, HEW had stopped the federal funds for about 200 southern school districts. However, the agency failed in its investigation of northern school districts (Salomone 1986, 64–65).

In 1957 the Chicago chapter of the NAACP issued a report about de facto segregation in the Chicago schools. The city's political machine responded by buying enough NAACP memberships to defeat a militant candidate for leadership in the Chicago branch. This muted any protest that the report caused (Orfield 1969, 154–155).

In 1961 the superintendent of Chicago public schools refused to allow black students in overcrowded schools on the west side to transfer to underutilized white schools. The NAACP sued to allow black students to use the empty classrooms in the white schools. In 1962 the U.S. Civil Rights Commission issued a report outlining segregation in the Chicago schools. The Chicago Urban League issued a similar report. When the school board ignored these complaints, a federation of civil rights groups organized a boycott (Orfield 1969, 156–157).

To end litigation and protests, the board sponsored a study of integration in the city. Presented in 1964, the study revealed serious problems. More than 40 percent of the students in the city schools were black, but less than 10 percent of the schools were integrated. Eighty-four percent of the African American students attended segregated schools. Most important, school board policies furthered segregation, allowing school attendance boundaries to follow racial lines through the neighborhoods. For example, the board placed mobile classrooms in predominantly black schools instead of placing these structures near other buildings where the new space could be used to enhance integration. The study also noted that the school system needed almost $60 million to improve teaching in all the buildings (Orfield 1969, 157–158).

Despite the bad news from the study, in 1965 the Chicago school board reappointed the superintendent who had ignored civil rights concerns during his tenure. When the board reappointed him, liberals began to protest. In June 1965 local civil rights leaders asked the U.S. attorney general to investigate de facto segregation in Chicago. In July 1965 U.S. Congress representative Adam Clayton Powell held hearings in the House Education and Labor Committee to investigate Chicago schools. During those hearings, some witnesses testified that the school board was unprepared to initiate desegregation. Other witnesses cited several instances when school attendance boundaries were drawn to maintain racial segregation. News media displayed the controversy to the nation (Orfield 1969, 159–167).

In 1965 HEW decided to act against the Chicago school district because they had some information about it. HEW sent a team in September 1965 to study the problems in Chicago. Before the study was completed, the commissioner of the U.S. Office of Education in HEW told the Illinois state superintendent of public instruction to defer further grants to Chicago. The state superintendent complained publicly about careless federal infringement on state authority. He demanded the Office of Education produce the information that justified the decision. Unfortunately, the Office of Education did not have the information (Orfield 1969, 162–189).

The controversy spread rapidly from Chicago to Washington as Chicago school people and Illinois congressional representatives criticized the HEW action. Newspapers carried stories of the arguments. The mayor of Chicago, Richard Daley, accused the Office of Education of taking drastic actions without giving explanations. He said the result was intolerable federal intrusion. Daley complained to U.S. President Johnson, who met with the commissioner and requested an immediate settlement. Interpreting this as a directive to get out of Chicago, the secretary of HEW delegated negotiators to meet with school officials. Chicago school officials agreed to do what they were doing already, and HEW released the federal funds. HEW surrendered so quickly that supporters did not have time to come to the department's defense (Orfield 1969, 189–196).

In January 1967 HEW released a report of the Chicago schools. It did not make any ultimatums and offered only general observations. Noting the complexity of the problems, the report listed several recommendations. The school board replaced the superintendent. In April the new superintendent submitted a plan to increase pupil and teacher desegregation in Chicago schools. White Chicago residents complained and the board applied the desegregation plan to only 249 students in one section of the city (Orfield 1969, 198–206).

The problems in Chicago marked the end of HEW influence in school desegregation. In 1969, President Richard Nixon's Justice Department and HEW announced that they would not withhold federal funds on account of segregation. They would rely on litigation to cause a school district's compliance with the Civil Rights Act. This announcement was an understatement. The number of

Title VI compliance reviews conducted by HEW dropped to twenty-eight in 1969. By 1974 HEW conducted no reviews. Civil rights organizations tried to prod the executive branch into action in 1970. The NAACP Legal Defense Fund sued HEW for failing to enforce Title VI. The U.S. District Court found that HEW backed down on promises to desegregate 113 school districts. The Office of Civil Rights agreed to meet a series of deadlines in discrimination cases. However, in 1981 the NAACP and the Women's Law Center sued the newly created Department of Education for ignoring the deadlines (Salomone 1986, 66–67).

Besides acting as a mechanism to force school districts to desegregate racially, the U.S. Civil Rights Act of 1964 offered to ease desegregation. In Title VI, the Civil Rights Act demanded that school districts racially desegregate. However, in Title IV, the Civil Rights Act promised federal grants to districts to hire specialists and to state departments of education to set up centers for teacher training and other technical assistance to aid in racial desegregation. Some consultants were to be people known and respected among the school districts. They were to offer suggestions to combat segregation and educational disadvantage. Unfortunately, until 1967 HEW pressed Title IV staff and support into the more negative task of reviewing the compliance of school districts. In November 1967, the Office of Education set up the Division of Equal Educational Opportunity to direct projects in such areas as individualized education or interpersonal relations (U.S. Commission on Civil Rights 1973, 1–3).

Although Title IV offered a unique and valuable approach to equal rights, it never fulfilled its potential for four reasons. First, the annual budget for Title IV programs in the nation never exceeded twenty million dollars. Second, HEW never had adequate staff to monitor Title IV activities. Third, program directors tended to disburse funds despite the merit of the proposals. As a result, people at state and local levels began programs unrelated to desegregation through Title IV support. Fourth, Title IV programs avoided hiring experts from outside the systems that requested the help. As a result of hiring personnel who came from the school districts, the resulting Title IV programs were timid or wrongheaded (U.S. Commission on Civil Rights 1973, 41–44).

The failure of Title IV suggests how far the executive branch of the federal government moved away from school desegregation. In 1972 HEW decided that its experts could not design desegregation plans for school districts even when a judge ordered them (Metcalf 1983, 143–144).

Then U.S. President Richard Nixon profited from and contributed to the unpopularity of school desegregation. In February and in March 1972 Nixon asked courts to call a moratorium on efforts to achieve racial balance. Instead, Nixon offered $2.5 billion to aid disadvantaged urban children. In October 1972 the U.S. Congress defeated Nixon's proposed moratorium on busing. Nonetheless, federal agencies ignored the racial desegregation of schools. Further, the proposition helped Nixon in his second presidential campaign. His opponent, George McGovern, said citizens must pay for a century of segregation with school busing for racial balance. Capitalizing on the unpopularity of school desegregation, the Republican party called for a constitutional amendment to outlaw busing for racial desegregation. Nixon won by a landslide (Metcalf 1983, 144–145; 428).

When Nixon made his stand against busing, newspapers warned that the popular wrath to which he was playing could get out of hand. Although the newspaper predictions came true in Boston, Massachusetts, Nixon was not to blame. The problems began in July 1965 when HEW could not withhold funds from Chicago's public schools until they desegregated. At that time, conservatives saw that political resistance would defeat school desegregation in northern cities (Orfield 1969, 152–153).

Boston, Massachusetts

Massachusetts was the only state to have a law requiring school districts to operate racially balanced schools. Passed in 1965 by the Massachusetts legislature, the Racial Imbalance Act defined a racially imbalanced school as one that had more than 50 percent nonwhite students. To ensure compliance, school districts sent annual censuses of students to the state board of education. It could suspend funds going to any system with racially imbalanced schools (Formisano 1991, 35–36).

According to the first racial census in 1965, Boston had forty-six racially imbalanced schools. There were only nine other racially imbalanced schools in the entire state. The Boston school committee submitted a racial desegregation plan to the state board of education in December 1965. Finding the plan inadequate, the state board suspended the Boston schools' state funding in April 1966. Both sides sued in Suffolk Superior Court in August. At first, the school committee won, but lost on reversal in the state superior court. When the Boston school committee sent a plan outlining little more than token desegregation, the state board approved it. Boston schools received state funding while the number of its racially imbalanced schools climbed from forty-six in 1965 to seventy-five in 1972 (Formisano 1991, 44–47).

The Racial Imbalance Law proved ineffective because the conservative members of the Boston school committee encouraged mass demonstrations and rallies against the legislature and the state governor. Because of the public pressure, the legislature voted to repeal the Racial Imbalance Act in April 1974. Subsequently, in May 1974 the governor announced that he would replace the imbalance act with a plan calling for voluntary busing and magnet schools (Formisano 1991, 60–64).

In December 1971 investigators from the U.S. Department of Health, Education, and Welfare found Boston's middle schools or junior highs enrolled white and black students in a discriminatory way. HEW's Office of Civil Rights asked the Boston school committee to change its practices. Seven months later, HEW initiated formal administrative enforcement proceedings. In March 1973, an administrative judge upheld these findings of the Office of Civil Rights. However, soon after, the U.S. district court ordered the racial desegregation of the Boston schools (U.S. Commission on Civil Rights 1975, 106–108).

In March 1972 the NAACP filed the case known as *Morgan v Hennigan*. The U.S. district court judge decided in June 1974 that the Boston school committee maintained racially segregated schools. He noted that white children from a predominantly white and overcrowded junior high school moved to another overcrowded school with mostly white students. However, there were empty seats in a nearby junior high school where most of the students were black (U.S. Commission on Civil Rights 1975, 70–71). On a list of twenty-seven northern school districts found guilty of discrimination by federal courts from 1956–76, the Boston school committee committed the most violations (Orfield 1978, 19–23).

In court, the Boston school committee blamed the segregated nature of the city for the unbalanced composition of the schools. According to the 1970 census, of the four areas of the city important to the racial desegregation of the schools, three were predominantly white and one was predominantly black. Charleston had seventy-six black residents out of a total population of 15,353 people. South Boston had 388 black residents out of a total population of 38,488. Roslindale had 39,558 people, of whom 750 were black. Of the 65,528 people in Roxbury, 52,661 were black (U.S. Commission on Civil Rights 1975, 24–25).

Residents of the neighborhoods tended to have strong ethnic ties, complicating the racial desegregation of Boston's schools. Thirty-one percent of Charleston's residents were foreign-born or the child of a foreign-born person. Thirty-seven percent of South Boston's and 47 percent of Roslindale's population were from recent immigrant backgrounds. Yet in Roxbury, only 17 percent of the people were from families new to the United States (U.S. Commission on Civil Rights 1975, 24–25).

The Boston school committee members claimed that they adopted policies to preserve neighborhood schools, and they expressed surprise at the segregative effects of its policies. The court rejected this defense for three reasons. First, the Boston schools adopted programs such as magnet schools and citywide schools that contradicted the idea of neighborhood schools. Neighborhood schools in Boston served segregated areas. Second, in 1973, in *Keyes v School District No. 1,* the U.S. Supreme Court said that a court could not accept the excuse that the school board's actions preserved neighborhood schools. Third, in 1962 the school committee commissioned a study of housing patterns that predicted the changes in racial composition that took place through 1970. The existence of this study suggested that the school committee intentionally segregated children by their races (U.S. Commission on Civil Rights 1975, 73–75).

The U.S. district court ordered the schools to set up a desegregation plan that the school committee developed earlier. Implemented in September 1974, the plan required the busing of about seventeen thousand students out of the eighty thousand in the system. Although the busing plan did not reorganize the schools, it had controversial features. For example, it paired Roxbury High School, in the heart of a black area, with South Boston High School, the pride of a white Irish enclave (Formisano 1991, 66–75).

Protest parades streamed out of South Boston before schools opened. Nearly ten thousand people gathered on Boston Common and marched to City Hall Plaza to protest the coming school desegregation. When the schools opened, the plan went smoothly except in such places as South Boston, where mobs threw stones at school buses bringing black children from Roxbury. The problems seemed to take place in only a few schools. Average attendance for 1974–75 fluctuated between forty and sixty thousand. The total potential enrollments were eighty thousand students (Formisano 1991, 75–82).

On 10 May 1975 the U.S. district court judge accepted a plan that increased the number of bused students to twenty-four thousand. Again, schools opened in September 1975 to more marches and protests in Charleston, South Boston, Hyde Park, and West Roxbury (Formisano 1991, 98–104).

People surrendered to the inevitability of desegregation. In 1976 a mayor's commission on violence reported that 150 out of 165 schools in Boston functioned smoothly. Furthermore, by 1977 school busing lost its influence in city elections. Then a moderate candidate won the most votes for school committee. The hard-line conservatives opposed to busing lost their seats on the city council. In 1982 the U.S. district judge turned the guidance of the Boston schools to the State Board of Education. Since 1975 the judge had guided the schools, issuing over four hundred orders. Yet his desegregation order withstood all appeals against it. He gave control of the schools back to the school committee in 1985 (Formisano 1991, 203–212).

In Boston the busing controversy had three important effects. First, there was a shift in the party allegiance of the voters in the wards where the strongest resistance to busing occurred. Instead of casting ballots for Democratic candidates in national elections, voters supported the Republican party of Gerald Ford and Ronald Reagan. Second, the socioeconomic level of the students dropped

until, by 1985, 93 percent of the students in Boston's schools qualified for free or reduced lunches. Third, the racial desegregation of
schools accelerated white flight. Cardinal Medeiros directed Catholic schools not to accept students whose transfer would aggravate
racial imbalance in the public schools. Yet during the first two years
of busing over two thousand white children fled to the Catholic
schools. Also, white families moved to the suburbs and enrolled their
children in those schools. As a result, the racial composition of the
Boston public school changed, from 1973, when 60 percent of the
students were white, to 1980, when 35 percent were white. The
decline of white students continued so that in 1987, 26 percent of
the students were white, and these students were in schools that
experienced little busing (Formisano 1991, 196–214).

Boston was susceptible to white flight. It was one of the small-
est of the nation's cities in relation to its metropolitan area because
Boston stopped annexing outlying areas after the 1870s. As a result,
neighboring communities were physically close but politically separate (Warner 1970). However, school desegregation was not the only
thing to cause white people to move. From 1950 to 1970, before
carrying out Boston school's racial desegregation plan, jobs and population flowed to the suburbs. A state highway, Route 128, ringing
the city, supported many high-technology companies (Formisano
1991, 225–227).

Similar migrations of people took place in other cities. The federal government encouraged people to move to suburban communities in three ways. First, after World War II, the GI Bill offered
money for home purchases to military veterans. The Federal Housing Authority insured loans for people who could not use the GI
Bill. However, until 1950 the agency refused to lend money for homes
in racially integrated areas. Second, the federal government sponsored the construction of interstate highways that allowed people
easy travel from town to city. Third, federal funds paid for the building of sewer and water systems in new suburban developments.
However, those funds would not pay for the repair or the enlargement of urban sewer and water systems. The result of these federal
practices was to direct white people with money to live in the suburbs and abandon African Americans without sufficient income in
the city.

White Flight

As the people in South Boston resisted racial desegregation, social scientists publicly debated the effects of school busing on white families. The controversy began in April 1975, when James S. Coleman delivered a paper to the American Educational Research Association describing the effect of school desegregation on white enrollment. By June 1975 headlines appeared in several leading newspapers contending that the man who started busing decided that the policy backfired. Coleman wrote articles for popular journals and appeared on television talk shows discussing school desegregation causing white flight. He submitted affidavits in federal courts, and in October 1976 he testified before the U.S. Senate Judiciary Committee hearings on a proposed antibusing amendment (Pettigrew and Green 1976).

Coleman and his colleagues thought that a school desegregation plan influenced the migration of white families for only one year. However, they added that the plan had secondary effects. When white families left the city and its schools, their departure increased the proportion of black students in the schools. As the percentage of African Americans increased, more white families left, making the city increasingly black and the suburbs increasingly white. This disparity added to white flight (Coleman et al. 1975, 73).

Coleman and his fellow researchers found that the effects of racial desegregation differed in different cities. Small cities had a significantly smaller loss of white population than large cities did. When African Americans predominated in a city and whites lived outside in the suburbs, white migration could be severe. Interestingly, more white children left elementary schools than withdrew from secondary schools (Coleman 1975, 78–79).

Other social scientists disagreed. In February 1976 Thomas F. Pettigrew and his colleague Robert L. Green pointed out that researchers such as Reynolds Farley came to different conclusions using the same statistics. Coleman used the information from 1968–69 to make his analysis of trends while the other researchers included data for five years or more. As a result, Pettigrew and Green argued that, after five years desegregation plans did not hasten migration of middle-class people from the city or to private schools. Pettigrew and Green added that desegregation plans that include a city and its surrounding suburbs do not cause white flight. However, they feared

Coleman's statements could encourage white families to move from the cities by creating an atmosphere where such behavior seemed legitimate (Pettigrew and Green 1976a, 20–26; 40; and 1976b).

In May 1976 Coleman said the situation was worse than he had supposed. After five years of school desegregation, white people continued to leave the cities to avoid school desegregation plans. He attributed the discrepancy between his conclusions and those of his critics to different ways of tracing the losses. Coleman suggested that the creation of more metropolitan desegregation plans would not lessen white flight. Data on such districts came from places that were growing and had few black residents (Coleman 1976).

In August 1976 the U.S. Commission on Civil Rights accepted Pettigrew and Green's version of events. The commission said school desegregation did not cause massive white flight. At least since the 1950s, white people had been leaving the cities for the suburbs. The commission noted that four factors fueled this migration: relocation of employment to suburban areas; desire for more living space; higher incomes; and the unfounded fear that property values in cities declined as minorities moved into a neighborhood. Finally, the commission cited a 1972 U.S. Supreme Court decision holding that the fear of white flight could not prevent an extensive desegregation plan (U.S. Commission on Civil Rights 1976, 161–162).

Interestingly, white families may not have left the cities as much as white families avoided the cities when buying a new home. In the 1970s more than one-sixth of the people in the United States moved every year. Consequently, all neighborhoods had to attract new home buyers continually. If white home buyers felt reluctant to settle in a city or if realtors steered them to the suburbs, a formerly integrated neighborhood soon became segregated (Orfield 1978, 97).

Most important, the effectiveness of metropolitan desegregation plans varied by region. For example, in 1975 Coleman noted that less white flight followed racial desegregation in northern cities than in southern cities. The experiences of two cities illustrated this distinction even when the racial desegregation of schools took place throughout the metropolitan area. Wilmington, Delaware, joined the other school districts in New Castle County to form a racial desegregation plan. Fortunately, limited numbers of white students went to other school districts or private schools. Nashville, Tennessee, joined those school districts in the suburbs of Davidson County. However, white students chose to attend public schools where the white students were in the majority, or they left the public school system to enter private schools.

Wilmington, Delaware

In 1954 Delaware schools were part of the *Brown* case. By 1956 the city of Wilmington had officially desegregated all the grades. On the other hand, the school districts in the southern part of the state resisted the order. To end this practice, a black parent sued Clayton school officials in federal district court. Because of the suit *Evans v Buchanan* the State Board of Education recommended that the legislature approve a new school code eliminating enrollments based on race. When the legislature failed to draft the new code, the state board of education of Delaware closed many small school districts and eliminated the segregated school districts in two rural counties in 1965–67 (Raffel 1980, 42–44).

In 1968 the Delaware state legislature adopted the Educational Advancement Act. While this law gave the state board authority to reorganize school districts, it contained two important provisions to limit redistricting. First, it required that the boundaries of the Wilmington school district coincide with the boundaries of the city. Second, it prohibited districts from having more than 12,000 pupils (Raffel 1980, 42–47).

The effect of these two provisions was to isolate the African American students in the Wilmington schools. Since these provisions in the Education Act represented a legislative act to segregate the schools, the federal courts found the legislature guilty of de jure segregation in 1974.

The events began in 1971 when five black parents, helped by the American Civil Liberties Union, sued to reopen *Evans v Buchanan*. At first, the NAACP did not support the suit, for two reasons. First, black children would bear the burden of busing. Second, an interdistrict remedy would undermine African Americans' newly won power in the Wilmington schools. Nonetheless, the parents pressed their complaint that the state board had not eliminated segregation. In 1971, 72 percent of Wilmington's students were black. Yet the 1968 Educational Advancement Act prevented them from being integrated with students in the surrounding white suburbs. The Wilmington school board joined the suit as an intervening plaintiff in 1972 (Raffel 1980, 45–47, 62).

On 12 July 1974 the U.S. district court decided that although Wilmington had adopted racially neutral attendance zones, segregation continued. The justices ordered the state board to submit desegregation plans for Wilmington alone and for the metropolitan area (Raffel 1980, 46–47). Thirteen days later, the U.S. Supreme Court issued its decision in the Detroit case, *Milliken v Bradley.* The Supreme Court held that lower courts have to show that public officials committed discriminatory acts before those courts can order interdistrict desegregation. This decision did not change the case in Wilmington.

The plaintiffs argued that the 1968 Educational Advancement Act prohibiting the Wilmington district from merging with surrounding schools represented official discrimination. The judges agreed and decided that the desegregation order could extend beyond the city. On 27 November 1975 the U.S. Supreme Court agreed (Raffel 1980, 48–51).

On 19 May 1976 the U.S. district court justices decided that the school districts had submitted inadequate desegregation plans. The judges constructed their own plan establishing a single reorganized school district for all of New Castle County except a small racially mixed district far from the city. In June 1977 the U.S. Court of Appeals for the Third Circuit decided the district court plan was too extensive. The appeals court gave a U.S. district court judge the responsibility of supervising the remedy, and he turned to local and state officials to construct the plan (Raffel 1980, 51–60).

Unfortunately, the local and state officials could not decide how to equalize the pay of teachers in different districts. They could not agree on how extensive the pupil desegregation should be. On 5 August 1977 the U.S. district court judge rejected the state's desegregation plan and created a five-person board to make the decisions. By 9 January 1978 the judge rejected the plans the new board sent him and set up technical guidelines to insure better desegregation. He called for programs to enhance communication skills, curriculum offerings that reflected cultural pluralism, building plans to prevent discrimination, programs to emphasize cultural pluralism, and reassignment of faculty and staff in racially integrated patterns (Raffel 1980, 73–80).

As the deadline of September 1978 approached, the suburban districts made last-minute appeals to the U.S. Supreme Court asking for more time to prepare. Justice Rehnquist at first considered and then denied the stay. On 11 September 1978 desegregation began. It was a success. There was no violence. Generally, students and teachers were pleased with the massive project. The redistricting involved ninety-nine schools with over 60,000 students, of whom about 20,500 were bused for desegregation (Raffel 1980, 3; 77–87; 174–5).

On 16 October 1978, a few weeks after the desegregation process began, the teachers in New Castle County struck for higher wages. Wilmington teachers crossed picket lines to work because they had the higher salaries. By 19 November 1978 the strike ended with the acceptance of a complex financial package. It should be emphasized that this strike was not a reaction against the desegregation plan. It was against administrators unwilling to equalize teachers' pay during the reorganization (Raffel 1980, 194).

Religious organizations, business organizations, and several coalitions supported the formation of a desegregation plan. The religious organizations encouraged people to comply with a lawful order and to be good examples to the rest of the nation. Religious leaders spread information. They urged people to keep the peace. They pressured public and school officials to prepare for the beginning of desegregation. The business community set up a separate organization, SANE, to seek peaceful compliance with the court decision (Raffel 1980, 120–153).

Opponents of busing organized into a single group called the Positive Action Committee (PAC) that enrolled almost ten thousand people. PAC had the greatest impact on the state legislature and may have influenced Senator Joseph Biden to adopt an antibusing view. Interestingly, the PAC may have encouraged peaceful implementation, because the group worked to influence elections and legislative bodies. This discouraged public disobedience (Raffel 1980, 154–173).

At best, limited white flight occurred. Some white families moved from the area before and after desegregation. In New Castle County, white enrollment in the schools dropped from 73,000 students in 1971 to 56,500 in 1977. Black enrollment rose during the same period from 16,400 to 16,700 students. Enrollments in nonpublic schools rose from 15,000 to 16,700 students. When the desegregation plan began in 1978, the number of white students in New Castle County public schools dropped by over 6,000 students. Some decline in white students reflects lower birth rates, the migration of families, and the growing popularity of fundamentalist schools (Raffel 1980, 175–187).

The experiences differed in Nashville, Tennessee. White flight was a problem there.

Nashville, Tennessee

In 1955 the city of Nashville and Davidson County operated dual school systems. Black students and white students attended separate schools. However, 40 percent of the people in Nashville were black, while in the surrounding independent suburbs the population was white. In March 1956 a U.S. district court judge ordered the Nashville city schools to desegregate (Pride and Woodward 1985, 54–55).

The school board chose to begin with the first grades and desegregate one grade per year. The plan assigned 115 black children to previously white schools and fifty-five white students to black schools. Furthermore, the board allowed children to request transfers. All the white children refused to go to black schools, and only thirteen of the black children agreed to attend white schools. Despite these severe limits, the citizens of Nashville reacted violently to the effort to integrate schools. Authorities such as the city attorney of Nashville tried to end violence by prosecuting segregationists who caused disturbances. Nonetheless, there were bombings and protests (Pride and Woodward 1985, 55–56).

In 1957 the U.S. district court ended the freedom of choice that characterized the first plan and made the grade per school per year plan compulsory. In 1960 the court ordered Davidson County schools to imitate Nashville's plan. The city and county school systems merged and the new board adopted the one grade per year plan in 1963. The new metropolitan board asked all schools in the county to integrate by 1966–67. This did not happen. In 1969, 83 percent of the white students in the county attended schools with only white children (Pride and Woodward 1985, 54–58).

In 1969 the plaintiffs ·in the original suit sued again in U.S. district court, complaining that the board used geographical school zones that hindered integration. As a result, black students attended inferior schools in the city, while white students went to newer buildings in the suburbs. In July 1970 the judge ordered the schools to desegregate the staff, to desegregate the students, and to identify school construction sites that would enhance desegregation. Although appeals continued, in August 1970 the board adopted plans to increase desegregation without requiring busing (Pride and Woodward 1985, 61–63).

To desegregate the elementary schools, the board decided to have larger schools that drew children from wider areas. For the secondary schools, they chose to build comprehensive schools that would attract as many different types of children to the same building as possible. In 1971 the U.S. district court judge rejected this plan. He asked a team of experts from the U.S. Department of Health, Education, and Welfare to draw one (Pride and Woodward 1985, 64–70).

The HEW team followed two important elements the U.S. Supreme Court approved in 1971 in *Swann v Charlotte-Mecklenburg*. First, they transported students out of their neighborhoods to desegregate schools. Second, they used a mathematical ratio of black and white students to decide the appropriate level of desegregation. The HEW team paired schools in the city with schools in the suburbs to keep any of Nashville's schools from being all black. When they proposed busing 15,000 children, the public gasped (Pride and Woodward 1985, 69–74).

When schools opened on 5 September 1971, there was little trouble. However, the plan failed to desegregate the schools. Students in the entire county district represented a ratio of 75 percent white and 25 percent black. The buildings did not reach this level because that year 8,600 white students fled the system (Pride and Woodward 1985, 75–82).

There was no simple answer why white parents removed their children. Although wealthy parents were more easily able to withdraw their children than poor ones, to some extent the reasons for doing so varied according to the age of the child. Many of the fears that caused parents to withdraw their children were groundless. For example, some parents said that the racial integration would hurt academic achievement. However, the achievement of the children as measured by standardized tests improved after starting the desegregation plan (Pride and Woodward 1985, 106–125).

Some white children avoided the desegregation plan by moving within the public schools. That is, the children left their assigned public schools to enroll in public schools not touched by the busing plan because they served desegregated neighborhoods. Other white students enrolled in private schools. In 1969, 9 percent of the county's first-graders were in private schools. By 1978–79, this portion grew to 20 percent of the county's first-graders. In all, the private schools doubled their share of school enrollments during ten years of busing (Pride and Woodward 1985, 126–143).

Because of this rapidly growing interest in private education, several new schools opened in Davidson County. Of the forty-three private schools in the county, seventeen opened after 1969. Many of these private facilities were Christian schools, but they did not entirely exclude blacks. In one new Christian school, all of the 110 students were black. Interestingly, the parents sent their children to private schools hoping they would learn the values of self-discipline, hard work, and proper manners. They feared the values would disappear in racially integrated schools (Pride and Woodward 1985, 157–162).

Not surprisingly, parents whose children stayed in the public schools had a more favorable view of the desegregated schools than did the public. Yet approval of desegregation followed racial lines between parents and teachers. That is, black parents approved of desegregation more than white parents. White teachers thought desegregation hurt white students. Black teachers disagreed. Black teachers were more likely to say that busing improved race relations than were white teachers. However, neither group of teachers thought busing improved the self-esteem of black students (Pride and Woodward 1985, 142–165).

Among Nashville's high school students, the fear of another culture seemed to motivate transfers among the schools. In 1978 the plaintiffs in the original case complained the district violated the order by building schools in the white suburban areas of the county and by closing schools in the black urban areas. They added that the district allowed whites to avoid desegregation. The board replied that the suburban schools were integrated and offered comprehensive programs. The board contended white students transferred from black high schools in the city because those schools did not offer subject matter specialties found in the comprehensive schools in the suburbs. However, when asked why they left a high school in the city, the white students said the school was a symbol of black culture and they did not want to be part of it (Pride and Woodward 1985, 177–188).

On the matter of transfers, the attitudes of black students mirrored the attitudes of the white students. This became clear in August 1979, when the U.S. district court found that the 1971 court order caused resegregation. The judge ordered the schools to develop a plan to desegregate the entire county. The school board held hearings to determine how to organize the schools. African Americans asked for predominantly black schools for their children. To respond to the wishes of the two groups, the judge requested a plan with neighborhood schools in May 1980. The student enrollment of these neighborhood schools would have at least 15 percent black or white students. Consequently, some schools could have a white or a black atmosphere. In 1982 the court of appeals reversed this decision (Pride and Woodward 1985, 182; 183; 298–299).

The ten years of conflict in Nashville demonstrated that neither black people nor white people would willingly occupy the status of a minority culture. Each group wanted to dominate in schools and this desire caused problems. The middle-class white families were the most mobile, and they left the public schools for private academies. However, Nashville was not unique. The desire to maintain a cultural identity threatened desegregation efforts in other cities. For example, in San Francisco, Asian groups fought to maintain the neighborhood schools to preserve their cultural heritage.

San Francisco, California

In July 1971 San Francisco was the first large nonsouthern city ordered to racially desegregate its schools. The issue began in January

1962. Leaders from Congress of Racial Equality (CORE) and the Council for Civic Unity urged the San Francisco school board to admit to segregated schools, to declare this undesirable, and to prepare a desegregation program. The superintendent and the board refused (Kirp 1982, 85).

In September 1962, 1,400 citizens attended a meeting to demand that the school board set up a citizens' group to recommend ways to end racial isolation in the schools. The board refused to set up the committee. However, some members of the board formed an ad hoc committee to study the issue. The NAACP sued in U.S. district court, asking for district-wide desegregation (Kirp 1982, 87).

In April 1963 the ad hoc committee released its report acknowledging segregation in the San Francisco schools. Although the report denied that the segregation resulted from board policy, it recommended that racial balance be a criterion in drawing school assignment boundaries. This admission, along with the reassignment of several hundred minority students and the appointment of a black human relations officer, satisfied the civil rights groups. The NAACP let the suit lapse (Kirp 1982, 87–88).

In 1965 the Coordinating Council for Integrated Schools, a coalition of civil rights groups in San Francisco, asked the board to determine the extent of the segregation then in the city schools. When the board released the information, it documented a considerable amount of integration. To obtain an outside evaluation, the board commissioned a study from the Stanford Research Institute. The board ignored the study's conclusions. In July 1967 a new superintendent took office. He proposed building educational parks to improve the schools and to desegregate them. When several community groups argued against the parks, the board appointed a citizen's advisory committee to recommend action (Kirp 1982, 89–91).

In February 1969 the committee suggested integrating two middle-class areas or subdistricts where pupil reassignment would be easy because the neighborhoods were already racially mixed. Nonetheless, even this limited desegregation caused controversy, as San Francisco's mayor took a position against the busing needed to set up the integration. Because of the furor, in June 1970 San Francisco voters passed a referendum advising the board not to bus children for racial balance (Kirp 1982, 92–93).

On 24 June 1970 the NAACP sued again in U.S. district court to cause desegregation. On 22 September 1970 the judge postponed a decision until the U.S. Supreme Court decided *Swann v Charlotte-Mecklenburg*. In April 1971, after the higher court had concluded, he ordered the San Francisco schools to desegregate by September. The judge ordered both the district and the NAACP to prepare desegregation plans. When he received them, he allowed the school administrators to choose the plan they wanted to use, thinking that this would encourage community acceptance (Kirp 1982, 94–100).

As the plans were being prepared, ethnic politics came to the fore. In May 1971 Chinese American residents of San Francisco complained the desegregation would disrupt their community-based public schools, assaulting their ethnic identity. They filed a motion to testify about the effects of the proposed remedies. The judge denied them the opportunity (Kirp 1982, 103–104).

In September 1972, while the Ninth Circuit Court of Appeals considered the case, the San Francisco schools set up a desegregation plan. However, in 1971 one third of the elementary schools fell out of racial balance. By 1975 the percentage of racially imbalanced schools had risen to almost one half. This happened because in 1971, several schools were almost racially balanced. As white people left those neighborhoods, the racial proportions in the schools tipped. In 1981 about 40 percent as many whites attended the elementary schools as attended in 1970. In addition, trying to placate the irate Chinese, the board did not include them in the desegregation plan (Kirp 1982, 107–108).

Segregation within school buildings increased. Although the judge forbade the use of educational techniques that segregated students, the school district placed too many black students in special classes. For example, in 1981, 60 percent of the enrollment in classes for the educable mentally retarded and educationally handicapped were African Americans yet blacks made up only 27.6 percent of the district's students (Kirp 1982, 107–108).

On 22 June 1974 the appeals court decided to remand the case to district court. The appeals court justices thought that the district court had not shown that public officials deliberately caused the racial segregation of the schools. Unfortunately, the case ended because, by 1974, the people who had started it had lost interest (Kirp 1982, 106–107).

Bilingual Education and Black Power

The Chinese families in San Francisco who sought to preserve their neighborhood schools raised a significant language issue that affected other minority groups. In March 1970 the Chinatown office of the San Francisco legal services filed the case *Lau v Nichols.* They contended that the English-only instruction in the public schools harmed the nearly 3,000 students of Chinese origin who did not speak English. In 1974 the case reached the U.S. Supreme Court. The justices decided that the equality of education required by the 1964 Civil Rights Act compelled the schools extended special aid to students who did not speak English. While they did not specify what the necessary education should be, the justices precluded simple desegregation (Orfield 1978, 207; and Salomone 1986, 98).

To some extent, the decision in *Lau v Nichols* contradicted an earlier decision about Mexican Americans. Until 1973, federal courts had allowed school districts to treat Mexican Americans as white students. Consequently, Houston, Texas, integrated blacks and Chicanos, leaving Anglos in all-white schools. However, in *Keyes v School District 1 in Denver, Colorado,* the court cited a study by the U.S. Civil Rights Commission showing that blacks and Mexican Americans shared common problems. As a result, the city schools had to desegregate both groups and white students. The school district wanted to leave some Spanish-speaking children in special programs or separate schools. The U.S. Court of Appeals refused to accept these programs as a substitute for desegregation (Orfield 1978, 28–30).

In all these cases, the courts avoided judging the effectiveness of any educational program. They asked school districts to attend to the special problems faced by children who do not speak English. The decisions did not mandate separate schools because once the child learned English the problems disappeared. Furthermore, in 1978 in *Martin Luther King Jr. Elementary School Children v Ann Arbor School District,* the U.S. district court extended the problems of language to include black English (Salomone 1986, 102).

Cultural pluralism and the racial desegregation of schools are not mutually exclusive. School districts could have devised programs that allowed both. For political reasons, the policy directions appeared to contradict each other. The U.S. Department of Health, Education, and Welfare enforced its guidelines calling for bilingual education and neglected its guideline requiring racial desegregation. The unfortunate result was that increased bilingual education accompanied more racial segregation in schools (Orfield 1978, 220).

More important, several African Americans came to value cultural pluralism over racial integration. Before the 1960s, the civil rights movement represented an unwillingness to tolerate racial segregation. By 1962, however, disaffection with the NAACP led many African Americans to conceive of a variety of alternate responses (Lomax 1962). For example, the black power movement sought community control of the schools to help black children develop pride in their culture and to tailor compensatory education to their needs. The experiences in Oakland, California illustrated the growth of this movement.

Oakland, California

Black power advocates asserted that they did not choose segregation. They said that white people made separate schools the only alternative. This was the case in Oakland. During the 1960s, whites left the city of Oakland at a rate that made integration unlikely. Almost half of the sixty thousand children in the Oakland schools were white in the early 1960s. By 1979, less than 15 percent of the students were white (Kirp 1982, 218).

The controversy over desegregation began in January 1961 in Oakland, when Skyline High School opened in the wealthy, white section of the city. The NAACP complained that the attendance boundaries for the high school created a private school supported by public funds. The long-term white superintendent disagreed, saying the boundaries were reasonable and the neighborhood was changing to become socially heterogeneous. In 1962 the NAACP threatened to sue to cause desegregation. In May of that year the board agreed to establish a citizens' committee to study the issue. When the committee formed in January 1963, the board asked it to suggest ways to alleviate minority group concentrations. By that time, a newly appointed superintendent had time to propose an open enrollment policy designed to ease overcrowding in some buildings (Kirp 1982, 220–224).

The citizens' advisory committee recommended redrawing attendance zone lines in May 1964. White parents complained the suggestions would cause white flight. As a result, the board rejected the committee's plans. However, in October 1964 the California Commission on Equal Education recommended that the board change the controversial attendance zone of the Skyline High School. State education officials publicly rebuked the Oakland board and the Oakland Federation of Teachers. The NAACP and the Alameda County Central Labor Council urged the change. In January 1965 the board expanded the high school attendance zone, permitting students from mostly black junior high schools to attend the building. The board also agreed to prepare a master plan for desegregation. They set up nondiscriminatory teacher hiring and assignment practices to increase the numbers of minority teachers in the schools (Kirp 1982, 226–229).

By 1966 the school administration sought to hold on to the remaining white students in the district. Consequently, the open enrollment plan became a way for white students to attend schools with other white students. In 1966 and again in 1968, when proposals for interdistrict desegregation came to the board, the members did not attend to them. In 1977, the state department of education demanded that Oakland schools make progress toward desegregation. When the Oakland school board created a new citizens' advisory committee, its report said, "The time for integration was the 1960s. We're in the 1970s. Integration is outdated" (Kirp 1982, 230–232).

In the middle 1960s whites no longer dominated the politics of Oakland schools. Instead, minority groups came to the fore. Between 1966 and 1970 more than one hundred groups formed to influence school policy; most of them dissolved as quickly. In April 1966, twenty-one organizations joined as the Ad Hoc Committee for Quality Education. Although this umbrella group asked for several specific things to satisfy its constituent members, it turned discussions to questions of community control. Board meetings became heated and often violent confrontations as black activists complained that more money was spent on affluent schools than on poor schools (Kirp 1982, 233–235).

The education of deprived students became an explosive issue. Title I ESEA funds were supposed to be spent on the educationally disadvantaged. In 1966–67, Oakland school administrators spread $5.5 million of these monies throughout the schools. Officials in other communities did the same thing. However, when a state audit revealed this fact, black activists contended the Oakland school board was unconcerned about poor pupils. They said the only remedy was for community organizations to participate in board affairs. Consequently, in 1969 another umbrella group of community organizations called Community United for Relevant Education wanted to take a part in the selection of a new superintendent. The board rejected these proposals (Kirp 1982, 239–240).

Fortunately, the board selected as superintendent a black administrator, Marcus Foster, who could help African American schools without alienating the remaining whites. Foster did not see racial desegregation as the central concern. Instead, he established a series of citizens' committees that took their members from the various interest groups vying for control in the community. These committees gave the district suggestions about buildings, finance, and curriculum. Furthermore, Foster decentralized the district by dividing it into three regions. Each region was to have more control over its own buildings, making it easier for parents to resolve problems in the schools. In addition, Foster changed the distribution of resources. He gave more money per pupil to schools with more minority and disadvantaged children than to schools with white or advantaged children (Kirp 1982, 241–243).

Because of Foster's administration, public distrust of the schools declined, confrontational meetings disappeared, and new programs, such as bilingual education, began. However, these changes were more symbolic than real. The parents did not have more access because of the decentralization. Nor did changes in expenditures affect school achievement (Kirp 1982, 244).

Unfortunately, in 1973 a member of the Symbionese Liberation Army assassinated Foster. The board continued to disregard integration when in 1975 it appointed as superintendent a black woman who once taught in the district. She emphasized the needs of minority students and educational achievement instead of desegregation or citizen involvement. For example, she created an Instructional Strategy Council to develop curriculum guides emphasizing competence in literacy and arithmetic. In addition, she tried to make the teachers accountable for the students' performance (Kirp 1982, 244–245).

NAACP Suffers a Loss

Although black activists in Oakland lost interest in racial integration, the NAACP continued to push the U.S. courts to expand the rights of black children. However, in 1974 the U.S. Supreme Court balanced the supposed rights of black children to attend desegregated schools and the potential rights of white children to attend their neighborhood schools. In *Milliken v Bradley,* the court limited the extent of desegregation by deciding that the white children in suburban Detroit could not be forced to cross district lines to attend schools in the predominantly black city schools. Unfortunately, the only way to solve the problems of Detroit schools seemed to be to create a metropolitan district.

In 1965, a liberal board of education took office and tried to improve the schools. Supported by organized labor and by civil rights activists, this board increased the number of black administrators and teachers and mandated multicultural education across the curriculum. To help the board achieve its ends, newly elected Democratic representatives to the state legislature voted increases in state aid to the Detroit schools. Unfortunately, the board faced increased criticism about the failure of inner-city Detroit schools. Local news stories portrayed these schools as places where the classrooms lacked basic supplies, the teachers felt demoralized, and the students did worse on standardized tests the longer they remained in the buildings. Although the liberal board tried to improve the schools and move toward integration, black power advocates demanded community control of the schools (Mirel 1993, 294–306).

Six days of rioting began in Detroit on 23 July 1968. The rioting injured more than one thousand people and killed forty-three. Estimates of property damage reached $125 million. Views of the riot differed according to the race of the spectators. University of Michigan researchers found that white citizens thought the event was spontaneous criminal anarchy, while black residents saw the riot as a protest against mistreatment. In the hearings that followed, the liberal school board members and administrators contended that the problems were financial. They said it would cost at least $8.12 million to repair the schools. Many black activists rejected this liberal prescription. They urged African American parents to take control of the schools in their neighborhoods. As a result, a formerly effective coalition of white labor leaders, white liberals, and black leaders lost power as black activists campaigned to decentralize the control of the Detroit schools and the white working class broke from its own union leadership, refusing to vote for school taxes (Mirel 1993, 310–313).

In 1968, disregarding the recommendations from their unions, white laborers voted for the Republican party and against the liberal-proposed school tax increase. In October 1970, reacting to the possibility of racial desegregation of Detroit schools, voters elected a conservative school board. Faced with a $12 million deficit in 1971, the board eliminated such courses as art and music. They reduced the teaching force. In 1971, the appeals court ordered the state board of education to prepare a desegregation plan that included the school districts in Wayne, Oakland, and Macomb counties. Almost immediately, Robert W. Griffen, Republican senator from Michigan, introduced a constitutional amendment to ban busing for racial integration. Voters circulated petitions to recall Michigan's Democratic pro-busing senator. Facing anti-busing frenzy, the Detroit school board asked voters to approve a renewal and an increase of the school operating levies. Although the projected school deficit was $40 million and there was no organized opposition, the issues failed, as anger over school busing dominated all the elections. A poll of voters showed that they wanted money to be spent on school improvement, not busing. Many people said that refusing to give the schools money could delay desegregation (Mirel 1993, 345–352).

To help the nearly bankrupt district, the state legislature advanced $73 million to the Detroit schools. It gave the school board the power to levy a property tax and an income tax without voter approval in 1973. Instead of helping the schools, this new power contributed to popular fears that a business elite would foist taxes and racial desegregation on the city. A new school board took office with mostly black members. The new board imposed an income tax, but repealed it after voters approved a property tax increase to operate the schools (Mirel 1993, 353–356).

While the city school faced economic problems, the NAACP pushed for a metropolitan remedy for racial desegregation in the Detroit, Michigan, schools. The problem was that if racial desegregation of schools was limited to the city alone, the city schools would remain racially identifiable. By 1973 the school population in Detroit was 70 percent black. Yet, all the schools in the metropolitan area had a student population that was 81 percent white (U.S. Commission on Civil Rights 1977, 84–86). Some advocates contended that, in Detroit, a metropolitan remedy required little busing because the distances were short and costs low (Orfield 1978, 186). On the other hand, critics called the proposed plan the most ambitious desegregation proposal ever made. It covered three counties that included fifty-two suburban school districts and the Detroit schools. It involved about 780,000 students (Mirel 1993, 345).

At the U.S. Supreme Court, the justices did not consider the feasibility of the desegregation plan when they reversed the findings in the lower courts. Most of the justices said the evidence showed Detroit school officials committed constitutional violations. To protect the tradition of local control of schools, they felt the remedy had to stay within that district. The NAACP found one case where a suburban district sent black children to a black school in Detroit. The justices saw this as an isolated instance that involved only two districts. Further, the justices added that the state government's actions had not changed more than one district. This made an interdistrict remedy unnecessary (U.S. Commission on Civil Rights 1977, 87–89).

In *Milliken v Bradley,* the U.S. Supreme Court justices repeated their desire to remove only that racial segregation caused by specific official acts. The NAACP tried to expand that intention, arguing that all sorts of policies, such as federal mortgage insurance, had caused racial segregation. While the NAACP had not won on those grounds, they had forced the court to accept only effective desegregation plans.

Green v County School Board of New Kent County was a 1968 case involving a rural Virginia town with two schools. These schools had been racially distinct. To desegregate, the school board gave the children the freedom to choose which school they wanted to attend. The school board made it difficult for blacks to choose to attend the white school by doing such things as scheduling few open enrollment periods. If black parents persisted, white retaliation often scared them away. However, these actions did not influence the justices. The Court relied on statistical evidence to decide that the freedom of choice was illusory. Plans had to work (Salomone 1986, 46–47).

Statistical evidence did not influence the justices in *Milliken v Bradley* for a reason. The state of Virginia had mandated separate schools for black and for white students before 1954, while Michigan had not. This distinction between northern and southern states had not impressed the lower courts. In the lower courts, judges found the state of Michigan responsible for offering equal education to all its residents. They said the state had the power to consolidate school districts to provide relief. Unfortunately for the NAACP, most of the U.S. Supreme Court justices disagreed (U.S. Commission on Civil Rights 1977, 86–87).

The NAACP pressed ahead with its aims to desegregate the schools in the city. In 1973–74, 158 schools in the city had student populations over 90 percent black. Twenty-seven schools had student populations 90 percent white and forty-six schools ranged between 65 and 89 percent white. In January 1976 the schools began a program of racial desegregation. The judge introduced middle schools, made curriculum innovations, began construction of five vocational centers, and expanded bilingual education. Most important, he demanded that the state contribute $70 million because it had played a part in creating the segregation (Mirel 1993, 357).

Despite the school improvements that accompanied racial desegregation, white students left the system. Between 1971 and 1976 the number of white students dropped by 51,000. By 1984 the Detroit schools were an almost all-black system; fewer than 10 percent of the student population, or 19,000 students, were white (Mirel 1993, 359).

Milliken v Bradley had wide-ranging effects. The public furor surrounding the *Milliken* decision whipped up anti-busing sentiment in Detroit that hurt the local school finances. People who opposed busing expressed their opinions by defeating school tax votes

(Mirel 1993, 346). At the national level, the *Milliken* decision slowed the drive for racial desegregation as lawyers generally agreed not to take any case resembling Detroit to the U.S. Supreme Court. Further, the court's decision to limit desegregation among school districts ended the drive to adopt a constitutional amendment forbidding busing for racial balance (Orfield 1978, 391–395).

However, a ruling about metropolitan housing in 1976 called *Hills v Gautraux* raised questions whether plans to remedy segregation could include suburbs and cities. In their decision, the U.S. Supreme Court justices said the *Milliken* decision did not prevent the federal courts from ordering a remedial effort extending beyond municipal boundaries. Of course, metropolitan housing could not be a substitute for school desegregation. Minorities have limited opportunities to obtain housing in suburbs (U.S. Commission on Civil Rights 1977, 2, 98–99).

Although the U.S. Commission on Civil Rights approved of metropolitan plans, they were not panaceas. Even in successful programs, administrative details limited meaningful desegregation. The experiences in St. Louis, Missouri, illustrated this point.

St. Louis, Missouri

Like Delaware, Missouri had mandated racially segregated schools. However, in Delaware the Wilmington schools and the suburban schools were both in New Castle County. In Missouri the school districts that formed the metropolitan plan in St. Louis in 1982 were in two different counties. One was St. Louis City, an independent county with almost 60 percent of all African Americans in the metropolitan district. The other was St. Louis County, a collection that contained ninety-two municipalities, twenty townships, and twenty-three school districts (Monti 1985, 32).

From 1955 to 1971, school districts in the suburban county merged twice. The first was in 1960 when a predominantly white district, Berkeley, annexed Scudder School District, a district with many black youngsters and several industries. The second merger took place fifteen years later.

A University of Chicago team recommended in 1962 that the newly enlarged Berkeley district merge also with Kinloch, a small but poor and all-black district. The U.S. Department of Justice made a similar but futile appeal to local authorities. Finally, the U.S. district court ordered Berkeley, Kinloch, and Ferguson-Florissant to merge during the 1975–76 school year (Monti 1985, 36).

Although the public quietly accepted the merger of these three school districts, student enrollment declined by 38 percent from 1975 until 1982. However, in the reorganization, the school administration closed some schools and reduced staff by 25 percent. Other county school districts not under a desegregation order suffered declines in student enrollment during the same period, but public pressure prevented the administrators of those districts from making similar adjustments (Monti 1985, 102).

In part, problems arose because the court directed most of its attention to school governance during desegregation. The judge was careful to ensure that the new school board was composed of four members from the Ferguson-Florissant district, one member from Kinloch, and one member from Berkeley. In addition, a biracial advisory committee was to help in all matters related to desegregation. Former members from the three former districts sat on this committee. However, authority to handle most of the problems in forming the new larger district fell to the former administrators from the old Ferguson-Florissant. Most important, these administrators devised ways to act independently (Monti 1985, 105–106).

Initially, school officials sought the approval of leaders in the area. School administrators met with civic and religious groups, realtors, and media representatives. Accepting the professionalism of the school administrators, the leaders of the civic groups did not intrude or try to oversee the school reorganization. In addition, school officials held meetings with parents to answer questions about the plans. Believing these sessions reassured the parents about the changes, school officials did not talk in public once the meetings were over. They distributed information to the advisory committees that served the board (Monti 1985, 106–107).

However, since the desegregation programs lacked external review, some problems persisted. During the 1976–77 school year, project staff from the University of Missouri at St. Louis Center for Metropolitan Studies documented several problems. These included a higher suspension rate for black students than for white students, longer bus rides for black students, preventing them from participating in extracurricular activities, teachers using prejudicial language in classrooms, a lack of materials in an educational center in Kinloch, white staff relying on black staff to solve problems with black students, and a feeling of distrust among the parents of Berkeley and Kinloch toward the staff (Monti 1985, 110).

Instead of correcting the difficulties, school officials avoided taking action. For example, when black parents complained about the treatment of their children, the administrators asked black staff to promise that officials would look into the problem or point out to the parents that the children had made trouble previously. When white parents complained that a black principal was prejudiced against their children, the board of education listened to the complaints but did not act. The parents called federal and state officials who told them that they had to provide the names, dates, and times and descriptions of the incidents before any official investigation would begin. The parents placed an ad in the paper to gather such information; they were unsuccessful (Monti 1985, 112–113).

The court appointed biracial advisory committee to monitor the desegregation plans, yet the committee members relied on school administrators for information rather than visit schools. Another advisory committee concentrated on curricular issues; it depended on school officials to provide information and develop proposals also. Unfortunately, school officials would give information to the committee members and ask them to approve procedures at the same meeting, thereby allowing no time for an independent investigation of the issues (Monti 1985, 116–117).

In addition, some programs disguised school problems. For example, the advisement systems seemed to help white students, but they failed black students. Black students complained informally about the cursory treatment they received from counselors. As a result, there was no record of their dissatisfaction. The students may have complained informally because the court-mandated grievance system discouraged complaints. The only way parents or students became part of the grievance procedure was as complainants. Once a building supervisor made a decision, subsequent appeal upheld it. More important, the school officials did not tell parents or students about the grievance procedures that were available to them.

Despite these problems, the school's annual report noted the absence of complaints as a sign of student happiness (Monti 1985, 119–121).

In February 1972 a group called Concerned Parents for North St. Louis sued in U.S. district court to desegregate the St. Louis city schools. The board of education acknowledged that the schools were segregated, but contended that the schools' population changed too rapidly to build buildings or adjust attendance zones. Before the judge ruled, the parents and the board agreed to a compromise. In 1963 about 50 percent of the secondary students and more than 60 percent of the elementary school children were black. By 1975 the city's school population was half the size it had been in 1967. More than 70 percent of the students were black (Monti 1985, 39–41; 131).

On 24 December 1975, as part of the consent decree in U.S. district court, the school district agreed to do three things: reduce segregation by realigning the elementary buildings with the high schools, reassign staff to improve their racial balance, and establish magnet school programs that offered specialized curricula to students participating in racial desegregation. On 29 January 1975, the board approved a $7 million plan to fulfill the consent decree and establish nine alternative schools. An advisory committee of forty-seven people selected by the district selected the type, size, location, and details of the magnet schools (Monti 1985, 133–138).

The solution was unpopular with everyone: Groups who supported desegregation and people who wanted neighborhood schools disliked the idea. The NAACP, a parents' group, and the U.S. Department of Justice sued in U.S. district court for increased desegregation. They contended that the board changed attendance zones after 1954 in ways that maintained segregated schools. For example, some busing took place to relieve overcrowding in some schools. In transporting black students to a white school, the district sent an entire class and kept them apart from other students in the school. Despite these complaints, in April 1979 the U.S. district court judge agreed with the school district that it had done as much as possible. The Eighth Circuit Court of Appeals disagreed and reversed his decision (Monti 1985, 40).

In 1980–81 the St. Louis City schools began a desegregation plan for the district's sixty-three thousand students that cost about $23 million. Although the plan reduced segregation, problems remained. For example, two-thirds of the district's black students in the elementary grades attended segregated schools (Monti 1985, 40).

Nonetheless, in the magnet programs, the students got along well together because they chose to be there. Often, the students chose a school in their neighborhood for its nearness. They did not choose a school for its program. As a result, the magnet schools and nonmagnet schools had similar retention rates. Of the students who attended magnet schools in 1976, only half remained in the same school three years later. Further, sometimes the academic programs suffered because the specialty area was over emphasized (Monti 1985, 139–141).

The level of test results of children in the St. Louis magnet schools was higher than that of other students. However, these higher scores may not have come from the work done in the magnet schools. The youngsters who chose the magnet schools may have been more talented academically. In 1982 students in magnet schools in St. Louis had higher pretest scores than did their peers in nonmagnet schools. Interestingly, some nonmagnet high schools had students who had high pretest scores. These were schools in racially integrated areas (Monti 1985, 139–144).

In designing the reorganization, the planners designated schools near the predominantly white elementary schools in St. Louis's Southside as integrated clusters. In this way, they kept busing distances short and did not frighten the white students away by sending them to neighborhoods they feared to enter. However, the result was that schools in the northern third of the city remained segregated. Most important, these predominantly black schools contained the students with the least academic ability. Better prepared white students entered the magnets. The academically prepared black students remaining in the nonmagnet schools attended schools in integrated clusters (Monti 1985, 144–145).

In 1981 the board of education and the NAACP sued to form a metropolitan plan with several additional counties and more than forty districts. The U.S. district court ordered the St. Louis County schools to voluntarily participate in student exchanges with St. Louis

City to enhance desegregation. Although the order appeared para-doxical, communities that ignored or marginally obeyed the order faced the imposition of a desegregation plan. As a result, by the summer of 1982, eleven districts joined the city's plan. Other districts offered to join later (Monti 1985, 41; 147).

In 1981–82 three hundred white students from the suburbs attended city schools. During the same year, 240 black students from the city went to the suburban schools. These exchanges may not have reduced inequities. Suburban communities screened the students. The officials told less desirable candidates that they must repeat a grade. Nonetheless, the plan profited the districts that participated. In 1981–82, the state paid host districts $1,250 per student plus 50 percent of any remaining balance of the basic cost of education. As a result, the voluntary-mandatory metropolitan plan served to maintain racial inequalities in St. Louis. White students left. Students from lower social classes remained together (Monti 1985, 149–150).

Conclusion

There were many ways that people in different cities tried to bring about racial desegregation. Since the debates about school desegregation centered on such things as states' rights, judicial activism, cultural pluralism, and local control, few people thought about why black and white students should be together. In order to think about the needs of a human community, people needed an ideal that promoted human freedoms while it called attention to the needs of the society. Religion should have offered such an alternative. Sometimes, it did point to values all people could share. However, other times, religion appeared to justify segregation.

References

Ashmore, Harry S. 1994. *Civil Rights and Wrongs*. New York: Pantheon Books.
Bagwell, William. 1972. *Desegregation in the Carolinas*. Columbia: University of South Carolina Press.
Baker, Scott. 1995. "Testing Equality," *History of Education Quarterly* 1:49–64.
Bartley, Numan. 1969. *The Rise of Massive Resistance*. Baton Rouge: Louisiana State University Press.
Bates, Daisy. 1962. *The Long Shadow of Little Rock*. New York: David McKay.
Blossom, Virgil T. 1959. *It Has Happened Here*. New York: Harper and Brothers.
Coleman, James, et al. 1975. *Trends in School Segregation: 1968–1973*. Washington, D.C.: Urban Institute.

Coleman, James. 1976. "Correspondence: Response to Pettigrew and Green,"
    Harvard Educational Review 2:217–224.

Commission on Professional Rights. 1970. *Beyond Desegregation: The Problem of
    Power.* Washington, D.C.: National Education Association.

Formisano, Ronald. 1991. *Boston Against Busing.* Chapel Hill: University of North Caro-
    lina Press.

Freyer, Tony. 1984. *The Little Rock Crisis.* Westport, Conn.: Greenwood Press.

Kirp, David. 1982. *Just Schools.* Berkeley: University of California Press.

Lomax, Louis. 1962. *The Negro Revolt.* New York: New American Library.

Metcalf, George R. 1983. *From Little Rock to Boston.* Westport, Conn.: Greenwood
    Press.

Mirel, Jeffrey. 1993. *The Rise and Fall of an Urban School System.* Ann Arbor: Univer-
    sity of Michigan Press.

Monti, Daniel J. 1985. *A Semblance of Justice.* Columbia: University of Missouri
    Press.

Orfield, Gary. 1969. *The Reconstruction of Southern Education.* New York: John Wiley
    and Sons.

————. *Must We Bus?* 1978. Washington, D.C.: Brookings Institution.

Pettigrew, Thomas, and Robert Green. 1976a. "School Desegregation in Large Cities,"
    Harvard Educational Review 1:1–53.

————. 1976b. "Reply to Coleman," *Harvard Educational Review* 2:225–233.

Pride, Richard, and J. David Woodward. 1985. *The Burden of Busing.* Knoxville: Univer-
    sity of Tennessee Press.

Raffel, Jeffrey. 1980. *The Politics of School Desegregation.* Philadelphia: Temple Uni-
    versity Press.

Salomone, Rosemary. 1986. *Equal Education Under the Law.* New York: St. Martin's
    Press.

U.S. Commission on Civil Rights. 1973. *Title IV and School Desegregation.* Washing-
    ton, D.C.: U.S. Government Printing Office.

————. 1975. *School Desegregation in Boston.* Washington, D.C.: U.S. Government
    Printing Office.

————. 1976. *Fulfilling the Letter and Spirit of the Law.* Washington, D.C.: U.S. Gov-
    ernment Printing Office.

————. 1977. *Statement on Metropolitan School Desegregation.* Washington, D.C.:
    U.S. Government Printing Office.

Warner, Sam B. 1970. *Streetcar Suburbs.* New York: Atheneum.

Chapter Two
Private and Religious Schools

Controversies over the racial integration of public schools extended beyond the schools themselves. Sometimes, religious leaders played roles in the civil rights movement. Private schools were important. In the 1950s, in defiance of the U.S. Supreme Court decisions, the legislatures of North and South Carolina approved bills to grant tuition to students who wished to attend private schools. Without state aid, many private segregationist academies began when courts ordered the formerly white public schools to integrate. Fundamentalist Christian schools rapidly replaced these private academies. In time, the Christian schools accepted black students. In some ways, Catholic schools profited from the desegregation of public schools. However, busing controversies and white flight influenced urban Catholic schools in the same way they affected urban public schools.

While many religious leaders wanted to advance the civil rights movement, they had trouble calling people's attention to the religious reasons for racial integration. These problems appeared early in the struggle. In 1957, during the crisis at Central High School in Little Rock, twenty-seven local pastors of small Baptist sects sponsored a service to pray for continued segregation. The next day, nearly all rabbis, priests, and ministers sponsored city wide prayers for peace. Less than a week later, two researchers, Ernest Q. Campbell and Thomas F. Pettigrew, surveyed the participants from both services. They interviewed forty-two clergy from Protestant churches and Jewish synagogues in Little Rock. Catholic priests did not participate. The respondents tended to be community leaders and, apparently, were white (Campbell and Pettigrew 1959, 12–15).

Campbell and Pettigrew found that the clerics faced a dilemma. On the one hand, by the time of the crisis, the national organiza-

tions of major Protestant churches committed themselves unequivo-
cally to racial integration. On the other hand, the parishioners in
Little Rock did not want the clergy to support desegregation. To
solve the dilemma, these religious leaders reached an uneasy compromise with their parishioners. The parishioners did not try to force
the clergy to support continued segregation. However, most of the
church members wanted the clergy to remain silent on the race issue. If the clergy ignored this wish, the church members reduced
contributions, avoided services, or removed the minister. The pressure was the same in churches of all social levels. In more popular or
more stable churches, the ministers were less likely to speak out.
Further, if the church was in the middle of a fund-raising campaign,
the minister tended to remain quiet. However, when segregation
did not affect the parishioners, the minister was free to comment.
Ministers in working-class churches of some Baptist sects did publicly support segregation (Campbell and Pettigrew 1959, 121–136).

The silence of white clergy particularly hurt African American
religious leaders who demanded their fellow Christians to come to
their aid. For example, Martin Luther King Jr. asked the white ministers in the South to declare in a united voice the truth of the gospel
on the question of race. He thought this would speed the day when
people recognized they are all one in Jesus Christ (Campbell and
Pettigrew 1959, 132–133).

Although King frequently urged white ministers to help their
white parishioners realize that racism hides the truth that God loves
all human beings, he found many white ministers opposed to the
civil rights movement. While imprisoned, King wrote his letter from
a Birmingham jail to counter critical remarks made by several prominent Alabama clergy. In that letter, King noted that white religious
leaders misrepresented the leaders of the Montgomery, Alabama, bus
boycott. He added that the most support he ever received was when
southern religious leaders admonished their worshipers to comply
with desegregation because it is the law. He said he longed to hear
one such white cleric tell white parishioners to follow the U.S. Supreme Court's decree because it is morally right and because African
Americans are their brothers and sisters (King 1963, 90–93).

King was in the Birmingham jail because he had marched without a permit on Good Friday, 12 April 1963. He chose the Easter

weekend to protest racial segregation in the business district of the city for two reasons. First, it disrupted an important shopping day. Second, a new city administration had taken office, and King wanted the demonstration to set the stage for negotiations. He thought the nonviolent demonstration and the resulting economic problems would cause tension and lead to a settlement (King 1963, 65–82).

Birmingham, Alabama, was the symbol of racial intolerance across the nation. King and his colleagues in the Southern Christian Leadership Conference hoped that the protest in Birmingham could begin a nationwide process. They began their work because the pace of racial integration was slow. Although the U.S. Supreme Court called for desegregation in 1954, only 9 percent of the black students in the South attended racially integrated schools by 1963. Furthermore, the racial integration in most of these schools was token at best. Throughout the campaign in Birmingham, King and his colleagues did not pursue school desegregation. Instead, they focused on four major targets. First, they pursued desegregation of lunch counters, fitting rooms, and drinking fountains in city stores. Second, they sought upgrading and hiring of African Americans in business and industrial concerns in Birmingham. Third, they wanted all charges against demonstrators dropped. Fourth, they desired the establishment of a biracial committee to develop a timetable for desegregation in the city (King 1963, 18, 54, 102).

Throughout the month of April, the city police arrested demonstrators. At the height of the protest, on 2 May 1963, wave upon wave of demonstrators marched on the Sixteenth Street Baptist Church. By this time, more than 2,500 people had gone to jail. Frustrated, the police dropped the posture of nonviolence they had taken until then. On 4 May 1963 newspapers carried pictures and stories of police officers clubbing prostrate women, of dogs attacking young children, and of pressure fire hoses sweeping people down streets (King 1963, 100–105).

During the summer of 1963 the number of affiliates to the Southern Christian Leadership Conference jumped from 85 to 110. Demonstrations of solidarity took place in Washington, New York, Los Angeles, San Francisco, Cleveland, Chicago, and Detroit. The climax of the summer was the march on Washington in which nearly 250,000 people from every state came to the nation's capital. Several church organizations endorsed the march. These included the National Council of Churches of Christ, the American Baptist Convention, the Brethren Church, and the United Presbyterian Church. Representatives from these religious groups came to Washington to hear Martin Luther King Jr. on 28 August 1963 tell of his dream for a newly united land (King 1963, 110–125).

In his momentous speech, King offered his hope as a refrain: "When we let freedom ring . . . we will be able to speed up the day when all God's children, black men and white men, Jews and Gentiles, Protestants and Catholics, will be able to join hands and sing the words of that old Negro spiritual. 'Free at last! Free at last! Thank God almighty, we are free at last!'"

In this passage, King used gospel hymns to evoke the image of different people joining hands while singing about a republican value they share. Unfortunately, this value of freedom is not the transcendental good that religion could have given the civil rights movement. The different people in King's image are not singing about a value such as love that binds yet liberates them. They praise the right to be individuals.

In this regard, King was consistent. In his letter from the Birmingham jail, King compared himself to Paul of Tarsus who carried the gospel around the world. King said that he responded to the call from people to bring to them "the gospel of freedom" (King 1963, 77). An essential aspect of what he called the gospel of freedom was nonviolent resistance.

King called nonviolent resistance the sword that heals. It was a way for African Americans to refuse to sacrifice their humanity to the indignity of segregation. By resisting, the African American said, "Punish me. I will accept it to show the world that I am right and you are wrong." This refusal did more than free the black person. When the African American protester affirmed his or her humanity, the protest reminded the segregationist of the ideal of human community (King 1963, 27–34).

The principles of nonviolent resistance appeared in the commitment form that the Southern Christian Leadership Council asked demonstrators to sign. They appeared as ten commandments that included the following: Meditate daily on the teachings of Jesus. Remember that the protest seeks justice not victory. Talk the language of love because God is love. Sacrifice personal wishes so that all people might be free. Observe with friend and foe the rules of courtesy. Regularly perform service to others. Remain in good health spiritually and bodily. Follow the directions of the captain of the demonstration (King 1963, 37).

King thought that nonviolent resistance captured the spiritual traditions deeply held by African Americans. Further, the experiences of American revolutionaries and India's Mahatma Gandhi showed the effectiveness of boycotts and protests in toppling colonial powers (King 1963, 37; 64).

While King believed the technique of nonviolent resistance carried spirituality in it, such spirituality can be separated from the practice. This had to become a difficulty as King sought to bring together a wide range of people with differing views. If King expressed the religious reasons for racial integration in vague terms, he did not ignore them. He asked white clergy to remind white people that God created and loved black people and white people. Unfortunately, white clergy did not remind their parishioners of the religious reasons for racial integration. Sometimes they were overwhelmed by the antibusing fury.

In Boston, Massachusetts, clergy stayed out of the controversy. Many of the rabbis and Protestant ministers who favored the court order lived in suburbs untouched by the plan. Further, the residents of South Boston, where opposition to busing was most severe, were predominantly Catholic. While some priests supported busing, many priests aligned themselves with their parishes. The cardinal was politic. Before the public schools' desegregation, Boston's Cardinal Humberto Medeiros supported the Racial Imbalance Act. Once the plan began, Cardinal Medeiros did not strongly support it. The cardinal's caution was understandable. Catholic mothers marching past churches in Charleston called to priests to join them in the streets praying for an end of busing. At other times, the marchers did not want the priests to pray for them. One woman told a liberal priest that she and her fellow marchers did not need him; they dealt directly with God (Formisano 1991, 72–73; 164–165).

When they could support school desegregation, religious leaders seemed to make a conscious choice to not use their faith as a rationale. For example, during school desegregation in Los Angeles, religious leaders worked to prevent violence, to distribute information, and to prevent white children from fleeing into private religious schools (U.S. Commission on Civil Rights 1977). In a similar fashion, religious leaders in Wilmington, Delaware, encouraged people to obey a lawful order and to keep the peace (Raffel 1980, 120–153).

Most important, often clergy supported racial desegregation by transposing transcendental values into practical ones. The associate director of the Detroit Roundtable sponsored by the National Conference of Christians and Jews wrote a memo in March 1976 describing the peaceful desegregation of the Detroit schools. He said, "the success came through long, hard work by many people and organizations in every segment of the Detroit community." One such organization was the Coalition for Peaceful Integration, funded through a grant from the U.S. Department of Health, Education, and Welfare. The coalition developed community teams to support peaceful obedience to the court order. In the memo, he noted that "clergy preached on peaceful implementation and were able to get far greater results than if they preached in support of busing or the need for school desegregation." The director added that while "some clergy found it possible to talk about religious principles such as guilt or the sin of segregation . . . such preaching . . . did more to unnecessarily alienate people who could support . . . peaceful implementation." The author of the memo said that the religious principles that were fruitful in Detroit were to encourage people to hope that the schools could make it, to care that the children were safe, to become involved, and to get the truth in the form of accurate information (Radelet 1976).

The religious values the clergy in Detroit used to support desegregation are not transcendental. A traditional religious value supporting racial integration is that people must recognize all human beings are created in the image of God. Another religious value favoring racial integration is that all people share God's love. Instead of calling on these views, the clergy in Detroit used religious sounding ideas to support the desire to maintain an orderly society.

Since liberal religious leaders avoided using transcendental reasons to support racial integration, the pleas to absolute values seemed to come from conservative extremists. However, no matter how religious leaders viewed racial integration, the truth of creation as expressed in religion condemned racial discrimination. Consequently, when institutions such as nondenominational Christian schools offered a haven for white students to avoid public school desegregation, the nature of the religious school seemed to weaken segregation. In time, the school allowed some black students who accepted the value frame of the founders to enter the school.

Private and Christian Schools

Racism was a factor in the founding and maintenance of some Christian day schools. However, most Christian day schools flourished because evangelical Christians gave up their support of public school. They deplored the uncertainty about the sources of authority, dissolution of standards, loosening of custom, and government social engineering that they saw in society. They thought the public schools made these problems worse (Carper 1984).

Beginning in the 1960s Christian day schools grew at an amazing rate. One estimate was that two such institutions started every day. By 1984 there were from 9,000 to 11,000 such Christian schools with a student population of about 1,000,000. This rate of growth prompted one commentator to call them "the first widespread secession from the public school pattern since the establishment of Catholic schools in the nineteenth century." Interestingly, many of these Christian schools took over from private segregationist academies. However, by the 1980s most of the Christian schools professed nondiscrimination. Further, although the representation of African Americans among the students remained small, many Christian day schools enrolled some black students (Carper 1984, 111; 115; 121).

In the southern United States, private schools flourished because of desegregation. By 1970 most school districts in the South had to carry out some form of desegregation. In September of that year 38.1 percent of the black children in southern states attended previously all-white schools (Walden and Cleveland 1970). In response, many white students formed their own academies. The rate of white flight into these separate schools depended on the proportion of black children attending the previously white schools. From September 1969 to September 1970 in Alabama, when the percentage of black students increased in a school, the percentage of white students declined (Walden and Cleveland 1970).

When 25 percent of the students in a district were black, less than one percent of the white students withdrew. If the proportion of black students rose to 50 percent, 6 percent of the white students withdrew. The rate of white withdrawal increased as the percentage of black students rose. More than half of the white students left a public school when the student body became 75 percent black. In 1970 in Alabama, more than 25,500 children entered private academies (Walden and Cleveland 1970).

The private schools to which these white children fled varied widely. In 1971 in Alabama, there were about 140 private segregated elementary and secondary schools. Pupil enrollment ranged from nineteen to 500 students. Tuition ranged from $210 to $850. While some schools had attractive physical plants with fine libraries, others were old and small with inadequate libraries (Walden and Cleveland 1970).

In 1976, aided by the Ford Foundation and the Lamar Society, David Nevin and Robert Bills released the results of a two-year study of segregationist academies in thirteen southern states. Nevin and Bills contend that segregationist impulses helped all private schools during the 1970s. For example, in Memphis, a Church of Christ school grew to a system enrolling over 3,000 pupils in ten elementary schools and a high school. Catholic school enrollment held steady throughout the South. Nevin and Bills construe this as growth since Catholic school enrollments fell nationally at this time. In all, according to the 1970 census, over 940,000 children in the thirteen southern states attended private schools. By 1975 the number of private school students had grown to about 1,230,000 (Nevin and Bills 1976, 7–9)

Most important, Nevin and Bills found that fundamentalist Christian schools quickly replaced secular academies in southern cities. First, when public schools desegregated, private academies opened immediately. The founders of the private schools contended that they prevented violence by giving people the option of another school. Soon, the founders of the Christian academies saw a need to save children from inadequate private schools; they persuaded their church members to open Christian schools.

At first, private secular schools appeared in rural communities to take in white students. For example, Prince Edward Academy opened in Virginia in 1959. The first segregationist academy opened in South Carolina in 1964. By the 1970s schools espousing fundamentalist Christian theology took the places of the secular ones. These fundamentalist schools appeared in larger cities and soon outnumbered the secular academies (Nevin and Bills 1976, 5–7).

Some private schools advertised segregationist aims. For example, the enrollment application for a private school in Jackson, Mississippi said that "the curriculum of Council School Foundation is designed solely for the educational responses of white children" (Nevin and Bills 1976, 12–13). Despite these open declarations of discrimination, the schools received some government support. For example, several times before 1976, states such as Alabama, Tennessee, and Mississippi tried to give state aid to private schools. The U.S. Supreme Court set these attempts aside. Further, until 1970 a school's policy of racial discrimination did not prevent the Internal Revenue Service from granting the school tax exempt status. In 1972 the IRS began asking for a statement of nondiscriminatory policy from the school officials (Nevin and Bills 1976, 13–16).

Despite the segregationist intentions of private school founders, the fundamentalist Christian schools blunted the segregationist impulse over time. The experiences in Memphis, Tennessee illustrate the transition. In 1973, when the U.S. district court ordered the Memphis schools to desegregate, the Citizens Against Busing (CAB) opened twenty-six schools enrolling more than 5,000 students. When the public schools desegregated without violence, the Memphis Chamber of Commerce credited an anti-violence campaign. However, a member of CAB said its founding of private academies prevented violence. People had an alternative to the public schools and busing. In turn, the church people founded Christian schools to take the children's education out of the hands of people in CAB schools who appeared to be rabble rousers. By the next year, less than six CAB schools remained enrolling about 500 students. Once begun, the church schools grew quickly. For example, when busing began in the Memphis public schools, the pastor of the Elliston Baptist Church asked the church to found a school for the members. At first, the school had only 320 students. Soon, Elliston Baptist Academy allowed the public to apply for admission. Enrollment soared to 1,800 in twelve grades (Nevin and Bills 1976, 26–34).

In 1973–75, Nevin and Bills surveyed eleven newly developed private schools in South Carolina, Georgia, Alabama, and Tennessee. No denomination that had a tradition of parochial education sponsored these schools. Schools named "Christian" were similar to those schools named "Academy." Only two of the eleven schools had "Christian" in their titles. Literature for a third school claimed it was Christian and a minister was headmaster. However, the only sign of religion in the school was a picture of Jesus in the library. Most of the academies claimed to be Christian and interpreted this as reinforcing the "American way of life" (Nevin and Bills 1976, 113–114).

When Nevin and Bills looked inside the Christian schools, they found them infused with a mixture of patriotism and religion. The Pledge of Allegiance, praise of U.S. military activities, and Bible study formed important parts of the day. The teachers called themselves "born again Christians" and taught that evolutionary theory contradicted the Bible's truth. Students followed dress and hair codes. The administrators emphasized discipline (Nevin and Bills 1976, 37–45).

While the quality of the schools varied, the authors found many schools in poor condition. Many schools had an insufficient pool of families from which to draw financial support. The teachers were often inadequately prepared. Usually headed by untrained administrators, the schools offered a limited curriculum. Teachers left frequently, seeking higher salaries. Untrained headmasters often left when they could not meet the founders' rising expectations for the schools. At first, the parents founded the school to avoid racial integration. Once in place, the parents wanted the school to offer more opportunities to the children or provide increased value training. When the headmaster could not satisfy these expectations, he left (Nevin and Bills 1976, 98, 175–176).

The private schools did not face restrictive state limitations. Nonetheless, the teachers used traditional practices that their public school counterparts abandoned. Unable to meet the standards of departments of education in their states, the schools joined their own accrediting agencies. Ironically, despite the poor conditions, the students seemed to learn as much as did children in the public schools (Nevin and Bills 1976, 176–177).

Nevin and Bills found the students in these private schools differed greatly from students in public schools. The children in the private schools held higher ideals and expressed a type of morality that resolved situations by seeking moral absolutes. On the other hand, the children in public schools tended to consider situations by looking out for their interests. This difference in students' attitudes made up for other problems. In the private schools, the students looked upon the teachers as authority figures whose ideas warranted acceptance. Consequently, the students and their parents rated the private school teachers effective. The students and parents rated public school teachers as less effective even though teachers in the private schools were less prepared than teachers in the public schools. In all, the children in Christian schools cultivated a respect for authority. These private school children might have learned a less absolute view of morality if they had attended public schools (Nevin and Bills 1976, 180–184).

Since the private schools offered a haven to white middle class families leaving urban schools, the new schools damaged the public schools. When the black and white middle-class students left the public schools in Atlanta, the schools became 87 percent black. The teachers had to serve a new clientele with different and greater needs (Nevin and Bills 1976, 88).

In some ways, the simple existence of private or religious schools appears to weaken the effort to have racially integrated schools. Although not all commentators are as critical as Nevin and Bills, many complain that private schools reinforce segregation in some way. For example, in 1978 Gary Orfield noted that when a city school system desegregated, Catholic educators endorsed the plan and refused to accept transfer students from public schools. However, Orfield complained that Catholic schools impeded desegregation because those schools kept a substantial portion of the city's white children out of the public system (Orfield 1978, 61).

Catholic Schools and Racial Integration
Despite the misconception that Catholic officials think and act in similar ways, Catholic acceptance of racial integration varied from

diocese to diocese. For example, in New York, after the Brown decision in 1954 black parishioners supplanted white Catholics and individual priests and lay people tried to care for them. The chancery offices in New York ignored the changes. On the other hand, in March 1963 Cardinal Shehan of Baltimore told his faithful that Catholics had an obligation to remove injustices and discrimination (Buetow 1970, 354).

Like other religious groups, most Catholics hoped that everyone would recognize the love that God has for all people and stop prejudging other groups. Unfortunately, faith in the rejuvenating power of religion seemed to excuse Catholics from making more positive acts to cause racial integration. Consequently, although the U.S. Catholic bishops criticized racism, they never called for racial integration. Church leaders may have seen segregation as a prudent course of action until religious awakenings in the community ended the split between races.

In 1961 Ralph Gleason captured the attitude of leaders of the Catholic Church. He pointed out four reasons why racism is contrary to religious ideals. First, in Genesis, the story of creation shows that all the groups within the human race began together. Second, Christianity affirms that humanity will come together in the Kingdom of God. Third, while some differences in cultures and abilities among people are necessary, the members of each of these groups share human prerogatives and dignity. Fourth, a person cannot pray to "Our Father" and not recognize African Americans or Jews as brothers (Gleason 1961, 3–4).

Gleason contended that racism implies division and grading among groups of people. He added that any passages in the Old Testament such as those forbidding Jews to marry members of other groups were not calling for enforced segregation. These passages asked to preserve religious traditions. Further, Gleason said that in the New Testament, Jesus held up members of groups that most people despised to be examples of right thinking and acting. The parable of the Good Samaritan is one such case. Finally, Gleason noted that segregation violates the obligations people have to charity and to justice. When white people force African Americans to remain separate, the white people label them as inferior beings (Gleason 1961, 8–12).

Although Gleason said that even voluntary segregation without discrimination would appear contrary to the rule of unity and charity, he added that "the Church may tolerate segregation for a time since prudence may dictate that the common good requires toleration in particular temporary situations. . . . This does not dispense from the obligation to do at once what can be prudently done to remedy the evil" (Gleason 1961, 16).

This final caveat may explain why many church leaders reinforced segregation. They hoped that they were advancing the common good and ultimately removing racism. The experiences among Catholics in New Orleans illustrated this situation.

New Orleans differs from other southern cities in that within the city many African Americans are Catholics. This fact derived from the origins of the Louisiana territory. René-Robert Cavelier de La Salle claimed the area for France in 1682. The first Catholic parish was established in the territory in 1703. By 1769 Spanish troops had taken control of the Louisiana territory and by 1788 the area became part of the Diocese of Havana. In 1793 Louisiana and Florida became a new diocese. The point is that almost from its beginnings, Louisiana had a strong Catholic influence and its citizens generally held slaves. Further, following the theological thinking of the day, Louisiana's *Code Noir* required that masters attend to the religious instruction and moral behavior of their servants. Although often not observed, these requirements represented directions that missionaries tried to follow. However, a simpler Protestantism often attracted the slaves more than Catholicism. In addition, some plantations had too many slaves for the available clergy to serve them (Mills and Mills 1993).

During the late nineteenth century, relations between whites and blacks worsened. In 1888 Francis Janssens became the fifth archbishop of New Orleans. He was a former native of the Netherlands. Janssens decided to give black people in New Orleans a separate church as an experiment. He hoped that the separate church would foster more vocations for black priests and encourage an expansion of black leadership. The experiment seemed to work because separate black Catholic Churches flourished in Louisiana (Kasteel 1993).

In New Orleans, separate black schools became popular. Xavier High School opened for black students in 1915. Ten years later Xavier

College began. This is the oldest continuing black Catholic college in the United States.

In New Orleans, as elsewhere, the Catholic parishes followed specific geographic boundaries. When Janssens set up the separate black church in 1889, black people did not have separate parishes. African Americans living in white parishes in New Orleans attended a black church within the parish boundaries. Segregation by geography came in the early 1960s as white people moved to suburban parishes of Jefferson and St. Bernard while middle-class blacks moved into east New Orleans. The result was more churches in the city had entirely African American membership. However, at the same time, the designation of "Colored" disappeared from the National Catholic Directory (Niehaus 1993, 192–193).

In June 1949 the Seventh Synod of New Orleans forbade separating African Americans within a church while awaiting communion. It added that priests could encourage black parishioners to attend churches specially built for them. After the 1954 U.S. Supreme Court decision, New Orleans Archbishop Joseph Rummel acknowledged the wisdom of the decision. However, he cautioned that immediate desegregation would not be prudent. One reason for avoiding immediate change was that the state legislature threatened to withdraw all aid from any desegregated schools. As a result, desegregating Catholic schools may have ended the money for texts, transportation, lunch programs, and state approval. These cuts would have hurt the black Catholic schools (Kight 1994, 7–10).

In June 1955 Rummel appointed a committee of clergy and lay people to study racial segregation. The committee recommended a grade by grade introduction of integration beginning with first grade or kindergarten. Rummel issued a pastoral letter in February 1956 condemning segregation as sinful. Segregationists burned a cross near his home, picketed outside a local seminary, and turned in empty church support envelopes. They vowed to withhold contributions until assured there would be no school integration. Rummel canceled plans to desegregate the Catholic schools (Kight 1994, 10–12).

Rummel turned his attention to the national level, helping to formulate a statement on race relations. Issued by the U.S. bishops in 1958, "Discrimination and the Christian Conscience" reaffirms the moral and religious nature of the race question. It said that racism was an affront to the rights of human beings and it denied the love God has for all people. Recognizing the differences that exist among groups of people, the statement called for the economic and educational opportunities enjoyed by other immigrant populations. Still, the bishops urged prudence in making any plans to change society.

On 14 November 1960 the New Orleans public schools began a process of token desegregation (Weider 1986). The legislature did not remove state funding from those public schools. Assured the financial threat had passed, in 1962 New Orleans Catholic schools changed their enrollment policy to allow Catholic children to apply to any school in the New Orleans archdiocese. The schools desegregated peacefully as one hundred and fifty black children attended thirty formerly all white schools. When the White Citizens' Council protested, the chancery mailed letters to seven of the council's leaders threatening to excommunicate them if they persisted in their complaints. Four of these people stopped. Three continued and received letters of excommunication. One of these people retracted his racist position in 1968 and was absolved (Kight 1994, 19–22).

Conditions in Chicago paralleled those in New Orleans. In the 1880s thirty black Catholic families in Chicago began worshipping in separate services in St. Mary's Church. About 3 percent of the city was black, and the black Catholics were a fragment of the thirty thousand black residents of the city. A black priest educated in Rome came to minister the African American Catholics in Chicago in 1889. In 1912 the black parish of St. Monica's began a Catholic school with 150 students (Sanders 1977, 205–206).

During the First World War, industries in Chicago needed laborers, and the black population in the city doubled as African Americans fled the poor conditions in the south. Black Catholics spread beyond St. Monica's, entering other all-white parishes. Seeking to answer what he saw as a color problem in 1917, Archbishop Mundelein designated St. Monica's as an all-black parish. While African Americans could attend other parishes, they enjoyed full membership in St. Monica's. As a result, black children had no claim on any other Catholic school (Sanders 1977, 207).

Mundelein urged a German missionary order to take over St. Monica's and promote the growth of Negro Catholicism. Even though African Americans in Chicago tried to change this decision, Archbishop Mundelein supported St. Monica's. By 1922 the church and the school outgrew its facilities. In 1924 the entire congregation and staff of St. Monica's moved to a larger building nearby. As the only black church and school in Chicago, St. Monica's membership grew to 7,000 by 1930 (Sanders 1977, 208–209).

Mundelein tried to serve the black Catholics by moving beyond the confines of St. Monica's in 1932. He designated as all-black certain other churches in other parts of the city where black people lived. In 1939, when Mundelein, then Cardinal, died, there were six Catholic schools for black children with an enrollment of nearly 3,000 pupils. At first his successor, Cardinal Stritch, maintained the racial segregation. He had begun to move against it by 1930 (Sanders 1977, 214–217).

Cardinal Stritch opened the Catholic schools in Chicago to all students in 1945. Unfortunately, local policies continued to retain segregation. Sometimes, the cardinal interceded to force a white school to accept a black student. Unfortunately, when a parish acceded to the cardinal's wishes, racial tipping resulted. For example, a formerly white Irish parish accepted its first black students in 1945, and by 1949 three fourths of the enrollment was black. A formerly German school opened its doors to black students in 1947. In two years, the school was entirely black. On the other hand, some formerly Irish churches and schools admitted a few black people but remained predominantly white (Sanders 1977, 218–219).

The open enrollment policy in Chicago Catholic schools caused a related problem. African Americans saw the Catholic schools as superior to the public ones to which they would send their children otherwise. As the number of black people in Chicago grew, more black parents wanted to send their children to Catholic schools. As a result, by 1965 over 21,000 African American children enrolled in Chicago's parochial schools. One third of these were not Catholic. More important, there were few integrated schools. For example, twenty-three of the schools in the city had only black students. Another twenty-three schools had a few black students. The rest of the schools were in areas where the transition between white and black students promised to be swift (Sanders 1977, 219–220).

The situation was similar among the Catholic high schools. As the neighborhoods around the schools changed from white to black, white students left and not enough black students came into the school to compensate. Out of ninety-six high schools, by 1965 fifty-nine had some black students. Nine of these were more than 10 percent black and of these nine, three had no white students at all. Only six had fewer than 90 percent of one race (Sanders 1977, 221–222).

As the white Catholics moved away from urban neighborhoods, the Catholic schools they left behind became racially desegregated. Unfortunately, resegregation followed this period of racial desegregation. At first, a few black students would enter a previously all-white school. As the number of black students grew, the number of whites fell until the school became all-black. Desegregation was the period between the time when the first black came and until the last white left.

An example of this process of resegregation took place in the Academy of Our Lady, a school for young women on Chicago's southwest side. Founded in 1874 by the School Sisters of Notre Dame, the school accepted boarding students until the 1930s. It held continuous accreditation from North Central Association. Entrance requirements were high, standards were rigid, and almost all who entered went on to college. By 1967–68, enrollment rose to 1,800 young women, with seventy faculty. However, the neighborhood around the school began to change. In 1960, the area had a population that was 13 percent nonwhite. By the 1972–73 school year, the district around the school was almost 100 percent black. Black enrollment increased in the school (Moses 1978, 94).

In 1967 the Archdiocesan School Board of Chicago adopted an open enrollment policy. At first, this did not change the enrollment pattern of the Academy of Our Lady. As the neighborhood changed, the number of white applicants declined and black applications increased. From the 1968–69 to the 1972–73 school year, a total of 834 fewer pupils enrolled. This was a drop of 51 percent. More important, most of that decline was among white young women. Their numbers declined by 963 from 1968 to 1972. This was a drop of 71 percent. Black enrollment increased over the same period by 129 pupils or 49 percent. The increase in black enrollment did not rise dramatically in any one year; it was steady over the five years (Moses 1978, 95–96).

Thus, the pattern of enrollment in the Academy of Our Lady followed the pattern in other urban Catholic schools around the country. The total enrollment declined because an enormous percentage of the white students left. While there was a significant increase in the number of black students, the decline in total enrollment made the black enrollment seem larger than it was. Unfortunately, when enrollment changed, the financial picture worsened. In 1968–69, the annual budget of the Academy of Our Lady had a surplus of $30,000. In 1972–73 the budget had a deficit of around $100,000. Consequently, racial desegregation raised questions about the survival of the school (Moses 1978, 97–99).

Trying to preserve the Academy of Our Lady, the alumnae board wrote a letter to the associate superintendent of the Chicago archdiocese. The board recommended limiting black enrollment below 50 percent to maintain an integrated student body. In June 1972 the principal and a delegation from the parents' association met with the archdiocesan school board to propose a plan to maintain integration at the Academy. First, they sought an exemption from the open enrollment policy to allow the use of a quota in admissions. Second, they asked for a recruitment program and busing to bring white young women into the Academy from other high schools. The school board appointed a committee to study these possibilities (Moses 1978, 100–104).

The quota committee met during the summer of 1972, seeking testimony from a variety of sources. Associations of pastors and principals in white areas supported the plan. Similar groups in black areas opposed it, saying the plan was racist. One exception was a group of black parishes that supported the quota. The Provincial Chapter of the Sisters of Notre Dame declared opposition to the quota (Moses 1978, 104–106).

The committee sent questionnaires to the parents of the current and incoming first-year students in the school. Parents of incoming and first-year students returned 345 valid forms. Parents supported racial integration and approved of the quota to retain it.

More black parents approved of integration and the racial quota on admission than did white parents. The higher the education of the parents the more likely they were to support the racial quota. Parents who planned to send their daughter to college approved the quota more than did other parents (Moses 1978, 169–173).

The quota committee showed that most people concerned with the school accepted the strategies for retaining racial integration at the Academy. Nonetheless, in October 1972 the Chicago Archdiocesan School Board rejected the Academy's proposal to impose racial quotas on admission. They said the strategies did not appear to be viable (Moses 1978, 175–176; 244–245).

On 13 October an editorial appeared in *The New World* congratulating the school board for refusing to exempt one school from the archdiocesan policy of open enrollment. The editorial criticized the quota as something that would simply exclude black students. The editorial said the school could organize its own resources better, aggressively recruit, and transport white students to the school. In a published letter to the editor, the principal of the Academy complained that the paper was advancing a double standard. In the same issue, the editors had complimented a high school for producing racial balance by accepting certain percentages from each parish (Moses 1978, 244–245).

The principal of the academy attributed the rejection of the quota plan to two main problems. First, school policy makers such as the members of the school board did not attend to the research to support their decisions. Instead, they shifted their consideration to vague public relations and social ethical ideas. Second, without any clear understanding of how desegregation could work, proposals such as the quota appeared racist (Moses 1978).

Other Catholic schools shared the difficulties found in Chicago Catholic schools. The migration of Catholics from cities to suburbs was extensive. In 1965–66 Catholic school enrollment reached a high of 5.6 million students. This figure was 87 percent of the nonpublic school enrollment. In 1978 the enrollment in Catholic schools dropped to about 3.3 million students, or 70 percent of the non–public school enrollment. The drop continued so that in 1981–82 the Catholic schools had about 3.1 million students or 64 percent of the non–public school enrollment (Hunt and Kunkel 1984).

Andrew Greeley and his coauthors at the National Opinion Research Center (NORC) tried to discover the reason for this decline in enrollment. They found that it came from white flight to the suburbs, accompanied by the failure of bishops to build schools where newly affluent Catholics could attend. Greeley and his coauthors came to these conclusions by replicating an earlier study. In 1963 they sought the opinions of 2,071 Catholic adults, 990 students in Catholic high schools, and 700 of their parents. In 1974, the NORC sampled 1,128 adult American Catholics (Greeley et al. 1976, 5–11).

Greeley was concerned that the social and spiritual ferment causing evangelical Protestants to establish fundamentalist Christian schools had led Catholics to abandon their schools. He entitled his book *Catholic Schools in a Declining Church* because apostasy increased among Catholics while school enrollments declined. The NORC researchers found that the respondents in 1963 felt closer to the church than the 1974 respondents. Between 1963 and 1974, the Catholic Church changed considerably. Meeting from 1963 until 1965, the Second Vatican Council opened the Church to widespread reform by removing such apparent restraints as the Latin mass and meatless Fridays. While conservative Catholics blamed the liberalizing influence of the Council for the increased apostasy, Greeley did not agree. He said that the vacillating administration of Pope Paul VI caused many of the problems. Before his death, Pope John XXIII set up a commission to consider the question of birth control. His successor, Pope Paul VI, added people to the commission but forbade the Vatican Council to discuss the subject. The existence of a commission implied that birth control was possible for Catholics. However, in 1967 Pope Paul issued his encyclical, *Humanae Vita,* reasserting the traditional teachings.

Greeley found several reasons to think Pope Paul's encyclical weakened Catholics' faith in the church. First, Catholics disregarded the encyclical. In 1972, 81 percent of the Catholic women under forty-five used some form of contraception. Only 14 percent of those women followed the acceptable rhythm method. Second, the women using birth control pills seemed untroubled by their choice. They were more likely to receive communion than were the women who followed the prescriptions in *Humanae Vita.* Third, U.S. Catholics stopped going to church at a rate of one percent per year from 1965 until 1968. These were the years after the Council met. After the encyclical, from 1969 until 1971, church attendance dropped three percent per year. Similar changes appeared in the rate of priests resigning their vocations. In 1966, after the Council, 1.5 percent of the priests resigned. In 1969, after the encyclical, the rate of resignations rose to 5.2 percent. However, these declines might have been steeper. Using their own data from 1963 and 1974, the NORC researchers found that the Vatican Council increased people's affection for the Church and the encyclical reduced it (Greeley et al. 1976, 103–154).

These theological matters did not cause the decline in Catholic school enrollments. It came from other more practical matters, according to Greeley and his coauthors. The 1970s represented the end of the immigrant era among American Catholics. By 1974 Catholics lagged behind only Episcopalians, Presbyterians, and Jews in income, education, and occupation. With their newfound affluence, Catholics left the cities, abandoning the schools that they once attended. These migrating Catholics did not become racist. In 1963 the NORC attitude survey found Catholics expressing more sympathy to racial integration than Protestants in the northern United States. Although the differences were limited to college graduates, Catholic education appeared to cause a warming of racial attitudes. In the 1974 NORC replication, though, people who attended the schools for less time expressed more sympathy to racial integration. While modest, the differences implied that Catholic schools doubled the affection a person had for racial integration (Greeley et al. 1976, 65–74; 192–195).

Parents of Catholic school students and parents of public school students saw a need to work for racial integration. In the 1974 survey, 31 percent of the parents who sent their children to Catholic schools expressed an obligation to work for the end of racial segregation. Thirty-seven percent of the parents who sent their children to public schools took a similar position (Greeley et al. 1976, 224–225).

The NORC survey revealed that, in 1974, 41 percent of the parents who lived in racially integrated neighborhoods sent their children to Catholic schools. On the other hand, 34 percent of the parents in segregated neighborhoods sent their children to Catholic schools. Although all schools had a high level of racial integration, Catholic schools were more segregated. According to the 1974 NORC survey, the classrooms of 78 percent of the children in public schools were racially integrated. The classrooms of 62 percent of the children attending Catholic schools were integrated (Greeley et al. 1976, 226–227).

NORC researchers asked the parents why they sent their children to a Catholic or a public school. In the main, the respondents who used public schools said that Catholic schools were better than public schools, but the Catholic schools were inaccessible to them. That is, urban residents could not afford the tuition. Suburban residents could not find a school near their homes (Greeley et al. 1976, 242–243).

Greeley's discoveries offered a simple solution to the enrollment problems in Catholic schools. They did not offer a suggestion for problems of racial segregation. The question remained if separate schools could foster racial integration. An important element was the enrollment of minority children in the Catholic schools.

Public Values and Private Schools

In 1981, Reverend Virgil Blum described the results of study done by the Catholic League for Religious and Civil Rights. The researchers sampled sixty-four randomly selected Catholic elementary schools in Los Angeles, New Orleans, Chicago, Milwaukee, Detroit, New York, Newark, and Washington, D.C. Seventy percent of the students enrolled in these schools were either Hispanic, black, or Asian. Interestingly, 72 percent of the families who sent children to these schools had annual incomes of less than $15,000. Average tuition in these schools was $390. Tuition payments to Catholic schools for inner city residents often totaled 10 percent of the family income. Families did this because they thought the Catholic schools' environment was superior, the teachers expected more from the students, the discipline was firmer, and the school emphasized moral development (Blum 1981).

Unfortunately, urban minority groups do not have the same chance to go to Catholic schools that suburban white people have.

Families that can afford to pay tuition do not, and families that have few resources face the highest tuition costs. This is the result of an unfortunate irony. Dioceses and archdioceses supplement the finances of low-income, inner-city schools in accord with such policy statements as the 1986 U.S. bishops' pastoral letter, "Economic Justice for All." However, diocesan money is spread thinly. On the other hand, wealthy suburban parishes reduce the tuition using money from weekly contributions and fund-raising activities to support the schools.

In the 1994–95 school year, a predominantly black Catholic inner-city elementary school, Dayton Catholic, charged an annual tuition rate of $2,178. Serving three urban parishes, the school enrolled 162 students. A suburban Catholic school in nearby Springfield, Ohio, St. Teresa's, served an upper-middle-class, predominantly white parish. St. Teresa's charged an annual tuition of $375 and enrolled 220 students. The Cincinnati Archdiocese extended a total of about $130,000 to help Dayton Catholic and to reduce its tuition. In addition, the three parishes that it served contributed about three or four thousand dollars. On the other hand, St. Teresa's gave $341,000 in parish tuition aid. This meant that St. Teresa's spent about 74 percent of its total budget operating its parish school. As a result, African American families with children attending Dayton Catholic paid a lot; white middle class families sending their children to St. Teresa's paid little. Such inequities have long existed among Catholic schools. Consequently, in the 1970s inner-city Catholic schools closed at a rate about five times higher than that of other urban schools.

Some inner-city Catholic schools went through a remarkable process to stay alive. For example, in Milwaukee, St. Leo closed as a Catholic school in 1970. It became St. Leo Community School, declined to seventy students and closed again. In 1977 it reopened with 280 students, 98 percent of whom were black and 90 percent of whom were Protestant (Blum 1981).

Similarly, in 1968 an elementary school in the section of New York City called Harlem closed as a Catholic school. It became a community school subsidized by the New York archdiocese for three years. In 1971 the parents began their own fund raising program. Fortunately, St. Thomas Community School won approval from the

New York Board of Regents in 1973. As a result, they qualified for foundation and corporate grants (Taylor 1981).

Despite the fragile support for inner-city Catholic schools, in 1981, 6 percent of the minority students in the United States attended Catholic secondary schools. Ten percent of the minority children attended Catholic primary schools. Furthermore, in 1981 the rate of integration in Catholic schools mirrored the racial integration in public schools. However, African American students in Catholic schools scored higher on academic achievement tests than their counterparts in public schools. While some of this improvement was the result of family differences, a significant amount came from the Catholic school (Greeley 1981).

The High School and Beyond study coordinated by James Coleman demonstrated the effectiveness of Catholic schools. Begun in 1980, this study sought to answer if the private sector schools contribute to segregation. In 1982 Coleman and his colleagues found that senior level high school students in Catholic schools did better on standardized tests in reading comprehension, vocabulary, mathematics, and writing than did similar-age students in public schools. This was especially true of disadvantaged children. In 1987 Coleman compared public schools, Catholic schools, and independent private schools. Looking at schools' abilities to serve disadvantaged students, he found that Catholic schools raised the academic achievement of blacks, Hispanics, and children from families with lower socioeconomic standing. Catholic schools were more successful in this regard than public or other private schools. He thought the communal character of Catholic churches and schools reduced the likelihood that minority or disadvantaged children would drop out (Coleman 1987, 147–148).

Coleman found Catholic schools to be more effective in several ways. Not only did the Catholic students show higher academic achievement, Catholic schools sent more students on to college. Catholic students were more likely to succeed in college once they got there. Of those students who entered the work force, graduates of Catholic schools were more likely to have higher wages and remain in their first jobs. Coleman said that the advantage Catholic schools have is a "community on which social norms arise out of the social structure itself, and both reinforce and perpetuate that structure" (Coleman 1987, 7). This means that the parents of the students go to the same church and take part in many activities together. This parental interaction reinforces the schools' message to the children.

While several articles appeared in journals for Catholic educators celebrating the success of Catholic schools, Coleman's reports seemed to inspire some misunderstanding and doubt. William Bennett, then secretary of education, missed the point of the studies. Bennett cited Coleman's report to recommend that Catholic educators launch a campaign to educate the disadvantaged students and seek public funding for the service (Goldberg 1988). Unfortunately, the disadvantaged children that Bennett mentioned were not Catholic. Their parents had less reason to associate with the parents of the other children who attended Catholic schools. As a result, their presence would reduce the Catholic schools' social capital and make it more like the less effective public or private schools that Coleman studied. Other researchers disagreed with Coleman's conclusions.

In 1989 Robert Crain and Christine Rossell used information drawn from Chicago, Cleveland, and Boston to disagree with Coleman. Coleman had concluded that although minorities were underrepresented in private schools, the private schools were racially balanced. Crain and Rossell argued that, in Catholic schools, segregation was as high in 1981 as it had been in public schools in 1968 before those school districts desegregated. Further, despite white flight, Crain and Rossell noted that the public schools were more desegregated than they had been. For example, Boston public schools showed a 50 percent lower level of segregation in 1981 than appeared on the same measures in 1968. Interestingly, Crain and Rossell found segregation more common in the Catholic elementary schools than in the Catholic high schools; Coleman studied the high schools (Crain and Rossell 1989).

Although their evidence implies that Catholic schools cause segregation, Crain and Rossell recommend a more complicated conclusion. They think that private schools further segregation under some conditions and encourage racial integration under other conditions. An example of the latter case might be the following: When an urban school district begins desegregation, white families may choose to enroll their children in private schools but remain living in the school district. In a few years, the parents may return their children to the public schools and enhance desegregation (Crain and Rossell 1989).

Conclusion

Many liberal-minded religious leaders worked hard to make the racial desegregation of schools successful. For example, one researcher found that "case studies almost unanimously assert that actions by local officials and elites may prevent racial violence, enhance community support, smooth implementation, and bolster beleaguered school personnel." On the other hand, she noted that "despite convincing anecdotes, aggregate data show little effect of elites on citizen's response to a desegregation order . . ." (Hochschild 1984, 114; 116).

However, the U.S. Commission on Civil Rights disagreed. "In 532 school districts which had desegregated . . . the level of opposition among local leaders just before was far greater in districts which reported serious disruptions . . ." (U.S. Commission on Civil Rights 1976, 92). The leaders were in business, in politics, and in religion. In those cases where there were no serious disruptions, 87 percent of the religious leaders were supportive or neutral. In those cases where there was violence, 66 percent of the religious leaders were supportive or neutral. Interestingly, more than 60 percent of the business and political leaders in the peaceful districts were supportive or neutral. On the other hand, only 30 percent of the business or political leaders in the disrupted districts were supportive or neutral.

The U.S. Commission on Civil Rights survey showed that, in all communities, religious leaders tended to support desegregation more than they disapproved of it. Unfortunately, the survey also implied that the clergy were less likely to influence the outcome than were other types of local elites. The commission did not draw this conclusion. Instead, the report declared that "the process of school desegregation is significantly affected by the support or opposition it receives from the local communities' leadership" (U.S. Commission on Civil Rights 1976, 92).

Although religious leaders supported the racial desegregation of the schools, often they chose not to express that support in religious terms. Further, religious leaders often had problems racially integrating their own schools. These leaders may have feared the schools would close if desegregation went too quickly. On the other hand, they may have hoped that religion would have a calming influence on people. They might be correct. Fundamentalist schools that started as segregationist academies soon accepted black students. The school people decided that a religious orientation was more important than race. Perhaps this shows the power of ideals. -

References

Blum, Reverend Virgil. 1981. "Why Inner City Families Send Their Children to Private Schools." In Edward Gaffney, *Private Schools and the Public Good*. Notre Dame: University of Notre Dame Press, 17–24.

Buetow, Harold. 1970. *Of Singular Benefit*. London: Macmillan Co.

Campbell, Ernest Q., and Thomas F. Pettigrew. 1959. *Christians in Racial Crisis*. Washington, D.C.: Public Affairs Press.

Carper, James. 1984. "The Christian Day School." In James Carper and Thomas Hunt, *Religious Schooling in America*. Birmingham, Ala.: Religious Education Press, 110–129.

Coleman, James, et al. 1987. *Public and Private High Schools*. New York: Basic Books.

Crain, Robert, and Christine Rossell. 1989. "Catholic Schools and Racial Segregation." In Neal Devins, ed., *Public Values, Private Schools*. New York: Falmer Press.

Formisano, Ronald. 1991. *Boston Against Busing*. Chapel Hill: University of North Carolina Press.

Gleason, Robert W. 1961. "The Immorality of Segregation." In Joseph O'Neill, *A Catholic Case Against Segregation*. New York: Macmillan Co., 1–17.

Goldberg, Kirsten. 1988. "Catholic Schools Challenged to Educate the Worst," *Education Week* 13 (April): 4.

Greeley, Andrew. 1981. "Catholic Schools and Minority Students." In Edward Gaffney, *Private Schools and the Public Good*. Notre Dame: University of Notre Dame Press, 6–16.

Greeley, Andrew, et al. 1976. *Catholic Schools in a Declining Church*. Kansas City: Sheed and Ward.

Hochschild, Jennifer. 1984. *The New American Dilemma*. New Haven: Yale University Press.

Hunt, Thomas, and Norlene Kunkel. 1984. "Catholic Schools." In James Carper and Thomas Hunt, eds., *Religious Schooling in America*. Birmingham, Ala.: Religious Education Press, 1–34.

Kasteel, Annemarie. 1993. "Archbishop Francis Janssens and the Americanization of the Church in Louisiana." In Glenn Conrad, *Cross, Crozier and Crucible*. New Orleans: Archdiocese of New Orleans, 156–169..

Kight, Joseph. 1994. "How About September." M.A. thesis, University of New Orleans.

King, Martin Luther, Jr. 1963. *Why We Can't Wait*. New York: New American Library.

Mills, Elizabeth, and Gary Mills. 1993. "Missionaries Compromised." In Glenn Conrad, *Cross, Crozier and Crucible*. New Orleans: Archdiocese of New Orleans, 30–47.

Moses, James C. 1978. *Desegregation in Catholic Schools*. Ann Arbor: University Microfilms International.

Nevin, David, and Robert Bills. 1976. *The Schools that Fear Built*. Washington, D.C.: Acropolis Books.

Niehaus, Earl. 1993. "Black and Catholic." In Glenn Conrad, *Cross, Crozier and Crucible*. New Orleans: Archdiocese of New Orleans, 183–193.

Orfield, Gary. 1978. *Must We Bus?* Washington, D.C.: Brookings Institution.

Radelet, Joseph. 1976. "Religious Leadership and Detroit School Desegregation," 27
    March. Mimeographed memo, Dayton School Desegregation Series, American
    History Research Center, Wright State University.
Raffel, Jeffrey. 1980. *The Politics of School Desegregation.* Philadelphia: Temple Uni-
    versity Press.
Sanders, James W. 1977. *The Education of an Urban Minority.* New York: Oxford Uni-
    versity Press.
Taylor, Barbara. 1981. "The St. Thomas Community School." In Edward Gaffney, *Pri-
    vate Schools and the Public Good.* Notre Dame: University of Notre Dame Press,
    44–48.
U.S. Commission on Civil Rights. 1976. *Fulfilling the Spirit and Letter of the Law.*
    Washington D.C.: U.S. Government Printing Office.
———. 1977. *A Generation Deprived.* Washington D.C.: U.S. Government Printing
    Office.
Walden, John, and Allen Cleveland. 1971. "The South's New Segregation Acad-
    emies." *Phi Delta Kappan.* December: 236–239.
Weider, Alan. 1986. "A Principal and Desegregation," *Equity and Excellence* (Sum-
    mer): 125–129.

Part II

Racial Desegregation in Dayton, Ohio

City Government, Schools, and Churches

Chapter Three
City and School Administration

During the first decades of the twentieth century, Dayton adopted forms of city and school governance designed to serve the common interest. In the past, leaders had cultivated constituencies within wards or precincts. Under the newer, progressive model, citizens esteemed by the entire community set policy. Experts managed day to day affairs. Copied from businesses and factories, this model of administration served many groups. However, the administrators guiding civic affairs reinforced the racial segregation that had been present in the city. In 1966 African Americans living in depressed areas complained about this elite form of government. Unfortunately, many Dayton residents came to think that any effort to bring different people together resulted in elitism rather than integration. As a result, some efforts to end racial segregation exacerbated differences among groups.

Located forty-five miles north of Cincinnati, Ohio, straddling the Great Miami River, Dayton ranked eighty-ninth among cities in the United States in 1980. Unfortunately, by then the city had lost many of its residents. In 1960 Dayton had a population of 262,332 people, and 19.6 percent of the residents were nonwhite. In 1970 the population dropped to 243,459. By 1980 the city's population had fallen to 193,536, though the land area increased in those ten years a little over ten square miles to 48.4 square miles. Although the percentage of African Americans in the city increased, the number of black people in the city fell from about 74,000 in 1970 to nearly 70,000 in 1980.

The causes for the exodus are not hard to find. Many middle-class residents fled the city from 1960 until 1980 during the civil rights protests. More important, though, from 1970 to 1980 several

companies such as National Cash Register, Dayton Tire, and
Frigidaire shut their doors. They took one half of Dayton's 800,000
manufacturing jobs to other parts of the country and abandoned
factory buildings. In addition, in 1988 Douglas Massey found the
housing patterns in Dayton to be the third most racially segregated
among fifty other metropolitan areas. Only Cleveland and Chicago
were more segregated (Thomas 1988).

The pattern of segregation was simple. In 1970 the black population occupied the west side of the Great Miami River that divides
Dayton. In addition, African Americans lived in two northern suburban communities. A few whites lived there as well. There were
pockets of black families living on the east side of Dayton and a few
African Americans in the southern suburbs. However, these areas
were almost exclusively white (Usher 1971b).

The Impact of City and School Reform on Segregation

Until 1913, the elected officials of the city included the mayor, the
auditor, the treasurer, the solicitor, the judge, the clerk of the court,
and fifteen members of the city council. Voters in each of the then
twelve wards elected a representative. Three more council members
ran for election at large. The move to change this council–district
form of government began in 1896. John H. Patterson, then president of National Cash Register, said that people skilled in business
management should run municipal affairs rather than Republicans
or Democrats. Dallas, Texas; Des Moines, Iowa; Staunton, Virginia;
and Sumter, North Carolina, had turned city affairs over to appointed
managers. In 1912, the state of Ohio added to its constitution a
home rule amendment allowing changes in municipal government.
Patterson had his chance.

The Dayton Chamber of Commerce appointed a committee of
the five most prominent business leaders, with Patterson as the chairperson, to consider plans. This committee grew to include one hundred members. The Chamber of Commerce withdrew to prevent its
sponsorship from prejudicing working people against the reforms.
Patterson personally financed a Bureau of Municipal Research to
find instances of poor management by the council–district government. The flood of 1913 gave Patterson the chance to make his case
to Dayton's voters (Bolling 1940).

When the flood emergency began, Ohio Governor James Cox declared martial law in Dayton. Cox named Patterson head of the Flood Emergency Commission even though Patterson was under sentence of the U.S. District Court for violation of the antitrust act. Patterson acted heroically. He turned his factory, located on high ground, into a relief station. His workers made boats and rescued people stranded by the high water. His buildings became dormitories, hospitals, and dining rooms. Despite such efforts, the flood killed 400 people and destroyed $100 million worth of property. As he performed his good deeds, Patterson used his position as head of the emergency commission and the state of martial law to achieve his political ends. He closed the Socialist newspaper, silenced criticism of himself or the plans for a new style of city management, and advertised the benefits of a business-style city government (Sharts 1922).

A few weeks after lifting martial law, the city held the election to change city administration. Patterson's proposal won by a large margin and the decision was never reversed. In 1922 a vote of 17,000 to 26,000 defeated the last major attack on the charter. In that election, even people who had opposed the charter, such as the Socialists, upheld it (Bolling 1940).

According to the new charter, legislative powers rested with a commission of five members who were elected from the city at large. The commission member receiving the most votes became mayor. The commission appointed the city manager for an indeterminate length of time. Although the city manager was supposed to "end government by deficit," the city had an unbalanced budget from 1917 to 1922. Nor did the new charter end the influence of political parties. The first council was composed of men chosen by the Citizens' Committee whose task was to select prominent individuals who had the ability and the desire to help the city. However, after that election, the winners were usually candidates sponsored by the Citizens' Committee and endorsed by the Republican and Democratic parties (Bolling 1940).

The progressive city administration came to serve the interests of the many ethnic groups that lived in Dayton with one exception. African Americans never came into the mainstream. Although many black immigrants said that working conditions were better in Dayton than in the states such as Mississippi which they left, African Americans were restricted to the west side of Dayton, where they faced underemployment, poor housing, and inadequate city services (Ayres 1973).

In part, the patterns of racial segregation resulted from personal choice. Black people created havens in a harsh land, and these ghettos perpetuated themselves. However, the federal government took two steps against African Americans that it did not take against immigrants from Europe. First, the Federal Housing Authority (FHA) required covenants restricting African Americans from ownership for property before it would offer financing. Usually the clauses simply said, "the buyer agrees not to sell, transfer, lease or rent said premises to any person of negro descent." These covenants appeared in deeds to houses in the North, East, South, and Dayton View areas. Consequently, black people had difficulty buying a home anywhere except on the west side. This restriction was in force from about 1910 to 15 February 1950 when the FHA stopped the practice. However, as late as November 1969 the U.S. Department of Justice wrote title companies serving the Dayton area warning them these covenants should not influence a sale nor be included in a deal (Clark 1990; Hemmelgarn 1972; Jerris 1969).

The second way the federal government reinforced racial segregation was through the construction of housing projects and the recruitment of government employees. In 1944 during the Second World War, the federal government recruited workers for defense efforts in Dayton and housed them in projects controlled by a local agency. In 1944 out of a total of fourteen projects, black people occupied four and white people occupied ten. When the projects for black people were filled on 22 August 1944, the chairperson of the War Housing Committee, O.B. Reemelin, asked the U.S. Civil Service not to recruit "Negro workers, requiring family housing units . . . for this area, until housing facilities . . . have been provided." Part of Reemelin's concern came from his observation that the number of African Americans in Dayton had grown. In 1940 the census showed about "21,000 Negroes." A survey in 1944 by the Federation Council of Churches showed an increase to 31,682, he said (Reemelin 1944).

Consequently, the racial segregation in Dayton was not simply the result of local pressures. The federal government encouraged racial separation as the officials serving in the FHA tried to protect investments. In the war housing office, the directors wanted to protect the families of the workers. As a result the price of unity among other factions was the segregation of black people. This was also the case in school affairs in Dayton.

Dayton School Administration and Racial Segregation
Officially, Dayton's city council did not control school business. In 1855 the charter was changed in accordance with the laws of Ohio allowing the direct election of two school board members from each of the then six wards in the city. Despite the official split, a pattern of reform similar to the reform of city governance took place in the public schools. First, the school board was reorganized in an effort to bring unity to the system. Second, the newly centralized, business-like school administration placed African American students in separate schools with black teachers.

Dayton's first school board had been appointed by the city council in 1842. It was composed of one representative from each of the then five wards. The reform of 1855 increased the size of the board to twelve members with two members elected directly from each of the wards. At the same time, the district added a superintendent whose task was to give unity to the system. Several board members favored the idea of a superintendent, saying the board could not take care of day to day problems; it mismanaged funds. The teachers opposed the creation of the office of the superintendent, and some people argued that a superintendent represented an unnecessary expense. In what may have been an effort to meet the objections, the board appointed the principal of the high school to be superintendent half time. He became full time superintendent in 1858, resigned in 1859, and the position was vacant until 1866 (Sollenberger 1935).

The supervision of the schools was further centralized by the state of Ohio in 1904, when the legislature voted that city school districts of more than fifty thousand inhabitants should have boards of education of not less than two members or more than seven members elected at large and of not less than two or more than thirty members elected from the subdistricts as they were then called. The

Dayton board decided to make the then ten wards into ten subdistricts, each with two elected representatives, and to have two members elected at large. In 1920, the state of Ohio completed the centralization of school administration for districts by reducing boards of education in cities to a total of seven members, all of whom were elected at large (Sollenberger 1935).

The centralization of school governance reduced the differences among some schools in some neighborhoods. However, the board of education reinforced the racial segregation of the Dayton schools. In this regard, they operated within the limits of state law.

Until 1849 in Ohio, state law did not provide for the education of black children who were kept out of the public schools. In that year, school authorities could set up a separate school district supported entirely by African American taxpayers and managed by directors chosen by black male voters. On this basis, a school opened in Dayton and continued to operate until 1853. Then state law directed boards of education to establish separate schools for black students sustained from the general fund (Steele 1889). Through the efforts of two African American state representatives, segregated schooling ended in Ohio on 22 February 1887. The Ohio General Assembly adopted a resolution saying no regulation about education "can be made that does not apply to all children, irrespective of race or color" (McGinnis 1962).

Unfortunately, the law did not change the practice of separating black students from their white counterparts. Writing in 1889, former president of the Dayton Board of Education Robert W. Steele said that from 1853 until 1887, black students enjoyed facilities equal to those offered to white students in Dayton. Steele noted that black youth could have claimed entry into any white school after 1868, when the Fourteenth Amendment became part of the U.S. Constitution. He added that no black parent claimed that right. Speaking of his own time he claimed, "Colored youth now attend without objection the schools in the district in which they reside."

If Steele's remarks are true, they did not reflect the conditions of the twentieth century. As the city grew, the board of education built schools to serve the neighborhoods. Because of segregated neighborhoods, African Americans stayed apart from whites. Further, as the racial composition of a neighborhood changed, school policy changed to keep the races apart, and the conditions in the separate schools were not equal. Two examples illustrate how the Dayton board maintained segregation even when it was illegal in Ohio. First, as more black students entered Willard School, the board suggested in 1919 that black students and a black teacher set up classes in the basement. The board rejected this idea when the parents and the teacher protested.

Second, in 1918 black students moved into the attendance area of Garfield School. The board of education converted a two-story frame house located behind the brick school building into classrooms for the black children. In 1922 the parents of a black child sued in Montgomery County Court protesting this segregation. Deciding the case in 1926, the Ohio Supreme Court ordered the child move into the brick building. From then until 1932, when the board of education closed the frame house, black children whose parents complained entered the brick building and joined integrated classes. Most black children remained in the frame house. However, the population of Garfield School changed so rapidly that by 1936 only African American children attended (*Brinkman v Gilligan* 1972). Throughout the 1930s, as the black population in the Garfield School attendance area increased, white students could attend another school outside their expected attendance area. Black students could not.

The pattern of racial segregation in the high schools was different from the pattern in the elementary schools. The difference was that elementary schools served a specific geographic area. Until the 1920s high schools did not have specific attendance boundaries; they served the entire city. The first public high school, Central High School, opened in Dayton in 1850. Enrollments were small, with only a handful in each graduating class until 1893, when 60 students received diplomas. Then, Steele High School opened, and the students from Central moved to the new building. Steele High was designed to hold 800 students, but more than one thousand were enrolled by 1896. East High School was opened in 1906 and more construction followed. By their nature, high schools took in students from the various elementary schools in the city. Dayton city schools flirted with intermediate schools from 1874 until 1886, but the board decided to retain grades seven and eight within the district or elementary schools. Since one or two high schools served the entire city, those few African Americans, such as Paul Lawrence Dunbar, able to go to high school studied with white students. However, until 1923, few Daytonians went beyond grade eight.

Ohio enacted its first compulsory school attendance law in 1877. However, the General Assembly waited until 1890 to require children under fourteen years of age to attend school for twenty weeks per year. In the same year, the General Assembly required boards of education to employ truant officers. School enrollments in Ohio grew slowly until 1921 when the state adopted the Bing Law, requiring all children between the ages of eight and eighteen to attend school. In Dayton high school enrollments grew by 520 students in one year. Before the Bing Law, in 1920–21, 3,217 students attended high school. The number of high school students grew to 3,737 in 1921–22 (Sollenberger 1935).

From 1910 until 1923 Dayton did not add any school buildings. However, in the following nine years, the board of education built seven schools. The first of those buildings, Roosevelt Junior and Senior High School, was on the west side in a then predominantly white area. This matched the east side school, Stivers, built in 1908. Roosevelt contained grades seven through twelve. The board of education thought this would offer economy in costs of construction and school operation. The new building offered an opportunity to incorporate a then nationally popular educational movement to have a junior high school. Roosevelt occupied two city blocks and contained over four hundred rooms with one and one half miles of corridors. In 1933, the number of black people in the neighborhood increased. Less than three quarters of a mile away, the board of education built Dunbar Junior and Senior High for African Americans (Sollenberger 1935).

Located on South Summit Street in West Dayton, Dunbar was to take seventh and eighth grade black students from Garfield and Willard Schools. When the other high schools had attendance zones, Dunbar allowed black students from other parts of the city to enroll. White students who lived in the immediate area of Dunbar could choose to go elsewhere. The entire faculty, the student body, and the principal of Dunbar were black. Until the mid-1940s, athletes from Dunbar were forbidden to play teams from other Dayton high schools. They had to compete against teams from all-black high schools in other cities.

Not all the black high school students in Dayton went to Dunbar. However, when they went to other schools, they stayed apart. For example, in the high schools, all students had to take swimming. Because it was large, Roosevelt had two swimming pools: one was for young men and the other was for young women. As African Americans enrolled in the school, black students used one pool and white students used the other. In 1950 the practice of maintaining these separate pools ended as swimming became an elective program.

In this way, Dayton city schools maintained a segregated system. During the 1951–52 school year, Dayton had a total of forty-seven schools, with a total enrollment of 34,948. Of those forty-seven schools, thirty-eight had enrollments of 90 percent or more students from one race. Four of the schools were black, with a total of 3,602 students. Thirty-four of the schools were white, with a total of 23,514 students (*Brinkman v Gilligan* 1972a).

However, the board of education refused to acknowledge that it maintained segregated facilities. In 1951 the board adopted a policy saying it "is opposed to racial segregation." The policy promised to make every effort "to introduce some white teachers in schools in Negro areas . . . but it will not . . . force white teachers . . . into these positions." The policy said it would "introduce Negro teachers, gradually, into schools having mixed or white populations when there is evidence . . . communities are ready to accept Negro teachers." The same policy from 1951 concluded, "The Board of Education does not consider a school to be segregated when . . . the school . . . contains children of only one race." Although Dunbar High School held only black students and black faculty, it was not considered a segregated school because attendance "is voluntary." However, not all students at Dunbar voluntarily enrolled. For example, in 1949 black students from a children's home traveled on buses a distance of eight or ten miles to Dunbar. The NAACP protested and the board of education stopped the practice.

Efforts to Racially Integrate the Schools

Reflecting the energized national civil rights movement in 1954,

Dayton voters elected the first black school board member, Reverend J. Wellby Broadus of Bethel Baptist Church. Until 1965, Reverand Broadus remained one of the seven members of the board, all of whom were elected at large.

Appeals to desegregate the schools came to Dayton's board. Mr. Charles Francis, then president of the Dayton branch of the NAACP, wrote Dr. Robert French, then superintendent of Dayton public schools, on 15 November 1954. Francis asked French and the school board "to reexamine the patterns of segregation that exist in Dayton schools in light of the . . . U.S. Supreme Court decision . . . [which says] segregation [of children] from others of a similar age and qualification solely because of their race generates a feeling of inferiority . . . unlikely to be undone." Francis made his plea for the benefit of all of Dayton.

On 2 December 1954 Superintendent French drew up a report for the board of education to discuss integration. French noted all elementary schools had definite boundary lines. In 1952 "the policy of transfers from one school to another was abolished when the boundaries of several west side elementary schools were shrunk or reduced, permitting a larger number of Negro children to attend mixed schools." He said, "the schools keep no records of racial identification." Consequently, French used school census information to find there were 8,295 black children between the ages of five and seventeen in Dayton. As far as teachers are concerned, French said that Dayton schools "employ 168 Negro teachers out of a total of 1,577 . . . which is 10.6 percent." All but seventeen of the African American teachers taught in all-black schools. Eight white teachers worked in black buildings, but only three of these were full time. French attributed the failure to assign white teachers to Negro schools to a "reluctance on the part of white teachers to accept assignments in west side schools and [an absence of] any pressure to force teachers to accept such assignments."

The racial integration of faculty advanced slowly. On 24 July 1956 the schools were reported to have "at least forty Negro teachers in mixed or all white positions." On 25 March 1958 the Dayton schools claimed "We no longer keep records of staff by race," but estimated that "the number of Negro teachers teaching in mixed or all white situations has grown from one in 1951–52 . . . to seven, eleven, eighteen, thirty-two, fifty-three, and seventy-six in succeeding years." The total in 1957–58 was seventy-six. On 1 September 1958 the assistant superintendent for personnel assigned 111 Negro teachers to twenty-eight schools having integrated or all-white student bodies. The assistant superintendent noted, "While we still encounter some opposition . . . , we feel that our integration . . . has been accomplished with a minimum of turmoil . . . " (Royer 1958).

Gradual change persisted in Dayton. Superintendent French wrote on 21 December 1959 that "to the best of my knowledge Dayton has never maintained legally segregated schools. . . . In 1933, Dunbar High School was built and, unlike other schools, given no boundary lines. . . . For all intents this school has been a Negro school." In this letter, French promised "this school will be replaced by a new high school in 1961–62 with definite boundary lines." Unfortunately, these boundaries did not cause desegregation. The new Dunbar High School opened in 1962 "with a virtually all black staff and pupil population and in 1963–64 enrolled a pupil population 99.6 percent black" (*Brinkman v Gilligan* 1972b).

On 1 August 1963 Superintendent French said "progress has been made." French said the Negro teachers were accepted with a lack of controversy. However, he admitted there were several difficulties. Some "Negro teachers hesitate to accept assignments in white neighborhoods," he said. "White teachers . . . might feel out of place . . ." in Negro communities, he added. As far as the integration of pupils is concerned, French said, "nothing has ever been done to deliberately segregate pupils." He said that, several years ago, an attempt was made "to promote integration of pupils by building new schools . . . on the fringe of Negro areas. . . . Soon after construction . . . the composition of the entire area became predominantly Negro. . . ." Despite this complaint, racial integration may not have been an important part of planning schools. When French listed the criteria for establishing school attendance boundaries, he noted three considerations that entered the decision. These were capacity of the building, number of pupils to be served, anticipated demographic changes in the area, and distance from school (French 1963).

Complaints about segregation came to the board of education regularly. In 1964 Charles Tate, then chairperson of the Dayton Al-

liance for Racial Equality, sent a letter to Robert Kline, then chairperson of the board of education, saying, "the observable actions of
the school board . . . codified the pattern of segregation. . . . The
locating of the new Dunbar High School in the middle of one of the
worst 'slum areas' in the United States and in an all Negro community is a case in point. . . . The construction of McNary Elementary
School in an all Negro community can only be interpreted as a deliberate plan . . . to perpetuate segregation. . . ." Tate concluded that
while housing segregation contributed to school segregation, "the
opposite is also true."

Superintendent French and the board of education responded
by adopting a policy that claimed they had done all they could. In
1964 the board adopted a policy of staff integration saying, "Beginning in 1951 . . . we began staff integration when one Negro teacher
taught an integrated group of students." While the program had
grown steadily, the policy statement added that the Dayton schools
would "not increase it in response to pressures of minority groups,
majority groups, or law enforcement agencies. . . . " The reason why
the board was hesitant to act quickly is that the effort to desegregate
staff caused "excellent white candidates [for teaching to refuse] positions . . . because of fear of placement in predominantly Negro
schools." Nonetheless, the board felt it could assign Negro teachers
to any school, and the percentage of Negro teachers in the schools
had risen to 27 percent of all employment.

The board reported in October 1965 that only two schools were
without some degree of integration among teachers. The problem
was "some schools have almost no turnover. . . . However, as time
passes, more opportunities will open." Those opportunities must
have come rarely because teacher segregation remained a problem
until 1971 when the administration moved 650 teachers to comply
with an HEW ultimatum. Pupil segregation increased as more black
students entered the Dayton schools. Of the four schools 90 percent
or more black in 1951–52, all continued 90 percent or more black
in 1972–73. Of the thirteen schools 90 percent or more black in
1963–64, all remained 90 percent or more black in 1972–73. In
this period, the student population of the Dayton schools went
through a rise and fall. In 1951–53 there were 34,948 pupils in
forty-seven schools. During 1963–64, there were 59,091 students

in sixty-six schools. In 1971–72, the number of students dropped to 55,142. The number and the percent of black students rose steadily from 6,628 or 10 percent in 1951–52 to 15,987 or 27.8 percent in 1963–64 to 23,544 or 42.7 percent in 1971–72. The proportion of minority students continued to rise after that but the numbers declined so that in 1987–88 the percent of minority students was 62.7. Minority students totaled 18,942. Although twenty schools opened after 1950, the district became more racially segregated (*Brinkman v Gilligan* 1971b).

Pressure for Change Increases

On 1 September 1966 the impetus for integration increased dramatically. In the early morning, a black man, Lester Mitchel, standing on the sidewalk in front of his apartment, was shot to death by white men in a passing car. In response to the senseless killing, a riot broke out on the west side of Dayton. The violence ended by noon, although some incidents of looting and fighting continued into the afternoon. Seven hundred National Guardsman arrived in the late afternoon and stayed until 7 September 1966 ("National Guard" 1966).

Compared to eruptions elsewhere, Dayton's civil disturbance was not serious. However, it shook Daytonians. Religious leaders of African American churches walked into the crowds and tried to bring peace. These included the Catholic priest from predominantly black St. James parish and several Protestant ministers. One minister said that the city administration panicked and overreacted. He thought the police could have restored order (Ayres 1973; Palmer 1966; Whitfield 1966).

City leaders and civil rights leaders blamed each other. For example, Mayor Dave Hall and Ohio Freedom Movement leader W.S. McIntosh yelled at each other on the street. McIntosh said he held the mayor and the police chief responsible because they would not come down to the west side to meet with people about the problems facing African Americans. Hall replied that the accusation was wrong. Later, there was some debate whether McIntosh furthered the unrest or quelled the storm (Neuman 1966; Walker 1966).

McIntosh was an important figure in the civil rights movement in Dayton. He had a reputation for being a forceful leader. He formed the West Side Citizens' Council in 1952 to complain about police brutality. In 1953 his organization began picketing companies like Sohio to open jobs for blacks. McIntosh continued his drive to make large companies hire more black workers. His organization became a chapter of CORE in 1963 (Pensonk 1975).

Although McIntosh argued that the black people rioted because they needed better housing and equal employment opportunities, black people on the street expressed immediate and personal feelings. They were disgusted with high prices in local stores. They wanted a city hospital nearby. They were angry with white men seeking black prostitutes (Tate 1966).

It seemed clear, though, that the people in city administration had not treated the African Americans on the west side of the city fairly. For example, C.J. McLin Jr., prominent African American politician and business leader, selected members for the Mayor's Ad Hoc Riot Study Committee: "McLin called an evening meeting . . . at a tavern in the heart of the Inner West Dayton area. Approximately 90 people attended. . . . " McLin held six more meetings. At each meeting, three people joined the study committee. This group interviewed business people. They attended assembly sessions with all high school seniors in Dayton. The members questioned school dropouts and prison parolees. The committee divided itself into four subcommittees, each dealing with a specific area: housing, education, employment, or public services. In the area of housing, the committee complained that the zoning board did not inspect homes or apartments adequately. They said the city allowed business and industrial interests to abuse the area with air pollution and junk yards. They complained the city selected the west side as the only area in which to place two municipal dumps. The committee added that sanitation services were inadequate and there should be more recreational facilities on the west side. Other complaints included police brutality and high rates of underemployment and unemployment.

The mayor's Ad Hoc Riot Study Committee made twenty-two recommendations about education. It suggested schools buy "texts that emphasize the contribution of Negroes to society and organizing inservices to help teachers work with disadvantaged youth." It called for more innovative teaching, more guidance counselors and more black people in school administrative posts. It also recommended forming a citizen's committee to evaluate the entire Dayton school system. The committee was silent about desegregation. Finally, the committee recommended that a new organization called "Man on the Street" monitor welfare agencies and provide increased communications between the citizenry and the city government. This became a formal organization (Mayor's Ad Hoc Riot Study Committee 1966).

In addition, the Ohio State Advisory Committee to the United States Commission on Civil Rights asked the Dayton Committee on Civil Rights to study racial relations in Dayton. Mayor Dave Hall served as the honorary chairperson. In April 1967 the Dayton committee issued its report, entitled *A Call to Action*. It said that people were aware of conditions allowed to breed and multiply through years of apathy and were ready to act. Concentrating on education, employment, housing, police–community relations, municipal services, and health and welfare, the committee noted that all six areas had to be considered together.

First, in the area of education, the *Call to Action* said that schools failed "to educate the deprived ghettoized child [and by that] perpetuate the problems. . . ." The report added, "Segregation deeply affects the quality of education. . . . The solution to the problem of segregated housing would . . . provide . . . integrated . . . education." The committee saw progress in education. The signs included Operation Head Start, increased tutoring programs, and increased recruitment of teachers from predominantly Negro colleges. *A Call to Action* recommended five steps to improve education: hire quality teachers for depressed area schools, substituting the idea of an educational park to desegregate the schools, develop alternate ways to educate children who drop out, open school buildings after hours for community use, use more counselors and home visiting teachers in schools, and, finally, set up a community-wide board of review of the schools. Education played a role in the second area, unemployment. Vocational training could help (Dayton Committee on Civil Rights 1967).

A Call to Action did not bring peace to Dayton. H. Rap Brown came to Dayton to speak in June 1967. For two nights following his appearance, disturbances shook the west side (Keppel 1990). Regardless, *A Call to Action* became the blueprint for proposed changes. For example, the public schools began to try to reduce the importance of the neighborhood school. This was a difficult fight. The first steps were timid.

On 10 August 1967 Dayton's board of education made a hesitant commitment. It adopted a statement of intent listing five points of action. First, the board affirmed a desire to "seek to achieve a more nearly balanced racial composition within the areas served by its schools." Second, it maintained "the selection . . . of teachers [or] administrators will be on merit only." Third, it called for "curriculum materials . . . which emphasized the creative and positive contributions made by various ethnic groups." Fourth, the board encouraged "dialogue . . . among the varied ethnic and cultural facets of our system." Finally, the board intended to "actively engage all governmental, social, and community agencies which aim at implementing the policies stated above" (Board 1967).

Although people understood this statement as recommending the racial desegregation of the schools, the resolution reads as a measure to enforce fair housing codes. The decision to cause racial balance in schools is one resolution among four others. The second statement about teachers and administrators appears to affirm past practices of only gradually desegregating the faculty. Still, change was in the air.

The year 1967 represented the last of Dr. Robert French's administration. He retired in 1968 after twenty-one years as superintendent. One board member's comment was, "Dr. French belonged to a period that was not with us any longer. I knew that storm clouds were gathering." The new superintendent was not selected to desegregate the schools. However, while he was visiting, he heard comments that led him to think "the community must be seriously thinking about the problems [of racial and social segregation] in schools and wanting to do something about them" (Price 1990; Carle 1990).

A New Approach

On 14 June 1968, the new superintendent attended his first board of education meeting. The evening foreshadowed future problems. Attending the meeting were thirty white students from different colleges who were part of a project called "Summer in the City." It was sponsored by a church federation to work on Dayton's racial problems. They demanded more Negro history in schools and a Negro principal for Roosevelt High School. At the same meeting, a black civil rights leader, Rev. U.A. Hughey, African American pastor of the Greater Allen A.M.E. Church, "promised to renew his . . . campaign for an end to school desegregation." The new superintendent soon appointed five African Americans to be building principals and eleven black educators to be assistant principals (Lashley 1968).

In June 1968 the board of education decided to set up a Citizens Advisory Council. Though the council's primary task was to suggest ways to solve racial imbalance, the resolution creating the council did not mention integration or desegregation (Worth 1968a).

While the board of education was tentative in drafting policies, in July 1968 four members said why they thought Dayton needed racial desegregation. One reason was that racial integration was the law of the land. Another reason was studies showed that black and white children learned more when they went to school together. The only black member of the board of education in 1968 gave a stern warning. He would vote against any measure to strengthen West Dayton schools while keeping them segregated (Worth 1968b).

Despite the efforts to change, racial problems in the Dayton schools increased. In 1968, the disparity between minority representation between pupils and faculty continued. About 39 percent of the 52,000 students were black but only 29 percent of the faculty and staff were African Americans. More important, desegregated schools became segregated again. Roth High School had been 50 percent white when it opened in 1959. In less than ten years, it was almost exclusively black. There were four reasons for the change: First, integration never occurred in the 1960s, though blacks and whites mixed. Second, the neighborhood quickly changed into a predominantly black area. Third, white parents withdrew support from school activities. Fourth, there was a rise in violence among students going to the school (Polite 1968; Worth 1968c).

The U.S. Department of Health, Education, and Welfare pushed Dayton schools toward desegregation. In a Title IV Compliance Review conducted 12–22 November 1968, the acting director of the Office for Civil Rights issued a warning. "An analysis of the data . . .

established that [the school board] pursues a policy of racially motivated assignment of teachers and other professional staff. . . . All
Negro principals . . . [and] Negro teachers are assigned to schools
where Negroes constitute 92 percent of the total enrollment." The
letter added a similar complaint about the distribution of pupils:
"Of a total of 5,627 Negro high school pupils . . . 85 percent are
concentrated in 3 schools. . . . Similarly, 85 percent of the Negro
elementary pupils attend 20 out of the 53 elementary schools"
(Henderson 1969a).

In May 1969 a team from the U.S. Division of Equal Educational Opportunity announced it would come to Dayton to serve as
advisers to the board of education. The superintendent asked surrounding districts to help, saying, "the problem of integrated education does not rest solely with the central city schools. . . . This problem must be a metropolitan [one] . . ." ("U.S. to Help" 1969). He
got an almost immediate reply from the superintendent of Dayton
area Catholic schools who agreed to join the study ("Catholics Join"
1969).

Unfortunately, violent confrontations took place among students when the administration took tentative steps to desegregate
them. The problems arose out of a change in the attendance zone
for Stivers High School located near the downtown on the predominantly white east side. Because of redistricting, about thirty black
students attended the school. The U.S. Office of Civil Rights approved the redistricting. It improved desegregation of students at
Stivers and eased enrollment at Dunbar and Roth (Board of Education 1969).

After schools opened, black parents complained to the Model
Cities Planning Council that white students attacked their children.
The project director of the Model Cities Education Component took
it upon himself to intervene. Unfortunately, he intensified the situation. Entering the Stivers building on 9 September 1969, he encouraged thirty black students to march to the school district's administrative building about a mile away. They occupied the building.
After a time, they returned to Stivers where a crowd estimated to
number 1,000 people had gathered. The crowd began throwing objects, and police arrested the former project director (Board of Education 1969).

To cool things down, the administration closed Stivers the next day. However, the project director returned to the administrative offices downtown. He advised students not to go to school until he settled the matter. The crowd tried to block school employees from entering the building (Board of Education 1969).

Isolated incidents of violence continued to occur. For example, African American youths from Dunbar and Roth, which were black schools, came to the racially integrated Colonel White High School. They drove around the building, and attacked white students in the yards of nearby homes ("Racial Disturbances" 1969).

Although the superintendent warned him to avoid schools, the project director continued his campaign. He visited four schools from 11 September until 25 September 1969 (Board of Education 1969).

At the October meeting of the board of education, the superintendent recommended suspending the project director from the Dayton school's part of the Model Cities Education Component. Several high school and university students, faculty members, and staff workers spoke in support of the former project director. Some warned that such action could result in serious consequences. Nonetheless, the board suspended the director and gave him notice of intent to cancel his position (Board of Education 1969).

On 10 October 1969 the superintendent reaffirmed his belief that the integration of the schools was essential to the future of the society. He complained that the screams of bigotry from whites or blacks drowned out the voices of genuine concern. He added, "When racial disturbances materialize, we need to have solutions leading to the resolution of them not to the heightening of them" (Goodman 1969b).

The U.S. Department of Health, Education, and Welfare maintained its pressure. The Education Branch chief of the Office of Civil Rights complained that the school reinforced segregation under community pressure. Defending the actions, the school superintendent said thiry-four black students left Stivers and returned to predominantly black Roth and Dunbar at their parents' request. In addition, thiry-six white students left Roth when injury or harassment interfered with learning. While the superintendent acknowledged the importance of reducing racial isolation, he complained that federal agencies did not help reduce separatist pressures during a crisis (Henderson 1970; Carle 1970).

Faculty Desegregation and Student Enrollment

From 1969 until 1972 the Dayton Board of Education moved toward desegregation. At different times, several members said that any action to desegregate Dayton schools had to include the suburban schools. Otherwise, it would encourage white people to leave Dayton. In early 1969 the board members said they did not want to bus students. As a result, desegregation plans moved from teacher desegregation to student integration. Finally, they suggested busing students across school district lines.

The first effort was to desegregate teachers. The U.S. Office for Civil Rights had sent the Dayton schools a warning. It was in Dayton's best interest to assume the obligation for desegregation of teachers. By entering into a binding agreement in 1969 to desegregate the faculty and staff, Dayton had two years to work out the problems. It avoided the cost of an administrative hearing. Furthermore, the Dayton Board of Education did not have to admit to causing segregation (Ciolli 1970; Dayton Public Schools 1970).

The board of education adopted a resolution on 22 August 1969 to promote faculty desegregation by voluntary methods. While minority teachers agreed to transfer to white schools, white teachers resisted assignments to black schools. Consequently, the U.S. Office of Civil Rights suggested the board change guidelines for teacher assignment. The board hesitated because a unilateral change would violate the board's agreement with the Dayton Classroom Teachers Association. The teachers would interpret it as an unwillingness to share in the decision. Nonetheless, on 19 December 1969 the board adopted specific deadlines for teacher desegregation (Henderson 1969a; Henderson 1969b).

The school administration and the Dayton Classroom Teachers Association formed a task force to decide the best course of action. Convening on 4 October 1970, the members of the task force read copies of the letters between the Dayton school administration and the U.S. Office of Civil Rights. The goal was for each building to have staff that reflected the racial composition of the district staff as a whole. In 1969–70, the total staff was approximately 30 percent black and 70 percent white. This required a total of 669 transfers in the 1969–70 school year. In 1970–71 the schools still needed 594 transfers (Felton 1970; Polite 1970a; Task Force 1970).

The problems were among older teachers apprehensive about new assignments. Without difficulty, the board assigned new teachers to buildings in ways that would enhance racial balance. In 1970, the president of the Dayton Classroom Teachers Association made two separate requests to extend the deadline for teacher desegregation. The deadlines remained ("Carle Must Sell" 1970).

The board solved the problem in part by opening five middle schools. These changed the K–8 organization Dayton schools followed since the 1940s. In addition, the administration offered inducements such as special preparation for teachers who would volunteer. It gave permission for teachers to go in groups to another school. The board gave teachers release time to visit the new schools. In the end, the board forced only eighty or ninety teachers to move. Out of the six hundred that transferred, twenty teachers asked to return to their former school after one year (Ressler 1988; Haws 1988)

National organizations of teachers such as the National Education Association and the American Federation of Teachers supported racial integration by the 1960s. The Dayton Classroom Teachers Association did the same. On 12 April 1971 the executive committee passed a motion unanimously "demanding that the Dayton Board of Education enter into negotiations with the U.S. Office of Education to develop and to adopt a comprehensive student plan that will result in the desegregation of the Dayton Public Schools" (Ohio State Department of Education 1971). Nonetheless, teacher desegregation succeeded because the federal government demanded it.

To desegregate the students, the school board tried two things. First, it adopted a freedom of enrollment policy. Second, it created middle schools.

The freedom of enrollment policy failed. During four years from its beginning in the 1969–70 school year until 1972–73 only 1,453 students transferred. Of these four years, 1971–72 was the year of the most requests and the most approvals. During this year, only forty-eight nonminority students applied. The board approved thirty-nine of these. At the same time, 757 minority students applied. The board approved 460. Unfortunately, many nonminority students wanted to transfer to schools where their presence would not improve racial balance. Many minority students sought admission to buildings lacking space.

Freedom of enrollment policies could be abused. For example, problem students saw the program as an escape hatch. Teachers and administrators misused the program to dispatch undesirable students. Coaches could use the program to recruit athletes. In Dayton, building principals agreed to adopt criteria for students to meet. They also agreed that students transferring would lose some eligibility to play interscholastic sports (Goff 1972; Worth 1970b).

To encourage children to apply for transfers, the board held city-wide human relations council sessions. Newspapers obliged by publishing stories about how students who went across town liked it. Newspapers also reported that systems such as Evanston, Illinois; Oakland, California; and White Plains, New York, experienced success using open enrollment. The newspapers described the first year of a program of open enrollment and voluntary exchange among Dayton area Catholic schools. As will be seen in a later chapter, the program involved forty white suburban children and forty black urban elementary school students (Goodman 1969b; Worth 1969a).

Ironically, the Freedom of Enrollment Policy contained no explanation of why racial balance might be beneficial to a school. According to the standards for evaluating a request for transfer, a desire to bring about racial balance was the third point to be considered. Students residing in the attendance area had first priority. Students meeting requirements for a course available in a particular building had second priority, and those students whose requests enhanced racial balance had third priority.

By January 1970 with a freedom of enrollment plan, Dayton was the second most segregated school district in Ohio behind Cleveland. More African American students attended predominantly white schools. However, a greater percentage of black children attended black schools and a greater percentage of white children attended white schools. While a drop in white enrollments caused some segregation, the superintendent blamed the segregation on the city and the absence of official integration programs (Worth 1970a).

The second step to desegregate the pupils was the reorganization of the curriculum through a middle school program. This was an old idea proposed on 19 October 1965 by then superintendent, Robert French. The schools' research department devised a plan creating middle schools containing grades five through eight. The board did not adopt it.

On 4 March 1971 the board of education decided to set up six middle schools in existing buildings. They did not require renovation. The new organization did not call for any increase in total staff. Middle school reorganization offered an opportunity to bring in several innovations in the curriculum. Starting with the needs and interests of children, the planners hoped to provide opportunities for students to become self-directing. They set up team planning among teachers (Board of Education 1971a).

To prepare for the opening of the middle schools, central office staff worked eighty and ninety hours per week. The middle schools had the flavor of an elementary school. This allowed a transition period for the students moving through the grades. The team planning used specialists in different subject areas to develop appropriate curricula and teaching methods such as individualized education (Rogus 1988).

Several teachers felt the programs were imposed on them rather than developed with them. Parents seemed to feel the same imposition. Consequently, in an effort to protest this lack of control, parents and some teachers threw marshmallows at the school board at a meeting on 18 January 1971. The marshmallow-throwing idea came from a series of black and white encounter sessions that the administrative staff had to attend. One of the features of the sessions was, if someone acted in a racist manner, other participants would throw marshmallows at the offender (Mangan and Hunt 1988; Polite 1971).

Conservative school board politicians complained that the new organization was socially wrong. They said that in elementary schools children in seventh and eighth grades and younger children stayed together. This represented a poor market for drug dealers. The conservatives feared that when adolescents grouped together, they faced more social difficulties such as prostitution and venereal disease (Turk 1971b).

Unfortunately, the middle schools increased the racial segregation of the students. However, they could have enhanced racial balance as magnet schools with 15 percent of the space reserved for transfer students. Only in one area, Dayton View, where some natural integration was present in the neighborhood, did middle schools cause desegregation (Ohio State Department of Education 1971).

An Admission of Guilt

On 29 April 1971 the Dayton board admitted to having unequal educational opportunities for minority students. It asked the Ohio State Department of Education to recommend a course of action. The State Department said that Dayton had "an affirmative duty to comply with the constitution . . . [and] eliminate from public schools all vestiges of state-imposed segregation." It praised the Dayton schools for seeking its aid to reduce racial and economic isolation of pupils. The authors of the report congratulated "the Dayton Board of Education for being the first of the state's large urban systems to move affirmatively toward elimination of racial isolation and its evil effects." The report noted, "some members of the . . . Dayton Board of Education have consistently and persistently pursued a policy of eliminating racial . . . isolation. . . . Other members [unfortunately] . . . have been less outspoken. . . . yet have consistently denied opposition to integrated education." Nonetheless, the State Department recommended the Dayton board design a plan to remove racial segregation. Such a plan should be done in stages with community support. Consequently, the State Department recommended establishing a community advisory committee that would hold open forums to receive suggestions from citizens (Ohio State Department of Education 1971).

The board had an advisory committee. Known as the Committee of 75, the advisory group held its first meeting at the local Frigidaire plant on 30 August 1971. The president of the board of education addressed this opening meeting. He assured the participants that they were free to come up with any suggestions they thought best to eliminate the unequal educational opportunities in the Dayton school district. He said it was better for the citizens to make a plan than to have one imposed by the courts.

Turning their report in three months later, the committee recommended that Dayton's board of education "initiate action with
the boards of education of suburban communities surrounding Dayton, looking toward possible consolidation." Furthermore, the report urged the board to initiate action with the State Board of
Education to consolidate these districts. Since quality, integrated
education should be available to all children in the metropolitan
area, such consolidation was necessary. However, if some people
did not agree with that assumption, the report said, consolidation
with suburban schools was necessary so "there will be no place to
run from the changes that must be made" (Advisory Committee
1971).

The Committee of 75 called for drastic action for two reasons.
First, segregation led to riots and violence. Second, racial isolation is
illegal. The report noted Dayton had done little to correct racial and
economic isolation. The committee warned that federal courts had
ordered the desegregation of schools in other cities. U.S. courts were
likely to order Dayton schools to desegregate. Ending with a plea,
the committee said that a 1969 update of the Kerner report declared
the nation remained divided into two armed camps; one was black
living in cities and bankrupt. The other was white and fleeing to the
suburbs. This had to change, the committee said, "the opposite of
integration is disintegration."

On 3 December 1971 the editors of the *Journal Herald* wrote
an editorial giving the committee's report mild praise. The editors
noted that "the major recommendation is for the establishment of a
metropolitan school system . . . But the committee, while proposing a worthy goal, does not . . . tell us how to achieve it." The editorial went on to say if school integration is to work, the neighborhoods will have to change. *Journal Herald* editors believed "What is
needed in Dayton is a community commitment to integration in all
spheres" (Editorial 1971).

Receiving the report on 8 December 1971, the school board
acted quickly. It adopted three resolutions. First, the board called to
end segregation in the schools and to admit to having acted in ways
that encouraged segregation. Second, the board asked the Ohio State
Board of Education to develop a plan of metropolitan desegregation
that would include Dayton and the surrounding suburbs. Third,

the board directed the superintendent to desegregate the Dayton public schools by September 1972. In making these resolutions the board affirmed that "racial and economic integration of student bodies in each school is imperative to providing equal educational opportunity, a broad curriculum capable of serving their individual needs of pupils, and a democratic environment in which future citizens can be prepared to live in America's multiethnic society" (Board of Education 1971c).

On 10 December 1971 an editorial in the *Journal Herald* said that the resolutions calling for desegregation were inevitable and reasonable. It warned the actions could cause problems. The editorial noted that southern states spent millions of dollars fighting desegregation, yet it happened. "Those of us in the North might do well to profit from the South's experience," the editorial went on. Furthermore, Dayton's board of education could only control the Dayton schools, not the suburban ones. Consequently, the editorial said, they had to desegregate their own schools first. The editorial approved of the appeal to the other districts and to the state of Ohio to cause metropolitan desegregation that the editorial called the ultimate goal. The editorial added that this appeal had some basis because "a recent court decision in Detroit could lead to the metropolitanization of the schools. . . ." However, this editorial was critical of the way the board of education went about making its decision. "The move comes on the heels of the passage of a tax levy and an election in which those who feared the board might do just what it has done were allowed to believe that while the goals were clear no action was imminent." The editorial went on to say that the decision was bound to increase the public feelings of distrust in the board. Worse, the editorial noted, if the gamble did not pay off, "Dayton may find itself a city approaching an all-black population along with a starved school system."

Interestingly, the *Journal Herald* was one of Dayton's two large daily papers. Being conservative in style and policy, the *Journal Herald* came to support a conservative political party named Serving Our Schools (SOS). However, in 1972 the paper's position seemed moderate. However, the board that decided to desegregate the schools was a lame-duck board. At the election in November, a member of SOS had defeated a liberal candidate. As a result, in January 1972 a new board was going to take office, and it threatened to reverse the efforts to encourage desegregation.

The Conservative-Liberal Split

The party Serving Our Schools began in 1969. Two people formed the party because the All Dayton Committee (ADC) that selected candidates for public office refused to endorse them for a school board campaign. The ADC derived from the 1913 city charter, although it was then the Citizen's Committee. In 1969, when the ADC rejected these conservatives, they started their own party complete with membership dues, contributions, and ward-like organization. With the creation of this party, school board elections took on the traditional campaign style. For more than a decade, they stopped being nonpartisan in Dayton (Usher 1971a).

In November 1969 three members of Serving Our Schools won election to the school board. The fourth SOS candidate who lost was the only African American to campaign under the SOS banner. When the three victorious members of Serving Our Schools took office in January 1970, they began attacking the policies of the superintendent and the four liberal members. For example, in January 1970 one SOS member unsuccessfully asked to change the freedom of enrollment policy to a policy that disregarded race (Allbaugh 1970).

The split between the superintendent and the SOS members of the board grew quickly and publicly. Part of the controversy was financial. Often, the former superintendent, Robert French, had maintained a budget surplus. His replacement faced deficits. SOS members blamed him for unnecessary innovations. The SOS members campaigned against school tax levies no matter how the liberals tried to prove the financial need.

Public exchanges between the superintendent and the SOS board members were sometimes rough. In a public board meeting on 3 April 1970 he criticized SOS board members for using busing as a scare word. He said "Dayton schools have as much de jure (intentional) segregation as some systems in the South, but Dayton could be a model of the new American city." SOS members resisted his requests for tax levies. After one failed on 5 May 1970, he defended the need to pass a levy to an SOS board member. "There are some people who care about the kids and their education and we're not giving it to them now. We're giving them a racist education" (Worth 1970c; Turk 1970a).

While the election of the SOS members and repeated defeats of tax levies suggested that Dayton residents did not want to desegregate the schools, this was not true. For example, on 8 February 1970 an umbrella group called the Congress of Representatives of East Dayton Organizations presented the school board with a statement in favor of racial integration and busing. Dayton schools were busing more than four thousand children because they lived far from their neighborhood schools. The schools used buses to take nearly 700 more children away from their overcrowded neighborhood school. Despite this busing, it was not for racial balance. In Ohio at that time no city bused for racial integration (Worth 1970b).

SOS members used financial problems to bring the four liberal members to support conservative positions. For example, in July 1970 after a levy failed on 5 May, an SOS board member said he might support a bond levy if the board stated it would not bus or transfer students to achieve integration. The board said that in the term of the current members no busing program would be enacted. Another 10.5-mill levy went up in September 1970. It failed as well. On 31 December 1970 Carle announced that 633 school jobs would be cut because the schools faced a thirteen million dollar deficit (Turk 1970b; Polite 1970b).

In February 1971 the president of SOS, who was then an employee of the school and could not be on the school board, sought to legally enjoin the board from borrowing against 1971 revenues. He did not want to support what he saw as nonessential programs. These included the Living Arts Center, an innovative program; incentives to encourage teachers to transfer for racial balance; and a contract to rehire the superintendent. The suit was unsuccessful. In April 1971 the superintendent recommended removing the president of SOS from his position as assistant principal at E.J. Brown Elementary School and reassigning him as an industrial arts teacher. The board approved this recommendation by a vote of four to three (Turk 1971a; "Goodwin Demotion" 1971).

Dr. Willard Fox, then executive director of the Ohio School Board Association, and Ronald Campbell, then a professor at the Ohio State University, called the split between the conservatives and the liberals on the school board incurable. The Dayton Chamber of Commerce hired these men to find grounds for mutual agreement between the factions on the board. Fox and Campbell found the liberal majority believed the schools had to change to serve pupils from disadvantaged families better. They found the conservatives thought the schools had worked well under Dr. French, the previous superintendent. They also found the liberals wanted to desegregate schools but the conservatives refused to go beyond neighborhood schools. Consequently, Fox and Campbell could not find any grounds for agreement between the groups. The only solution that they could offer was for the voters to decide at election time the direction they wanted the board to follow ("Split Defies Cure" 1971).

The fighting on the board became intolerable. In August 1971, the superintendent resigned. He withdrew his resignation on 2 September 1971 after he received a vote of confidence from the board. At the school board meeting on that date, the superintendent listed the good decisions they had made and the plans they agreed upon. The major problem that lay ahead, he said, was to put a tax levy on the ballot and work for its passage (Board of Education 1971b).

The school levy passed in November 1971, but it took some intense pressure. State Superintendent Martin W. Essex authorized the Dayton schools to close on 5 November of that year. Essex based his decision on a state auditor's report showing that the Dayton schools would be out of money on 27 October. The board put a 10.5-mill levy on the same ballot that carried the election for three seats on the school board (Turk 1971c).

The liberals had tried to organize to prevent the victory of the conservatives. By one measure, they had succeeded. They formed a coalition, calling themselves Independent Citizens for Good Schools (IGS), used market research, employed a professional campaign strategy, and bought media exposure. In reward, three of the liberal candidates received strong support from the *Journal Herald*, a conservative paper, and, at the polls, two of these liberals won by overwhelming margins. Out of a total of 164,123 votes cast, the liberals received 62.3 percent and the conservative SOS received 37.7 percent. Unfortunately, the liberals offered four candidates for the three available openings. The conservatives offered only three. The extra liberal candidate diluted the liberal vote enough to allow the conservative

Goodwin to edge out two of the liberal candidates. This made the SOS the majority party (Goodman 1971a).

Both liberals and conservatives offered black candidates. U.A. Hughey of the NAACP and State Representative C.J. McLin Jr., both prominent black leaders, supported the liberals and worked within the organization. As a result, the liberals received more support from predominantly black West Dayton. The SOS found the predominantly white East side to be its stronghold.

Although C.J. McLin was a seasoned politician and a powerful force among African American voters in Dayton, he could not prevail over the squabbling factions among the liberal candidates. A pre-election survey by the Independent Citizens for Good Schools had shown that Joseph Seaman, a white two-term board member who held moderately liberal views, could not win the election. Consequently, the leaders of the IGS did not want to support him. Seaman refused to withdraw from the election. After some highly charged and unfortunately public meetings, the Independent Citizens endorsed three candidates and Seaman ran alone (Goodman 1971b).

The east side support for SOS had been a surprise in 1969. There were four popular explanations why it occurred. First, the east side was predominantly Catholic and "though Catholics deny voting against support for public schools, many east siders say this is the reason for the area's early opposition to money issues." Second, they felt the bulk of new construction for schools and allocation of school services went to the west side. Feeling deprived, the people in east Dayton voted against these necessary services. A third explanation for east end support of SOS was that older homeowners who show little congeniality to costly school reform populated the area. Fourth, Appalachian migrants who did not value education lived on the east side and voted against school spending (Herd 1971a).

On 16 December 1971 Dayton school board president and the superintendent met with an attorney serving the NAACP in other cities and the counsel for the Dayton branch of the NAACP. The newspaper warned that "when conservatives took over from liberals in Detroit [as they will in Dayton] the integration plan was shelved. That's when the NAACP went to court and won the case" (Polite 1971).

Unfortunately for the liberals, as the NAACP increased its attention to the desegregation of Dayton schools, the then U.S. Department of Health, Education, and Welfare reduced its concern. On 22 December 1971 the *Dayton Daily News* reported that the civil rights division of HEW temporarily halted its investigation of pupil integration in Dayton schools. The same story quoted an attorney from the Cleveland office of HEW saying there was ample evidence of de jure segregation or that caused by lawful formal action. The attorney added that the notable example is the site selection and attendance patterns of Dunbar High School. However, the U.S. Department of Health, Education, and Welfare never reopened this case (Herd 1971b).

Liberals needed an external reason to racially desegregate the schools. To explain the reasons for faculty desegregation, the liberals pointed to pressure from the U.S. Department of Health, Education, and Welfare. Unfortunately, HEW stopped enforcing its guidelines before the board could desegregate students. Liberals turned to the courts thinking that the U.S. Constitution provided the reason for desegregation. However, the Fourteenth Amendment does not say that people from different races have to live together. The courts only said that officials could not force children to remain apart. In this way, the controversy over racial desegregation became a conflict of rights. Liberals contended that it was illegal to allow racial isolation to continue because children had a right to an education in a racially integrated setting. Conservatives countered by saying children had the right to attend schools near their homes. In neighborhood schools, children knew each other and teachers had met the rest of the family.

Most important, the liberals and the conservatives agreed that something was wrong with the organization of the city and the schools. Liberals claimed that Dayton's progressive model of administration was flawed. People in 1913 promised that everyone would benefit when public institutions imitated businesses. However, the people selected for supervisory positions adopted policies that ignored the needs of African Americans. The liberals wanted to extend the benefits of efficient management to all people. In a similar way, conservatives complained that the elite groups who controlled the city and schools trespassed on the wishes of white middle class people. To prevent administrators from catering to other groups, the conservatives fought against tax levies. They thought they could serve the schools by keeping them local neighborhood institutions. While neither side won completely, they changed the style of city and school politics in Dayton.

References

Advisory Committee to the Board of Education. 1971. *Report of the Committee of 75.* Dayton Board of Education: Dayton, Ohio.

Allbaugh, Dave. 1970. "School Board Liberals Defeat Attack," *Dayton Daily News,* 23 January.

Ayres, B. Drummond, Jr. 1973. "Cities North and South Show Progress," *The New York Times,* 28 August.

Board of Education of City School District of Dayton, Ohio. 1967. Minutes, 10 August: 414–417.

———. 1969. Minutes, 3 October: 339–344.

———. 1971a. "Resolution Establishing Middle School Sites," 4 March.

———. 1971b. Minutes, 2 September: 300.

———. 1971c. Minutes, 8 December: 416.

Bolling, Landrum. 1940. *City Manager Government in Dayton.* Chicago: Public Administration Service.

Brinkman v Gilligan. 1972a. "Request for Admissions." Unpublished.

———. 1972b. Plaintiffs Exhibit 2A, "One-Race Schools and Classrooms in One-Race Schools, 1972–73."

———. 1977. 446 F Supp. 1232.

"Catholics Join School Study." 1969. *Journal Herald,* 14 May.

"Carle Defends Pupil Placing." 1969. *Dayton Daily News,* 24 April.

"Carle Must Sell Proposal." 1970. *Dayton Daily News,* 13 December, 15c.

Carle, Wayne. 1970. Letter to Lloyd Henderson, 20 February.

———. 1990. Interview with author, 11 February.

Ciolli, Frederick. 1970. Letter to Wayne Carle, 14 October.

Clark, Edwina. 1990. "Title Clauses Still There," *Dayton Daily News,* 11 July: 1, 6a.

Dayton Committee on Civil Rights. 1967. "Call to Action." Dayton, Ohio: April.

Dayton Public Schools. 1958. "Facts and Figures Regarding Staff Integration," 25 March.

———. 1964. "Staff Integration Policy." August.

———. 1965. "Staff Integration Policy." October.

———. 1970. "Task Force on Staff Desegregation." Vols. 1–3. Dayton, Ohio.

Editorial. 1971. "Committee of 75," *Journal Herald,* 3 December.

Felton, John. 1970. "School Integration," *Journal Herald,* 17 August.

Francis, Charles J. 1954. Letter to Mr. Robert French, 15 November, Unpublished.

French, Robert. 1959. Letter to Mrs. F.A. Stermock, 21 December.

———. 1963. "Integration," Dayton Public Schools, 1 August.

———. 1965. Letter to Members of the Board of Education, 19 October.

Goff, William H. 1972. Letter to William Stover, 28 February.

Goodman, Denise. 1969a. "Voices of Concern Stifled," *Journal Herald,* 10 October.

———. 1969b. "Across Town—'I Like It,'" *Journal Herald,* 10 November.

———. 1971a. " How Bill Goodwin Won," *Journal Herald,* 7 January.

———. 1971b. "SOS Foes House Is Divided," *Journal Herald,* 16 August.

"Goodwin Demotion Approved." 1971. *Journal Herald,* 30 April.

Haws, G. Keith. 1988. Interview with author, n.d.

Hemmelgarn, Joseph H. 1972. Affidavit, *Brinkman v. Gilligan,* 10 November.

Henderson, Lloyd R. 1969a. Letter to Carle, 17 March.

————. 1969b. Letter to Carle, 28 March.

————. 1970. Letter to Carle, 23 January.

Herd, David. 1971a. "SOS Got Surprise Bonus," *Dayton Daily News*, 30 August: 25.

————. 1971b. "Integration Look Delayed," *Dayton Daily News*, 22 December.

Jerris, Leonard. 1969 Letter to George Scott, 7 November.

Keppel, David. 1990. "Rap Brown Returns," *Dayton Daily News*, 1 September.

Lashley, Jim. 1968. "Carle's Debut on Board," *Dayton Daily News*, 14 June.

————. "School Administrative Staffs Integrated," *Dayton Daily News*, 28 June.

Mangan, Michael, and Marianna Hunt, 1988. Interview with author, 27 October.

Mayor's Ad Hoc Riot Study Committee. 1966. "Preliminary Report." Unpublished.

McGinnis, Frederick. 1962. *The Education of Negroes in Ohio*. Blancester, Ohio:
    Curless Printing Co.

"National Guard on the Way," 1966. *Dayton Daily News*, 1 September: 1.

Neuman, Ladd. "Hall, McIntosh Yell Accusations Amidst W. Third's Broken Glass,"
    Dayton Daily News, 1 September.

Ohio State Department of Education. 1971. "Recommendations of the State Depart-
    ment of Education to the Dayton Board of Education," 7 June.

Palmer, Craig. 1966. "Negro Ministers in Front Line," *Dayton Daily News*, 2 Septem-
    ber.

Pensonk, Judy. 1975. "Activists Page Way Generation Ago," *Dayton Daily News*, 16
    November.

"Plan Studied." 1971. *Journal Herald*, 18 December

Polite, Dennis. 1968. "Dayton Schools' Racial Portrait," *Dayton Daily News*, 22
    October.

————. 1970a. "School Board Meeting," *Dayton Daily News*, 17 December.

————. 1970b. " School Jobs," *Dayton Daily News*, 31 December.

————. 1971a. "Pickets, Lunches on Board Fare," *Dayton Daily News*, 18 January.

————. 1971b. " Expert Queried," *Dayton Daily News*, 16 December.

Price, Reverend Gordon. 1990. Interview with author, 29 January.

"Racial Disturbances at Col. White H.S." 1969. *Dayton Daily News*, 30 September.

Reemelin, O.B. 1944. Letter to Milliard Greulich, 22 August. *Brinkman v Gilligan*,
    Plaintiff's Exhibit 143A.

Ressler, Paul. 1988. Interview with author, 4 October.

Rogus, Joseph. 1988. Interview with author, 28 December.

Royer, Homer. 1958. "Staff Integration." Dayton Public Schools, 1 September.

Sharts, Joseph W. 1922. *Biography of Dayton: An Economic Interpretation of Local
    History*. Dayton, Ohio: Miami Valley Socialist.

Sollenberger, D.L. 1935. "The Development and Growth of the Public Secondary
    Schools of Dayton, Ohio from 1850–1935." M.A. thesis, Ohio State University.

"Split Defies Cure." 1971. *Dayton Daily News*, 14 July.

Steele, R.W. 1889. "Educational." In *History of Dayton, Ohio*. Dayton, Ohio: United
    Brethren Publishing House, 217–261.

Task Force on Desegregation. 1970. Minutes, 4 October.

Tate, Charles. 1964. Letter to Robert Kline.

Tate, Florence. 1966. "Rights Chiefs Off Course," *Dayton Daily News*, 4 September.

Thomas, Scipio. 1988. "Dayton Third Most Segregated," *Dayton Daily News*, 24 No-
    vember.

Turk, Paul. 1970a. "Carle Labels Schools Racist," *Journal Herald*, 24 May.

————. 1970b. "Levy Deal Proposed," *Journal Herald*, 20 October.

————. 1971a. "Injunction Denied," *Journal Herald*, 12 February.

————. 1971b. "Carle Hit as Using Children," *Journal Herald*, 1 March.

————. 1971c. "State Unites School Board," *Journal Herald*, 20 October.

Usher, Brian. 1971a. "Grassroots Resprouting," *Journal Herald*, 5 June: 25.

————. 1971b. "City Remains Segregated," *Journal Herald*, 30 August: 21.

"U.S. to Help City Integrate Schools." 1969. *Journal Herald,* 9 May.

Walker, Doug. 1966. "West Side Leadership Struggle On," *Dayton Daily News,* 4
    September.

Whitfield, Vance. 1966. "Priest Fights Unrest," *Dayton Daily News,* 2 September.

Worth, William. 1968a. "Shifts in Faculty May Ease Negro Demands," *Journal Herald,*
    29 June.

———. 1968b. "Board Says Integrate," *Journal Herald,* 23 July: 22.

———. 1968c. "Roth Integration Dying," *Journal Herald,* 2 November.

———. 1969a. "Open Schools Only Part of the Answer," *Journal Herald,* 3 June: 1, 9.

———. 1969b. "Teachers to Study Inner City ABC's," *Journal Herald,* 24 June.

———. 1969c. "Panel Report Asks Rotation of Teachers," *Journal Herald,* 15 August.

———. 1970a. "School Segregation Rising," *Journal Herald,* 21 January.

———. 1970b. " Limited Busing OK, East Daytonians Say," *Journal Herald,* 8 February.

———. 1970c. "Carle: Busing a Scare Word," *Journal Herald,* 3 April.

Chapter Four
Community Control and Racial Integration

In 1913, to take politics out of public administration, Dayton adopted a progressive model of city and school administration. The hope was that officials elected at large and influenced by experts would advance the good of all people. Ironically, the federal government adopted two policies that challenged this model.

First, it encouraged suburban sprawl and allowed people to form separate communities without requiring that they cooperate in solving social problems. After World War II, when people wanted to return to mythical rural settings, the federal government helped them. Interstate highways allowed people easy travel from town to city. The GI Bill offered money for home purchases. Federal funds paid for the building of sewer and water systems in new suburban developments. However, those funds would not pay for the repair or the enlargement of urban sewer and water systems. Nor did the communities that received federal support have to provide housing for low-income families. Consequently, in northern cities, white people with money could live in the suburbs while African Americans without sufficient income stayed in the city (Bertsch 1994).

Second, when the federal government tried to rectify the urban problems that its policies aggravated, it supported a type of community control. In the guidelines for its renewal grants, it asked the people in the cities to decide what problems they faced and what course of action they should follow. In Dayton, this changed the focus of city and school administration. Instead of reinforcing the former ideal of centralized planning and control, it empowered citizens to decide what would be best for them.

The idea of community control contradicted the ideal of racial desegregation in other cities such as Detroit, Los Angeles, and New

York. However, those concepts could work together. In Dayton, the Model Cities Demonstration Project reinforced racial segregation. However, the Dayton View Stabilization Project sought to promote racial integration.

The Model Cities Demonstration Project

While the federal government intervened in a wide range of local community affairs throughout the nation during the 1960s, it did so in ways that sought to enhance local control. For example, the Economic Opportunity Act of 1964 was designed for urban and rural areas. It called for locally initiated comprehensive community action programs to focus a variety of resources on the roots of poverty. In each community, community action agencies would bring together separate efforts sponsored by the federal, state, and local governments to create a unified approach. Unfortunately, the job was too large for the community action agencies (Sundquist 1969).

The community action agencies were destined to fail. First, those agencies never occupied seats of authority in their local communities. For example, southern communities saw the community action agencies as extensions of the civil rights movement that the white leadership distrusted. Second, the federal government encouraged the chaotic growth of community action agencies because the Office of Economic Opportunity (OEO) approved individual projects without looking at comprehensive plans. The OEO asked only that these smaller projects not be inconsistent with the comprehensive plans that might arise. Consequently, individual communities did not study their problems but submitted applications indiscriminately. In response, the OEO required communities to develop proposals that used such existing national programs as Operation Head Start, legal services, comprehensive health services, foster grandparents, and Upward Bound. As a result, community action agencies could not devise plans to fit the local conditions (Sundquist 1969, 39–42).

Not surprisingly, less than three years after forming community action agencies, the federal government created the Model Cities program to give special grants to cities that developed comprehensive plans enlisting federal, state, local, and private resources to transform blighted areas into useful ones. In January 1966 President Lyndon Johnson sent the proposal for the Demonstration Cities and Metropolitan Development Act, also known as Model Cities, to the Congress. The Model Cities program included two important changes from the community action agencies. First, Model Cities required that comprehensive and coordinated planning take place before any action began. As a result, cities applied for planning grants to submit proposals. If the U.S. Department of Housing and Urban Development (HUD) accepted a proposal, it gave the winning city another year to perfect five-year action plans. Second, the Model Cities program insisted that there be citizen participation in the planning and execution of the program (Sundquist 1969, 79–81).

Although the War on Poverty was no longer popular, the U.S. Congress approved the Model Cities program in November 1966. However, Congress reduced the supporting funds and eliminated the requirement for each city to have a federal coordinator. Most important, Congress removed requirements that encouraged racial integration. For example, the Congress dropped a provision calling for racial integration of housing, and it prohibited HUD from requiring school busing as a precondition of assistance (Sundquist 1969, 82).

By 1 May 1967 nearly 200 cities had applied to HUD for the planning grants. Dayton was among seventy-five cities that received first-round funding. Columbus and Toledo were the two other cities in Ohio chosen to receive Model Cities grants. Cleveland was not selected (Rotterman 1967).

Part of the reason Dayton's grant was successful was the city had the appropriate personnel. In March 1966 Dayton's city manager hired an administrative assistant to coordinate all federal programs and keep abreast of federal resources the city might use. The assistant soon learned of HUD's plans to offer a Model Cities program. He wanted to apply because the city had just finished a five-year study funded by HUD that fit the thinking of the Model Cities program. This study recommended improvement of the city's economic base, aggressive enforcement of building codes and housing rehabilitation, and extension of self-help programs to urban dwellers. Consequently, this study looked toward social planning efforts to improve housing, employment, and receipt of services to improve the city (Marshall Kaplan, Gans, and Kahn Inc. 1969).

In May 1966 Dayton's city commission assigned an agency named the Special Committee on Urban Renewal to prepare a draft application. Known as SCOUR, the agency hired a university professor as a consultant. Immediately, he picked West Dayton as the focus of the Model Cities application because it appeared unjust to help the entire city. For example, the West Dayton area contained 30 percent of the substandard housing and about 27 percent of the families living in poverty; however, it would have received only 13 percent of the money for these renewal efforts (Marshall Kaplan, Gans, and Kahn Inc. 1969).

As described in chapter three, residents of West Dayton shook the city by rioting briefly but dramatically on 1 September 1966. The television and newspaper accounts confirmed the view that West Dayton should receive the attention of the Model Cities program. However, when SCOUR released the preliminary draft in December 1966, a group of militant African Americans complained that the residents of the area had not been involved in the preparation of the document. They claimed the program shortchanged the residents. A young black man who later became the coordinator for the Model Cities planning council made these complaints most strongly. Fortunately, there was time to satisfy this objection. HUD distributed guidelines for the program in January 1967. Dayton's administrative assistant and the chairperson of SCOUR revised the draft application to include the concerns voiced by the African American activists. On 12 April 1967 Dayton submitted the Model Cities planning application asking for about $250,000 (Marshall Kaplan, Gans, and Kahn Inc. 1969).

In the 1967 Model City application, SCOUR asserted that Dayton was different from other large cities because its problems were less pronounced and therefore solvable. The application added that neighborhood associations created a system of indigenous leadership. Most important, the city had a new city manager, a new police chief, and a new superintendent of public schools who would create new ways of working and would cooperate with the project. The plan designated an area immediately west of the downtown covering about two and one-half square miles, and containing

32,500 residents to receive the attention from the grant. This represented 9 percent of the city area and 13 percent of the city's population (Special Committee on Urban Renewal 1967).

Although the SCOUR application pointed to the 1966 riot to prove the needs of West Dayton. it added that the specific causes of the disturbance were unimportant. The central concern was for the problems listed by an Ad Hoc Riot Study Committee set up by the Dayton city commission at the urging of C.J. McLin Jr., a local African American business person and politician. McLin's group collected a long list of complaints from over 400 residents of West Dayton. SCOUR's application noted that the problems listed by McLin were "compounded by the long continued existence of racial prejudice and discrimination. This condition interacts with the depressing physical environment, widespread health and social problems, economic discrimination in job securing and advancement, and low educational attainments." SCOUR's plan was to set up programs to assure freedom of choice in housing, job opportunity, and job training. Most important, SCOUR's application offered two innovative suggestions: a planning council composed of elected residents and a foundation to raise private money to add to the programs (Special Committee on Urban Renewal 1967).

While SCOUR's application was under consideration in Washington, two disturbances broke out in the designated program area. The first was in June 1967. The second was in September 1967 and led to some looting, fighting, and destruction of property. Police arrested about 100 persons. In October 1967, while HUD deliberated, the city hired an interim Model Cities project coordinator, opened offices, and initiated a housing inspection program in West Dayton. City administrators said these actions would increase the chances of Dayton being selected to receive the federal support. In part, though, the city may have hurried the Model Cities project to stop further violence (Dressler 1967).

The project coordinator appointed an Ad Hoc Advisory Committee to structure elections of residents for the planning council. He organized the Model Cities policy committee consisting of representatives from local public agencies, such as the city commission, the board of education, and the county board of commissioners. According to the project coordinator's ideas, the policy committee was going to supervise the actions of the planning council. On 16 November 1967 Dayton was picked to receive a federal planning grant. Unfortunately, HUD awarded the city only $125,000 of the $250,000 requested in the application (Shere 1967).

In January 1968 a young black assistant principal with the Dayton schools complained to the city commission about the Model Cities organization. He said that the professionals on the policy committee could overrule all the decisions made by the residents on the planning council. In the middle of February another controversy arose. The Ad Hoc Advisory Committee accused the city administration of ignoring them. They said that the city manager applied for federal money to fund the Concentrated Employment Program by himself. After a long meeting, the city commission abolished the policy committee; this gave the residents on the planning council the power to make the policy decisions for the Model Cities program (Marshall Kaplan, Gans, and Kahn Inc. 1969).

When first proposed, the election for the planning council generated widespread enthusiasm among residents in the project target area. Seventy-one candidates ran for twenty-seven seats. On election day, 14 March 1968, fully 24 percent of the eligible voters came to vote. No other Model Cities program in the nation had a higher turnout of eligible voters than cast ballots in Dayton. Once elected, the planning council seemed to turn to young or militant black people for leadership. They hired as the planning coordinator a twenty-year-old teacher from a local elementary school. Furthermore, the chairperson of the planning council tried to garner support by appealing to groups called Negro militants. In one meeting, he said, "We must have it crystal clear that behind the council is the muscle of FORCE" (Marshall Kaplan, Gans, and Kahn Inc. 1969).

The name FORCE was an acronym for Freedom, Organization, Rights, Citizenship, Equality. They claimed to be an "organization of organizations in the Black community to unite Blacks for the purpose of shaping their own destiny." The group argued that the city commission took a paternalistic interest in the west side of Dayton "without participation of the Black community." FORCE formed during an institute on community organization led by Saul Alinsky in Chicago in June 1967. In August 1967 FORCE claimed to represent forty-five organizations in Dayton. It had an affiliated group of white supporters named FORCE Associates (Proposal 1967). Critics complained that although the FORCE claimed to be nonviolent, the group included two juvenile gangs. As a result, at least one reporter from a suburban newspaper claimed that FORCE encouraged riots. More distressing to the reporter was the allegation that FORCE Associates had raised thousands of dollars for FORCE; furthermore, a tax-exempt nonprofit corporation, Malachi, directed by a pastor of a local Presbyterian church, sponsored the seminar that inspired FORCE (Ulich 1968). No matter how the media viewed FORCE, Model Cities wanted its help, and FORCE enjoyed the recognition from Model Cities. FORCE issued a statement of support that legitimized both the planning council and FORCE (Marshall Kaplan, Gans, and Kahn Inc. 1969).

Despite the chairperson's effort to garner support, the residents in the community accused the planning council of being aloof and unresponsive. The coordinator and the council's personnel committee appointed the brother of the council chairperson to be the assistant coordinator. He was a lawyer suspended from practice for failing to file income tax returns. On 24 April 1968 angry residents complained that the Model Cities program was violating their trust, making decisions in closed sessions, and neglecting their own constituency (Goodman 1968a). These people collected 246 signatures on petitions asking that their neighborhood associations no longer be considered part of Model Cities. The petitions were withdrawn because the planning council promised to meet with the angry residents to find ways to settle the difficulties (Dansker 1968a).

As part of the proposal, Battelle Memorial Institute was commissioned to evaluate the early stages of the project. In June 1968 it released a report of Dayton's Model Cities program. The study repeated the charge that the planning council failed to involve the residents in decisions. The report said that a few people made the major decisions about programs. Furthermore, the Battelle report said the planning council had a poor public information program that caused area residents to form unrealistic expectations. Battelle's report laid the blame on the Model Cities planning council; it said the members had developed internal solidarity fighting for a strong role. Unfortunately, those same members tended to ignore important programmatic considerations, and they had weak ties to the community (Goodman 1968b).

The power the planning council held made the Dayton Model Cities Demonstration Project unique. No other program approved by HUD allowed target area citizens to have equal authority with the city administration. To some extent, federal officials saw this as a risk. The director of Model Cities administration in New York said that "it is the city's responsibility to delineate the extent of citizen responsibility." He saw citizen participation as dangerous when the group decided to act on its own. While he praised Dayton's coalition between citizens and city hall, he noted that his confidence was "based on the city manager's ability to stay on top of the program" (Goldwyn 1968).

Since nonprofessionals made up the planning council, they followed an unusual process to write the proposal. Their suggestions differed from those professional urban planners would have submitted. They were so different that in 1969 an evaluator praised the city officials and residents for setting up a program. The evaluator said that the act of writing the proposal was an intensive training process in working together. The problems derived from the fact that the council members saw things differently than the city and federal government officials. That is, the evaluator said, the "residents of Dayton's Model Neighborhood viewed problems in individual terms." Rejecting measured or planned change, they saw life as a series of crises that had to be solved. As a result, the residents wanted an approach that would be as comprehensive as possible, even if that meant working with each individual one by one. On the other hand, the evaluator said that city and federal officials looked at social problems in terms of percent unemployed, infant deaths per thousand, and school dropouts per some enrollment base and looked as well for measured improvement in these statistics. Nonetheless, the evaluator concluded that a measure of success was that Dayton did not experience any more riots in the streets. The evaluator thought that Model Cities had attracted the participation of blacks whose anger provided the basis for the earlier disorders (Marshall Kaplan, Gans, and Kahn Inc. 1969).

It took a long time to write the project application for which Dayton had received the first year planning grant. Following HUD's guidelines, the Model Cities comprehensive program was to consist of three components. Part I was a set of problem statements. Part II consisted of the five-year objectives and the strategies of implementation. Part III described the first action programs, budgets, and personnel needs. Part I was due on 1 August 1968; it was not submitted until December. Further, in order for Part I to be completed, a team of writers hired from nearby Antioch College to compose the report had to fill a managerial vacuum. They coordinated the activities of each of the subcommittees set up by the planning council (Marshall Kaplan, Gans, and Kahn Inc. 1969).

Although Part I was completed four months late, it was acceptable. On 14 June 1968 HUD approved Part I of Dayton's proposal and allocated $2,949,000 (Rotterman 1968). The remaining parts of the comprehensive plan were finished and approved by the planning council and the city commission by 19 February 1969.

Consultants for Marshall Kaplan, Gans, and Kahn Inc. revealed the unique nature of Dayton's Model Cities Demonstration Project in a comparative study of similar programs in eleven cities. Commissioned by HUD and released in 1970, the Kaplan study placed the planning methods of the different cities along a continuum. This began on one extreme with professional "staff dominance." It ended on the other extreme with "resident dominance." In the middle, the categories ranged from "staff influence" to "staff and resident parity" to "resident influence" (Marshall Kaplan, Gans, and Kahn Inc. 1970).

Atlanta, Georgia, was an example at one end of the continuum of a Model Cities program city with staff dominance because the mayor's office in that city maintained sustained interest in and commitment to the Model Cities program. In Atlanta, the residents did not join together to initiate things, nor did they protest that they had not been consulted. Four cities represented examples in the middle where city administrative staff was influential but not in control. These cities were San Antonio, Texas; Pittsburgh, Pennsylvania; Gary, Indiana; and Detroit, Michigan. Four other Model Cities programs were also in the middle with the city administrative staff and the residents having parity. These cities included Denver, Colorado; Richmond, California; Cambridge, Massachusetts; and Reading, Pennsylvania. Resident influence characterized Rochester, New York. The only program at the other extreme where the residents dominated the planning responsibilities was Dayton, Ohio (Marshall Kaplan, Gans, and Kahn Inc. 1970).

The comparative study found that several factors influenced which type of system would develop. These factors included the size of the city, the type of local government, the previous experience with federal programs, and the level of turbulence in the environment as shown by such things as demonstrations. The writers said that in Dayton's case, the existence of a cohesive resident base enabled them to exert dominance. The consultants also pointed out that Dayton's city manager was continually involved in the Model Cities program, offering visible public support. In other cities, the chief executive became involved only during crises. When the report tried to detect how each system responded to HUD's process, product, and performance requirements, they found that different systems offered different advantages. For example, in cities where the staff dominated the project, the comprehensive plan was finished within the allotted year and with few variations from the guidelines. On the other hand, there were many benefits for cities where parity existed between the city's professional staff and the residents: A variety of agencies was involved, the participants developed common strategies for planning, and they used categorical programs in their budgets. The problem with the domination by the residents in Dayton's program was that the proposal ignored many of HUD's guidelines. As a result, the report suggested that parity between staff and residents led to a better planning process and a stronger product (Marshall Kaplan, Gans, and Kahn Inc. 1970).

Resident domination caused problems in the development of the education component of Dayton's Model Cities program. At first, the Model Cities planning council and the Dayton Board of Education tried to appease each other. For example, on 27 June 1968 the board announced the creation of an integration advisory council to report directly to the board. The members of the advisory council came from all sections of the city including Inner West (Lashley 1968). In July 1968 the then newly appointed Dayton school superintendent paid his first visit to a meeting of the Model Cities planning council. He praised the program as "a unique opportunity for achievement in the inner city." In return, the education consultant to Model Cities tried to help the public schools. The school board asked the voters to approve a school tax levy in December 1968. The Model Cities consultant suggested using some Model Cities program money to help the schools in the entire city (Dansker 1968; "Model Cities Levy Linked" 1968).

At the November 1968 meeting Dayton's board of education declared its desire to participate actively in the Model Cities program. Although this was only tentative approval, it was essential in order for Model Cities to receive federal support. Unfortunately, it was not clear who would control the schools in the Model Cities area. In 1968 the board of education approved the formation of community school councils. In each school building, the council included six parents elected from the area, the principal, the community school director, representatives from the two teachers' organizations then in the schools, and, in the high schools, a member of the student council. The purpose of these community school councils was to encourage citizen participation in school affairs. On the other hand, the Model Cities people expected these councils to do more than encourage citizen participation. They wanted these school councils to have final authority over whatever happened in those schools ("Projects Listed" 1968).

The planning council moved to take this control. In April 1969 the chairperson of the Model Cities planning council explained how untrained citizens could direct schools. He said that the purpose of the elected councils should be to set policy for the schools and to let the educational technicians carry it out (Harris 1969a). The planning council set up programs to prepare residents to serve on the community school councils. In June 1969 the project director of the educational component reported success in teaching residents "to participate fully in the development of new educational programs for the entire community." The residents who took part in this program learned to make decisions about site selection of schools, design of schools, purchase of materials, and designing curricula. According to the report, the participants viewed the program as one that was moving toward positive school reform (Thomas 1969).

Dayton's school board resisted giving the Model Cities planning council the authority the latter group wanted. For example, the planning council wanted a young African American man, then an assistant principal in a Dayton school, to be the director of the education component. The board was unwilling to name him, although they agreed to do so on 10 June 1969 (Harris 1969b). However, the school board reversed a decision the director made about job announcements for positions in the Model Cities education staff in July (Allbaugh 1969).

The Model Cities education director fought the board, saying that the school board should not control the project. He said the City Demonstration Agency controlled Model Cities since the federal money went to this group; the city commissioner and the superintendent of Dayton schools disagreed. Although he lost that battle, the education director publicly accused the superintendent and the Dayton school board of trying to destroy Model Cities (Felton 1969).

After nearly eight months of rancor, the board agreed that all proposals affecting schools in the target area would be agreeable to the Model Cities planning council. Two months later, the school board fired the education director of Model Cities because he interfered at the riot at Stivers High School described in chapter three (Worth 1969).

When the school board ignored the protests of the planning council, the planning council sued in common pleas court. They complained that the board of education had violated the agreement to share decision making with the planning council. The judge ruled in November 1969 that the board could not enter an agreement to share the power to select personnel; the school board could not abdicate the responsibility to hire, retain, or dismiss staff. In January 1970 the planning council returned to court and contended that federal program guidelines stipulated that the board of education and the planning council share power. The judge said that federal guidelines could not force people to enter illegal agreements ("Ruling Backs School" 1970).

The Model Cities planning council hired the former director as a consultant despite his being fired by the board of education. Later, he went on to secure a doctorate and build a career in higher education ("Thomas to Draw Pay" 1970; Martindale 1974).

Educational programs continued as anticipated in the Model Cities neighborhood during and after the controversy. However, the dispute between Dayton's board of education and the Model Cities planning council over the firing of the project director threatened the federal funding. An official of HUD visited the city in January 1971 and warned the school board and the planning council that Dayton could lose $750,000. In February 1970 the board and the planning council agreed to turn to a process of mediation when a dispute arose (Goodman 1970).

Unfortunately, this agreement did not eliminate the hard feelings that had developed between Model Cities members and the school board. They increased pressure to retain segregated schools in Dayton. For example, when the board fired the Model Cities education director, a member of the Model Cities planning council joined the newly formed conservative Serving Our Schools Party. Supported strongly by white people on the east side of Dayton, SOS members favored retaining neighborhood schools (Allbaugh 1973). Most important, as will be seen in chapter five, African Americans began supporting the SOS during school board elections.

In August 1970 the planning council claimed progress toward resident control of the schools; the council and the board of education had formed a joint hiring panel. In its second year plan, the planning council added that the community school councils enabled residents to participate in the planning and operation of programs in the schools. Consequently, the issue of control continued to be a controversial part of the education program in Model Cities. Other projects in the schools continued successfully. In 1970 of all the aspects of Model Cities in inner west, the biggest share of the total $2,949,000 budget went into the education component. It used $555,000. Job development was second with a total of $512,000.

The money for education was spent on several projects. For example, the community schools program kept five schools open from seven in the morning until ten at night. During this time, the buildings held adult education classes, set up recreational activities in the gyms, and allowed residents to offer personal services to other people in the neighborhood. These programs served over 1,000 people and were run by residents of the area. In this way, the community schools employed and trained people who might not otherwise have had jobs (City of Dayton 1970).

Two projects run by the education component tried to change the personnel in the schools. First, a program recruited African Americans to become change agents in inner city schools. These people became administrative interns. While earning credits toward school supervision certificates, the interns took sensitivity training and they studied the perceptions of neighborhood residents. Second, the education component of Model Cities retrained teachers. In another program, teachers in Model Cities schools learned to develop innovative teaching techniques and team teaching. During the first year, teachers attended inservices focused on Black Awareness (City of Dayton 1970).

Finally, several programs tried to raise the students' self-concepts. For example, programs of guidance and counseling prevented children in the upper elementary grades from developing negative attitudes. The education component invited prominent black Americans to visit the schools to inspire the children to succeed. Some of these programs were from other agencies such as an early education program that employed one hundred and sixty-four people "to develop perceptual, social, and verbal skills in the child" and Head Start, which enrolled almost fifteen hundred children from the target area (City of Dayton 1970).

Many of these programs were successful. The students in the summer youth tutoring program gained from six months' to two years' reading ability because of sixty hours of instruction. Between 1969 and 1971 eighteen interns received master's degrees in administration from local universities with special emphasis on inner-city schools (Tyson 1973).

It is difficult to say why the programs worked. People felt a sense of mission and they tried hard. For example, administrative interns were constantly on the job. They set up student council courts to help the students handle the discipline problems themselves. The interns arranged for municipal court judges to visit the schools and officiate at mock trials to show how the criminal justice system worked. Through the student council courts, the children in the school took a share in building management, and they learned important lessons in civics. The interns made home visits to try to help children who were having trouble, and they conducted inservices to help teachers realize the problems the children faced at home. Because of this work, school attendance rates improved and discipline problems declined. Further, Model Cities contracted a branch of the Kettering Foundation, /I/D/E/A/, to teach teachers and administrators how to introduce individually guided instruction into the schools (Revere 1994).

These activities increased to the point that in 1974 the education component secured more funds in partnership with other agencies than any other aspect of Model Cities. These partnership monies created opportunities for middle school children with reading problems to teach reading to primary school children. Other partnerships included recruiting students from nearby colleges to serve as teachers' aides and encouraging a local, historically black state university to open a branch campus in the designated project area. As a result, many people obtained an education or job training that they would not have received otherwise (Martindale 1974).

Unfortunately, the Model Cities program implied that the schools should remain segregated. Four examples illustrate these segregationist tendencies. First, in spring 1967 Edison Elementary School, in a black neighborhood in West Dayton, was partially destroyed by fire. During the summer of 1968 some Model Cities activists contended that Edison School should be rebuilt on its original site and improved. Their view was that if the school was an excellent one, white children would ask to come to Edison. Reverend U.A. Hughey, who was also a black activist, wanted Edison School to be relocated closer to white neighborhoods. Hughey's view was the school would promote integration by its location. Hughey lost that debate, as Edison was rebuilt on its original site (Goodman 1968b).

Second, members of Model Cities thought that school desegregation was unnecessary. For example, in February 1970 the chairperson of the Model Cities education subcommittee announced the formation of an alliance for quality. This new group asked two representatives from each of Dayton's ten high schools to compile a report. Their aim was to show the school board that the school's quality was more important than racial balance among its students. The chairperson's rationale was that if all schools were of high quality, "the black child will have no difficulty being accepted in the white school and vice versa" (Allbaugh 1970).

Third, in May 1969, when the U.S. Department of Health, Education, and Welfare asked Dayton's school board to desegregate the faculty, the Model Cities planning council resisted the school board's plan to move teachers. The council sent a letter to the school board saying there had been a "concentrated effort on behalf of the coordinator to orientate and further sensitize teachers to the neighborhoods' educational problems. It is important the present teachers be allowed to stay in their positions if they so desire" ("Model Cities Council" 1969). Consequently, in the eyes of the planning council, the special training of the teachers outweighed the benefits of a desegregated faculty.

Fourth, the important expression of segregationist ideas was the attempt to design educational programs to reducing educational disadvantage and to provide educational services necessary to serve the poor in the community. This point is the subject of chapter eleven. For this discussion, it is enough to note that the Model Cities Demonstration Project in the inner west section of Dayton contradicted efforts to provide for racial integration.

In Dayton's Model Cities Demonstration Project the concept of community control reinforced racial segregation. Further, as noted earlier, the U.S. Congress permitted this by removing any guidelines from the Model Cities legislation requiring racial integration. However, community control did not necessarily bring with it such results. In fact, the U.S. Department of Housing and Urban Development funded a project to improve a residential area adjacent to inner West Dayton. Directed by residents of the area in a manner similar to the Model Cities project, the Dayton View Stabilization Project tried to maintain racial and economic integration.

The Dayton View Stabilization Project

The land immediately across the Miami River from Dayton was once considered as the site of a rival city. In 1816 one of Dayton's first clergymen plotted a town that he called North Dayton and established a ferry to help people across: his speculation failed. A toll bridge was built in 1819, and by the turn of the century the area was renamed Dayton View. Prosperous citizens settled there and built palatial homes in the area (Lynch 1958).

In 1960 Dayton View had a population of 15,650 people living in 5,417 dwellings, of which 55 percent were rentals. By 1965 the population had increased by 800 people and the number of dwelling units increased by 241. The new construction in the area con-

sisted of housing for the elderly, multiple-story apartment buildings, and one-story ranch-type apartments. The most noticeable social change was the movement of African Americans and Appalachian families into the Dayton View area. However, "through the
efforts of the Neighborhood Council and the Negroes themselves
integration is taking place." As a result, it seemed in 1965 that "the
white population of Dayton View is not as likely now to become
part of a mass movement to evacuate when faced with the prospect
of Negro neighbors as it would have been ten or even five years ago."
Unfortunately, the increased population pressured services like sanitation, police protection, and education. The question remained
whether the cooperation enjoyed between the neighborhoods in
Dayton View and the city could lead to the development of beneficial programs (Neighborhood Master Plan 1965).

On 1 September 1966 rioters gathered on West Third Street,
and National Guard troops stood on the bridge over Wolfe Creek to
keep them from walking into Dayton View (Shere et al. 1969a). As
described earlier, in this chapter and in chapter three, the riot shook
people throughout Dayton.

In January 1968 the presidents of three local groups sent a letter
to the city manager outlining the need to stabilize the neighborhood
of Dayton View. They wanted Dayton View to retain the racial integration it had achieved by this time. Consequently, they defined
stabilization as the elimination of the fear of physical blight, the fear
of poor schools, and the fear of the neighborhood losing its racially
integrated character. Once these fears were gone, they hoped, the
fear of white flight would also disappear. They asked the city to set
up an office and hire an individual with a small staff to coordinate
the stabilization program with other agencies (Rihm 1968).

The city manager forwarded this request to the city commission on 9 February 1968. In his proposal, the city manager noted
that there were four related activities to improve the area. First, the
Dayton public schools received $973,654 for the Multiple Motiva-
tion Program to help the children in the area. Second, the city planned
to spend $284,382 to build a playground in the area. Third, HUD's
Code Enforcement Grant offered $949,224 to hire staff and make
low-interest home improvement loans available in the area. Fourth,
the housing program of the city's human relations council sought to

reduce panic and exodus in culturally changing neighborhoods. The city manager recommended that the city establish a site office with a full time director, a secretary, and other staff to coordinate renewal activities and enhance communication between the residents and the city commission (Watt 1968).

Two of the five city commissioners objected strongly to what they saw as special treatment of one neighborhood. The black commissioner complained that "we're not protecting neighborhoods. We're protecting a neighborhood." He added that "the place that needs it the worst is the last place to get it" (Hopcraft 1968). Despite the controversy, the city commission adopted the plan, and in April Joseph D. Wine resigned as a city commissioner to become the coordinator. He opened the office in May 1968.

Wine displayed what the city manager called an evangelistic fervor in his early reports to the city commission. On 23 April 1968 Wine explained that "discriminatory practices of the real estate profession have insured that there is no free market for Negro housing, and that the Negro population in our urban centers is increasing faster than the availability of living space to house it." Wine added that white people fear their property values will decrease with integration. He concluded that these factors caused "complete neighborhoods to go from white to temporary integration to black." He said the Dayton View project was a two-pronged effort to keep the city from becoming a black center ringed by white suburbs. The first approach was to open housing for Negroes in and around Dayton besides Dayton View. The second approach was to keep Dayton View a desirable place to live. He believed his new office could serve as a laboratory to show practical ways to make inner-city neighborhoods stimulating places where families could make their homes and raise children (Wine 1968a).

In a subsequent report, Wine said that he set up his office with a secretary, four neighborhood counselors, a specialist in sanitary engineering, and several trainees. Through the Code Enforcement Grant he got eight housing inspectors, a supervisor, and loan counselors. By August 1968 he claimed that inspectors had evaluated one third of the structures in the area and the owners were making the needed repairs. Wine said that there were six different sections of Dayton View's 412-block area. Each section had its own mix of architecture and people: Some had large homes. Some had small homes. Some were densely populated. Others were more sparsely populated. Some had rich people living there. Others had young families with low incomes living there. Some neighborhoods were black; others were white. Faced with the problem of effectively serving each neighborhood, Wine recruited a person on each of the 412 blocks in Dayton View to act as block contact. This contact distributed the project newsletter, *The Keystone*, and gathered information for the project. In lower Dayton View, Wine recruited neighborhood residents to form the Screaming Eagles. This citizens' patrol used radios to alert local police about crime as it occurred in the area. He hired children ranging in age from eight to twelve years old to clean up the neighborhood and named this group the Rat Patrol. Wine began a campaign to ensure that realtors' signs were not obtrusive and remained the required twelve feet from the street. He sought ways to control stray dogs. He successfully prosecuted a "slovenly commercial owner who displayed little regard for the character and health of the neighborhood" and acted to maintain restrictions on liquor permits in the area (Dayton View Project 1968).

Trying to expand influence, Wine formed the Dayton View Coalition to serve as a board of directors for the stabilization project. The coalition consisted of about forty members and it was weighted toward the participation of professionals such as physicians, university professors, and business people. The idea of this coalition grew out of the MALACHI organization that fostered the formation of FORCE and FORCE associates who were active in the Model Cities Demonstration Project. Wine attracted professional people to the Dayton View Coalition where policies could be debated. Wine invited the people who were socially conscious but who wanted to participate in direct activities to form such groups as the Screaming Eagles. This group later became a citywide institution called Neighborhood Assistance Officers. They received training from the Dayton police department and cooperated with the uniformed officers to reduce local crime (Zsambok 1994).

An editorial in the *Journal Herald* on 28 September 1968 praised Wine for selecting individuals with different views to serve on Dayton View Coalition. Provocative discussions filled the meetings. For example, the coalition considered imposing a quota system requiring people to sell their houses to people whose racial identity would enhance integration. A sale would be forbidden if it would move the ratio of black and white people in a neighborhood beyond a certain point (Goodman 1968c). The group dropped the quota plan because it conflicted with the more important ideal of opening the metropolitan area to free and open housing programs (Dansker 1968c).

The greatest controversy arose when the coalition considered busing children to different schools. On 31 October 1968 Wine introduced to the Dayton View Coalition a memo addressed to the superintendent of Dayton public schools. Wine was concerned with two problems. First, two Dayton View schools had more students than the buildings could hold. Second, most of the lower-class Appalachians and African American students in Dayton View attended only one of the six elementary schools. Wine wanted to form four clusters of schools. Each cluster would include one school in Dayton View and three other schools from the northwest quadrant of Dayton. Each school in a cluster would specialize so that in one school only students six to eight years of age would attend. In the second school, the students would be eight to ten. The third would have children ten to twelve years of age. The last would be for children twelve to fourteen. All schools would be nongraded, although the remaining two schools in the northwest quadrant would be preschools. Wine hoped that schools would exchange teachers and the best equipment for its specific age or skill groups would concentrate in each school. In addition, he thought that all schools would have small proportions of problem children or students from culturally deprived backgrounds. Consequently, the teachers could spend more time individually with them (Wine 1968b).

The next day, the *Journal Herald* reported that a delegation from the coalition would take the memo to the superintendent. The memo never officially reached him. Almost immediately, petitions bearing hundreds of signatures from the areas of Dayton that would have been part of Wine's plan swamped the school's central office. Parents said they wanted to protect their children. They feared "Wine would sneak the proposal past the board of education" (Harris 1969c). An assistant principal from a school in the Dayton View area said racial bigotry was not the problem. He thought parents opposed the "uprooting of 15,000 children every two years" ("Opposition not Racial" 1969). The setback did not end Wine's interest in schools or racial integration.

Since Wine saw the Dayton View Stabilization Project as a laboratory, he looked for connections among the many parts of urban renewal. He thought that education was central to community improvement because it reduced juvenile crime and young homeowners wanted good schools for their children. As a result, he saw a federal grant program, Multiple Motivation, as an important feature of the effort though the Dayton Board of Education administered it.

The U.S. Department of Health, Education, and Welfare funded Multiple Motivation from February 1968 until February 1971 under Title III of the Projects to Advance Creativity in Education. The grant was to increase educational services and dispel the myth that neighborhood change caused school deterioration. Money went to a Catholic elementary school, St. Agnes; a private Jewish school, Hillel Academy; and five public schools in the Dayton View area. Each of these schools formed a school community committee and the grant paid for a coordinator to improve activities in the school and correct problems in the neighborhood. The schools became community centers providing services for children and adults in the community. Each school got learning center and language development resource teachers who acted as change agents. The schools had teachers' aides to help with individualized instruction for all children (Chamberlin 1970).

Unfortunately, Multiple Motivation did not survive beyond its original three years federal funding period; the school board could not pick up the costs for the program after February 1971 (Turk 1971). In part, the problem was financial. Dayton's voters would not pass school levies although the four liberal members of the school board kept warning the money was needed. The three conservative members often disagreed, saying the money went for programs they saw as wasteful. The state superintendent closed Dayton's schools for a lack of funds on 5 November 1971. On 12 November a school levy passed. While Multiple Motivation might have been revived then, it was also a victim of the political efforts of the Dayton View Coalition.

In 1969 the Dayton View Coalition campaigned for the liberal candidates in the school board election. To stop them, the conservative party, Serving Our Schools, complained to the city commission that the coalition was using city money to advance political campaigns (Daley 1969). Members of the Dayton View Coalition said they formed a separate organization to raise their own campaign funds (Adler 1994). Nonetheless, the three conservative candidates who won in the 1969 election did not forget who their enemies were. In November 1971 the school levy passed, but the Serving Our Schools party won a fourth seat on the school board, making the conservatives a majority. Not only did the conservatives on the board disband the liberal programs that remained, they would not revive a program that their detractors wanted.

While it existed, Multiple Motivation inspired many varied and important activities. According to a program description that appeared in the Dayton View Stabilization Project newsletter, *The Keystone*, there were two main aspects to the Multiple Motivation project. First, it tried to enhance cooperation. Four school community coordinators and a block contact organization enhanced community involvement. This organization controlled rumors and made routine communications easy. Further, each school had an advisory board that sent representatives to the cluster advisory board and to a coordinating council.

Second, Multiple Motivation stressed what was called learning for the whole child. Addressing the whole child meant offering a wide range of courses and activities. Multiple Motivation supported a total of 152 school community center classes that enrolled 4,349 students, one third of whom were adults, in such things as flower arranging, photography, and French. Curriculum innovation addressed the whole child. For example, Colonel White High School began block time scheduling to allow more flexibility. At the elementary level, St. Agnes introduced a completely individualized program. Through the cooperation of the Good Samaritan Mental Health Clinic, the students in the elementary schools had an extensive guidance counseling program (Held 1969).

At least two schools in Dayton View earned widespread fame because of the success of the programs that grew out of Multiple Motivation. One of these schools was St. Agnes and the second was

Longfellow. In both schools, the principals recruited faculty and built programs of individualized or nongraded education. These schools took on a model called Individually Guided Education sponsored by the Kettering Foundation. Under this model, schools allowed students to go on at their own speed. The teachers worked in teams or learning communities in such ways that they served as advisors or guides for the children.

The principal of St. Agnes had been a member of the Sisters of Notre Dame since 1949. At first, the principal tried to consolidate St. Agnes with other Catholic schools in the area because she felt the survival of the school was in doubt. With the approval of the Multiple Motivation grant, St. Agnes became part of the league of seven schools to try to improve schools in the rapidly changing neighborhood. Before the grant was in place St. Agnes had grades two through eight. With the grant, the nine teachers, five aides, and four adult volunteers grouped the 275 students according to their interests. They took out all the walls that could be removed. On the upper floors, the students pursued language arts. On the lower floor, they studied science and social studies. Two thirteen-year-old students sat as voting members on the twelve-member school board for the parish (Polite 1972). Intramural activities began as the students in St. Agnes joined reading groups with students in Hillel Academy. Sixth graders debated such questions as the important message in Kipling stories about Mowgli and the jungle. One student noted these activities gave them opportunities to meet children of other religions (Brucken 1969). A prominent journal of Catholic schools, *Today's Catholic Teacher,* extolled the virtues of St. Agnes in a series of articles by Dan Geringer (1969). He claimed the program was exciting because the children were continually examining controversial questions such as whether Jews act as if they were the enemies of people of other religions. But Geringer acknowledged that St. Agnes had problems as well. For example, individual study became the rule because students had trouble breaking away from one-to-one relationships with teachers. The students seemed unable to work cooperatively with other children.

When visitors toured the facility, they loved what they saw. In 1969, the director of innovative programs for the Kettering Foundation asked the principal and the staff of St. Agnes to serve as consultants. He wanted them to explain what they did to people in schools in other cities.

Despite the praise, the people at St. Agnes faced two severe problems. First, money was always short. In 1972 the budget was only $73,000 per year. As a result, primary teachers who needed a wide range of materials had to scrounge things or make their own phonics tapes rather than purchase materials. Second, political problems arose when the school strove to teach children to accept differences. The staff did not always teach traditional values. For example, in a first-grade classroom a get-well card to a teacher read, "I hope you get well and come back soon. But if not, that's the way it goes." This lack of charity and the disrespect for authority offended many traditional Catholics. One teacher noted the children "know the school is theirs. They are not taught to fear anyone" (Geringer 1969). These parents complained to the Cincinnati Archdiocese. When the archdiocese received complaints questioning the orthodoxy of the teaching of religion, the officials sent a priest other than the one assigned to the parish to examine the teachers.

In December 1972 the principal resigned from her position, citing a lack of financial support from the archdiocese and from her order. She also complained of a general unwillingness of the Catholic hierarchy to support racial and social integration (chapter seven will discuss this more fully). An editorial in the *Journal Herald* mourned her resignation, saying "the school had become a model of harmonious, socially constructive integration," but it seemed "ironic that the problems the principal coped with so ably at St. Agnes still plague the archdiocesan school and are the reasons for her resignation." She moved to the Good Samaritan Hospital where she became the director of an innovative Learning Center that provided help to children with severe behavior problems. In 1975 she left the religious order because she did not want to be identified with an organization that refused to confront the problems of racial segregation (Fanella 1990).

The other Dayton View school that tried to reinforce racial integration by being a place where children learned to enjoy school was Longfellow Elementary School. This school became highly regarded despite two significant drawbacks. First, it was overcrowded. Some of its more than two thousand children walked to nearby churches to attend classes because they could not fit in the building. Second, it was located on a busy intersection. The principal took advantage of this location and turned the building into a billboard complete with catchy signs. One said, "This is Longfellow, where we have equal educational opportunity for all." Another sign advertised the school as the home of "MM" for Multiple Motivation when that program was in force.

As with St. Agnes, the principal was part of the success. He stood on the corner every day helping the children cross the street. He served playground duty, and walked into nearby stores to make sure his children did not cause problems for the businesses. During the school day his main concern was to maintain control. After school, he worked long hours with teachers and staff encouraging innovative instruction. The principal believed the slogans on the building and his visibility started a chain of success stories. The parents and children took more pride in the school and they volunteered to do more things: they offered courses in sewing or made objects to sell for Christmas. Using the money from these projects, the principal offered trips for the students or to buy equipment for the school. The principal selected his staff from a large pool of applicants. Since the school district had to desegregate the faculty, many teachers applied to come to Longfellow because it was considered a black school but it did not have troubles with discipline. (Caras 1994).

After 1971 Longfellow became the home of IGE, Individually Guided Education, for Dayton. As discussed in chapter nine, representatives of the Kettering Foundation came to Longfellow in the early 1970s. They made a film, *Somebody Special,* to show how IGE could work to make children happy and successful. Students from private schools and from the outlying suburbs applied to come to the school. This success did not come easily. The administration and the faculty put in long hours each week. They started work well before the children arrived and ended long after the children had gone (Caras 1994).

The film *Somebody Special* conveys a dangerous half truth. It implies that teachers and the principal brought the parents into the school because of the openness of the Individually Guided Education process. The truth is that Longfellow was embedded deep within a genuine community constructed by the Dayton View Stabilization Project and the Multiple Motivation workers. Part of the success of Longfellow came from the long hours of toil from the teachers and the administrators and the openness they showed teachers and students. But another important part of Longfellow's success came from Joe Wine and his colleagues, who made the residents realize that Dayton View was a place to make a home. It also came from all the workers in the Multiple Motivation project who introduced people from all walks of life to the benefits of social involvement. Without these supportive efforts, Longfellow would not have been as successful as it was.

While the instructional success that Multiple Motivation enjoyed was important, its community relations aspect was crucial. It helped reduce the disturbances that plagued the Dayton View schools. For example, in October 1968 125 African American students at Colonel White took over the cafeteria. They refused to leave until a teacher apologized for saying that the school was better before the black students arrived. The teacher would retire at the end of the year, and he had made the remark in a private conversation ("Col. White Students Offended" 1968). A little more than three months later, students in Jefferson Elementary School pounded tables in the cafeteria and chanted "Say it loud, I'm black and I'm proud." The police were called and the presence of the officers enraged the students. The principal closed the building as children marched through the main building turning over furniture (Worth 1969).

Administrators from the schools, the police, Multiple Motivation personnel, and the director and staff of the Dayton View Stabilization Project met at Jefferson school. They heard complaints from the students and discussed the difficulties that existed. They made seven suggestions: offer a black history course in the school, provide more sensitive leadership, give counseling tailored to black students, hold human relations inservices for teachers, hire teachers aware of the students' culture, avoid severe reactions to discipline problems, and increase the respect for the office of principal (Jefferson Meeting 1969).

Consultants from universities conducted the inservice training. Staff from the Dayton View Stabilization Project introduced the teachers to the sociology of the area served by the schools. Teachers boarded buses for a tour of the area. The staff workers explained how the parts of Dayton View differed from each other. They told what amenities the area offered and how the area affected the children for good and ill. Many teachers were "surprised to see the number of good homes" in lower Dayton View instead of the tenement-filled ghetto they imagined ("Teachers Tour" 1968).

In 1970 the Southwestern Ohio Educational Research Council evaluated the Multiple Motivation project in Dayton. The evaluators found that the students thought the Multiple Motivation made school more fun. Further, the students enjoyed the opportunity to learn independently, and they wanted to spend more time in learning centers. Because of their popularity, learning centers threatened to compete with regular classrooms for space and materials. The teachers were working in teams although it had been difficult to create learning communities. The evaluators found Multiple Motivation's greatest success to be establishing a communications network with the community through the board system. In part the success of the system was that the advisory boards selected members from each geographic region of the school's attendance zone. In this way, the committees ensured the participation of parents of other than middle-class white people. Finally, the evaluators noted that the project director and the school community coordinators worked long and hard to make the programs work. Fortunately, residents appreciated the efforts because they enrolled in the programs (Wiley 1970).

A measure of success of the community relations aspect of the Multiple Motivation program was the Dayton View voter response to school tax levies. Newspapers asserted that Dayton View residents opposed school or city tax levies (Goltz 1971). Although this was generally true, an analysis of the voter returns for a school tax that failed in 1970 showed Multiple Motivation influenced voter attitudes. The levy received overwhelming support from residents in the heart of Dayton View and in the center of Multiple Motivation cluster schools. High-income whites and blacks and low-income blacks gave the most support for the levy. Middle- and low-income whites voted against the levy. Unfortunately, the tax levy failed because it ran poorly outside the Multiple Motivation area (Woodie 1970).

Despite the success of Multiple Motivation, the Dayton View project did not clearly reduce fear of integration, of poor schools, or of crime. For example, white families who initially resisted the efforts of "blockbusters" to sell their homes began to move. Some of them found their African American neighbors intimidating ("Couple Moves" 1969). Second, Multiple Motivation was not a magic cure for the schools. For example, the supervisor of guidance and testing for the Dayton public schools acknowledged some drop in test scores of pupils in two Dayton View schools. She said, "The schools are getting more numerous children out of the white middle-class cultural mainstream." She added "they are working as well as can be expected" (Harris 1969d). Third, despite Wine's efforts to reduce crime, police statistics suggested crime was higher in Dayton View. Wine said the police reports were wrong. He contended that the police statistics included sections other than Dayton View, and when only Dayton View was considered, the rates were lower. In addition, the police report concentrated on felonies while the stabilization project concentrated on misdemeanors as the precursors of serious crimes. Wine said the project had reduced minor offenses ("Crime Report" 1969).

The argument over crime rates illuminated the methods of the Dayton View Stabilization Project. Wine operated on the premise that interconnected conditions caused urban decline. That is, Wine asserted that small unnoticed things were often most important. For example, he made signs saying "stray dogs breed crime." His rationale was that stray dogs, like junk cars, cause people to give up on keeping their surroundings neat, then the sloppy neighborhood invites instability (Shere et al. 1969a). Unfortunately, such an argument was difficult to prove.

The project lacked other signs of success. The federal government had approved none of the sixty-seven applications for loans to repair homes and accepted only eight of the eighty-three applications for grants to improve structures. Under President Nixon, federal agencies tried to withhold such grant monies. However, the city commission refused to fund the project adequately. The director, Joe Wine, earned a salary of $13,000 per year that was equivalent at the time to the salary of an assistant accountant or waste collection supervisor (Shere et al. 1969b).

The city commission may have underfunded the Dayton View Stabilization Project because the project challenged the commissioners. For example, on 10 April 1969 members of the Dayton View Coalition rebuked the city commission for seeking to raise the municipal income tax from one percent to 1.5 percent. They complained the city had not shown the need for the tax increase. At least one city commissioner accused the coalition of trying to kill the tax, and the mayor said they were not helping the city ("Dayton View Feedback" 1969).

In August 1969 the management services of the executive department of the city of Dayton released a review of the stabilization project. It concluded that the director and staff of the Dayton View Stabilization Project had not defined the problems they wanted to solve nor determined the strategies they should follow. The report acknowledged the project staff could not assess the needs of the neighborhood; external specialists were needed.

After reviewing the project, on 17 November 1969 the City Plan Board made its own recommendations to improve the stabilization effort. First, the city should increase its commitment to the stabilization project. Second, the Dayton View Coalition should have a broader base of citizen participation, and third, the project had to develop a more comprehensive program for physical change. Finally, the City Plan Board complained about the word, "stabilization," saying it implied the project resisted change. The Plan Board said the aim of the project should be to support the process of urban change (City Plan Board 1969).

For the next few months, there was an argument about the word, "stabilization." Participants in the project contended that the Plan Board misunderstood the word. They claimed that official policy statements in Dayton used the term "stabilization" to mean the elimination of fear. It did not mean trying to maintain a neighborhood as segregated. They refused to support urban change if that process meant the resegregation of Dayton View from a white neighborhood into a black community. Instead, they argued that "the only acceptable policy is one that effectively guarantees the opportunity for integration for the entire community." They said a planned program of urban change was one that enhanced the opportunity for residential integration (Dayton View Program 1970).

The city commission replied to the Plan Board's report on 26 November 1969 by setting up a task force to coordinate the project with other city activities. The commission appointed a management technician to evaluate the project. They designated a city planner as responsible for comprehensive planning for Dayton View. Finally, the commission applied for federal planning funds to help the project (Goldwyn 1969).

Wine's desire to enhance the racial integration of the entire community attracted national attention. For example, in December 1971 the *Kansas City Star* published a long article saying that Wine was looking for the formula to save America. If so, the formula was a familiar one: fight rats, abandoned buildings, and deterioration. Campaign against realtors who steer whites from critical neighborhoods. Keep youths happy. The Kansas newspaper noted that Wine added a new twist to these tried and true ideas. It was a housing dispersal plan that opened suburban neighborhoods to African Americans to relieve the pressure on Dayton View (Hammer 1971). Unfortunately, open and fair housing was not successful in Dayton.

For example, the migration of African Americans into Dayton View continued as illustrated by some school enrollment figures: in 1963 Longfellow and Cornell Heights elementary schools in Dayton View had student bodies with 5 percent and no African American students respectively. In 1968, those schools had student bodies that were 42.3 percent and 44 percent black. These figures implied that housing for African Americans was not available in other parts of the city and suburbs (Wiley 1969).

Open and Fair Housing Initiatives

In Dayton from 1910 until 1950, the titles for homes contained covenants against ownership by other than Caucasians. These covenants came into being because the Federal Housing Authority (FHA) refused to insure or finance houses in racially mixed areas. In 1950 the FHA reversed its policy and refused to insure or finance property when the deed carried a covenant restricting ownership to a certain race (Hemmelgarn 1972).

In September 1967 the Dayton City Commission approved a fair housing ordinance to make it easier for African Americans to buy homes in segregated areas. This ordinance made it unlawful for anyone to refuse to sell or to rent a home to someone based on race or religion. It also prohibited similar discrimination in lending money to buy or rehabilitate homes ("Fair Housing Text" 1967). Shortly after the fair housing ordinance became law in June 1969, the Dayton Metropolitan Housing Authority took responsibility to insure that the location of public housing would not perpetuate further segregation (Human Relations Council 1969).

In 1968, recognizing that fair housing had to be county-wide, 107 priests of the 132 in the Dayton Deanery signed a petition asking that all Montgomery County adopt policies opposing discrimination in buying, renting, or leasing homes (Lohrer 1968a). Consequently, all levels of government felt pressure to enact open or fair housing regulations. By June 1968 five Dayton suburban governments adopted fair housing policy statements. In addition, the four Dayton area representatives to the U.S. Congress aided the passage of the housing and civil rights bill. This bill was an attempt to help cities that had open housing requirements but were adjacent to suburbs that lacked such requirements.

Unfortunately, these laws offered little relief. For example, the Ohio Civil Rights Committee said the most benefit they saw from the passage of fair housing laws was from the publicity that accompanied them. This state agency lacked such important weapons as the power to prevent a sale of property someone complained about. Consequently, the Ohio Civil Rights Committee could not settle the nearly 600 complaints it received in a year either promptly or equitably (Dansker 1968d). The Dayton Human Relations Council had so little power they could only refer complaints to the American Civil Liberties Union that would offer legal assistance ("Plan to Put Muscle into Fair Housing" 1968). Instead of going to court, the Dayton Human Relations Council urged people willing to sell to African Americans to display a window sticker of the American flag (Goodman 1968e). Not surprisingly, a comparison of housing patterns in 1967 and in 1970 showed that the open housing policies were uneven at best. Almost no black families lived in the southern suburban communities of Oakwood, Kettering, and West Carrollton. Some African Americans had begun to move into the northern suburbs (Hall 1972).

It was more surprising that legislation did not change the segregated patterns in federally subsidized housing. Although this was an area the government controlled, federal officers did not encourage integration. A study of the effects in Dayton of sections 235 and 236 of the U.S. Housing and Urban Development Act of 1968 made this clear. These two programs reduced costs on rental and cooperative housing projects and provided for the construction and rehabilitation of homes for low and moderate income families. The study showed that families who benefited from these programs fell into two groups. The families who lived in suburban communities around Dayton were white. The families who lived in the city of Dayton were African Americans. Interestingly, the families in both these groups wanted to live in racially integrated settings but none was available (Eskew 1971). The directors of the Miami Valley Regional Planning Commission decided that Dayton was to be among the first communities to ask the suburbs to share economic or social integration.

In September 1970 the Miami Valley Regional Planning Commission (MVRPC) adopted Housing Goals and Policies for its five-county-area planning jurisdiction. In 1970 almost all of the 3,350 units of public and federally assisted housing were in the city of Dayton (Usher 1970). This plan was to make the distribution more equitable by building 14,000 low-income housing units throughout the region (MVRPC 1971). Residents in the towns where these low-income units would be built immediately criticized the plan. In September 1970 over one hundred residents of Oakwood, a southern suburb of Dayton, packed a council meeting to oppose accepting 634 low and moderate income housing units. One resident who opposed the introduction of subsidized housing yelled, "Those people can find homes if they are willing to work for a living." The audience applauded his comment (Bohman 1970). The supporters of the plan to disperse low-income housing tried to turn the prejudice against welfare into a means to advance the dispersal of low-income housing. They argued that the Federal Housing Authority subsidized the high property values of suburban communities through mortgage insurance. They called this middle-class welfare. As a result, they thought it fair to require each community to build some low-income housing projects before they could receive federally insured home owner loans (Wine 1990). However, the Miami Valley Regional Planning Commission's housing dispersal plan did not threaten to punish communities that avoided low-income housing. It offered rewards for compliance. As a result, it attracted national attention.

In June 1971 U.S. Secretary of Housing and Urban Development, George Romney, complimented Dayton's dispersal plan. He said it represented the way then President Nixon wanted to move on housing. Nixon approved of the plan using a formula to fairly allocate low-income housing to the suburbs. Further, he liked the fact that, instead of asking HUD to withhold funds from suburbs, the plan suggested rewarding suburbs for adopting the plan. Unfortunately, the mayors of most big cities, and even Dayton's own mayor, felt the plan did not go far enough (Usher 1971).

In 1972, the director of the MVRPC explained Dayton's dispersal plan to public administrators at a national conference. In his paper, the director said that the plan involved a network of simultaneous activities. Most important, he obtained an agreement from HUD to give bonus grant monies to suburban communities that accepted the housing dispersal plan. The director added that HUD was cooperative, but the local FHA officials were not. They required constant supervision. The director noted residents in suburban communities put pressure on public officials to prevent low-income housing from coming into their communities. Still, he concluded, the only way to succeed was to operate wide open to criticism (Bertsch 1972).

Unfortunately, it was easy for a community to frustrate the dispersal plan. For example, one developer noted that land was available at reasonable cost in most suburbs but it was not zoned for multifamily use. Consequently, "a developer had to go before boards, commissions, and city councils to get the zoning he needs and the agency that granted the approval has to take heat from the neighborhood residents who see the project as the end of the world" (O'Hara 1971).

Another problem was that pressure to keep the low-income families out of the suburbs exceeded the pressure to disperse the projects throughout the suburbs. A study conducted in 1971 showed that low-income residents of substandard housing in Dayton tended not to object to the dilapidated conditions (Smiley 1971). Consequently, while suburban residents fought to keep the low-income housing projects out, low-income families did not exert an equal, countervailing pressure to move to better facilities.

Ironically, suburban residents need not have feared that many different people would come into their communities. In 1973 a study showed that people who lived in the area before the projects were built tended to occupy federally subsidized housing. Sometimes, these people qualified for low-income housing after retirement. At any rate, there was no migration of new people into the area (Harris et al. 1973). Still, the suburbanites were afraid of newcomers. The northern suburbs of Dayton accepted the first units built following the low-income housing dispersal plan. The southern suburbs resisted (Bland 1971). However, in the southern suburb of Centerville, construction began on a subsidized housing project with 232 units. It was Chevy Chase.

Despite the careful and open manner in which the MVRPC carried out the housing dispersal plan, it stalled almost immediately. In 1972 officials from HUD complained that Dayton's open housing plan called for more low-income units than the area needed. Manufacturing jobs had left the city, and population in the counties around Dayton declined (Fritz 1972). Further, on 5 January 1973 the Department of Housing and Urban Development froze monies for the construction of subsidized housing, halting Dayton's dispersal plan (Bland 1973). The Nixon administration wanted to substitute a form of direct cash subsidies to the poor for organized building projects. Without federal money, the MVRPC could not offer bonuses for communities that complied with the plan.

The MVRPC revised its estimate of the number of units of low-income housing needed in the region, and they changed the fair share allocations for each community. The MVRPC acknowledged that since 1970 the city of Dayton had "absorbed several hundred units more than its original goal." Southern suburbs had not taken as many as they should. For example, one suburb to the south of Dayton, Oakwood, had a fair share allocation of 361 units, but by 1973 it had not built any. Despite this lack of cooperation, the MVRPC held that spreading low-income housing projects through the suburbs "can be done only through increased levels of responsibility on the part of other local governments" (MVRPC 1974). Unfortunately, even mild steps met antagonism. For example, in 1975, when the Dayton Urban League proposed that a task force be set up to act as a watch dog for fair housing laws, the special projects advisor for the Montgomery County Commission would not present it to the commission. He feared "the white suburbs would balk" (Martindale 1975).

In 1974 the U.S. Housing and Community Development Act required that local communities develop their own housing plans calling on community block grants. While this system was supposed to allow more freedom to communities to decide how to spend the federal money, there was less to use. For example, in 1974 Dayton received $6.8 million in community development grants. These replaced a total of $13 million that included the Model Cities program. This represented about half of the federal money once given to a range of services such as job training, small business loans, and crime and delinquency programs. Further, the new federal monies could not be spent on many of these programs; the city had to pay their expenses or drop them (Martindale 1974b). In this way, the block grants created a market of competing social needs, and open housing could not compete with job training programs. Consequently, although by 1973 there had been gains in fair or open housing, those improvements fell away.

In 1978 the low-income housing dispersal program came back to life. The U.S. Department of Housing and Urban Development gave the MVRPC a $2.5 million bonus grant. The director hoped that "if a community agrees to build low-income housing, they could offer block grant money as an award" (Lowenstein 1978). In this spirit, the MVRPC offered a third edition of the housing and dispersal plan. In this new plan, the MVRPC did not call for new housing projects. It recommended using existing or rehabilitated units. Unfortunately, this made dispersal throughout the suburbs more difficult. The city of Dayton had lost more population than the suburbs and had more housing units to rehabilitate (MVRPC 1978). Unfortunately, the MVRPC did not have time to work on that problem. Federal funds continued to decline. In 1981 as part of general cuts in domestic spending, the Reagan administration cut the operating budget of the MVRPC. The commission lost half of its staff and reduced many programs (Dykes 1981). The low-income housing dispersal program ended. Open or fair housing remained an ideal rather than a reality.

Consequently, in 1985 the Montgomery County Fair Housing Center completed a study showing that despite "improvements in housing opportunities and the increased migration within the county, there was still a tendency for most migrating black households to concentrate in a few communities, rather than dispersing all over the county as did white households. This indicates that even in 1980, blacks probably did not fully have equal housing opportunity" (Montgomery County Fair Housing Center 1985, 1).

Despite the failure of fair or open housing initiatives and the problems with the Dayton View Stabilization Project, the city of Dayton expanded the Dayton View Stabilization Project into a city-wide program. Two staff members of the Dayton View Stabilization Project wrote the City Wide Model Cities Planned Variations. They adapted the neighborhood organization of the Dayton View Stabilization Project into the proposal. In 1970 the City of Dayton created priority boards as neighborhood organizations. In the Model Cities Planned Variations, the priority boards became replicas of the Dayton View Stabilization Office (Woodie 1994). However, in what some people saw as punishment for past offenses to city hall, the city commission overlooked Joe Wine as director. He became Task Force Management Coordinator.

The City-Wide Model Cities Program

On 29 July 1971 the president of the United States, Richard Nixon, announced the selection of twenty cities to participate in a Planned Variations of the Model Cities Programs. He chose Dayton along with Butte, Montana; Des Moines, Iowa; and Erie, Pennsylvania. Nixon said that his revenue sharing proposals to the Congress made basic changes in the administration of federal grants. The aim of these variations was to "demonstrate what local government can accomplish in solving urban problems when given greater freedom from federal regulations." Nixon said that these variations would improve the operation of the federal grant system under existing legislation. There were to be three features to his proposals: First, all twenty cities would receive funds to build up the planning and management capacity of the local chief executive. Second, the Model Cities programs would expand to include the entire city. Third, there would be considerably less oversight by federal agencies. Nixon said this Planned Variations program represented "an important beginning step in the process of returning authority to local government" (Nixon 1971).

The administrators in the city of Dayton were careful to make sure that these changes did not affect the work going on in the Model Cities planning council in Inner West. In a memorandum of understanding, the city of Dayton and HUD agreed to maintain funding of the Model Cities Demonstration Project in Inner West. Further, the agreement noted that the partnership between the planning council and the city commission would not change during the planned variations trial.

The city received $5.2 million for the planned variations from HUD over the two-year period. A central administrative budget and four-member neighborhood teams in each of the five priority boards cost $1.4 million. The Model Cities Demonstration Project in Inner West continued on its own. In September 1971 a former special assistant with the HUD regional office in San Francisco became director of the Model Cities city wide program. The planning council in Inner West thought the head of their project should be the director of the citywide program. Residents in other areas complained that they were not receiving the same power to control the programs in their neighborhoods that the people had in Inner West. Dayton's city manager replied that the Model Cities planning council had an equal partnership agreement with the city because racial discrimination was the problem; such an arrangement gave residents access to power. He added that other neighborhoods would have informal power to select programs, but formal power would reside with the city ("Model Cities Director Appointed" 1971).

In December 1971 elections were held in the five new Model Cities neighborhoods and 149 priority board members elected. The new members underwent a two-day training session in contract preparation, group dynamics, and community organization. In May 1972 the city commission approved the $2.1 million budget for the first year. Unlike the Inner West program, school-related expenses were not a high priority. In the citywide project, funds were spent on the Dayton Museum of Natural History. Citywide money supported a community school program. This kept school buildings open to offer night classes and recreational activities for residents. Some money went to adult basic education. The citywide project did not employ the compensatory education projects developed by the Inner West planning council (Russ 1972).

Despite hopeful beginnings, Dayton's Model Cities faced problems with federal agencies. In 1973 President Nixon reduced Model Cities allocations by 45 percent. The National League of Cities recommended that people from Dayton tell the Housing and Urban Affairs Subcommittee of the Senate Banking, Housing, and Urban Affairs Committee about the benefits of the Model Cities programs. They considered Dayton's project a prime example of how Model Cities should work. On 10 April 1973 Dayton's city manager and the executive assistant to the city commission urged the subcommittee to protect the project. They feared that the progress achieved in Dayton by spending over $17 million would be lost (Crawford and Kunde 1973).

Unfortunately, it was not clear what progress Dayton's Model Cities projects achieved. In August 1973 a report by the evaluation component of Dayton's Model Cities Demonstration Project in the Inner West contended that "overall conditions within the neighborhood have gotten worse in each succeeding year since 1969." The mayor of the city complained that "a negative report just gives critics of the program a chance to say we've wasted all that money." A member of the planning council of the Inner West Model Cities Demonstration Project said the program had faced great odds: "It was a pacification program from the beginning. It was not supposed to do anything." The planning council member added that the federal government set up the program in fifty cities torn by riots "so white people would have time to see whether there was a black revolution" (Williamson 1973).

An independent study conducted by the Ford Foundation was more positive. The evaluators said Dayton's Inner West Model Cities Demonstration Project distinguished itself when compared to those of seven other cities. The report complimented the organization of the planning council and the various components such as education, housing, and health. The evaluators approved of these satellite corporations because they allowed the residents from the area to sit on the committees and control the budget (Wilson 1973).

Despite these positive reports, by February 1974 there were three bills in the U.S. Congress that sought consolidation of Model Cities monies into block grants. The sponsor of one of the bills was a Democratic representative from Toledo, Ohio. He complained that the money given to Dayton deprived the residents in his own city because they did not have such programs ("Model Cities Dead" 1973).

Dayton's Republican representative argued against his party in favor of the Model Cities grants. He defended the apparent inequities they caused, saying that there was no reason to give funds to an area that did not need them: "Bicycle paths are fine, but your basic needs are housing, health and education facilities" (Ordovensky 1974). Because of such comments, the central issue was not one of fairness in the congressional debates; the issue of waste was most important.

In early 1974 the Dayton City Commission tried to show that the program of Model Cities worked. They produced a forty-page progress report and accompanying slide presentation celebrating the success of Dayton's Model Cities projects. The brochure listed the successes of the various components of the two Model Cities programs in Dayton. For example, the brochure boasted of the community school program that served about fifteen hundred students throughout the city. The brochure pointed out that the education component of the Inner West project had experienced success with several activities. These included the community schools, early childhood education, a program of teacher inservices to improve teaching skills, scholarships, and the community school councils in which educators and residents worked together. These programs corrected institutional racism and met the special needs of the residents of Inner West, the brochure said.

Unfortunately, Dayton's brochure did not influence enough votes in the U.S. Congress. All of Dayton's Model Cities projects ended on 30 August 1975. The priority board system remained in place. Although many staff people left as the federal funding declined, some people stayed on. For example, an administrator of the Inner West Model Cities planning council became an administrator with the

Inner West priority board. Financial problems lingered from the substantial budgets given to the Inner West satellite corporations. There were accusations of misuse of funds, and the federal government sought to recover thousands of dollars misspent by the Inner West Model Cities planning council (Allbaugh 1975). This continued to be a problem. For example, in 1984 the defunct satellite corporation of the Inner West planning council, the Housing and Urban Development Corporation, had vacant properties scattered throughout the inner west section. The city administration of Dayton continued to send bills for upkeep and taxes that went unpaid (Erickson 1984).

Conclusion

The Model Cities projects and the Dayton View Stabilization Project made long-term impacts on Dayton city administration. City staff members claim that Dayton has one of the most resident-responsive governments in the nation because of its involvement in these projects. They offered the first work experience for many administrators who came to occupy important positions in Dayton's government in the 1980s and 1990s. More important, the officials maintained the belief that residents should decide what projects would benefit the city. The only caveat was that formal control was not shared with residents as it was in the Model Cities Demonstration Project. The city administration would spend the money the way the residents wished, but the administration kept control of the funds (Woodie 1994).

Unfortunately, neither the Dayton View Stabilization Project nor the Model Cities programs had a lasting effect on the racial integration of the metropolitan area. Every effort to bring about racial integration through open or fair housing failed or lost support. African Americans were isolated in the west side of the city, in a few neighborhoods such as Dayton View, and in the northern suburbs. Despite the failure of programs of open or fair housing, people who opposed school desegregation said the way to bring about racial integration was through changes in the housing patterns.

When suburban residents refused to allow low-income housing in their communities, integrated neighborhoods in the city were in danger of becoming exclusively black or poor. In such a setting, an intelligent response is to try to improve the lives of low-income African Americans in the places where they live. Unfortunately, such an attempt in Inner West Dayton was not clearly successful.

Nationally syndicated columnist William Raspberry illustrated the difficulty in assessing the impact of the Model Cities program. In 1977 Raspberry reported the conclusions drawn by a member of Congress from Georgia about Atlanta's Model Cities project. Evidence of the program's failure were clear, he said. Population in the target area declined. Housing in the area was demolished. The percentage of families on public assistance in the area was up. School records showed that the students from the target area did badly when compared to students from other parts of the city. In a subsequent column, Raspberry published a rebuttal. He argued that the statistics about an area may show that the people there were worse than when the program began. However, Raspberry noted that those statistics do not tell if the same people are still in the area. He said that the original residents may have moved on to better neighborhoods because of the opportunities Model Cities opened.

This argument applies to the city of Dayton. The statistical picture of Inner West matches the description Raspberry gave of Atlanta's Model Cities target area. While 42,000 people lived in the Inner West area before the Model Cities Demonstration Project began, 11,420 lived there in 1994. Unfortunately, Raspberry's rationale acknowledges that the Model Cities programs did not help the city; they helped people to escape from the city. Racial and economic segregation remained despite several million dollars' worth of compensatory programs aimed at reducing it.

References

Adler, Michael. 1994. Interview with author, 22 June.
Allbaugh, Dave. 1968. "Ousted Aide," *Dayton Daily News*, 14 December.
———. 1969. "Thomas Overruled," *Dayton Daily News*, 1 July.
———. 1970. "Model Cities Alliance," *Dayton Daily News*, 10 February.
———. 1973. "Model Cities Pioneer," *Dayton Daily News*, 25 July.
———. 1975. "HUD Audit," *Dayton Daily News*, 27 April.
Bertsch, Dale. 1972. "Housing and Area-Wide Planning." Miami Valley Regional Planning Commission Archives, Dayton, Ohio.
———. 1994. Interview with author, July 29.
Bland, Jim. 1971. "Housing Plan Working in One Direction," *Dayton Daily News*, 3 August.
———. 1973. "Housing Freeze," *Dayton Daily News*, 25 April.
Bohman, Jim. 1970. "Oakwood Says No to Housing," *Dayton Daily News*, 10 September.
Brucken, Georgia. 1969. "Hot Debate Builds Tolerance," *Dayton Daily News*, 29 May.

Caras, Gregory. 1994. Interview with author, 15 June.

Chamberlin, William P. 1970. "Multiple Motivation Project Information." Local Government Records, Dayton View Stabilization Project. American History Research Center, Wright State University.

City of Dayton. 1970. "Second-Year Action Plan." Model Cities Special Projects File, American History Research Center, Wright State University.

City Plan Board. 1969. "Dayton View Stabilization Project," 17 November. Local Government Records, American History Research Center, Wright State University.

"Col. White Students Offended." 1968. Dayton Daily News, 4 October.

"Couple Moves." 1969. Dayton Daily News, 28 April.

Crawford, Don L., and James E. Kunde. 1973. "Testimony on the Impact of Model Cities," 10 April. Model Cities Special Projects File, American History Research Center, Wright State University.

"Crime Report." 1969. Dayton Daily News, 13 June.

Daley, Robert. 1969. "Coalition Accused," Dayton Daily News, 8 October.

Dansker, Emil. 1968a. "Committee Will Tackle Grievances," Dayton Daily News, 5 June.

———. 1968b. "School Chief Praises," Dayton Daily News, 23 July.

———. 1968c. "Dayton View Coalition," Dayton Daily News, 11 October.

———. 1968d. "Publicity First Result," Dayton Daily News, 15 April.

"Dayton View Feedback." 1969. Dayton Daily News, 2 May.

Dayton View Program. 1970. "Status Report to City Commission," 12 March. Local Government Records, American History Research Center, Wright State University.

Dayton View Project. 1968. "Report to City Commission," 28 August. Local Government Records, American History Research Center, Wright State University.

Dressler, James. 1967. "Model Cities Office to Open," Dayton Daily News, 5 October.

Dykes, David. 1981. "MVRPC Prepares to Cut," Dayton Daily News, 30 May.

Erickson, John. 1984. "Model Cities Gone," Dayton Daily News, 28 November.

Eskew, William. 1971. "A Regional Analysis of Section 235." M.A. thesis, Ball State University, Muncie, Indiana.

"Fair Housing Ordinance Text." 1967. Journal Herald, 25 September.

Fanella, M. Margaret. 1990. Interview with author, 26 September.

Felton, John. 1969. "Tiff Stalling Project," Journal Herald, 8 July.

Fritz, Pat. 1972. "Subsidized Housing Needs," Journal Herald, 23 August.

Geringer, Dan. 1969. "We Are Actually Looking at Our Kids," Today's Catholic Teacher, 2 May: 11–15.

Goldwyn, Ronald. 1968. "Model Cities Gets $2.9 Million," Journal Herald, 12 June.

———. 1969. "City Makes New Commitment," Journal Herald, 26 November.

Goltz, Gene. 1971. "Tax Likely a Squeaker," Dayton Daily News, 2 October.

Goodman, Denise. 1968a. "Model Cities Meeting Interrupted," Dayton Daily News, 25 April.

———. 1968b. "Model Cities Community Failure Hit," Journal Herald, 7 June.

———. 1968c. "Forces Mobilize Against Negro Separatism," Journal Herald, 23 July.

———. 1968d. "Quota System Eyed," Journal Herald, 4 October.

———. 1968e. "Buyer Seller Issue," Journal Herald, 17 June.

———. 1970. "City Warned of Model Cities Cut," Journal Herald, 21 January.

"Groups Want Say." 1971. Dayton Daily News, 3 October.

Hall, Howard. 1972. "Movement of Blacks Slow," Dayton Daily News, 29 June.

Hammer, Charles. 1971. "Ohio City Battles Blight," Kansas City Star, 8 December.

Harris, Henry. 1969a. "Write New Policy," Dayton Daily News, 13 April.

———. 1969b. "Thomas Keeps Job," Dayton Daily News, 10 June.

———. 1969c. "Parents Protesting," Dayton Daily News, 22 January.

Harris, Henry, et al. 1973. "Outsiders Don't Fill Public Housing," Dayton Daily News, 23 May.

Held, Sue. 1969. "Moving with Multiple Motivation," The Keystone, 19 December.

Hemmelgarn, Joseph. 1972. Affidavit, *Brinkman v Gilligan,* 10 November.

Hopcraft, David. 1968. "Dayton View Priority," *Journal Herald,* 16 February.

Human Relations Council. 1969. *Guidelines in Housing for Public Agencies.* City of Dayton, June.

Jefferson Meeting. 1969. Minutes, 30 January. Local Government Records, Dayton View Stabilization Project, American History Research Center, Wright State University.

Lashley, Jim. 1968. "Schools Set Up Integration Advisory Unit," *Journal Herald,* 28 June.

Lohrer, Bill. 1968a. "Priests Request Open Housing," *Dayton Daily News,* 19 February.

———. 1968b. "Suburbs Back Open Housing," *Dayton Daily News,* 26 March.

Lowenstein, Douglas. 1978. "Bonus to Pay for Low-Income Housing," *Dayton Daily News,* 25 July.

Lynch, Mary Ellen. 1958. "Dayton View," *Dayton Daily News,* 14 October.

Marshall Kaplan, Gans and Kahn Inc. 1969. "Dayton Model Cities Case Study Evaluation," Model Cities Special Projects File, American History Research Center, Wright State University.

———. 1970. "Analysis of First-Round Cities," Model Cities Special Projects File, American History Research Center, Wright State University.

Martindale, Catherine. 1974. "Thomas Influenced Education," *Journal Herald,* 8 July.

———. 1974b. "The Plan," *Journal Herald,* 14 November.

———. 1975. "Officials Stymie Integration," *Journal Herald,* 5 March 1975.

Miami Valley Regional Planning Commission. 1971. *A Housing Plan for the Miami Valley Region.* Dayton, Ohio.

———. 1974. *Housing for the Miami Valley Region.* Dayton, Ohio.

———. 1978. *Housing in the Miami Valley Region.* Dayton, Ohio.

"Model Cities Council." 1969. *Dayton Daily News,* 9 May.

"Model Cities Dead." 1973. *Journal Herald,* 5 November.

"Model Cities Director Appointed." 1971. *Dayton Daily News,* 23 September.

"Model Cities Levy Linked." 1968. *Dayton Daily News,* 5 December.

Montgomery County Fair Housing Center. 1985. *Changes in Minority Residential Patterns 1970–1980.* Dayton, Ohio: Dayton Community Housing Resource Board.

"Neighborhood Master Plan." 1965. Local Government Records, Dayton View Stabilization Project, American History Research Center, Wright State University.

Nixon, Richard. 1971. "Statement by the President." Model Cities Special Projects File, American History Research Center, Wright State University.

O'Hara, Richard. 1971. "County Housing Woes," *Dayton Daily News,* 13 June.

"Opposition Not Racial." 1969. *Dayton Daily News,* 5 January.

Ordovensky, Pat. 1974. "Was It Fair?" *Journal Herald,* 9 July 1974.

"Plan Rebuked" 1968. *Journal Herald,* 28 June.

"Plan to Put Muscle into Fair Housing." 1968. *Journal Herald,* 8 December.

Polite, Dennis. 1972. "Love in the Classroom," *Dayton Daily News,* 17 November.

"Projects Listed." 1968. *Dayton Daily News,* 11 November.

Proposal for FORCE. 1967. Mimeographed copy, unpublished.

Revere, Amy. 1994. Interview with author, 22 June.

Rihm, Robert, et al. 1968. "A Stabilization Program for Dayton View." Local Government Records, Dayton View Stabilization Project, American History Research Center, Wright State University.

Rotterman, Lou. 1967. "Dayton Picked to Get Model Cites Grant," *Dayton Daily News,* 16 November.

———. 1968. "Model Cities Grant Approved," *Dayton Daily News,* 14 June.

"Ruling Backs School." 1970. *Journal Herald,* 30 January.

Russ, Bonnie. 1972. "Model Cities Projects," *Journal Herald,* 25 May.

Shere, Dennis. 1967. "Model Cities Fund Slashed," *Dayton Daily News,* 21 November.

Shere, Dennis, et al. 1969a. "Dayton's Mobilization Against Fear," *Dayton Daily News,* 30 April.

———. 1969b. "Kissoff," *Dayton Daily News,* 4 May.
Smiley, Gail. 1971. "Housing Value Gap," *Dayton Daily News,* 31 May.
Special Committee on Urban Renewal. 1967. *A Model Cities Plan for Dayton.* Miami
    Valley Regional Planning Commission Library, Dayton, Ohio.
Sundquist, James. 1969. *Making Federalism Work.* Washington, D.C.: Brookings Insti-
    tution.
"Teachers Tour." 1968. *Journal Herald,* 16 October.
Thomas, Arthur E. 1969. "Educational Leadership Program." Model Cities Special
    Projects File, American History Research Center, Wright State University.
Thomas, Richard. 1968. "Area Legislators," *Dayton Daily News,* 11 April.
"Thomas to Draw Pay." 1970. *Dayton Daily News,* 6 January.
Turk, Paul. 1971. "School Innovation Program," *Journal Herald,* 26 February.
Tyson, Carl. 1973. "Report of Model Cities Activities." Model Cities Special Projects
    File, American History Research Center, Wright State University.
Ulich, Jill. 1968. "Race Group Not Bargain," *Kettering Oakwood Times,* 21 March.
Usher, Brian. 1971. "Nixon Hope," *Journal Herald,* 15 June.
Watt, Graham. 1968. Memo to City Commission, 9 February. Local Government
    Records, Dayton View Stabilization Project, American History Research Center,
    Wright State University.
Wiley, Edmund, and Herman Torge. 1970. "Multiple Motivation Evaluation Report," 31
    March. Local Government Records, Dayton View Stabilization Project, American
    History Research Center, Wright State University.
Williamson, Dan. 1973. "Model Cities Gets Good-Bad Critique," *Dayton Daily News,* 1
    August.
Wilson, Cammy. 1973. "Model Cities Here Rated Successful," *Dayton Daily News,* 10
    October.
"Wine Hoping." 1969. *Journal Herald,* June.
Wine, Joseph D. 1968a. "Dayton View Stabilization Project," 23 April. Local Govern-
    ment Records, Dayton View Stabilization Project, American History Research
    Center, Wright State University.
———. 1968b. Memo to Wayne Carle, 28 October. Local Government Records, Day-
    ton View Stabilization Project, American History Research Center, Wright State
    University.
Woodie, Paul. 1970. Letter to Wm. Chamberlin, 19 January. Local Government
    Records, Dayton View Stabilization Project, American History Research Center,
    Wright State University.
———. 1994. Interview with author.
Worth, William. 1969. "Board Model Cities Bury Ax," *Dayton Daily News,* 2 August.
———. 1969b. "Disturbance Disrupts," *Journal Herald,* 1 February.
Usher, Brian. 1970. "Dispersal Is Key," *Journal Herald,* 23 July.
Zsambok, Carol. 1994. Interview with author, 22 June.

Chapter Five
School Board Elections and Racial Integration

When liberal board members tried to racially desegregate Dayton's public schools, conservative politicians complained that elite Dayton citizens imposed policies on other people but exempted their own children. Forming a political party, Serving Our Schools, the conservatives appealed to lower- and middle-class white residents. When SOS members won control of the board, liberals organized to defeat them. The liberals fought bitter political campaigns searching for a mandate to desegregate the schools; they never got it. SOS members did not have that problem. They won elections by opposing progressive educational reform.

On 8 December 1971, before the conservatives took control, the liberal-dominated school board adopted three resolutions. First, it accepted blame for segregation. Second, it decided to desegregate the city schools. Third, it asked the state Department of Education to set up a metropolitan plan of desegregation. The superintendent announced that he would ask the Dayton Classroom Teachers Association to form a committee to work on mandatory teacher inservice training. He asked the Dayton Advisory Council on Education to set up a committee to review progress toward desegregation. Most important, on that same Thursday, he wrote personal letters, on plain stationery and at his own expense, urging 435 area religious leaders "to make . . . personal witness—now in behalf of the desegregation of public schools and economic integration of pupils in the Dayton metropolitan area." The superintendent said he appealed to clergy as a private citizen who believed segregation violated the Judeo–Christian value of the worth of each individual. In his letter, he said, "I know of no force greater than the spiritual one that finds expression through leaders like you" ("Carle Asks Clergy" 1971).

Like the Little Rock clergy discussed in chapter three, religious leaders in Dayton remained silent on the issue of desegregation. Only two clerics wrote letters to the editor of the newspaper. A religious reporter surveyed the clerics' responses in February 1972. When asked how they felt, the religious leaders displayed a range of views. The more fundamentalist preachers went further than calling the idea of forced busing immoral. For example, a Baptist minister said Biblical law in the Old Testament spoke against intermarriage for Jews. He added that the New Testament told people to come out from them and be separate. A Presbyterian said all social separations are un-christian. Pastors of the two largest Protestant churches in Dayton would not answer. The spokesperson for an ecumenical council, Metropolitan Churches United, said the group set up a task force to consider the issue but had no answer yet. Catholic priests of the Dayton Deanery announced their support of integration in a state-ment issued the week before the article appeared (LaBriola 1972).

The board hired a desegregation consultant to draw up a plan to desegregate Dayton's city schools. It was ready for the board meet-ing of 3 January 1972. The consultant said that "planning in Day-ton is easy . . . because . . . travel between any two points [is usually] less than a half-hour . . . and Dayton is pretty square" ("Dayton Plan Easy" 1972; Foster 1972).

However, the new school board did not consider the plan. Domi-nated by SOS members, the new board reconsidered the three reso-lutions that had called for the desegregation plan. It defeated them, and, in the place of those resolutions, adopted three different ones. The conservative resolutions contradicted the liberal ones.

First, the liberal board accepted blame for desegregation, while the first conservative resolution called for the development of plans providing for the equality of instruction in all schools at a reason-able cost. Second, the liberal board called for a mandatory desegre-gation plan, while the second conservative resolution suggested of-fering free transportation to students who wanted to transfer to another school to improve racial balance. In place of calling for met-ropolitan school consolidation, the third conservative resolution in-vited students in the surrounding districts to enroll in Dayton to improve the racial balance of schools in the metropolitan area (Board of Education 1972).

In support of these resolutions, a conservative board member urged the board to support basic principles of instruction that had worked in the past. She added that the school board did not cause racial imbalance in the schools. Federal agencies did not require Dayton schools to desegregate. She said that busing for racial balance would cost thousands of dollars not included in campaigns for school taxes. She concluded by saying that the board now supported neighborhood schools and believed the freedom of enrollment program was successful (Board of Education 1972).

Newspapers criticized the actions of the new school board to reverse desegregation. On 5 January 1972 the *Journal Herald* published an editorial reviewing the action of the new board. By rescinding the three resolutions calling for desegregation, the editorial said, the board virtually ensured a court fight. This might not be in the best interests of the community because it might remove the voices of local people in making the plan. In the place of planned integration the school board now offered freedom of choice, which the editorial called "a feeble substitute." Furthermore, the editors said they wished "the board had taken a look at [the desegregation plan] instead of dismissing it without so much as a glance" ("New School Board" 1972).

The superintendent tried to make the board look at desegregation. On 1 February 1972 he sent a letter to the editor of the *Journal Herald.* Referring to a previous news story, he listed the views of a party of white supremacists. He explained why each reason to oppose desegregation was wrong except that desegregation may involve sacrifice, fear, or trauma. He claimed a human relations program and a commitment to a multiethnic society reduced fear. He repeated his plea to religious leaders to state the correctness of desegregation. Finally, he said that in overturning the previous board's policies, the conservative board did not consider the desegregation plan. Since it would only take the use of seventy-six more school buses to put this program into effect, the superintendent concluded he would place this purchase among his recommendations. He warned the only reasons to oppose it were the reasons of white supremacists.

He never got his buses. Since the liberal board members implied segregation was a matter of policy, a court could force sweeping changes in the district. To counter this possibility, the conservatives adopted resolutions designed to absolve the board of any blame (Schumacher 1972a). Nonetheless, NAACP spokespeople expressed interest in using the Dayton to pursue statewide desegregation in Ohio. In this context, on 3 February 1972 the school board voted four to three to use school funds to defend itself against the anticipated NAACP suit. The liberals voted against the measure, arguing that no one had yet sued the schools. In a strange twist of logic, SOS members responded that they were simply trying to save taxpayers money (Schumacher 1972c)

In December 1971 the liberal board asked the State of Ohio to set up a metropolitan plan of school integration. The thought of busing students into Dayton brought howls of rage from suburban communities. On 25 January 1972 the Kettering school board adopted unanimously a resolution opposing busing across district lines to achieve desegregation. The resolution said, "Transportation of students across school district lines to achieve racial or socioeconomic balance is both artificial and counterproductive." The resolution promised to take whatever legal defense might be necessary to preserve the autonomy of the district. However, Kettering's resolution promised action to encourage integration among racial groups within the community. It asked the superintendent to prepare recommendations to promote increased human understanding (Schumacher 1972b). The Northridge Board of Education took a similar stand. Other districts tried to appear more reasonable. For example, Mad River and Wayne Township passed resolutions recommending establishment of a committee to study area-wide integration while maintaining district autonomy ("Area School Integration" 1972).

Resolutions did not stop the protest. Complaints flooded the suburban boards of education as the question of busing spread. PTA meetings that normally would have passed with little attention became seats of controversy. In Kettering, for example, on 22 February 1972, a month after the board of education passed its resolutions opposing busing, several hundred people showed up at a PTA meeting to express their objections to metropolitan area busing for racial balance (Kline 1972). Wayne Township agreed to take nonwhite students from Dayton. However, the Wayne board would not send white students to Dayton. Wayne Township had an enrollment of

8,374 students. Its black enrollment totaled 141 students. The biggest problem was that Dayton spent twice more per pupil than Wayne Township did. Officials of Wayne Township schools worried about having to reimburse Dayton ("Wayne Township to Study Busing" 1972).

Suburbanites admitted that they feared sending their children to Dayton. For example, on 19 April 1972 a panel composed of former members of the Committee of 75 met at the Central YWCA in Dayton. Their report justified the resolutions for pupil desegregation and metropolitan area busing. Safety came up repeatedly. A white mother said, "The problem is not racial, it is cultural. It's OK with me to bring in children of different backgrounds, as long as my children aren't harmed. . . . I'm not saying all blacks are toughs, but the crime rate is higher in West Dayton" (Carlson 1972). Interestingly, suburban parents often asked that their children ride a bus to protect them from dangers they would face on the way to school. Except one community, Oakwood, the schools in all of Dayton's suburbs bused more than half of their students. When busing was done for racial balance, it became controversial (Polite 1972a).

The antibusing forces called for neighborhood schools. They pointed to an Ohio law that asked the school board to locate schools in places convenient to the most students. However, as one newspaper reporter noted, "One interesting consequence of the busing battle is that many who once opposed open housing are now calling for just such a measure as a better way to integrate schools." The same reporter noted that fear of busing was causing white flight. He said, "There are a lot of homes on the market in Dayton. But most of the sales, according to figures obtained from Dayton Board of Realtors, are in the suburbs." The head of the board of realtors said this was not white flight. A sluggish local economy and an unstable financial picture caused many people to put their homes up for sale (Polite 1972b).

On 13 March 1972 a conservative newspaper, the *Journal Herald,* supported the idea of a metropolitan plan, saying the promised benefits of busing outweighed valid objections. The editors said that America needed national leadership to come to grips with the issue of compulsory integration of the public schools. The public endorsed school integration, the editorial claimed, while it opposed busing.

They acknowledged that complaints about inconvenience and cost were valid. The most compelling argument against compulsory busing was that it was an intrusion on personal liberty. People had the right to live out their prejudices, including the imaginary right to select their children's schools. However, the Coleman Report found integration to be more helpful to youngsters' learning than programs of compensatory education. Even if some scholars disagreed with the Coleman Report, the editorial added that America could not maintain a divided society. Public schools had an assimilative mission. They should work this way for black people ("School Busing" 1972).

On 21 March 1972 another editorial followed, saying the U.S. Supreme Court should speedily decide cases involving Denver, Colorado, and Richmond, Virginia. These included the issue of de facto segregation and the question of busing across school district lines to achieve racial balance in a metropolitan area. The editors believed neither Congress nor the president should step into this issue until the Supreme Court made a decision. Elected officials responded to public pressure rather than contemplated definitive action ("Time for Reason" 1972).

Reason did not prevail at school board meetings; there was more heat than light. The March 1972 meeting drew nearly 600 spectators. The *Dayton Daily News* claimed the meeting was more like the Broadway farce *Hellzapoppin* than an august assembly. It turned into a three-hour session, with citizens alternately castigating and praising three items: the superintendent, encounter sessions for administrators, and efforts to desegregate schools ("School Board Meeting" 1972).

Dayton's U.S. Representative, Charles W. Whalen, a Republican, was careful not to take a side in the controversy. On 25 February and again on 6 March 1972, he said busing for racial balance should be reserved for cases where segregation is involuntary. When segregation is due to a violation of rights, Whalen said, "such a means as busing may be used to correct it" (Hamilton 1972; "Whalen Backs Busing" 1972).

On the other hand, Dayton's superintendent did not avoid controversy. On 17 March 1972 he called a news conference in reaction to then President Richard Nixon's nationally televised speech. Nixon had called for an end to busing in schools for racial balance and for congressional curbs to court powers to order busing as a remedy. In his speech, Nixon promised to allocate $2.5 billion for aid to schools in economically depressed areas. Carle announced in his news conference that he planned to ask for $112 million to make Dayton schools equal to surrounding schools. Dayton's superintendent noted that the cost of desegregation would be less (Polite 1972b).

The superintendent's news conference received national attention. A nationally syndicated columnist, Carl Rowan, picked up the story and used it in his column (Rooney 1972). In response, a conservative SOS school board member called the superintendent and asked him to resign and to fire two assistant superintendents. The superintendent refused. To explain why the board wanted to fire these men, another board member said the board could not fire the superintendent. It could tie his hands ("SOS Pressures Carle" 1972). Although the assistant superintendents kept their jobs, the editors of the *Dayton Daily News* called the SOS members incompetent and willing to kick the system apart to get at the superintendent. First, before negotiations about teachers pay began, one SOS board member announced that all teachers should get at least the 5.5 percent raise the pay board allowed. This announcement encouraged the teachers' union to try to better the 5.5 percent. Second, the board forbade Carle to shift principals in mid year to adjust to enrollment shifts. This cost taxpayers $110,000. Third, the SOS refused to hire guards for three high schools though SOS members talked about a need for discipline. Finally, SOS members tabled an application for a $426,000 federal grant for vocational education. They said they did not understand the grant, though they had lengthy talks with the project director ("Dayton Board's Bungling" 1972).

These accusations did not seem to bother SOS supporters. On 24 May 1972 a survey made by the Public Opinion Center for the Community Communications project showed that Dayton residents who favored the SOS respected their school board members. These people agreed that discipline was a problem in schools. They thought the educational programs were not working. They thought busing was bad. Liberal voters had no such strongly held beliefs ("SOS Backers Unhappiest" 1972).

The Former Superintendent Returns with a Vengeance

On 6 April 1972 the SOS suffered what could have been a setback when an SOS board member died of a heart attack. At least forty-seven people applied for the vacant post. Since the board could not select a candidate within the thirty-day period allowed by state law, the decision fell to the judge of probate court. The judge took thirty-six days to make his choice. He selected a person who had not applied: Dr. Robert B. French, age seventy-two, the former superintendent. The judge said French was not committed to either of the divided groups on the board of education (Polite 1972c).

French had been superintendent of the Dayton schools for more than twenty years before being replaced. In interviews, French gave no comment to questions about his feelings toward the then present superintendent. French said he thought busing was a questionable means to achieve racial balance; he preferred open housing or changes in attendance boundaries. He denied being an advisor to SOS members and said his philosophy was good schools for kids. The judge did not explain how he selected French. Newspaper reporters speculated that the two men shared many ideas, having come to know each other through long careers in Dayton public affairs (Usher 1972).

At his first board meeting, French sided with SOS members to kill a proposed individualized mathematics program (Herd 1972). With his vote, the SOS board members voted against applying for federal funds for programs and they refused to allow the superintendent to appoint administrators (Polite 1972d).

On 2 January 1973 the conservative president of the board of education introduced a resolution of intent not to renew the superintendent's contract that expired in 1973. Liberals complained that the president of the board had refused to answer the superintendent's request for a formal evaluation. The superintendent had listed the goals the board had set for the schools. He showed how he and his administrative staff had tried to meet them. Despite these efforts, the board voted against the superintendent. The former superintendent, Dr. Robert French, voted with the conservatives (Board 1973a).

Using a parliamentary maneuver, a liberal board member moved to reconsider the votes. The reconsideration took place two nights later, on 4 January 1973. Despite the lack of time to prepare, the liberals amassed a surprising show of strength. Liberal board members read editorials from both Dayton papers.

The editorial from the *Dayton Daily News* spoke in favor of a letter-writing campaign. Such a campaign would show the SOS they were not listening to the voices of Dayton's citizens. Further, it could be a show of appreciation to the superintendent who had worked hard for Dayton schools. The editorial listed his progress in educational efficiency, in progress toward improvement of student reading skills, in improved teacher inservice, in enrichment of the curriculum, and in teaching methods. Although these accomplishments would not influence the SOS board members, concluded the editorial, they should realize they were indulging private willfulness.

In the *Journal Herald*, the editors called Robert French's vote a disservice to the school system he had served. They said French's "inability to accommodate emerging social and educational priorities in his last years as superintendent left the system floundering and led to his abrupt retirement six years ago." The editorial continued to say that French had not changed with the passing of time; it was ironic that French criticized the superintendent for trying to deal with controversial problems that "French had left unattended during his superintendency." The editorial added that SOS members betrayed their own conservative supporters: "There are reasonable conservative attitudes in the community, but they have not been expressed on the board. There has been only mulish resistance to [the superintendent], to district-wide integration, and to educational innovation." Finally, the editorial warned against damage to the system because of mass resignations of other school administrators.

Another liberal board member introduced a letter signed by the entire faculty of United Theological Seminary in support of the superintendent. Several citizens addressed the board appealing for the superintendent's reinstatement. Several of these people represented larger groups or agencies in Dayton. However, one person reminded the board that petitions against Carle with signatures in excess of 20,000 were still on file. These petitions dated from 1971 when the liberal superintendent supported cross-district busing in December 1971 (Board 1973b).

As expected, the board voted four to three not to reconsider the dismissal. Without any type of job search, the conservatives immediately named the principal of a Dayton city high school to be the superintendent after June 1973. The three liberal members said they did not know about the hiring. They walked out of the meeting while the remaining conservatives including French voted for the new superintendent (Board 1973b).

Flurries of protests continued in Dayton. Some church people tried to circulate a petition recalling the SOS board members. These were unsuccessful. On 8 February 1973 the *Dayton Daily News* published a lengthy story about a nearby suburb of Cincinnati, Princeton School District, whose superintendent led a successful merger of his white district with the predominantly black district of Lincoln Heights. The story quoted the superintendent as saying, "The big difference between us and the Dayton situation is that I had the board behind me all the way" (Reisinger 1973).

Newspaper editorials portrayed the fired superintendent as a victim of circumstances who absorbed an unbelievable amount of abuse with courage and dignity. They said he did not appreciate the scope and intensity of public reaction to actions that he made through humane, dedicated professional judgments ("Carle's Ouster" 1973). Liberals promised to help him in the next school board election.

The Liberal Counterrevolution

For the 1973 election a broad-based coalition of moderates and liberals formed a group called "Citizens for Better Schools" (CBS) to oppose candidates backed by the conservative party Serving Our Schools. Enrolling several people who had been part of the 1971 school board campaign, the new liberal organization was broad-based. It included executives from local corporations such as Mead and the president of the local chapter of the NAACP. They decided not to repeat the error made in 1971 of fielding more candidates than contested seats ("New Group Fights SOS" 1973; "School Group Picks Bowman" 1973; Polite 1973).

In 1973 the SOS had difficulty with too many candidates. SOS members interviewed several possible candidates on 21 and 22 May 1973 in the Sheraton Dayton Hotel ("SOS Begins Job of Picking

Ticket" 1973). From these prospects they chose two incumbents and two newcomers to fill the four openings on the board. An unendorsed conservative individual ran as an independent, threatening to dilute the SOS vote. On the other side, the liberal CBS offered four candidates, one of whom was an incumbent and three were newcomers. Among the liberals was Reverend U.A. Hughey, the only African American running for the school board.

In August 1972 the conservative *Journal Herald* ran an extensive five-part series on problems in Dayton's schools. Although the paper highlighted interviews with school board members, two SOS members who were to be candidates in the upcoming election refused to take part in the interviews. The three liberal board members spoke for the liberal view. Entitled "The Missing Majority," the interviews showed the candidates disagreed as to what were the major problems facing the schools.

The school board campaign started on 11 September 1973 when two dozen persons attended a debate in the basement of the North Riverdale Lutheran Church. Another debate took place on 19 October 1973 at the Corinth Boulevard United Presbyterian Church. These debates represented an innovation in Dayton's school board campaigns. The religious leaders tried to set up a format designed to get around acrimony and accusations that had characterized Dayton school board politics for most of the previous five years. The general plan of the debates was simple. The candidates were to listen to the audience and then respond to the points the people in the audience made. Often, a questionnaire was used to which the candidates responded earlier as a tool to show areas of agreement, disagreement and points of compromise.

In addition to hosting debates, an ecumenical church group, Dayton Metropolitan Churches United, conducted a survey of the candidates views that was published in 7 October 1973 issue of the *Dayton Daily News*. The debates and the survey of candidates represented the contribution religious leaders made to the racial desegregation of schools. Apparently unable to support racial integration, they tried to inform the public about the issue. While far less than Martin Luther King Jr. may have wanted, this nonpartisan approach built on a faith that people would decide intelligently when they knew the facts.

Three factors worked against the clerics' faith in people. First, the debates did not go as planned. Instead of staying within the format, candidates fell into a debate about the worth of Individually Guided Education or whether the process followed by the SOS in firing the superintendent and hiring a replacement was unprecedented (Schumacher 1973a). Second, poor attendance marked the sessions. Third, the local press characterized candidates who made public addresses as ideological (Schumacher 1973b).

The debates may have harmed the candidates. At least one candidate, Robert French, had nothing to do with debates or any form of electioneering. French's unwillingness to speak to the issues led one CBS candidate, U.A. Hughey, to call French a racist who disliked people who disagreed with him (Smith 1973; Wilson 1973). Nonetheless, when the votes were cast, French polled the second highest number.

The newspapers had long complained of a liberal-conservative split on the school board. The general view of this division was that the words of all candidates only contradicted those of the opponents. This accusation of ideology appeared to hurt the liberals more than the conservatives, who had an emotional antibusing stand to help them. Complaints about an ideological split weakened support among teachers and among African Americans who had been advocates of the liberal position.

The views of teachers are difficult to discern. On 12 April 1971 the executive committee of the Dayton Classroom Teachers Association passed a resolution calling for the desegregation of students in the Dayton schools. However, on 26 April 1973, at a school board meeting, the president of the Dayton Classroom Teachers Association accused liberals of being obsessed with the goal of desegregation. He accused the conservatives of making resistance to busing their primary goal. At issue was a school board threat to cut back on teaching staff to correct a budget problem. "Neither one puts children first." He explained, "The liberals want massive desegregation and the conservatives are not going to let the liberals push them into abandoning their no busing policy" (Board 1973c; Haws 1988).

While this speech represented a break from the earlier endorsement, teachers from at least one Dayton school worked hard in 1973 to elect liberal board members. They passed out leaflets, walked door to door, and urged people to vote for CBS. After the 1973 election, they expressed regret they did not push a little harder because the outcome was close (Summer 1988). However, teachers at other schools never took an active interest in school board politics beyond following the events and discussing them among themselves (Calhoun 1988; Smith 1988). The union president's speech may have reinforced apathy among his colleagues.

In the same way, some African Americans abandoned the desegregation issue. The leaders of the Model Cities Demonstration Project had said that integration was not an important concern for young African Americans. In any racially desegregated school in the city, black children would be in the minority (Hanna 1973). The separatist view became more popular in the predominantly black west side of Dayton and during the 1973 election, voters from the predominantly black West Dayton did not support the liberals as the CBS leaders had expected. For example, U.A. Hughey, a former officer in the NAACP and the only African American running for the school board in 1973, polled 6,618 votes from West Dayton. African Americans in West Dayton did not vote for conservatives. Hughey polled 5,500 more votes than the strongest candidate from SOS had from the same area. However, Hughey was not as popular among black voters as he should have been if those voters held a concern for the liberal views on the school board. In the same election, Mayor James McGee, a liberal black man, ran for reelection. He received 8,690 votes from West Dayton. This means that more than two thousand voters from West Dayton supported the liberal mayor but refused to cast a vote for a liberal school board candidate (Schumacher 1973c).

To some extent, the liberal candidates themselves gave evidence that the campaign was over trivial issues. The candidates endorsed by Citizens for Better Schools would not speak actively or loudly about school desegregation. They repeated that busing was a false issue; the schools must abide by any decision made by the courts. The candidates confided that the strategy behind this maneuver was that people favoring desegregation knew the liberal position. Emphasizing busing could only help SOS candidates. Unfortunately, this prevented CBS candidates from making clear statements about social justice. They let opportunities to score points against conservative SOS members go by without a comment. For example, at one debate, a member of the audience accused an SOS member of supporting segregation. CBS members stayed out of the discussion (Schumacher 1973d).

Instead of raising desegregation, CBS waged a campaign focused on specific educational issues such as the need for more counselors in elementary schools to help with discipline. SOS members felt that counselors were too costly. On the other hand, SOS members made busing the issue and called CBS the party of busing advocates. SOS candidates warned that liberals on the board could initiate a busing plan to destroy neighborhood schools even if the courts did not order it (Schumacher 1973d).

Liberals thought they could remain silent about busing because they thought they were the party of the majority. In 1971 liberals had done well. They polled 60 percent of the vote. They lost one seat because they had an extra candidate who diluted the vote. In 1973, having narrowed their field of candidates, they thought they would win if they could hold what they had.

On election day, 6 November 1973, the liberal party, CBS, lost by an extremely slim margin. The conservative Josephine Groff and Robert French won with nearly 21,000 votes each. A new CBS candidate came in third. For the all-important fourth seat, the president of Serving Our Schools edged out the liberal incumbent board member by seven votes with a total of 18,171. As a result, SOS retained four of the votes on the seven-member school board.

The loss came despite extra effort made by the liberals. CBS spent almost twice as much as SOS on the campaign. The liberals paid more than $25,000 for expenses while the conservatives spent less than $13,000. Contributors to the liberal cause were among the most prestigious citizens of Dayton. These donors were a retired chair of a large department store, president of a downtown clothing store, chair of a savings and loan company in Dayton, and a president of a manufacturing concern. These people gave about $200 each. The largest donation came from a Dayton elementary school principal who gave $1,000 to CBS. He felt he should put his money where his heart was (Begley 1990). Conservative SOS campaigners gathered most of their money from membership fees and three fund raising dinners (Carlson 1973).

The loss of black votes in West Dayton hurt CBS. However, moderate to liberal voters living in the north-central part of the city were most important in the SOS victory in 1973. In previous elections, these people had split their votes. In 1973 voters from these wards came out strongly for the SOS. According to election analysts, the fear of busing was the big factor (Schumacher 1973d).

Trying to maintain courage, Citizens for Better Schools did not disband after the election. They vowed to remain as a watchdog with the defeated incumbent candidate as chairperson. Other liberals despaired. In 1975 the SOS needed to elect only one member out of three seats coming up then to retain the majority (Smith 1974).

CBS could not act as a watchdog. On 26 February 1974 CBS sent a letter to the board asking to retain good teachers and sound educational programs in spite of financial problems (Schumacher 1974). They tried to watch over the promotions that the new conservative administration made, but there was little they could do. On 10 July 1974 the remaining liberal board members complained that Dayton schools were removing blacks and people who supported liberals from positions of authority in the school system: "All staff reductions were for personnel who had been actively involved in supporting liberal school board members and all staff additions were those who supported SOS" (Kinneer 1974a). Nonetheless, the CBS group looked to the election of November 1975 to tip the scales. In July 1975 CBS announced its slate of candidates for the school board. They faced a difficult situation.

In 1975 Daytonians had an ambivalent attitude toward the school board. On one hand, they did not want to have busing to achieve racial balance. On the other hand, they disapproved of the way the conservatives were running the schools despite the fact those conservatives were fighting desegregation. For example, in the fall of 1972 Dr. Jeanne Ballantine, Dr. Leonard Cargan, and Dr. Hardin Ballantine of Wright State University surveyed 400 Dayton residents. They found 41 percent of the people contacted said they would not comply with the order to send their children to a different school. Another 30 percent would comply reluctantly and only 25 percent could see merit in busing. Fifty percent of the people thought busing would create racial problems. The authors noted the results were tied to social class. That is, the higher the socioeconomic level of the respondent the more positive the person was about desegregation (Kinneer 1974b).

Another survey in August 1975 found even more dismaying results. Reporters for the *Journal Herald* contacted 397 parents with school children in Dayton. Sixty-one percent of those surveyed thought the schools were doing a fair or a poor job; yet 45 percent of those parents did not know the names of any school board member or the superintendent. Further, more than half the parents surveyed did not agree with either the liberal CBS party or the conservative SOS. However, when the parents favored a party, blacks tended to approve of CBS and whites tended to support SOS and these supporters were divided regionally. Those who supported SOS lived on the east side. Those who supported CBS lived on the west side and in Dayton View ("Board Gets Low Marks" 1975).

To some extent, CBS candidates modified their positions to fit the contradictory attitudes of the voters. For example, on 15 and 16 August 1975 the *Journal Herald* printed edited versions of interviews with spokespersons for the liberal CBS and for the conservative SOS. Surprisingly, there was little difference between the positions of the two parties. For example, the SOS spokesperson said "there is no cause to desegregate the schools [because] there is no violation." Instead of disagreeing, the CBS spokesperson equivocated. "When I was first elected to the board . . . I said . . . we're going to have to have some busing. After four years, I don't hold that position any more. . . . I'm not too fond of busing." When asked if racially segregated schools could provide equal education, the SOS spokesperson answered "Why not?" The CBS spokesperson softened earlier pronouncements. "I don't think you can define quality education in terms of a desegregation plan." Finally, when asked about aims, the SOS spokesperson said his group wants to turn the schools back "to what they were before . . . to serve the people of all races." The CBS spokesperson said his group is not a liberal organization because the members have varying views but in general they agree on seeking "equal opportunity for all kids" (Lawson 1975; "Douglass" 1975).

CBS ran into more problems. On 27 September 1975 a court-appointed school desegregation consultant, Charles Glatt of the Ohio State University, was shot six times by a former mental patient. The man pleaded guilty to shooting Glatt and three black residents of West Dayton; he said he killed in protest of desegregation ("School Board Campaigns Halted by Glatt Slaying" 1975; McInnis 1985).

Both parties canceled events planned for the months of September and October, hoping to diminish the emotional atmosphere that people feared had led to Glatt's shooting. The silence hurt the CBS people more than the SOS candidates. The first debate among the candidates took place on 20 October 1975 in United Theological Seminary. This was the only debate held by church people. Three other debates took place in high school auditoriums. Church people did not publish analyses of candidates' views. The newspapers filled the gaps. As in years past, few people attended the debates ("School Candidates Debate" 1975).

When the campaign began again, one SOS candidate returned to his hyperbolic style. He implied that the former superintendent had caused student riots and school closings. Further, he said that former superintendent had set up reading and math programs that lowered the scores of children on standardized tests. The SOS candidate charged that liberals wanted to bring that former superintendent back to Dayton. The liberal candidates replied that the SOS candidate was seeking revenge because he had lost his position of assistant principal of a Dayton school in 1971.

A newspaper reporter tried to verify the SOS assertions. She found that police reports attributed the violence at Stivers to changes in attendance boundaries that mixed Appalachian and black students. The reporter added that other school districts in Ohio closed buildings at the same time so the problem was not unique to Dayton. The reporter could find "no one in the central administration to confirm whether any program resulted in lower test scores." Although one liberal board member had phoned the former superintendent, no one had spoken to him since Glatt's death. By 1975 the former superintendent had become a university professor away from the turmoil of school desegregation (Littleton 1975).

The biggest blow to the CBS campaign was that they lost the financial support they had enjoyed in 1971 and in 1973. On 21 October 1975 the CBS finance chief reported his groups had collected only $6,000, while SOS reported contributions totaling $9,700. A new campaign law limited both sides to expenditures of about $14,000. Unfortunately for the liberals, the Area Program Council members deserted the CBS cause. In 1973 these business, industrial, and civic leaders contributed over $7,000 to CBS. In 1975 the Area Program Council decided not to help CBS. The president of the Dayton Area Chamber of Commerce asked the Area Program Council to remain neutral. The Chamber of Commerce president said his group had a working relationship with the conservative school administration and did not want to jeopardize it (Alexander 1975a). This decision brought sharp criticism from a CBS candidate who said that if business people think they have SOS's ear, it's a one-way conversation (Alexander 1975b). The Area Program Council did not change its position. The members wanted to stay in the good graces of the likely winners.

The election was a disaster for CBS. The only CBS candidate to win was an African American. He garnered more votes than anyone else, with a total of 23,141. Two conservative SOS candidates won for SOS with 21,206 and 21,134 votes respectively. The other two liberal candidates were more than two thousand votes behind. The CBS campaign manager said, "If West Dayton voters who voted for (the African American candidate) had pulled the levers for (two more liberal CBS types)," CBS would have won (Kinneer 1975b).

After the 1975 election Citizens for Better Schools disappeared. In 1977 a newspaper reporter tried to find the organization. The former chairperson told the reporter that the group was inactive. There was no reason for it to exist between elections. However, the African American candidate who won under the CBS banner denied the party's existence. He said that CBS and SOS were myths created by the press whose passing he would not mourn (Adams 1977a).

Busing for desegregation began in Dayton in September 1976. This caused an immediate decline in political partisanship on the school board. Restraint from both sides may have had a calming effect that allowed the desegregation program to be successful. However, an SOS member offered another explanation for the decline in controversy. He said the liberals brought busing that caused white flight and, as a result, the people who had voted for SOS were no longer Dayton voters (Adams 1977a).

Three school board members who had been part of the liberal–conservative debate retired in 1977. In December 1976 Robert French, the former superintendent, resigned from the school board, citing ill health (Odom 1977a). On 23 June 1977 Josephine Groff, an early SOS school board member, decided not to seek reelection (Odom 1977b). A member of CBS elected in 1973 announced that he would not seek reelection. He cited frustration with being systematically excluded from decision-making on the board by SOS members (Adams 1977b).

At election time, Dayton schools had finished their successful program of cross-district busing for racial balance. SOS had a full slate of candidates. CBS did not appear. The candidates opposing SOS candidates ran as independents. Only one independent, a black woman, won a seat on the board. Consequently, in 1978 two board members were black and without political affiliation. The other five people on the school board were white members of the SOS.

Newspaper editorials from 1971 until 1977 reflect the shift in people's attitudes toward the SOS party. On 22 October 1971 the *Journal Herald* said the SOS might not be racist but they had never disowned the racist groups who tied themselves to the SOS. The editorial went on to say the SOS favors natural integration but brands all administrative reforms with the forced integration label, "no matter how farfetched that characterization might be." This editorial concluded its description of the SOS by saying the members do not seem to have the courage to be leaders ("Dayton School Board" 1971).

By 1977 this criticism had changed. The *Journal Herald* lambasted liberals on its editorial pages. Harold Piety, then associate editor, said the CBS people had been misguided in their struggle to control the schools. According to Piety, CBS wanted integration and SOS formed to save schools from the liberals' determined effort to bring it about. He noted the SOS board members were too negative in their attacks on the former superintendent. Nonetheless, he thought SOS was a populist movement that represented the will of the people. Piety said that "people detected the odor of fraud about CBS." Piety excused SOS people for not showing they are serious about bringing good basic education to Dayton. He said SOS members were occupied with the challenge of racial integration. In making their endorsements for the 1977 school board campaign, the

Journal Herald picked two SOS candidates and two independents. Though this split would allow SOS to retain a majority, the *Journal Herald* said the paper endorsed the competent candidates.

The SOS held the majority until the school board election of 1979. The party again tried to run a coordinated campaign for the three vacant seats on the school board. The party asked the candidates it supported to pledge their loyalty. One member resigned from the party and a second SOS member resigned from the school board. As a result, three SOS members remained on the board. In the election, SOS candidates made their worst showing. One of the founders of the party lost his bid for reelection.

There were three reasons for the loss. First, although the SOS called for financial responsibility, its administration appeared to mismanage funds. For example, in the summer of 1978, the district claimed a financial emergency. Employees could not have raises, and residents would have to pay more taxes. But in January 1979 the district revealed that it had saved $6.8 million from the previous year. Although part of this saving came from a teacher's strike, there was enough confusion that state officials called for a reorganization of the clerk-treasurer's office. Second, the issue of busing for racial balance was over. Although the SOS claimed to be more than a single-issue party, their support softened when controversy over busing disappeared. Third, antagonized parties were stronger. The Dayton Education Association, formerly Dayton Classroom Teachers Association, endorsed the independents and many teachers worked to elect them by distributing handbills calling for the election of all three. The Democratic Party did not endorse anyone in the election, but at the last minute precinct workers distributed the independent candidate's literature (Hill 1979a; Hill 1979b).

After January 1980 only two members of SOS were on the school board. These members complained that the other board members made decisions in private. Whether these accusations were true or not, the new board made many changes. It instituted a system-wide management review. It conducted a search for a new superintendent to replace the former SOS appointee who was to retire in June 1981 (McKelvy 1981). For the first time in eight years, the superintendent was to be an outsider. None of the six finalists selected for the position was from Dayton. The board used a consulting firm to find the most qualified candidates rather than promote someone from within the organization (Ray 1981).

The SOS party never reappeared. In the years to come, former SOS members ran as independents for school board offices as it returned to a nonpartisan status. In the 1970s some members of the SOS party had looked at the school board as a stepping stone to other political offices. It never was, and the party never participated in any other campaigns than school board elections (Goodwin 1990). Since SOS never went beyond Dayton school board politics, when they lost there, they disappeared.

Conclusion

From 1972 until 1980 a populist political party dominated school affairs in Dayton. In opposition, liberal groups tried to form parties. They were less successful. Not surprisingly, the political campaigns did not help people understand why racial integration was necessary. Liberals who favored racial desegregation tried to avoid angering opponents. Conservatives repeatedly accused the liberal superintendent of causing problems. Religious leaders strove for fairness. African Americans became alienated from the contests. Finally, everyone expressed irritation with both sides of the controversy in a way that ultimately tolerated racism.

However, liberals looked to the courts and to the elections for reasons to racially integrate the schools. Despite their initial hopes, the justices disappointed them as the voters did.

References

"Across Town—'I Like It.'" 1969. *Dayton Daily News,* 10 November.
Adams, Steve. 1977. "77 May to See End of CBS," *Journal Herald,* 4 January.
Alexander, Andrew. 1975a. "School Race," *Journal Herald,* 21 October.
———. 1975b. "Ex-Backers of CBS Blasted," *Journal Herald,* 30 October.
"Area School Integration Study Urged." 1972. *Dayton Daily News,* 14 January: 11.
Begley, Roy. 1990. Interview with author, 20 July.
"Board Gets Low Marks." 1975. *Journal Herald,* 27 August.
Board of Education of the City School District of Dayton, Ohio. 1972. Minutes, 3 January: 15–26.
———. 1973a. Minutes, 2 January: 29–32.
———. 1973b. Minutes, 4 January: 32–38.
———. 1973c. Minutes, 26 April: 159–160.
Calhoun, Barbara. 1988. Interview with author, 5 October.
"Carle Asks Clergy." 1971. *Dayton Daily News,* 11 December.
"Carle's Ouster." 1973. Editorial, *Journal Herald,* 3 January.
Carlson, Bill. 1972. "Pupil Mix a Must," *Journal Herald,* 20 April.

————. 1973. "Loss Was Costly for CBS," *Journal Herald*, 22 December: 1, 38.

"Dayton Board's Bungling Cost." 1972. *Dayton Daily News*, 20 March.

"Dayton Plan Easy." 1972. *Dayton Daily News*, 4 January.

"Dayton School Board." 1971. Editorial, *Journal Herald*, 22 October: 4.

"Douglass: Education Comes First." 1975. *Journal Herald*, 16 August .

Foster, Gordon. 1972. "Desegregation Study, Dayton Public Schools." Unpublished report presented to Dayton Board of Education, 3 January.

Goodwin, William. 1990. Interview with the author, 14 February.

Hamilton, Clem. 1972. "Whalen Calls Involuntary Busing Segregation Key," *Dayton Daily News*, 6 March.

Hanna, Sam. 1972. "Thomas Asks Respect," *Journal Herald*, 31 March.

Harris, Henry. 1969. "Personalities Cloud School-Race Issue," *Dayton Daily News*, 3 October.

Haws, G. Keith. 1988. Interview with author, n.d.

Herd, David. 1972. "French Supports SOS Arithmetic," *Dayton Daily News*, 23 June.

Hill, D.J. 1979a. " Mutual Aid," *Dayton Daily News*, 11 November.

————. 1979b. "SOS: A Seesaw Ride," *Dayton Daily News*, 26 December.

Kinneer, Larry. 1974a. "School Board Liberals Rap Promotion," *Dayton Daily News*, 10 July.

————. 1974b. "Survey Finds Big Busing Split," *Dayton Daily News*, 17 February.

————. 1975. "SOS Holds 5 Board Seats," *Dayton Daily News*, 5 November.

Kline, Benjamin. 1972. "Kettering PTA Leans Away from Busing," *Dayton Daily News*, 23 February.

LaBriola, Carrie. 1972. " Busing and the Clergy," *Journal Herald*, 26 February.

"Lawson: Integrate Schools with Minimum Transportation." 1975. *Journal Herald*, 15 August.

Littleton, Jane. 1975. "Ghost," *Journal Herald*, 30 October.

McInnis, Doug. 1985. "School Planner's Death Recalled," *Dayton Daily News*, 19 September.

McKelvy, Vince. 1981. "Dayton School Board Still Divided," *Journal Herald*, 12 January.

"New School Board." 1972. Editorial. *Journal Herald*, 5 January.

"New Group Fights SOS." 1973. *Journal Herald*, 7 April.

Odom, Maida. 1977a. "French Sees Good Days for Schools," *Dayton Daily News*, 4 January.

————. 1977b. "Groff Will Not Run Again," *Dayton Daily News*, 23 June.

Polite, Dennis. 1972a. "To Ride a Bus or Not," *Dayton Daily News*, 14 August.

————. 1972b. "Carle Takes Nixon at His Word," *Dayton Daily News*, 17 March.

————. 1972c. "Ex-Superintendent French Appointed," *Dayton Daily News*, 14 June.

————. 1972d. "Straghler Still Struggling," *Dayton Daily News*, 26 December.

————. 1973. "Coalition Aims at SOS Seats," *Dayton Daily News*, 6 April.

Price, Reverend Gordon. 1969. Letter to William Levy, 19 December.

Ray, Karen. 1981. "Superintendent Candidates," *Dayton Daily News*, 23 January.

Reisinger, Sue. 1973. "Talk Smoothed Road to Integration in Cincy Suburb," *Dayton Daily News*, 8 February.

Rooney, Pat. 1972. "Writer Cites Carle in Criticism of President," *Dayton Daily News*, 25 March.

"School Board Campaigns Halted by Glatt Slaying." 1975. *Dayton Daily News*, 27 September.

"School Board Meeting." 1972. *Dayton Daily News*, 3 March.

"School Busing." 1972. Editorial, *Journal Herald*, 13 March.

"School Candidates Debate." 1975. *Journal Herald*, 20 October: 34.

"School Group Picks Bowman." 1973. *Journal Herald*, 17 May.

Schumacher, Robert. 1972a. "School Decision," *Journal Herald*, 8 January: 1, 14.

————. 1972b. "Cross-District Busing Out in Kettering," *Journal Herald*, 26 January

————. 1972c. "Schools Brace for Suit," *Journal Herald*, 4 February.

————. 1973a. "School Candidates Flunk Test for Quiet Meeting," *Journal Herald,* 19 October.

————. 1973b. "School Race Bogged in Script," *Journal Herald,* 31 October: 1, 40.

————. 1973c. "Conservatism Rules School Vote," *Journal Herald,* 13 November.

————. 1973d. "Busing Issue at Issue," *Journal Herald,* 30 October: 23, 30.

————. 1974. "School Liberals Lose a Round," *Journal Herald,* 26 February.

Smith, Jay. 1973. "Candidates Serious Even if Voters Aren't," *Dayton Daily News,* 4 November.

————. 1974."Rejected Liberals Muse Gloomy Choices," *Dayton Daily News,* 4 November.

Smith, Wertha Duuger. 1988. Interview with author, 13 December.

"SOS Backers Unhappiest." 1972. *Dayton Daily News,* 24 May.

"SOS Begins Job of Picking Ticket." 1973. *Dayton Daily News,* 5 May.

"SOS Pressures Carle." 1972, *Dayton Daily News,* 18 March.

Summer, JoAnne. 1988. Interview with author, 25 October.

"Time For Reason." 1972. Editorial, *Journal Herald,* 21 March.

Turk, Paul. 1972. "Carle Hopes to Stalemate SOS," *Journal Herald,* 22 March.

Usher, Brian. 1972. "Zimmer's School Move," *Journal Herald,* 15 June.

"Wayne Township to Study Busing." 1972. *Dayton Daily News,* 10 March.

"Whalen Backs Busing." 1972. *Dayton Daily News,* 25 February.

"White Board Lamented." 1969. *Journal Herald,* 6 November.

Wilson, Gammy. 1973. "Hughey Wants French to Quit," *Dayton Daily News,* 1 November.

Chapter Six
Dayton Goes to Court

In January 1972 the conservative Dayton school board rescinded the liberal school board's motions to desegregate the city schools. In response, the executive secretary of the local NAACP "called on the general counsel of the NAACP to assist in challenging the SOS program of continued segregation and the state board's default." Nathaniel R. Jones, then general counsel of the NAACP, agreed. When he was in the Air Force, Jones had been stationed in Dayton; he knew the segregated conditions in the city. More important, he hoped that the case would be an opportunity to show that apparently accidental segregation resulted from policy decisions of local authorities ignored by state officials (Dimond 1988, 125).

Conservative school board members accused the liberals of seeking to obtain from the courts what they could not get from the polls. The liberal members of the school board and the liberal superintendent helped the NAACP fashion the case against the school board after they lost the majority of seats on the school board. However, the liberals thought the public wanted to reduce racial isolation in the schools. In November 1971 liberal candidates for the school board collected more votes than the conservatives did. Unfortunately, the courts did not give the liberals the mandate they wanted. At best, the court decision was a partial victory for them.

On 18 April 1972 NAACP lawyers sued in U.S. district court, calling on state officials to draw a metropolitan desegregation plan for Dayton for fall 1975. The NAACP patterned the suit after similar actions in Richmond, Virginia, and Detroit, Michigan. Nathaniel Jones said, "We're asking the court to declare education in Ohio a statewide responsibility [by] seeking metropolitan relief that goes beyond the Dayton school system" (McDiarmid 1972).

The idea of integration with the suburbs preceded the NAACP suit. In 1971 the Dayton Board of Education's Committee of 75 said that metropolitan integration was essential for meaningful racial desegregation. The committee noted that in other cities "whites are fleeing to the suburbs and the inner city [is] left black and bankrupt." The committee noted that the same process was taking place in Dayton. With a sense of urgency, the committee declared that "the initiative in the struggle against segregated education belongs to the Dayton Board of Education. We cannot wait for housing and job patterns to change." Therefore, the committee urged the Dayton school board to work with the boards of the surrounding communities and with the state Board of Education to consolidate (Advisory Committee 1971).

Metropolitan desegregation was not an issue in court. In June 1972 U.S. District Judge Carl Rubin "deferred all questions concerning the state defendant's responsibility and metropolitan segregation until any clarifying decisions might issue from the Supreme Court" (Dimond 1985, 126). Rubin justified his decision to separate district desegregation from metropolitan integration by saying that he wanted to obey the U.S. Supreme Court. There may have been another reason; the U.S. district court judge disagreed with the lawyers for the NAACP about the role the courts should play in desegregation cases.

The NAACP lawyers felt that if the board caused some segregation, the entire district had to desegregate. On the other hand, U.S. District Judge Carl B. Rubin believed that the courts should not enter local school matters. Consequently, he wanted to correct only those faults that NAACP lawyers showed the board caused.

Rubin issued his first opinion on 13 February 1973. Rubin acknowledged that from the 1920s until the late 1940s the school board acted in violation of an 1887 Ohio law forbidding separate schools for "colored children." Rubin noted these acts included separate buildings at Garfield School, denying black children access to high school swimming pools, and excluding black high school athletic teams from city conference games. Since the board corrected these problems before 1954, Rubin thought they did not apply. A more recent problem was the question of having separate teaching faculties in black and in white schools. However, Rubin noted, this was corrected in 1971 (*Brinkman v Gilligan* 1977).

Despite the list of abuses caused by the school board, Rubin felt the board solved most of the problems. The remaining segregation in Dayton schools was not the board's fault. He said that the schools had racially unbalanced student populations consistent with the neighborhood population. In the question of the selection of school sites, Rubin concluded that the NAACP did not show that construction caused segregation. The board provided schools in white neighborhoods that remained mostly white and schools in black neighborhoods that remained mostly black (*Brinkman v Gilligan* 1977).

Rubin acknowledged that the board had made several errors. He said that optional attendance zones reinforced segregated schools. Children in these zones could choose from two or three schools. As a result, parents in those zones chose schools with racial considerations in mind. The freedom of enrollment plan offered slight contribution to racial integration, Rubin added. Although in 1969 Dayton schools employed more black teachers than any of the twenty largest school districts in Ohio, Rubin felt other employee positions presented problems (*Brinkman v Gilligan* 1977).

Consequently, Rubin said the Dayton school board had to remove the optional attendance zones, restate the criteria for selecting children under the freedom of enrollment plan, maintain faculty desegregation, and change the hiring practices so the ratio of black and white employees mirrored the ratio among students. Rubin added that he hoped the school board would do more (*Brinkman v Gilligan* 1977).

To the surprise of many observers, the board did more than Rubin ordered (Polite 1973a). On 29 March 1973 the conservative board members adopted a plan to eliminate optional attendance zones, to change freedom of enrollment priorities, to restrict faculty assignment practice to maintain desegregation, and to rewrite hiring policies. In addition, the plan called for six programs to provide interracial experiences for the students attending neighborhood schools. First, the conservatives constructed an environmental science program for all elementary school children who would attend regularly in a racially balanced mix. Second, they expanded a vocational high school in the center of Dayton by joining Stivers and Patterson together. Third, they offered a district-wide music program called a Musical Stereopticon that would include combined marching band, gospel choirs, and musical theater groups. Fourth, they offered integrated athletics. Fifth, they required teachers to take courses in minority language to aid in their instruction of black students. Sixth, they assured the continuation of the racially integrated Living Arts Center, an innovative program that had been a target of conservative attacks (*Brinkman v Gilligan* 1973).

Although critics labeled the plan as gimmicky, the proposal represented considerable flexibility for a political party dedicated to basic instruction and neighborhood schools. For example, the science centers occupied four buildings around the city staffed by fifty persons. About 11,000 pupils in grades five through eight and their teachers would make the trip once every two weeks to a center. Children in grades one to four visited annually. A mobile unit reached students who could not come to any center. Five hundred high school students served as teachers' aides. All these students attended in racially mixed proportions.

The plan represented a tempering of the conservative agenda. In fact, a former member of SOS who was running an unsuccessful campaign for mayor claimed the party promised to remove the Living Arts Center and disband Individually Guided Education Programs. Now, these programs were part of the conservative desegregation plan (Polite 1973b). However, these ideas contained some benefits. For example, a former music supervisor said that substantial opportunities existed and students played some wonderful concerts. These opportunities ended once busing began (Flamm 1988). An NAACP attorney called the conservative plan an insult to black children. He said the plan contained the mythology that blacks are good for singing and dancing (Schumacher 1973a).

The conservative majority drew up its plan in a deceptive manner. They excluded the three liberal members of the school board from the conference where the plan was formed. Although the school administration supplied information that was used, it did not help in drawing up the plan (Board 1973).

The liberals offered an alternative desegregation plan that included busing. They recommended bringing in more middle schools, reassigning students for racial balance, improving the curriculum, extending support and student counseling services, and offering teacher workshops and inservices. Seeking aid from the state of Ohio and from the federal government, the liberal plan was inexpensive. It added the state should desegregate the metropolitan area. Without such a plan, "the school districts of Montgomery County will take on the appearance of a black hub and a white rim" (Sterzer et al. 1973). Although the conservative majority rejected the liberal plan, the liberal minority submitted their plan without the endorsement of the board.

Judge Rubin selected the conservative plan even though it did not affect the racial balance in any school. The elimination of optional attendance zones affected only small numbers of students. For example, in the high school most affected by these zones, white enrollment declined by only 1 percent to 54 percent. The students in optional attendance zones moved to a mostly black high school (Turk 1973). Furthermore, the conservative plan had no budget. The conservatives hoped the state and the federal government would help pay for enrichment programs such as the science centers. This did not happen. As a result, the costs to the board rose to $700,000 (Polite 1973c).

In June 1973, the board postponed carrying out the science centers ("School Board Shelves Plan" 1973). It did not ask for state or federal aid, and the members doubted that Rubin would approve their plan. To meet a budget crunch, the board released 273 teachers (Schumacher 1973b). To force the issue, a coalition of private community groups called Project Share applied for federal aid for desegregation (Polite 1973d). The U.S. Department of Health, Education, and Welfare rejected the application because it did not include a plan for desegregation. After U.S. District Judge Rubin approved the conservative plan in July 1973, the Board of Education announced the science centers would be ready by October 1973 at an estimated cost of $350,000 (Schumacher 1973c). This estimate was low.

In February 1974 the conservative school board president announced the board would apply for federal funds (Schumacher 1974). Unfortunately, it was too late. The application deadline of 26 December 1973 had passed. In addition, the application threatened to hurt the board's effort to win the desegregation case on appeal. On 3 April 1974 HEW turned down Dayton's request for two reasons. The Dayton board did not maintain faculty desegregation, and it still had racially identifiable classes. NAACP lawyers planned to file briefs telling the appeals court about this decision (Smith 1974a). On 19 April 1974 the Miami Valley Regional Planning Commission tabled the board's request for $6.1 million to pay for the conservative desegregation plan, saying it did not reduce the racial isolation of students ("Planner's Move" 1974).

It was about twice as expensive to try to keep neighborhood schools as to move toward a desegregated system, and the conservative plan did not improve the situation. For example, the science centers for elementary children cost $1,771,410 to operate for one year. A comprehensive busing program to integrate the schools for two years would have cost $2,000,000 (Smith 1974b). Few students asked to transfer schools so the freedom of enrollment plan made no difference. In 1973–74 black enrollment in Dayton schools rose 1.7 percent, to 46.3 percent. However, three high schools had more than 90 percent black students and four high schools had less than 25 percent black enrollments. Furthermore, there was no evidence the special interest centers improved student learning.

When the four science centers opened in September 1973, all fifth- through eighth-graders attended the centers for fifteen days in the year. A curriculum specialist claimed that at one center the students saw science in a natural way by walking through the twenty-three acres surrounding the school. The students looked at the relationships living things had with their environments. They saw how those surroundings changed which they tracked on graphs and charts. At another center, the emphasis was on art and nature. The third center engaged students in earth and space studies. In the fourth center, the students concentrated on environmental studies (Smith 1973). Some teachers seemed to approve of these visits and the minority language programs, others disagreed and found them less helpful (Calhoun 1988; Dugger-Smith 1988; Thompson 1988).

Unfortunately for the conservatives, there was little objective evidence to show the value of the centers or the minority language programs. In 1974 the school board called the centers a success because tests of the students showed that they learned something. There were no tests from previous years or of students in other situations to show that the centers had made the difference. Furthermore, the attendance rate of children at the centers was about 10 percent lower than it was for all elementary schools. The minority language program for teachers seemed to cause teachers to accept different student languages, although the improvement the teachers showed did not reach statistical significance on tests (Smith 1974c).

U.S. Sixth Court of Appeals

While the conservative board tried to save neighborhood schools, the NAACP lawyers thought they could cause some form of system-wide desegregation. They felt that Rubin was wrong to conclude that the school district could cause a little discrimination and not have to change attendance patterns throughout the district. They were sure that they would win on appeal (Dimond 1985, 154). U.S. court of appeals justices agreed that a school board that caused segregation had to do more to cause racial integration than correct the specific abuses.

Chief Judge Phillips of the U.S. Sixth Circuit Court of Appeals wrote the decision on 20 August 1974. Phillips said Rubin was guided in his actions by a principle derived from another desegregation case, *Swann v Charlotte-Mecklenburg Board of Education.* This principle held that "it is the function of the federal courts only to eliminate a deprivation of constitutional rights; it is the duty of local school boards to operate and maintain integrated school systems."

However, Phillips said Rubin overlooked the decision in another desegregation case, *Keyes v School District I, Denver, Colorado.* In this case, the justices said, "once plaintiffs have shown that state-imposed segregation existed [in 1954], school authorities automatically assume an affirmative duty to eliminate [it]." Phillips also said the district court should not have dismissed state officials from being named defendants in the case. They were involved because the state provided some funds to Dayton schools while segregated conditions remained. As a result, Phillips remanded the case to U.S. district court (*Brinkman v Gilligan* 1974).

Before Rubin issued another opinion, he held hearings on 17, 19, and 20 February 1975. In his second opinion, he disagreed with Phillips' decision and strengthened his previous opinions. Rubin said he had two plans. One was designed by the liberals on the school board who worked with the NAACP. It would have assigned students in a ratio of black and white within 15 percent of the district average. Although he complimented the care taken in drawing up the plan, Rubin felt the integration was more than was necessary. He said the U.S. Supreme Court had already ruled that dismantling a dual system does not require any particular racial balance in each school. Rubin went so far as to say that the busing it would require would be forbidden by the Equal Educational Opportunities Act.

The second plan came from the conservative majority on the school board. It had two components Rubin found most important. First, it offered a magnet high school. Second, he liked the learning centers for foreign languages, business education, career motivation, and science. Although the magnet school and the learning centers might further segregate Dayton, Rubin approved these ideas for the following reasons: They are innovative. They offer the opportunity for alternate quality education. The board majority proposed them.

The U.S. district court of appeals disagreed again. On 24 June 1975 it remanded the case back to Rubin. Chief Judge Phillips wrote in this appeals court decision that although the justices omitted the phrase "de jure," the Dayton school system was guilty of de jure segregation practices. Therefore, the Dayton board had to take more remedial action. Phillips added Rubin was wrong to say the Equal Education Opportunity Act prohibited busing. He said the 1974 act did not limit remedies appropriate for constitutional violations. Phillips noted that the Dayton case differed from cases where courts prohibited busing. Finally, Phillips said the desegregation that Rubin accepted would maintain the pattern of one-race schools (*Brinkman v Gilligan* 1975). The appeals court justices ordered the Dayton school to adopt a system-wide plan by 31 December 1975.

The Dayton school board appealed to the U.S. Supreme Court. On 2 December 1975 the justices declined to review it. When the case went back to Rubin, he suggested that Charles Glatt, a professor from the Ohio State University, construct a desegregation plan. The Dayton Board of Education rejected this idea. On 11 September 1975, the school board authorized Dr. William Gordon to prepare a plan (Littleton 1975a). At the same time, the NAACP asked

Gordon Foster to submit a desegregation plan (Kinneer 1975). Rubin went ahead and appointed Glatt to draw up a plan.

On 19 September 1975, as described in chapter five, Charles Glatt was shot and killed while working on his desegregation plan in Dayton. This did not stop his ideas from coming forward. Glatt's widow, a student, and several other people compiled a 197-page report from his notes. Glatt's plan called for some changes in student assignments, restructuring grades to create middle schools, and for some curriculum development to incorporate black students. The plan called for closing three elementary schools and for busing over 20,000 pupils (Littleton 1975b).

On 2 December 1975 William Gordon gave the Board of Education a package of proposals to desegregate the Dayton schools. Gordon had noted three ways to desegregate high schools. These were to expand magnet programs, revise attendance zones, or consolidate schools. Gordon recommended a plan of metropolitan desegregation using three elementary school campuses with 10,000 students in each. This county-wide program would have cost $28 million, and it offered a chance to stop white flight. To oversee this consolidated county system, Gordon recommended forming a three-member authority with power to oversee the districts (Kinneer and Smith 1975a). Although the conservative majority refused to endorse his suggestions, they presented the package to Rubin (Kinneer and Smith 1975b).

Dissatisfied with the proposals he received, Judge Rubin opened hearings on 9 December 1975. Rubin said he did not want to run the schools; he was concerned only with constitutional deprivation. During the hearing, he accepted a motion from the Ohio State Department of Education asking the court not to order metropolitan desegregation (Littleton 1975c).

On 20 December 1975, Rubin issued his order. He said the board could use any plan it wanted providing the enrollment of each school fell within 15 percent of the ratio of blacks and whites in the district. At that time, Dayton school enrollment was 52 percent white and 48 percent black.

At first, Rubin said high school students need not be included. He set a limit of 15,000 students who could travel a distance requiring less than twenty minutes. Then, there were 45,810 students in the district (Kinneer and Smith 1975c). Rubin revised his order shortly after issuing it, exempting only the eleventh and twelfth grades. Rubin appointed John Finger as Master of the plan for the U.S. district court, and Rubin asked the U.S. Justice Department to provide consulting aid. The Justice Department sent a woman who had worked with Charles Glatt ("Rubin Gives" 1975; Littleton 1976a).

Although restricted to activities in Dayton, Finger wrote the Master's Report suggesting a metropolitan plan. He noted that Ohio had been consolidating districts. In 1931–32, there were 2,093 school districts in the state. By 1951–52, the number dropped to 1,429. In 1965–66 there were 738, and by 1975 there were only 617. Finger criticized the Ohio State Board of Education for neglecting to conduct studies to see if districts could be consolidated around Dayton. Furthermore, he noted that schools in the metropolitan area were withdrawing from cooperative activities with Dayton because they feared being drawn into a consolidation plan. Finally, Finger criticized Rubin, saying the court could order a metropolitan plan (Finger 1976).

Looking at the desegregation of Dayton schools, Finger said the easiest and best way was to pair schools on the east, or white, side of town with schools on the west, or black, side. Such a proposal required rides of around twenty minutes. Finger's suggestion was to transfer entire classrooms of elementary school children from one school to another for one half of the year. Thus, a child would remain with the same classmates and teacher but would be in two different buildings for a school year. Finger exempted kindergarten and disabled students from being bused. At the high school level, Finger recommended continuing magnet programs. Although only in the planning stage, the Metropolitan Education Center for the Communication Arts appealed to Finger because it would include the districts surrounding Dayton. Finger recommended the U.S. district court intervene and direct the Montgomery and Greene County boards of education to fund the endeavor (Finger 1976). Unfortunately, the Center was never established.

At the time, Dayton had ten high schools. Finger said students from four of them should be bused. These four schools could be matched in pairs since two of them had mostly white enrollments and two had mostly black enrollments. The exchange involved a total of 1,350 students in grades nine and ten between the paired schools during the first year of desegregation (Finger 1976). The total number of students exchanged was roughly equal to the number who rode buses when the schools were not under a desegregation order (Kinneer 1976a).

Finger hoped that pairing schools and switching entire elementary school classrooms every half year would bring schools on different sides of town closer together. If parents, teachers and students of a white school joined with their counterparts in a black school, they could contribute to the life in both buildings. Unfortunately, several people complained about this idea. On 16 March 1976 representatives of the Dayton Principals Association and the Dayton Education Association complained that switching in midyear would waste instructional time. At the same meeting, a parent of two school children complained that Finger's proposed pairings were going to lead to trouble. "You got Edison School paired with Franklin," she said. "Both schools have kids from low socioeconomic neighborhoods. That's not right" (Kinneer 1976b). In addition, when superintendents of school districts around Dayton heard that Finger recommended consolidation of their districts with Dayton, they strongly objected. Without exception, they said it would not work. Several superintendents noted they would recommend legal action to prevent it. Some superintendents said they had not withdrawn cooperation from Dayton. Most of the districts involved had less than five percent black enrollments (Kline and Fusco 1976). Rubin modified Finger's recommendations on 24 March 1976. He said the board did not have to shift whole classrooms for half year periods nor did they have to use magnets. Rubin never considered metropolitan desegregation.

Rubin set up a panel in February 1976 to monitor the desegregation. Called the Dayton Citizens' Advisory Board, this panel represented a cross section of Dayton's citizenry. The chair was the president of Wright State University. The other fifty-four members included architects, homemakers, business people, and a local bus driver. They had prior involvement in civic affairs (Littleton 1976b; Miller 1976).

Shortly after being called together, some members of the advisory panel accused Dayton school administrators of going slowly. However, the chairperson of the citizens advisory group said he saw no evidence of dawdling by public school administrators (Kinneer 1976c).

Things did go quickly in Dayton. In April, children in elementary schools made visits to their new schools. The school board announced the new attendance zones for high schools. The public received the information at a series of meetings. Unfortunately, few people attended the sessions. The Dayton school officials planned a door to door campaign to contact the parents. This canvassing project seemed doomed because in July the schools had less than 150 volunteers out of the two thousand needed (Kinneer 1976d; Kinneer 1976e).

A local Dayton group whose focus was on Appalachian history, Common Heritage Inc., disagreed with the plan to bus students. Still, it announced it would support peaceful compliance with a lawful order (Littleton 1976c). Local businesses chipped in. A locally based paper company paid for the publication of a four-page brochure written as questions and answers explaining the coming desegregation program. In addition, the same firm paid the salary of the community relations specialist. Part of the company's involvement arose from the fact that the head of that firm was on the citizens advisory panel (Kinneer 1976f). A newly-formed Citizen's Coalition for Peaceful Desegregation offered help in June 1976. The Interfaith Task Force of Metropolitan Churches United held a meeting where eighty religious groups and churches publicly signed a statement calling for the pursuit of peaceful measures. Pledges of support came in so rapidly from so many business and community organizations that the citizens advisory panel asked one of its members to coordinate the efforts of the various groups ("Groups" 1976; Kinneer 1976g).

The ministers of two churches, one on the east side and the other on the west side of Dayton, joined to form a two-week summer day camp. They selected children who would attend school together during the busing program (Adams 1976a). At the same time, most new directors of local television and radio shows avoided stories about the upcoming school desegregation. They feared that they might cause self-fulfilling prophecies (Bednarski 1976).

As the date for desegregation approached, elected officials began to speak publicly. On 8 July 1976 chairpersons of Dayton's Priority Boards agreed to a carefully worded resolution pledging support as individuals to peaceful implementation of the court's order ("Priority Board Chairmen" 1976). On 27 July 1976 the city's mayor, a liberal black man, made a televised speech asking Daytonians to avoid the agony of South Boston and Louisville. He urged them to be sensible like the people in Detroit, Memphis, and Denver. He said that citizens do not have to agree with the law to obey it. He added that critics of busing should pursue peaceful means to change the law (Adams 1976b).

The mayor's speech was well received. There was no indication that the busing would be greeted by anything except calm. Then Dayton Police Chief Grover O'Connor said he could nqt believe how quiet the community was; it scared him (Kinneer 1976h). Evidence of this quiet anticipation was that from 29 March 1976 the amount of controversy coming from the Board of Education declined. The conservatives on the board noted that they had appealed the decision to the U.S. Supreme Court. Nonetheless, they wanted a peaceful achievement of the plan they disliked. The conservative superintendent said the board's legal appeals calmed citizens who opposed busing (Kinneer 1976i).

On 16 August 1976 the board of education previewed the prospects for the busing plan. It was the first day of activities such as football, band, and drill team for students in the four paired high schools. Few students rode the buses provided. The only problem was that the bus left without fifteen band members and this infuriated the parents ("Wait" 1976). Most students who went from school to school for athletics during August said it was fine. They liked the system (Moore 1976).

Before the busing started full-scale, schools had open houses to allow parents and new students see what their new school would be like. Selected students were trained to resolve conflicts that might arise. Adult monitors were recruited to stand at bus stops, ride with children and keep the peace. Unfortunately, few people volunteered for this duty.

On 1 September 1976 Dayton area churches held prayer vigils. The mayor attended one such vigil to pray for peace, goodwill, and understanding (Kinneer and Odum 1976). Parents called Dayton schools' central offices to ask questions about bus stops and routes and tied up the phone lines.

On 2 September 1976 the school doors opened and buses rolled. "It was wonderful," said an African American teacher as she faced her first racially integrated class in her thirty-one years in Dayton schools (Sidlo 1976). On all measures the program was a success. On the first day, estimated attendance was 75 percent. The rate climbed to levels above the average for previous years in the days to come. The problems were minor: motorists sometimes forgot to stop for a school bus and some residents complained the children made noise at a bus stop.

There was no violence nor any threat of it, yet police promised to maintain helicopter surveillance. Police remained armed with tear gas and long batons They used a mobile ground command post. The police had taken eighteen months to prepare for this day; although things were running smoothly, they would not withdraw (Heller 1976).

To reduce problems, school administrators had required one half of the students to attend the first day and the other half attended on the second. On the third day, the entire student body appeared in Dayton schools. With attendance at 80 percent of enrollment, Dayton became a national symbol. *The New York Times* and the Associated Press carried stories congratulating Dayton for its success. Then chief of the U.S. Justice Department Civil Rights Division said "Dayton has one of the most successful large city school desegregation plans in the country." He credited the success to advance planning, local leadership, and cooperation between police and school officials. He also noted that Dayton lacked the degree of ethnic poverty found in other cities that could have increased the chances of violence (Adams 1976c; "Pottinger" 1976).

Other cities shared the success Dayton experienced. Dallas, Texas, and Flint, Michigan, and several other cites desegregated for the first time in 1976. Not one of them experienced violence or disruption. The chair of the U.S. Civil Rights Commission said this was evidence to support his commission's verdict that desegregation was working ("Panel Finds" 1976). Nonetheless, people in Dayton were proud of themselves. The head of the Citizens' Advisory Committee praised Dayton's mayor, saying his television speech was the turning point (Adams 1976d). The Dayton Civitans gave the superintendent of Dayton Public Schools a desegregation report card with all A's. Despite the success he enjoyed, the school superintendent continued to disapprove of busing. In April 1977 he said that things could still blow up because 60–70 percent of the people in Dayton dislike desegregation ("Maxwell" 1977).

In November 1977 public disapproval of busing came out in the defeat of a school tax levy. Dayton voters had not approved a tax levy since 1971. School tax levies continued to fail in Dayton until June 1983, when a 9.9-mill property tax increase for Dayton schools passed by a margin of 154 votes out of 37,042 cast (Brown and Ancona 1983).

If voters opposed busing, high school students did not. At the end of the 1976–77 school year, high school sophomores who were bused had a chance to return to their home schools. Of these students, 48 percent chose to return, but the patterns of the choice were uneven. Eighty-four percent of the white students attending the formerly all-black Dunbar asked to return to their home school, a formerly all-white high school on the east side. Only 48 percent of the white students from another all-white high school in the east side asked to leave the new school that was mostly black. The white students at Dunbar may have been more uncomfortable than were those at the other all-black school because Dunbar was an historically black school. Unlike the white students, black students wanted to stay in the formerly all-white high schools they now attended; less than 30 percent of the black students asked to return to their home schools ("48% Choose" 1977).

The Legal Appeals Continued

The success of the public school busing program did not stop the legal appeals. On 26 April 1977 the Dayton case came before the U.S. Supreme Court. The justices remanded the case back to Judge Rubin in U.S. district court for two reasons. First, the findings of constitutional violations did not justify system-wide relief. Second, there was confusion about applicable principles and appropriate relief in the district and in the appeals court.

In 1977 the Supreme Court did not make its decision on the merits of the case alone. Justice Rehnquist said that the case raised questions about the proper functions of a federal district court and a federal appeals court. In the Dayton case, the district court found racially imbalanced schools, optional attendance zones and recent board action to be "cumulatively in violation of the equal protection clause." This is not a clear violation. A judge could use a cumulative violation to justify an extensive remedy or to justify very little change. The court of appeals compounded the problem. It agreed with the vague term "cumulative violation" but ordered a system-wide remedy (*Dayton Board of Education v Brinkman* 1977).

Rehnquist went on to say that the court of appeals had no warrant to impose a severe penalty on unclear findings because it falls outside the role of an appeals court. Such a court may decide the findings of a district court are erroneous and put them aside. On the other hand, an appeals court can accept the findings but reverse the verdict because of legal errors it found. In this case, the appeals court did neither. While the appeals court did not specify a remedy, it implied to the district court that the schools had to transport approximately 15,000 students daily. Rehnquist concluded the court of appeals imposed a remedy out of proportion to the constitutional violations it found. Justices Stevens and Brennan concurred with Rehnquist. Brennan wrote that he agreed with the decision to impose a system-wide remedy. He was troubled, though, that the justification for such action came from evidence outside the cumulative violations (*Dayton Board of Education v Brinkman* 1977).

When the case came back to Rubin, he dismissed the complaint saying that the problems he had found were not constitutional violations warranting any remedy. Rubin noted in his decision on 15 December 1977 that the discrimination black people suffered in Dayton from 1910 to 1950 would be constitutional violations if they still existed. The plaintiffs failed to show how those practices influence present practices. As far as the racial imbalance of schools was concerned, "such imbalance above does not establish a violation." Further, Rubin said that the board did not cause segregation by sending black teachers to teach black students. The pupil population made the schools racially identifiable, not the composition of the faculty. Nor did the board cause segregation by changing the attendance zone, Rubin wrote. The NAACP argued that the school board had a duty to build schools or make additions that would provide for desegregation. Such planning would be speculative because people move around. As far as the actions of the board rescinding the 1971 desegregation resolutions, Rubin felt the former board members tried to manufacture a constitutional violation (*Brinkman v Gilligan* 1977).

Rubin discussed other accusations the NAACP made. First, he observed that the number of white students expelled from Dayton schools (1,910) was almost half the number of black students expelled (3,499). Rubin noted the NAACP did not show that this was a change in patterns. Second, plaintiffs asserted there were few black administrators in the central office. Rubin countered that the number of black administrators rose from 23 percent in 1973 to 40 percent in 1976 (*Brinkman v Gilligan* 1977).

Rubin concluded that courts can do no more than remind people of their moral obligations. When people disagree about how to meet those obligations, they must resolve the arguments with other means than legal suits. With that admonition, Rubin dismissed the case, telling each side to bear its own cost (*Brinkman v Gilligan* 1977).

The busing among Dayton schools continued as the case returned to Chief Judge Phillips and the Court of Appeals of the Sixth Circuit. On 27 July 1978 Phillips said that the NAACP had pointed out a system-wide pattern of intentional segregation. As a result, Dayton must reinstate its system-wide desegregation plan. Phillips wrote "that to the time of *Brown I,* defendants intentionally operated a dual system and never fulfilled their affirmative duty to eliminate . . . segregation." For example, sending black faculty to black schools is a violation of constitutional rights, according to the U.S. Supreme Court's decision in *Swann v Charlotte-Mecklenburg.* Phillips added that even if the school board caused segregation in the past, this is relevant. Unless corrected, past actions cause later segregation. Phillips noted that Rubin ignored the principle coming from *Keyes v School District 1,* which holds that, once a court finds a district intentionally segregated students, the school district must prove other acts did not cause segregation. Thus, instead of seeing if actions caused segregation, the district court should have considered if the actions reduced segregation. Phillips concluded, "with one exception, no attempt was made to alter the racial characteristics of any school in Dayton in the twenty-four years since *Brown I*" (*Brinkman v Gilligan* 1978).

Phillips said the district court misinterpreted other acts of the school board such as the use of optional attendance zones. It did not view the acts in light of the racial imbalance present in the system. The same was true of site selection for new schools. Phillips quoted a precedent from another case, *NAACP v Lansing Board of Education,* showing that school construction that promotes racial imbalance implies de jure segregation. Phillips added that the district court did not think opening middle schools caused segregation. The point should have been that this program failed to desegregate Dayton schools.

Phillips said that Rubin misinterpreted the earlier order from the U.S. Supreme Court. Those justices had said the lower courts should fashion a remedy that would rectify the incremental segregative effect of the violations for which the school district could be found guilty. While Rubin interpreted this to be a different standard than he applied earlier, Phillips said it was not. According to Phillips, Rubin should not have considered each error independently. He should have looked at the total effect. Further, Phillips said the NAACP did not have to prove the board caused segregation. The school board should have been forced to prove that its decisions did not cause the racial imbalance. Phillips concluded that the impact of the acts of the school board was district-wide. Therefore, he thought a district-wide remedy appropriate such as the desegregation plan complete with busing (*Brinkman v Gilligan* 1978).

Lawyers for the Dayton school board pressed on and asked U.S. Supreme Court Justices Stewart and Rehnquist for a stay in the judgment. This would have stopped busing in Dayton schools. On 28 and 30 August 1978 the justices refused. Justice Rehnquist had granted a stay to the Columbus, Ohio, board of education a few days earlier. The Dayton, Ohio, case was different in an important respect. Columbus had not started busing, while Dayton was entering its third year of such a program. Since maintaining the present situation was an important consideration in granting a stay, both justices felt Columbus could wait but Dayton should continue busing (*Dayton Board* 1978).

On 24 April 1979 the U.S. Supreme Court heard the appeal in the Dayton case. On 2 July 1979 the justices decided there was no reason to disturb the decision of the court of appeals. The Dayton Board of Education had an affirmative responsibility to dismantle a dual system. In the decision, the court showed it was concerned about the proper relationship between a district court and an appeals court. Justice White, who wrote the opinion, said the district court and the appeals court had clarified points that were unclear when Rehnquist had written the earlier verdict. Agreeing with Rehnquist, White wrote that a court of appeals should defer to the fact-finding of the district court. However, White felt this standard implied a responsibility to evaluate those facts. White was not willing to agree with the court of appeals that the Dayton schools had a dual system before *Brown I*. The only evidence of a dual system was such practices as optional attendance zones and teacher assignments by race. These proved only an unwillingness to eradicate prior discrimination. White agreed with the appeals court that there was no need to prove widespread violations had taken place recently. He acknowledged that the school board had to correct the effects of discriminatory practices. Pointing out that the board never showed it tried to alter segregation, White concluded that there had been a misunderstanding in the first set of decisions. The appeals court had first noted a violation involving a few high schools that did not justify cross-district busing. The second appeals court decision made a sufficient case for current system-wide effort (*Dayton Board of Education v Brinkman* 1977).

Justices Rehnquist and Powell dissented. Rehnquist contended that the decision swept away the distinction between de jure and de facto segregation. Once the school boards have to prove they are acting affirmatively, there is no need for anyone to prove any school board action causes segregation. For Justice Powell, the problem with the decision was it extended the role of the federal courts in school affairs rather than limited the role (*Dayton Board of Education v Brinkman* 1977).

In 1971 the NAACP lawyers wanted to use the guilt of state defendants to lead to a metropolitan plan for desegregation. In June 1982 the Dayton Board of Education revived the question of state liability, seeking what is called "injunctive relief" against former Ohio

Governor John J. Gilligan, former Attorney General William J. Brown; former Superintendent of Public Instruction Martin Essex, the Ohio State Department of Education, and the Ohio State Board of Education. The school board wanted the state officials to pay the legal costs. U.S. District Judge Carl Rubin issued his opinion on this request on 24 May 1985, saying that "had the state defendants acknowledged their affirmative obligations to investigate and eliminate segregation and had the power to withhold state funds been exercised Dayton schools would not be [segregated]." Rubin added, "[This] failure of the state defendants was a cause of the plaintiffs' deprivation." Rubin dismissed the Ohio State Department and the Ohio State Board of Education on the grounds the Eleventh Amendment to the U.S. Constitution bars a suit against a state. As a result, Rubin ordered Dayton and the remaining state defendants to share equally all costs in remedying the racial segregation in the Dayton schools (*Brinkman v Gilligan* 1985).

The Effects of Busing

Initially, the effects of busing were beneficial. For example, newspapers carried stories of children in elementary schools making new friends with children of different races. The students in high schools were less willing to mix than were the younger children. Some high school students who moved from one building to another were unsure which team they should support in athletic contests. The Dayton schools tried to help the students adjust to their new surroundings. Each building had some human relations activities such as forming buddy systems for the new students, having teachers eat lunch with the students, or honoring individuals as students of the month. The early childhood department of a local community college offered to help plan humanistic fairs in which the students met different cultures (Konicki 1976).

One surprising change was in the pictures of heroes the schools chose for decoration. A newspaper editorial claimed the truth about segregation was on the walls. During the summer, when no children were present, a person could tell what race children attended by looking at the pictures on display. After the busing began, some African Americans were in classrooms whose walls implied that no one black person was ever famous. Principals traded pictures with each other in order for the classrooms to show racially integrated representations of famous people ("Truth" 1976).

Although desegregation did not turn into a bonanza for private religious schools, there were some increases. Temple Christian doubled enrollment to 425 students. This turned out to be a temporary increase, because by 1986 enrollment returned to 220. A system of five schools unaffiliated to any denomination, Dayton Christian Schools, began in 1971 and in 1976 had 350–400 new students. The superintendent said this was a normal increase not caused by desegregation. Hillel Academy remained small (Adams 1976e). Furthermore, the superintendent of the Catholic schools in Dayton announced that Catholic schools would not become a haven for students fleeing desegregation. He asked Catholic schools to close enrollments (Kinneer 1976j).

There is no doubt, though, that white flight took place. At first, it seemed that Dayton would be spared this disaster. Houses did not promptly go up for sale nor did many students apply to transfer to other schools. One area in the east side of Dayton served by three elementary schools did experience an upswing in houses going up for sale. The principal of one of the elementary schools in that area noted an increase in the number of applications for transfer of records from a usual average of 90 per year to nearly two hundred. This was small in a school district served by sixty-one schools with more than 45,000 students (Adams 1976e).

Although white flight did not take place dramatically, all at once, white families left the city and its schools. They seemed to leave more quickly from 1975–76, when busing came to Dayton. From 1968–69, 67.1 percent of the white students in Montgomery County schools were in suburban schools. The rest were in Dayton. In 1980–81, 81.7% of the white students in the county were in those same suburban schools. Busing influenced this pattern. From 1968–75, the percentage of the white students in the county who enrolled in suburban schools increased about 1 percent per year. From the 1975–76 school year to the 1976–77, when busing was set up, that rate jumped nearly 3 percent. It returned to the former rate the next year and stayed there until 1980–81 (Holm 1980).

Further evidence that fear of busing prompted white families to move is that the percentage of white pupils in Dayton schools declined in similar ways. In 1968–69, about 62 percent of the 59,527 students in Dayton were white. This percentage declined by about 1 percent per year until 1974–75. From the 1975–76 school year to the next year when busing came to Dayton, the percentage of white students enrolled in city schools declined by almost 4 percent. In the years after 1976–77 until 1980–81, the rate of decline of white pupils in Dayton schools returned to about 1 percent per year. By 1980–81, 43.4 percent of the 32,692 students enrolled in Dayton schools were white. Thus, Dayton schools lost students but they especially lost white students (Holm 1980).

The years from 1968–80 saw general declines in Montgomery County schools disguising white flight. Enrollments dropped from 137,053 in 1968–69 to 100,986 in 1980–81. Dayton's share of those students declined from 43.4 percent to 37.4 percent in the same period, in part because Dayton went through a severe recession in the 1970s. In 1969 there were 883,000 workers employed in manufacturing jobs in Dayton. By 1980 that figure dropped by more than half, to 387,000, as firms such as Dayton Tire and National Cash Register and Frigidaire moved their production facilities. Similar declines occurred throughout the sales and service industries. As a result, the population of the city declined from 243,459 in the 1970s to 193,536 in 1980, though the size of the city increased by 10.1 square miles in that time. The city remained predominantly white, although the schools did not. Sixty-two percent of the population was white in 1980. However, the percentage of people over sixty-five years of age increased from 10.7 percent in the 1970s to 11.8 percent in 1980 (U.S. Bureau of the Census 1988).

Nonetheless, economics did not explain segregation. In 1980 only 13.5 percent of the households in Montgomery County, in which Dayton lies, lived in integrated census tracts. Yet the Fair Housing Board found that the income of black families was not so low nor the price of houses so high that black families could ill afford to move to predominantly white areas. They said, "if income was the sole criterion determining where blacks lived in Montgomery County, blacks would be equally represented in each census track." They blamed this pattern on real estate practices of steering, blockbusting, or redlining (Montgomery County Fair Housing Board 1985).

Federal Courts and Racial Integration

Paul Dimond, an NAACP lawyer in the Dayton case, writes that the U.S. Supreme Court erred by forcing judicial inquiry to "be narrowly focused on wrongdoing by particular officials." Dimond complains that when remedies must be "carefully tailored to do no more than overcome the incremental effects of a particular defendant's specific wrong," the pervasive racial segregation in America will not be undone. Dimond notes that some judges were responsive to the problems of proving guilt. However, he contends that if the U.S. Supreme Court justices "will confront the wrong inhering in pervasive racial segregation, [U.S. citizens] could be inspired to do more than regret [their] apartheid" (Dimond 1985, 395–402).

Dimond expresses the view of the liberal school board members in Dayton. Unfortunately, they asked for more leadership from federal judges than judges could offer. Even people in institutions, such as churches, designed to give moral direction could not give reasons to confront segregation as a moral or spiritual wrong. To some extent, clerics showed this in school board elections and in trying to effect a peaceful busing program. At best, religious leaders encouraged fairness and obedience to a lawful order. The next two chapters describe the events in religious or church-sponsored schools.

References

Adams, Steve. 1976a. "Kids Camp Exercise Black and White Harmony," *Journal Herald*, 23 July.
———. 1976b. "Mayor Pleads for Peace," *Journal Herald*, 28 July.
———. 1976c. "Dayton Success: No One Is Sure How It Happened," *Journal Herald*, 26 October.
———. 1976d. "Success!" *Journal Herald*, 14 September.
———. 1976e. "School Attendance Problems Cropping Up,"*Journal Herald*, September 15.
———. 1977. "Metro Busing," *Journal Herald*, 21 March.
Advisory Committee to the Board of Education. 1971. "Report of the Committee of 75," Dayton Board of Education.
Bednarski, P.J. 1976. "Desegregation to Be Seen from Kid's Point of View," *Journal Herald*, 29 July.
Board of Education of City School District of Dayton, Ohio. 1973. Minutes, 29 March: 118–119.
Brinkman v Gilligan. 1973. "Plan Submitted by Defendant." U.S. District Court Eastern Division, Civil Action No. 72–137.
———. 446 1977. F Supp. 1232.
———. 503 1974. F 2d 684.
———. 518 1975. F 2d 853.

———. 539 1976. F 2d 1084.

———. 583 1978. F 2d 243.

———. 610 1985. F Supp. 1288.

Brown, Maureen, and Paula Ancona. 1983. "School Levy," *Dayton Daily News*, 8 June: 1, 6.

Calhoun, Barbara. 1988. Interview with author, 5 October.

Dayton Board of Education v Brinkman. 1977. 433 U.S. 406; 53 L. Ed. 2d 85i; 97 S. Ct. 2766.

———. 1978. 439 U.S. 1357; 58 L. Ed. 2d 65; 99 S. Ct. 27.

———. 1979. 443 U.S. 526; 61 L.Ed. 2d 720; 99 S. Ct. 2971.

Dimond, Paul. 1985. *Beyond Busing.* Ann Arbor: University of Michigan Press.

Dugger-Smith, Wertha. 1988. Interview with author, 13 December.

Evans, Jim. 1989. Interview with author, 4 January.

Finger, John, Jr. 1976. "Report of Master for Southern District Court of Ohio," *Brinkman v Gilligan*, 15 March.

Flamm, Ernie. 1988. Interview with author, 21 September.

"48% of Students Choose to Return to Home School." 1977. *Journal Herald*, 20 April.

"Groups to Aid Desegregation." 1976. *Journal Herald*, 11 June.

Heller, Ann. 1976. "Desegregation: Police Were Ready," *Journal Herald*, 11 September.

Holm, Reverend Duane. 1980. Letter to Sr. Christine Bruno, 20 April.

Kinneer, Larry. 1972. "Desegregation Fund Bill Fails," *Dayton Daily News*, 26 June.

———. 1975. "Divergent Board Facing Integration Bind," *Dayton Daily News*, 27 June.

———. 1976a. "Finger Plan Won't Increase Busing," *Dayton Daily News*, 15 March.

———. 1976b. "Lucas Rips Goodwin," *Dayton Daily News*, 16 March.

———. 1976c. "Schools Go Slow," *Dayton Daily News*, 3 April.

———. 1976d. "Neighborhood Canvass Planned," *Dayton Daily News*, 3 April.

———. 1976e. "Integration Volunteer Turnout Sparse," *Dayton Daily News*, 9 July.

———. 1976f. "School Kids Take Home Desegregation Booklet," *Dayton Daily News*, 4 June.

———. 1976g. "Specialist to Coordinate," *Dayton Daily News*, 29 June.

———. 1976h. "McGee Asks Daytonians to Integrate Peacefully," *Dayton Daily News*, 28 July.

———. 1976i. "Maxwell Asks Moratorium," *Dayton Daily News*, 10 August.

———. 1976j. "Prayer Urged for Easy Integration," *Dayton Daily News*, 27 April.

———. 1976k. "Kids Not Mixing," *Dayton Daily News*, 25 September.

Kinneer, Larry, and Maidai Odun. 1976. "Prayer Vigil," *Dayton Daily News*, 1 September.

Kinneer, Larry, and Jay Smith. 1975a. "Stability Sought," *Dayton Daily News*, 2 December.

———. 1975b. "Board Gets Grab Bag of Integration Plans," *Dayton Daily News*, 2 December.

———. 1975c. "Rubin Orders Dayton School Board," *Dayton Daily News*, 20 December.

Kline, Benjamin, and Pete Fusco. 1976. "Metro Idea Meets Heavy Criticism in Suburban Districts," *Dayton Daily News*, 15 March.

Konicki, Steve. 1976. "Kids Make New Friends," *Dayton Daily News*, 4 September.

Littleton, Jane. 1975a. "SOS, CBS Ask New Plan," *Journal Herald*, 12 September.

———. 1975b. "Glatt's Report," *Journal Herald*, 8 December.

———. 1975c. "Desegregation Hearing Opens," *Journal Herald*, 9 December.

———. 1976a. "Community Relations Specialist," *Journal Herald*, 14 January.

———. 1976b. "School Panel Is Appointed," *Journal Herald*, 13 February.

———. 1976c. "Appalachian Group Backs Plan," *Journal Herald*, 27 May.

"Maxwell: Most Here Oppose Busing." 1977. *Dayton Daily News*, 7 April: 7.

McDiarmid, Hugh. 1972. "Suit Asks City Metroplan," *Journal Herald*, 18 April.

Miller, Jonathan. 1976. "Busing Expert Surprised," *Dayton Daily News,* 13 February.
Montgomery County Fair Housing Board. 1985. *Changes in Minority Residential Patterns in Montgomery County.* Dayton, Ohio: Dayton Community Housing Resource Board.
Moore, Gregory. 1976. "Activity Busing," *Journal Herald,* 18 August.
"Panel Finds U.S. Schools." 1976. *Journal Herald,* 19 September.
"Planner's Move Endangers Fund." 1974. *Dayton Daily News,* 19 April.
Polite, Dennis. 1973a. "Ruling Could Have Little Impact on Present System," *Dayton Daily News,* 7 February: 1.
———. 1973b. "Fanning Blasts SOS Clique," *Dayton Daily News,* 16 February.
———. 1973c. "School Budget Hit Again," *Dayton Daily News,* 9 March.
———. 1973d. "Community Groups Asks U.S. Aid," *Dayton Daily News,* 3 May.
"Pottinger: Calm Here Helps Others." 1976. *Dayton Daily News,* 15 September.
"Priority Board Chairmen Back School Plan." 1976. *Journal Herald,* 8 July.
"Rubin Gives Planners Extra Aid." 1976. *Dayton Daily News,* 14 January: 25.
"School Board Shelves Science Center Plan." 1973. *Dayton Daily News,* 15 June.
"School Human Relations Groups." 1976. *Dayton Daily News,* 10 October.
Schumacher, Robert. 1973a. "School Plan Called Insult," *Dayton Daily News,* 10 April.
———. 1973b. "School Board Nixes Two Plans," *Journal Herald,* 27 April.
———. 1973c. "School Science Centers Back in Planning For Fall," *Journal Herald,* 19 July.
———. 1974. "Dayton Seeks Desegregation School Funds," *Journal Herald,* 22 February.
Sidlo, Steve. 1976. "It Was Wonderful," *Dayton Daily News,* 3 September.
Smith, Jay. 1973. "Dayton Pupils Study Science," *Dayton Daily News,* 22 September.
———. 1974a. "Denial of Funds Could Influence School Bias Verdict," *Dayton Daily News,* 3 April.
———. 1974b. "Rubin Ruling Doesn't Alter Segregated Class Picture," *Dayton Daily News,* 24 February.
———. 1974c. "Science, Language Units Qualified Success," *Dayton Daily News,* 15 August.
Sterzer, Jane, et al. 1973. "A Plan Designed to Desegregate the Public Schools." Manuscript submitted to District Court, April.
Thompson, Brenda. 1988. Interview with author, 22 November.
"Truth Was on the Walls." 1976. Editorial, *Dayton Daily News,* 9 October.
Turk, Paul. 1973. "Schools Forward Racial Plan," *Journal Herald,* 30 March.
U.S. Bureau of the Census. 1973 and 1988. *County and City Data Book.* Washington, D.C.: U.S. Government Printing Office.
"Wait." 1976. *Journal Herald,* August 17.

Chapter Seven
Racial Desegregation and Dayton's Catholic Schools

In Dayton, Catholic religious leaders, parishioners, and educators seemed unable or unwilling to bring religious perspectives to bear on the questions of the racial desegregation of schools. Although the U.S. bishops said race prejudice was a religious and moral problem, Dayton's Catholic school people took their ideas about racial integration from then-current events. As a result, they had difficulty going beyond the apparent conflict between parishioners' rights and the social value of racial integration.

As the civil rights movement became prominent in Dayton, it attracted Catholics in the same ways it captivated public school people. As described in chapter three, in September 1966 a brief but unsettling riot took place on the west side of Dayton in protest of segregated conditions in the city. The fear of further violence caused many people to consider ways to change the city. Public school officials made a hesitant commitment to racial desegregation and hired a superintendent who came to work hard to cause metropolitan desegregation. After the disturbance, Catholic parishioners asked their church leaders to help change the segregated conditions in their schools. A request came from a local African American parish.

In April 1967 Curtis Niles said he was going to ask Cincinnati Archbishop Karl Alter to abolish boundaries for parochial school attendance. Niles was an African American civil rights advocate who chaired the board of education in predominantly black St. James Catholic Church. He announced his intentions at a local conference called to discuss how the social action commissions in each parish should operate. The year before the archbishop had ordered each parish to begin such commissions, and they were just coming into place (Cole 1967).

In July 1967 following Niles' ideas, the school board at St. James adopted a resolution calling for a voluntary exchange program with other parish schools in the area. The resolution said the aim of this program was to reduce the racial isolation that the U.S. Commission on Civil Rights and the Second Vatican Council condemned.

Unfortunately, the St. James resolution did not explain how the Second Vatican Council condemned racial isolation. As noted below, the Council forbade racial discrimination. Chapter two discusses the theological problems facing the Catholic hierarchy as it approached the issue of racial integration.

On 12 October 1967 the principal of St. Agnes in Dayton affirmed that the people in her school agreed with the ideas of the people in St. James. She sent a letter to Monsignor Edward A. Connaughton, then superintendent of Dayton area Catholic schools, outlining a plan to consolidate her school and five others. The letter recommended faculty assignments, busing distances, curriculum plans, facilities use, and financing. It noted that the entire faculty of St. Agnes school approved the plan.

Any proposal to change the attendance patterns of Dayton's Catholic schools required approval of the archdiocesan school board in Cincinnati. In November 1967 Connaughton formed a broadly representative committee consisting of eight lay people, including Niles, taken from five different parishes in the Dayton area and a priest from St. Agnes. Called the De Facto Segregation Committee, it studied the segregated nature of the Catholic elementary schools and made recommendations.

The report of the De Facto Segregation Committee reached Connaughton in May 1968. It found Dayton's parochial schools segregated. Of the twenty-seven elementary schools, three schools carried 90 percent of the total African American enrollment of 467 students. Eighteen schools were all-white. The remaining schools had token integration. According to the De Facto Segregation Committee's figures, in 1968 there were 12,964 white students in the twenty-seven Catholic elementary schools in the greater Dayton metropolitan area. The three schools that contained most of the black students had the following enrollments: Resurrection School had a total of 315 students of whom 72 percent were black. St. James

School had a total of 164 students of whom 96 percent were black. St. Agnes School had a total of 304 students of whom 14 percent were black.

The De Facto Segregation Committee said in their report that "the Negro's push for equality" was one of the major dilemmas of our time. "If the public school is slow to respond . . . the Catholic school must face up to its moral Christian commitment to love its neighbor; and if necessary, to give its life that men might live together in dignity and harmony."

The report said that segregated schools implied the inferiority of the minority children. To make this point, the report cited Jesuit legal scholar Rev. Robert Drinan and the study by the U.S. Commission on Civil Rights entitled *Racial Isolation in the Public Schools.* In addition, the De Facto Segregation Committee quoted psychological evidence to show that segregated schools caused white children to become prejudiced early in their lives. The report said suburban children never learned to understand the rich diversity of American life because they attended schools only with other white children. The committee went on to argue that integrated schools are the "first step toward the realization of the American dream." It said the Catholic school has to show that the Catholic Church accepts the Kerner Commission's conclusion that America must stop being a racist society. The committee added that Catholics "must integrate their schools to show that Americans are fundamentally a decent and humane people." Furthermore, the De Facto Segregation Committee asked an important question: "Christian faith develops through contact with Christ in the living, sacramental Christian community. How can this contact possibly be achieved if, when we are to find Christ, through our brother, we discover we are segregated from him?"

Despite the religious nature of this last challenge, the report of the De Facto Segregation Committee contained few references to theological ideas. These noted that children in Catholic schools should confront social issues making the school "a laboratory through which [students] can explore reality to find God." The De Facto Segregation Committee did not refer to any of several statements about racial discrimination the United States Catholic bishops had published by that time.

First, in 1958 the U.S. Catholic bishops published a pastoral letter entitled "Discrimination and Christian Conscience" which argued that "the heart of the race question is moral and religious. If our attitude is governed by the great Christian law of love of neighbor . . . we can work out techniques . . . for making . . . educational adjustments" (National Conference 1983a, 202). This pastoral letter was signed by twelve members of the administrative board, including Karl J. Alter, the Archbishop of Cincinnati.

Second, in 1960 Archbishop Alter signed a "Protest Against Bigotry" as chairperson of the Board of the National Catholic Welfare Conference (National Conference 1983b). This short statement called upon all citizens to protest against defiling synagogues, churches, schools, and other buildings with symbols of religious and racial hatred.

Third, in 1973 the National Conference of Catholic Bishops of the United States reaffirmed the Catholic position that the race question was a religious one. They said, "Discrimination based on the accidental fact of race . . . cannot be reconciled with the truth that God has created all men with equal rights and equal dignity" (National Conference 1983c, 17). Listing positive steps toward racial harmony, the statement suggested, "we do our part to see . . . housing, education, and public facilities are freely available to every American" (National Conference 1983c, 19). The statement concluded, "above all, it is our prayer that the love of God may infuse our thoughts so that we may revere in every man the image of the eternal God" (National Conference 1983c, 19).

Fourth, in November 1966 the U.S. bishops issued a "Pastoral Statement on Race Relations and Poverty" to reaffirm earlier pronouncements. It added the observation that the pronouncements of Vatican II said "discrimination based on race, language, religion, or national origins is contrary to right reason and to Christian teaching" (National Conference 1983d, 85). This pastoral added the plea that poor people receive a quality education.

These statements of the U.S. Catholic bishops did not call for the desegregation of the Catholic schools. Within the statements, though, is a vocabulary to further the discussion of racial integration built upon religious faith. In 1968 the focus of attention was the importance of civil rights. More important, the members of the

De Facto Segregation Committee felt an antagonistic relationship with church administrators. Consequently, the committee members did not attend closely to the works of the clerics. They tried to educate the religious leaders about contemporary social concerns (Dorenbusch 1990; Regulinski 1990; Vera 1990).

Dayton's De Facto Segregation Committee gathered a great deal of evidence. The members estimated they spent 2,000 hours over fourteen months compiling information and writing the eighty-seven-page report with an additional twenty-two pages of citations. To see if desegregation could work, the committee sent members to visit Evanston, Illinois, and White Plains, New York, to see how desegregation of public schools worked. The reports these investigators made were cautiously optimistic.

Other members of the committee surveyed parents' opinions about the racial desegregation of Dayton area Catholic schools. They sent out 271 questionnaires to the parents of children attending the predominantly black parishes of St. James and Resurrection in Dayton. Of these, 239 questionnaires came back. The questionnaires revealed a contradictory attitude among the parents. Eighty-one percent of the parents agreed strongly that "integrated education should be sought for as many students as possible in Dayton's Catholic schools." However, a plurality of the parents agreed strongly that "the parish would do better to work at improving the quality of its own school instead of seeking integration with predominantly white schools." The Committee believed this last finding reflected dislike for busing, fear of separating children from friends, or reluctance to place black children in hostile environments.

Using the information they had compiled, the De Facto Segregation Committee made two suggestions to integrate the Dayton area Catholic elementary schools. First, for the coming school year, 1969–70, it recommended a program of open enrollment to begin desegregating the schools. Second, it called for consolidation of the Catholic elementary schools for the year 1970–71. The committee did not recommend any changes in the attendance patterns of secondary schools. Its report said the Dayton area Catholic high schools had been integrated for years.

While the three secondary schools within the city limits were integrated, the high schools outside the city were not. Yet, these high schools fell within the geographic area occupied by the elementary schools that the committee studied. In the city, Chaminade for young men and Julienne and St. Joseph Commercial High Schools for young women were integrated. Two suburban high schools, Carroll, which began in 1961, and Alter, which opened in 1962, carried an enrollment made up almost entirely of white students. By 1973 desegregation of these high schools concerned the Dayton area Catholic schools office.

To consolidate the Catholic elementary schools, the De Facto Segregation Committee proposed a plan similar to those tried in places where short distances separated schools. The committee inscribed the Catholic elementary schools in the greater metropolitan area within a circle and cut it into six pie-shaped sections. The committee suggested that children living within each section would attend one building for the primary grades, another building for intermediate grades and a third for junior high grades. To this plan, the committee added a magnet school for pre-primary, and primary levels of instruction in the then centrally located Emmanuel School. Since this plan would mix all children from each pie-shaped section of Dayton, the committee hoped that children from the inner city would attend classes with those living in the surrounding suburbs.

The committee gave five reasons why they thought such a plan could work. First, the schools were located within a circle with a three-mile radius. Second, the parochial school could undertake experimental programs without the same process of public approval that public schools needed. Three, urban and suburban schools fell within the boundaries. Four, the administrative system of Catholic schools was simpler than that of public schools. Finally, the committee said that desegregated Catholic high schools in Dayton have never suffered racial conflicts. Elementary schools should have no problems. The only difficulty the committee foresaw was the loss of the parish school. However, the committee saw greater gains of racial, social, and economic integration of students and of sharing resources among the schools to risk losing parish schools.

Controversy Greets the Desegregation Report
On 8 May 1968 the chairperson of the De Facto Segregation Com-

mittee explained the report to a public meeting. He received strong support from several hundred parents and educators. A significant number complained. For example, when the chairperson asserted, "Segregated education and Catholic education are contradictory terms. Let's agree on that." A man retorted, "We don't agree on that" (Ball 1968a).

Some criticism showed practical flaws in the plans. For example, one visitor pointed out that the committee's plan had placed 90 percent of all black children in Dayton Catholic schools in two of the six sectors. This meant the remaining 10 percent of the black, Catholic students would be distributed among the other four sections (Barmann 1968a).

Catholic school teachers held mixed opinions. A reporter for the Cincinnati Archdiocesan newspaper, the *Catholic Telegraph,* surveyed the opinions of some teachers in the Dayton area Catholic elementary schools. On one hand, he found that some teachers vigorously supported the plan to end de facto segregation. On the other, he interviewed teachers who preferred open housing to advance integration, not school consolidation (Barmann 1968a).

Editorials in the secular press were favorable, calling the report thorough and challenging ("Progress" 1968). In April 1968 a group called Witness collected seven thousand signatures at Catholic churches on a general statement supporting desegregation (Allbaugh 1968). On 13 May 1968 seven women representing Witness gave the petitions to the Most Reverend Edward A. McCarthy, auxiliary bishop of the Archdiocese of Cincinnati. The women acknowledged the signatures were collected before the De Facto Segregation Committee's plan became public knowledge. Consequently, the people who signed may not have endorsed the plan. Nonetheless, the seven women recommended it. Bishop McCarthy promised to give the petition and the report careful study (Ball 1968b).

This was not the first time that Bishop McCarthy received complaints from liberals in Dayton. In January 1968 seventeen members of Centerville Church of the Incarnation challenged the church's $800,000 building program. They wanted $300,000 of that money to be spent among the poor in the city of Dayton (Goodman 1968a). This challenge failed, and all of the monies were spent in building the church. That failure deeply hurt some people.

Phil Donahue, later a nationally known television personality, writes in his autobiography that he was among the people who approached Bishop McCarthy about the Centerville church. Donahue says that he and several of his friends pointed out the unfairness of suburban Centerville building a million-dollar church while, in Dayton, St. James students needed new textbooks. The bishop replied, "The poor we will always have with us" (Donahue 1979, 90). Experiences like this one, Donahue says, caused him to lose his faith. "Of the four couples who originally gathered to challenge the decision to build that church, two are divorced, one has moved to the country with an unlisted phone number and none, repeat none, goes to church" (Donahue 1979, 96). The ungenerous attitude he found among administrators of the Catholic church, Donahue claims, led him to recognize how his education in Catholic schools and subsequent participation in religious retreats retarded his ability to reach out to other people.

Not only was Bishop McCarthy reluctant to support the recommendations of the De Facto Segregation Committee, the priests in Dayton were even more cautious. On 27 May 1968 the then dean of the Dayton Deanery, the organization of Dayton's priests, and pastor of St. Helen's parish wrote a letter to Archbishop Alter asking how the plan was going to be carried out and how it would be financed (Kline 1968a). Some people took the priests' questions as serious criticism. One parishioner of St. Helen's Church wrote a letter on 21 May 1968 to the *Dayton Daily News* saying he was upset to read in the church bulletin that the De Facto Segregation Committee's recommendations were impractical. This parishioner thought it was practical to do everything possible to give children equal educations.

As the priests were questioning the desegregation proposal, liberals who supported it advocated the plan. At the time, the Cincinnati Archdiocese sponsored a series of speeches about the Catholic Church and social problems in Dayton called Project Commitment. On 29 May 1968 at a meeting of Project Commitment, Phil Donahue called for more involvement by parishioners and local women religious, whom he accused of being silent sisters. At the same meeting, the priest of St. Charles said that parishes were islands too concerned with themselves. One of two African American men on the De Facto Segregation Committee warned that the Catholic Church was dying in the black community (Ball 1968c).

Religious women voiced their support for the desegregation of the schools in which they taught. On 30 May 1968 the *Dayton Daily News* carried a letter signed by thirty Sisters of Notre Dame, including the supervisor of Dayton area Catholic elementary schools. The letter quoted the Second Vatican Council's "Declaration of Christian Education" affirming that each person has a right to an appropriate education. The Sisters felt this justified supporting recommendations of the De Facto Segregation Committee.

The secular press joined the argument taking the liberals' side. On 31 May 1968 the editors of the *Dayton Daily News* criticized the priests for writing to Archbishop Alter to complain about the De Facto Segregation Committee's report. The editorial said, "Between the lines is written some negative reaction of parishioners, the hard liners for status quo and those who harbor racial prejudices. The priests should never support that kind of anti-Christian attitude" ("Catholic Open Enrollment" 1968).

Finally, black non-Catholics appeared to support the De Facto Segregation Committee report. The chairperson of a militant black organization called FORCE (discussed in chapter four), an acronym for Freedom, Opportunity, Rights, Citizenship, and Equality, said the statement was a welcome contrast to the inaction of the Dayton public school system.

The Archdiocesan Board of Education in Cincinnati discussed the report of the De Facto Segregation Committee on 11 June 1968. It approved the policy of open enrollment, allowing black students to attend any Dayton area Catholic school with their parishes paying the tuition. The board would not extend this policy to new non-Catholic African American students. At the same meeting, the board approved a voluntary exchange program under which white students could attend predominantly African American schools in Dayton. The board did not answer the larger question of the reorganization of all Dayton area Catholic elementary schools. Nor did the members agree to start a magnet school in downtown Dayton. They asked the Dayton area Catholic schools to set up a task force to study these possibilities.

Shortly after the archdiocesan school board met, Archbishop Karl Alter sent a personal letter to the dean of the Dayton Deanery. It responded to the dean's questions about starting and financing school reorganization. In this letter, the archbishop said he agreed with the priest's reservations about the De Facto Segregation Committee's Proposals. The archbishop included in his letter a memorandum entitled "Reflections on Proposals for the Reorganization of the Parochial Schools in Dayton, Ohio." In his letter, the archbishop said he did not want to publicize these reflections, yet the memorandum was probably sent to all Dayton area priests. In these reflections, Archbishop Alter made five general points. First, if the black children in St. James and Resurrection schools were sent to suburban schools, either enough white children would have to enter these schools to replace the black children or the buildings would close. Second, it was difficult to see how racial integration of students would improve the quality of education. Third, departmentalizing instruction could be profitable. Fourth, the consolidation of the Catholic elementary schools was contrary to the patterns of parish schools on which Catholics built success. Busing the children to new schools would be expensive at a time when Catholic schools were financially pressed. Fifth, the Catholic Church could not be responsible for the education of non-Catholic black children. If Catholic schools were to take on this mission, they would lose their purpose and their financial support. Alter went on to say in his letter that the De Facto Segregation Committee had written a report favoring the biases of the committee members. He said there was "a fair amount of evidence to offset the position taken by the committee" (Alter 1968a).

There are three reasons that imply Archbishop Alter was correct in asserting the De Facto Segregation Committee produced a biased report. First, the report made desegregation appear as the only course of action. The authors saw no reason to maintain parochialism except convenience. Second, the report cited no dissenting studies, although they may have existed. For example, on 13 June 1968 Sister Rose Angela of the Catholic Commission on Poverty wrote a letter to the *Dayton Daily News*. She said the De Facto Segregation Committee overlooked the fact that African American leaders were no longer pushing for school integration. She added that a black child from a lower-class home could develop a poorer self-image in an integrated classroom than in a segregated school. Third, the De Facto Segregation Committee was composed of like-minded individuals who would know how to write a research report. Although the committee included two black men, five white men, and one white woman, these people came from similar social circumstances. They included two college professors, two publishers, a magazine editor, a pharmacist, a traffic management specialist, the director of a Montessori school, and the assistant pastor of St. Agnes, a racially integrated, reform-minded parish. They were all thirty to forty years old.

If the bias of the committee was a problem, the archdiocesan school board did not attack the bias directly. They met it indirectly by commending the most radical aspects of the plan to a task force for further study. On 25 June 1968 Msgr. Connaughton announced, "The Archdiocesan Board of Education directed that a task force be established to consider the possibilities of the De Facto Segregation Committee's recommendations." Connaughton added that the pastor and an elected representative from each parish in the Dayton area would serve on the task force. Connaughton said the task force would consider three things: evaluate the quality of education in the parochial schools, the committee proposals, and the effect of these proposals on the mission of the parishes (Connaughton 1968).

Almost immediately, critics complained that the board of education designed the task force to defeat desegregation. The critics made two points to justify their distrust of the task force. First, the twenty-eight parish priests had criticized desegregation. Second, there was no stated intention to put educators on the task force ("Catholics OK" 1968).

The task force did not meet until September 1968, but concern for social justice continued among Catholics in Dayton as the date approached. Early in July 1968, members of half of the Dayton Deanery's thirty-three parishes reflected on the success of Project Commitment, an archdiocesan program aimed at attacking racial discrimination through weekly lectures or workshop sessions. At the July meeting, the parishes noted plans for future activities asking for "a concerted effort to force improvement of housing conditions and for more person to person social contacts between whites and Negroes" ("Programs to Attack" 1968). Some parishes invited minorities to join parish societies. Other parishes decided to contribute money to mission work in Dayton. Some parishes organized movements to advance open housing.

Other Catholic groups formed to push for desegregation of Dayton's Catholic schools. Afraid the task force would defeat any movement toward desegregation, a twenty-three-year-old white teacher in Dayton's historically black high school, Dunbar, chaired the Ad Hoc De Facto Segregation Committee. This group came out of a trip in June 1967 sponsored by a local interdenominational organization, Malachi, which called itself an experimental educational movement to develop insight and perspective for full life in community. Several churches in Dayton contributed funds to support this excursion. In it, about thirty Dayton community activists went to Chicago to attend a two-week workshop on community organization led by Saul Alinsky. Curtis Niles, who had precipitated the effort to desegregate the Catholic elementary schools the month before, went on the trip.

Returning to Dayton, these activists found the report of the De Facto Segregation Committee and the formation of a task force to review it as important opportunities. Although they did not think they would succeed, they wanted to advance some proposals that were being considered. The Ad Hoc group made only one change in those proposals. They pressed for a pilot project of consolidation with three Catholic elementary schools. Originally, the De Facto Segregation Committee had recommended two distinct phases. First, it suggested a one year trial of voluntary exchange with open enrollment. Second, it suggested reorganizing all the Dayton area Catholic elementary schools into six consolidated districts in the next year. The Ad Hoc Committee suggested that the first stage of open enrollment be dropped. It wanted the Dayton area Catholic schools to consolidate one district the first year to see how it worked (Nealon 1990).

On 20 May 1968 the chair of the Ad Hoc Committee wrote a letter to pastors, clergy, principals, and parochial school board presidents outlining the committee's proposal. He suggested using Holy Angels School for grades two and three, St. Henry's for grades four to six, and Resurrection for grades seven and eight. To direct the project, he recommended a district board for the project that included the pastors of the three parishes, the school principals, and a teacher representative from each school. He advised hiring a coordinator for the project (Nealon 1968a). When asked by a newspaper reporter why his committee submitted the proposal, the chair of the Ad Hoc Committee said, "Open enrollment is a sellout, not a bridge. There's nothing that goes beyond open enrollment to consolidation" (Dansker 1968). He said in June 1968 that his Ad Hoc De Facto Segregation Committee had collected 8,000 signatures on petitions urging desegregation of Catholic elementary schools.

The Ad Hoc Committee members tried to find support for the pilot project of consolidation. On 18 July 1968 fifty parents from the predominantly black Resurrection parish disregarded the advice of their pastor. They voted to join with two other schools yet to be named in a consolidated trial project. The priest warned "it was presumptuous of the Ad Hoc Committee to make its proposal when new machinery is at work to integrate schools." The priest suggested the proposal should not be adopted but recommended to the task force that was set up to consider the integration for the Catholic elementary schools in Dayton (Heller 1968).

Despite the success, the Ad Hoc Committee had trouble interesting other parishes or the archdiocese in the pilot project. On 19 July 1968 the pastor of St. Mary's, a predominantly white church in the east side of Dayton, said the inclusion of his church in the Ad Hoc Committee's project came as a surprise to him. He read about it in the paper. "The least they could do was ask us," he said (Kline 1968b). Only the black parish of Resurrection was willing to be part of the Ad Hoc Committee's pilot project. On 6 September 1968 the chair of the Ad Hoc Committee wrote a letter to his committee members. He explained that the committee was looking for two more schools. It needed the schools because a working pilot project would stimulate pressure and interest in consolidation (Nealon 1968b). The committee submitted its plan for a pilot project to Archbishop Alter. He replied on 29 July 1968 that "all private suggestions or representations by self-appointed committees are being referred to the task force for evaluation." Alter (1968b) said the task force represented all legitimate interests, both legal and canonical.

During the summer of 1968, the Open Enrollment and Voluntary Exchange began. The De Facto Segregation Committee had suggested this exchange as the first step toward desegregation. The Archdiocesan Board of Education approved it. On 17 July 1968, 168 people attended an organizational meeting at St. James where the chairperson of the De Facto Segregation Committee explained the idea. Phil Donahue told how he was sending his two children to predominantly black St. James. Speakers told parents to become involved with the affairs of the parish to which they were sending their children for school. Everyone hoped this program would lead to consolidation of the Catholic elementary school. Stories appeared in July 1968 newspapers warning of a rapidly approaching deadline for application for voluntary exchange. Some parents complained that local pastors did not announce the program ("75 Students" 1968).

It was never clear who would pay the costs of transportation. On 26 June 1968 the assistant superintendent for business for the Dayton city schools said his office would pay for the open enrollment of the black children in the suburban schools. He would not cover the costs for the white children to leave the suburbs and come to Dayton. On 23 December 1968 Bishop McCarthy wrote Msgr. Connaughton to say the Ohio State Department of Education forbade the use of monies from the sale of church property to transport the white children from the suburbs to the urban schools.

For two years, several parents used their personal cars. Some of these parents say they did this on the idea that the archdiocese would pick up the costs, but this never happened (Cochran 1990). As a result, during the 1968–69 and 1969–70 school years, about forty white children took advantage of voluntary exchange and attended St. James. They were almost the only white children in the building. However, their numbers declined by fifty percent each year until only five white children were involved in the 1973–74 school year. Black children were more constant. From the 1968–69 school year until the 1973–74 school year, between forty and fifty black pupils from St. James or Resurrection went to Catholic schools in the suburbs.

Local newspapers heralded open enrollment and voluntary exchange. Stories noted the hardship of a forty-five minute bus trip each way for those white children leaving Ascension School in Centerville and traveling to St. James. Because of the exchange, white children learned that black children were like themselves. Black children learned to be friends with white children. In 1968 the total cost for transportation was $5,000. The Ohio School Bus Bill paid $30 per pupil. The rest came from contributions from parents and other charities (Carton 1968).

In 1969 the Dayton area Catholic schools hired an assistant professor at the University of Cincinnati to evaluate the Open Enrollment and Voluntary Exchange. Completed on 17 August 1970 the results were not surprising. By academic measures, all the children, black and white, in St. James and in two white suburban schools, did equally well or badly. Yet, the parents of black children thought their children received better educations in the white school than in their own parish school. Objective evidence did not show this happened (Cash 1970).

The report offered four recommendations. First, the Dayton area Catholic schools should form a decision-making board with parents, students, teachers, and administrators to direct the future of the program. Second, the teachers should enroll in six quarter hours of college-level courses in African American literature and history. They should introduce the information from these courses to the children. Third, the parents should engage in soul-searching to maintain such programs. Fourth, the schools should establish laboratories, workshops, and trips for students to increase their ability to talk with different peoples (Cash 1970).

In 1970 half the white children in the voluntary exchange program withdrew. They did not do this easily. On 11 November 1970 a parent wrote a two-page, single-spaced, typed letter to the assistant principal of St. James. She explained in plaintive terms the difficulties they had with travel and the expenses they incurred contributing to their own parish and to St. James. They gave to both churches because they did not want to ask the bishop to enforce the rule allowing families in the exchange program to pay only to one parish. She described her doubts about the worth of the venture.

On 17 August 1971 the mostly white Corpus Christi Parish withdrew from the voluntary exchange program. When parents complained to Archbishop Paul F. Leibold, who had replaced Archbishop Alter, he replied on 3 February 1971 that he could not help. Catholic schools are a loose federation supported by contributions from each parish. He said he could not become an administrator of a school system. He added that he was sorry, but he could do nothing unless the Archdiocesan school board chose to act. The last year of operation for the exchange was 1973–74, when one white child was involved.

The Task Force Meets

The task force to consider the consolidation of Dayton's Catholic elementary schools met as planned. On 25 September 1968 at Corpus Christi Recreation Center in Dayton, Bishop McCarthy addressed the audience. He said the task force enabled the archdiocesan school board to hear the opinions of the people of Dayton. Bishop McCarthy asked all members to approach the work with the purest of intentions. He warned the issue could split the community. However, McCarthy acknowledged that the members of the De Facto Segregation Committee had worked long and hard to make their recommendations. "Such serious effort deserves to be respected."

Msgr. Connaughton reviewed what the task force was intended to do. He said the task force was not to consider the value of nondiscrimination. That question was already answered. Instead, the concern of this body was the way desegregation should be accomplished. In this spirit, Connaughton warned the audience against placing so many obstacles in the path of desegregation that such opposition became a form of disguised rejection.

After the opening remarks, controversy erupted, though only members of the task force could speak. One delegate, a professor of English at the University of Dayton, proposed adding more parents whose children were involved in the voluntary racial integration program. The chair of the original De Facto Segregation Committee recommended seating all members of his committee on the task force. Two such individuals sat on the task force. However, a commentator noted that seating members of the original De Facto Segregation Committee on this task force would be analogous to having accountants audit their own books.

There was considerable discussion about the absence of women religious on the task force. For example, the chair of the De Facto Segregation Committee complained that the pastors who declared opposition to the De Facto Segregation report were on the task force yet the elementary school principals, who were women religious wearing habits and who supported the De Facto Segregation report, were not.

Several pastors replied that they supported the report. One pastor said the letter written in May 1968 by the deanery did not indicate the pastors' resistance to desegregation. It asked how the consolidation would be implemented and funded.

On the issue of seating women religious, one principal said, "Principals did not expect to be elected to the task force, but they should have been here as observers" (Barmann 1968b). Bishop McCarthy characterized Sr. Christina's remarks as constructive. However, the story in the *Dayton Daily News* said "Sister Christina Slaps Archbishop Rule." This brought forth several letters to the editor from other nuns in the Dayton area complaining the headline was misleading.

The Archdiocesan Board of Education had hoped that the task force would operate as a public school board, with teachers and principals as resource persons. However, on 4 October 1968 the newly formed Southwestern Ohio Association of Laymen adopted a resolution to support the seating of Dayton parochial school principals on the task force. To underscore this appeal, sixty persons—men, women, and children—from Dayton drove to Cincinnati and picketed St. Peter in Chains Church on 13 October 1968. The next day the pickets appeared in front of the Chancery building in Cincinnati carrying signs saying "Task Force Needs Nun Power" and "Halt Alter's Falter" ("New Proposals Offered in Dayton" 1968). The protest was successful, and in November 1968 women religious joined five of the six subcommittees making up the entire task force ("Dayton Area School Principals" 1968).

Archbishop Karl J. Alter added to the reaction against the task force while the group was meeting. On 12 November 1968, in a newspaper interview, Alter said dissident Catholics in Dayton who complained about inflexibility and pomposity in the church annoyed him. Alter estimated that there were 250 such dissidents, whom he called a fraction of 1 percent of the area's Catholics. Alter said they blamed him for decisions he did not make. For example, these dissidents criticized him for expensive building programs. He said local people initiated and conducted them. Besides, Alter asked, "Why should the government have lavish buildings and the church live in squalor?" As for Dayton schools, the Archbishop added, "the current open enrollment program fosters racial integration but the proposed consolidation of parish schools will hinder it and could threaten the very existence of Catholic schools." Further, Alter said of the Ad Hoc De Facto Segregation Committee that people from Dayton told him this was a conspiracy to destroy Catholic schools (Goodman 1968b).

Alter's newspaper interview grew out of a story the reporter had published the preceding day about liberals who were challenging the Church. These challenges included such things as trying to take some of the money raised to build Centerville's Church of the Incarnation and spend it on the education and feeding of poor people. Among the liberals the reporter had interviewed was the priest who served on the original De Facto Segregation Committee who said, "I don't think there will be too much change under the present leadership" (Goodman 1968a).

The newspaper interview with Alter and the series on liberal challenges may have made a difficult situation worse. On 13 November 1968 the Dayton Deanery Council decided to begin a program to familiarize people with the findings of the De Facto Segregation Committee. Brother Joseph Davis, an African American member of the Society of Mary, introduced this motion. Without such a public campaign, said Davis, the people would reject the recommendation for school consolidation. The dean of the Dayton Deanery resisted the proposal, saying it anticipated action being evaluated by the task force. Despite his plea for caution, the motion passed (Cole 1968b).

On 7 December 1968 the president of the parents' group involved in Open Enrollment and Voluntary Exchange had a letter to the editor published in the *Journal Herald,* protesting the remarks made by Archbishop Alter (Irvine 1968). More support for the De Facto Segregation Committee's proposals came on 30 January 1969, when the Association of Cincinnati Priests announced their support for the consolidation of the Dayton elementary schools ("Catholic School Merger" 1969).

However, conservatives passed petitions to show the correctness of Archbishop Alter. The *Catholic Telegraph* on 12 December 1968 told of a petition carrying 112 names that complained about the breakdown in respect for the hierarchy and clergy ("112 Sign Letter" 1968).

Archbishop Alter's remarks reached the task force in Dayton and led to the resignation of three of the four black members on the seventy-six-member task force. Calling themselves Black Catholics in Action, Brother Joseph Davis, SM, and two colleagues resigned from the task force on 26 February 1969. In their letter of resignation, they cited Archbishop Alter's remarks in his newspaper interview and the Auxiliary Bishop McCarthy's ridicule of the Priests' Association's endorsement of the consolidation of the Dayton schools. They added, "We are aware that the voices of black people call more frequently for separatism. This is a psychological reaction to the imposed physical separatism. In [this] view it is better to make use of a reality than grovel after a promise." Brother Davis and the others went on to say, although he and fellow black Catholics had lost faith in the task force, he had not lost faith that the church can provide moral leadership. Nonetheless, Davis and his colleagues accused the task force and the Catholic hierarchy in Cincinnati of being willing to do only as much to advance desegregation as would be popularly acceptable. They said, "You cannot put a moral question to a vote."

Despite his activism and critical stance, Davis remained in the Society of Mary and the Catholic Church until his death in 1992. In 1969, he left his position as assistant principal of Chaminade High School to become principal of St. James. The people in the school asked to have a black principal. He agreed to this move if the white woman religious who had been principal became the guidance counselor. She said this arrangement worked well. After serving as principal for one year, Davis went to Washington, D.C., where he developed the National Office of Black Catholics. Looking back on these events some years later, Davis said that he resigned from the task force because the archbishop made the issue an economic one. According to Davis, Alter had signed pastorals opposed to discrimination. However, he let the people in the pews who would vote with their pocketbooks make the decisions about desegregation. Davis thought this contradiction in Alter's views was common for people in leadership positions. "When they deal with the question on a universal level, they assume very correct moral and theological positions. When it comes down to affecting particular institutions, they become reluctant" (Davis 1990; Dreerup 1990).

At any rate, immediately after Davis and his colleagues left the task force, the chairperson of the original De Facto Segregation committee resigned as well. The secular press greeted the task force resignations with foreboding. An editorial in the 8 April 1969 *Dayton Daily News* warned the resignations were indications "the group may be moving toward an unsatisfactory compromise." The editorial added "the Task Force, though weakened . . . still can pull out victory if its membership faces reform needs honestly." The parishioners of St. James tried to push the task force toward approving the consolidation of the elementary schools. On 13 April 1969 they adopted a resolution that asked the task force to submit plans consistent with the original intentions of the De Facto Segregation Committee. They sent the resolution to Archbishop Alter. Brother Davis, then principal of St. James's School, said the parishioners would not continue participating in the Open Enrollment and Voluntary Exchange Program without a commitment from church leadership that more extensive desegregation would follow (Harris 1969).

The Ad Hoc De Facto Segregation Committee tried to organize liberal Catholics to pressure the task force. On 7 October 1968 the Ad Hoc Committee sent letters to at least seventeen people or groups. It proposed forming a coalition. One recipient of the invitation, an elementary school principal and religious woman, replied with surprise that one day the Ad Hoc Committee denounced her for prejudice and the next day invited her to join them (Christina 1968). The chair of the De Facto Segregation Committee feared that a newly formed coalition might undercut the efforts of groups such as Witness already going on. Instead of a coalition, he proposed open communication among all the recipients of the Ad Hoc Committee's invitation (Regulinski 1968).

The chair of the De Facto Segregation Committee repeated his desire for open communication in a newspaper interview. He complained about the slowness with which the executive committee of the task force worked and the secrecy under which they operated. In response, a sixth subcommittee joined to work in the area of public relations (Regulinski 1968)

Although priests denounced the Ad Hoc Committee, the members maintained a hopeful outlook. In a newspaper interview, the chair of the Ad Hoc Committee said he felt archdiocesan officials contrived representation on the task force to work against desegregation. He said his committee wanted to work at the parish level to stimulate people's interest in the De Facto Segregation Committee's report and the ideas of consolidation. He denied his movement was an underground affair because they were working within the accepted framework. Acknowledging that he endured public criticism, he hoped that the effort would broaden pastors' concern for civil rights (Goodman 1968c).

The Ad Hoc Committee invited to Dayton Rev. James F. Schuster, superintendent of schools for the Altoona-Jamestown Diocese in Pennsylvania. Schuster created one of the first consolidated parochial school systems by merging twenty-two schools into nine consolidated administrative districts. Schuster came to the University of Dayton to deliver a speech on 26 November 1968. Schuster told his audience that parish schools were an important feature of the previous century's church of immigrants in America. Parish schools provided a way to bring these newly arrived people into contact with American culture gradually. Schuster said that in the twentieth century consolidated schools could provide a new direction. However, Schuster warned, such schools are not panaceas. They can be more expensive than parochial schools because of costs of coordinating textbooks. Yet, the expenses may level out and lead to such benefits as more efficient use of faculty, Schuster said ("School Consolidation Proposed" 1968).

At first, Schuster's lecture was a victory for the Ad Hoc Committee. However, on 11 January 1969 Schuster sent the chair of the Ad Hoc Committee a statement that he should look over the integration issue to the primary purpose of consolidation. This was the provision of quality instruction within a Christian framework. The chair of the Ad Hoc Committee defended his view, saying, "A Christian framework cannot mean an all white or an all black or all one nationality situation" (Cole 1969).

The task force was directed by a twelve-member executive committee whose meetings were closed to the public. In addition, there were six subcommittees. Each subcommittee elected its own chairperson and enjoyed autonomy in conducting its assigned tasks. The subcommittees were assigned as follows: public relations, quality education, finance, legal aspects, grouping of schools, parish life and Catholic education ("Dayton Area School Principals" 1968).

The task force announced a tentative proposal on 24 April 1969 that involved consolidating only four parishes. These schools were close to each other and one was experiencing a dwindling enrollment. The subcommittees on the task force presented equally tentative findings. The legal committee could find no reason in state or church law or in the Ohio Fair Bus Law to prohibit any action the committee might take. The finance committee said it was difficult to consider costs until a uniform system was adopted. The problem the finance group found was that school costs were mingled with parish costs. The quality education subcommittee endorsed the notion that any good school contains representatives from all social and economic levels found in the community. The main points of these reports were published in bulletins produced by the public relations subcommittee distributed in each parish. They produced little controversy.

On 27 March 1970 the task force produced its final report, which differed from the tentative proposals. For example, the suggestion to consolidate four parishes did not appear. Entitled "Evaluation of the De Facto Segregation Committee Recommendations for Consolidation of the Dayton Area Catholic Schools," the fiftysix-page report was a synthesis of the final reports of the six subcommittees. Each of these subcommittees conducted its own independent study of the original De Facto Segregation Committee's report. The final report of the task force divided the recommendations of the De Facto Segregation Committee into eleven suggestions. The first six of these recommendations involved the open enrollment and voluntary exchange program. Recommendations seven, eight, nine, and ten had to do with the reorganization of the Dayton area Catholic elementary schools into a centrally administered system with six pie-shaped districts. Each district would have a controlling board. Each school within each district had either primary, intermediate, or junior high grades only. The final recommendation was to convert Emmanuel School, located in the center of Dayton, into a citywide magnet school with pre-primary and primary grades.

Beginning with the recommendation to consolidate the elementary schools, the task force noted that each subcommittee acknowledged the value of the racial and socioeconomic integration of students. One exception was the subcommittee on parish life. They agreed sociological mixing had educational value, but they warned it did not supersede all other values. The primary values of Catholic schools had to be religious ones. The parish life subcommittee said that the value of the parish with its relation to the children and their homes superseded racial integration. The subcommittee on parish life had noted that in the parish, pastors and parents cooperate with God in begetting the child in baptism, in nourishing the child in communion, in preserving the child from sin in the sacrament of reconciliation, and in bringing the child to worship. This subcommittee feared that consolidation of the elementary schools would prevent such cooperation among the priest, the children's parents, and the children's teachers. While they acknowledged that some reasons may require the breakdown of parochial ties, these motives would have to be carefully selected.

The task force's subcommittee on quality education conducted a fact-finding survey. The quality education subcommittee surveyed the Dayton area Catholic schools. It found that the accelerating local trend toward social stratification prevented children from learning about people who are economically, ethnically, culturally or socially different. Such isolation could cause children to accept unchristian ideas. Because of these findings, the final report of the task force endorsed the principles underlying the effort to consolidate the schools.

The committee on legal aspects found that canon law required the local Ordinary, here Archbishop Alter, to supervise all ecclesiastical goods in his territory. This meant the archdiocesan school board and Archbishop Alter could consolidate the elementary schools over parishioners' objections. All canonists did not share this view. The report quoted a scholar contacted by Archbishop Alter who said such an action could weaken the role of parishes. The subcommittees on finance and grouping of schools found consolidation would increase the cost of Catholic elementary schools. However, the increase would not be prohibitive.

Despite these encouraging findings, the task force did not recommend consolidation because the specific plan would not provide adequate overall integration. Further, the quality education subcommittee feared the idea of grouping all the children of two consecutive grades together in one building was pedagogically unsound. The legal aspects subcommittee thought such an organization would not present problems to the Ohio State Board of Education. For purposes of certification, the entire system could be considered one school if each child spent two years in each one of three schools.

Instead, the task force recommended an alternate proposal made by the quality education subcommittee. This proposal was to begin nongraded, child-centered learning centers in various schools. Each would have a different theme. One school might concentrate on the humanities. Another school might focus on the fine arts. A third school could emphasize math and science. These centers would work as magnet schools encouraging integration within the existing parish schools. Although the final report approved this alternate proposal, the task force did not make a study to test its feasibility. The task force agreed with the De Facto Segregation Committee's recommendation to centralize administration of the parish schools in the Dayton area. Since each parish had its own governance board, there were bound to be inequities among the schools. Inefficiencies resulted from the duplication of services. The task force rejected the idea of the primary grade magnet school as unnecessary if parish schools had development centers.

A minority report from the executive committee disagreed with the development centers. Like consolidation, these would take the parish school away from the very parishioners who contributed to a building fund to construct the parish school. The minority report urged respect for this property right. Further, it quoted Pope Paul VI calling the parish a responsible body of necessary finality that takes care of everybody. In his view, the parish was an institution of high moral value.

In 1970 the Cincinnati Archdiocesan School Board approved

the establishment of a development center as the task force recommended. However, the schools came to face a financial crisis accompanied by dwindling enrollments. When several schools in the Dayton area closed, the board dropped plans for the development center in Dayton ("School Teachers to Be Trained" 1972). However, in October 1972 the Archdiocesan School Board set up a school board for the Dayton area Catholic schools. The archdiocesan board reviewed the actions of this board. Although parish schools retained their own boards, the creation of this decision-making body in Dayton moved toward centralizing the governance of parish schools (Felton 1972b).

A New Strategy

In October 1971 Reverend Gail A. Poynter succeeded Msgr. Connaughton as superintendent of the Dayton area Catholic schools. Msgr. Connaughton received a great deal of pressure to cause the change while he was superintendent. To alleviate that injustice, a woman religious wrote newly appointed Archbishop Joseph Bernadin in Cincinnati, on 1 February 1973. Msgr. Connaughton had recently suffered a heart attack and his death moved her to write. She said the archdiocese had done a grave injustice to Connaughton. "In fact, we were killing him. We were asking him to combat racism in our school system without hierarchical support and without a staff," she wrote. She feared the same thing was happening to the new superintendent. However, the teachers and administrators accepted the slowness in moving toward desegregation more than they had. The new superintendent acted more quickly than Connaughton had (Dreerup 1990).

When he was appointed, Rev. Poynter said parochial schools had to move toward racial integration. He admitted he did not have a master plan but wanted to explore possibilities ("School Teachers to Be Trained" 1972). On 16 February 1972, about four months after he became superintendent of Dayton area Catholic schools, the superintendent invited teachers and administrators in the Catholic schools under his suasion to encounter sessions where they could learn about the black experience.

Dayton area Catholic schools engaged the services of the same African American consultant who provided black-white encounter sessions for the Dayton public schools. At the invitation of the liberal superintendent of Dayton city schools, Poynter attended one of those sessions. Because of that experience, he came to see things differently. An editorial on 1 March 1972 in Dayton's *Journal Herald* praised the encounter program in the Catholic schools. The editorial said that "while the Dayton area Catholic school system has not exactly been in the Vanguard of the school integration movement, it is beginning to face up to the need with some intelligence." The editorial concluded that the encounter program "can help people get to know one another in an atmosphere free of the tensions that usually arise once any larger scale integration effort is underway" ("Integrating Schools" 1972).

Most important, the encounter program seemed to work. A Dayton school psychologist studied 297 teachers, presenting them with sixteen problem situations. He found that white teachers who had been through the encounter sessions were more able to anticipate the perspective a black person might have than were white teachers who had not been in an encounter session ("Encounters Help Span Gaps" 1972).

At first, Rev. Poynter saw encounter sessions as a step toward the desegregation of Catholic schools. In 1973 he said he hoped that the NAACP suit would result in an order for busing students. "It would make my job easier in bringing about a better integration of our schools." However, by 1977, one year after the buses rolled to desegregate the city schools, he gave up his hopes of anything causing Catholic schools to desegregate. The encounter sessions became a substitute for physical desegregation for him.

On 21 October 1977 Rev. Poynter delivered a paper entitled "What Position Should Your Diocese/Parish Community Take Toward School Desegregation?" to the Ohio Catholic Education Association (OECA) convention in Cleveland. In this paper, the superintendent pointed out that physical desegregation was difficult for Catholic schools. He said that civil laws do not force Catholic schools to desegregate. Although the National Conference of Catholic Bishops condemned racism in several pastoral letters, he said, they were silent about desegregation of schools. Further, there might not be a large enough number of black students in Catholic schools in any area to cause meaningful desegregation (Poynter 1977).

Believing Catholic schools could integrate, Poynter defined integration in a way to make the physical mixing of the races unnecessary even if beneficial. He called it a personal quality of the students that allowed them to respect the differences existing among groups of people. Inservices for teachers and multicultural programs for students could inculcate this quality even in segregated settings, he said (Poynter 1977).

Rev. Poynter made some suggestions to achieve physical desegregation of the schools. First, school people should formulate policies to prohibit white students from entering Catholic schools to avoid public school desegregation. Second, they should create open enrollment programs to welcome black students. They could adopt incentives to encourage white students to attend black schools, though by 1977 these exchange programs had little appeal. Third, Catholic schools should recruit black teachers and staff. Fourth, he noted the multicultural programs and inservice programs on racism could become necessary steps, especially if the school is "mono-racial." Other suggestions included promoting racial balance whenever consolidation of schools took place and instituting parish programs on the social values found in the Gospel (Poynter 1977).

Rev. Poynter's paper to the OCEA in 1977 represented a surrender to the problem of segregation, at least when compared to the report of the 1969 De Facto Segregation Committee. On the other hand, his views followed the hope common to religious thought that people can learn to recognize good and true things. Looking back over the struggles, he said the encounter group sessions changed many people as they changed him. He had been in Cincinnati before coming to Dayton so he knew the controversy Msgr. Connaughton had overseen, and he saw how Archbishop Alter and Bishop McCarthy reacted to the problems. Poynter said if they had been through the encounter program, they would have realized what "was blocking them from doing many of the things they could have done" (Poynter 1990).

Rev. Poynter thought the encounter group sessions enabled other members of the clergy to recognize the problems of racism. He attributed those sessions to causing the members of an association, Metropolitan Churches United, to take an active part in helping to segregate the public schools. He said, "I will not say the encounter sessions were religious experiences, but they were the closest things to it" (Poynter 1990).

In Dayton the Catholic schools consolidated as the De Facto Segregation Committee suggested. Steadily declining enrollments forced the remaining schools to merge. Unfortunately, the consolidation did not cause racial integration. Among the elementary schools, enrollment declined steadily from 1963–72. In the Dayton area Catholic elementary schools there was a total of 15,397 students in twenty-five schools in 1963. By 1972 they had declined to a total of 11,101, though the area expanded to include two elementary schools not formerly in the district. During those nine years three schools had closed and five new ones opened. All the schools that closed were located in the center city. The new ones were located in the suburbs (Kline 1973).

The elementary schools that consolidated joined schools that were already racially integrated or mostly black. In September 1974 St. Agnes, St. James, and Assumption joined to form a middle school on the campus of St. Agnes. Assumption took the children from K–5 grades that would have studied at St. Agnes. This made Assumption a more integrated school.

Among the high schools the picture was similar. In 1974 Chaminade High School for young men and Julienne High School for young women merged into one school in the building occupied by Chaminade in the center of Dayton. This meant the two high schools that were integrated were the ones that merged. The two white high schools remained unchanged. There were fears Chaminade–Julienne would become all black. This did not happen, in part because the school maintained an open enrollment policy rather than an affiliated parish system that the other two high schools in the area, Alter and Carroll, followed.

At any rate, the Dayton area Catholic schools were not physically integrated. In 1973, five years after the De Facto Segregation Committee made its report, 360 of the 651 black students in Catholic elementary schools currently attended either St. James or Resurrection. Eight schools were all white and thirteen had token integration. Only four elementary schools were integrated. The picture was not much better among the high schools. In 1973, Chaminade High

School for young men was 12 percent black. Julienne for young women was 18 percent black, and St. Joseph's for young women 11.5 percent black. However, Alter High and Carroll High in the suburbs were almost all white. Alter had eighteen black students out of a total of 1,224. Carroll had twelve black students out of 1,119. Furthermore, by 1977 it was clear that the court-ordered desegregation of public schools would not revitalize interest in desegregating Catholic schools.

In 1977 two schools, Dayton Catholic and Resurrection, contained 84 percent of the 749 black students enrolled in elementary grades. Chaminade–Julienne High School contained 164 black students out of a total enrollment of 1,904. Suburban Catholic high schools retained token black enrollment. Alter had fifty-four black students out of 1,212 and Carroll had eleven black students out of 1,188. These patterns continued into the 1980s, although Corpus Christi Elementary School became increasingly integrated as white people moved from the neighborhood.

Liberal Catholics had become discouraged with the lack of progress toward desegregation long before 1977. For example, in February 1973 a newspaper quoted the principal of St. Agnes, a woman religious, saying, "There has always been a committee working. . . . A report gets done and there's another committee to study that report." She said she could not stay in Catholic education and be honest: "The Church can promulgate in every other area, but on racism they respond to the people" (Schumaker 1973). She resigned her principalship in 1974.

The Catholic Schools and the Public Schools

Although facing problems of racial desegregation among their own schools, Dayton's Catholic educators tried to offer assistance to those people who wanted to desegregate the Dayton city schools. In March 1972 the priests of the Dayton Deanery pledged their help in removing economic segregation in the schools and community. This pledge was in response to a letter that the liberal superintendent of Dayton public schools sent on 20 December 1971 to 435 area religious leaders on plain stationery at his own expense. He asked them to bear witness in behalf of a resolution calling for desegregation of the Dayton public schools. In their pledge, the priests quoted a pastoral statement of the U.S. bishops saying, "Segregation implies people of one race are not fit to associate with another by the sole fact of race. We cannot reconcile such a judgment with the Christian view of man's nature." However, an editorial in the *Dayton Daily News* noted the priests said nothing for or against busing for racial balance ("Priests' Stand Moral, Sensible" 1972).

Most important, the Catholic schools in Dayton tried hard not to become a haven for white citizens seeking to avoid desegregation. On 3 March 1972 Poynter, as the superintendent of Dayton area Catholic schools, asked each school principal to present an admissions policy to his or her school board to prevent white students from using Catholic schools to flee public schools as they desegregated. Furthermore, Poynter tried to reinforce the position of other educators who spoke out in favor of desegregation. Notable in this regard is his support of the liberal superintendent of Dayton public schools. To garner support for metropolitan desegregation that would consolidate Dayton and suburban schools, the liberal superintendent made speeches in the surrounding towns. At Alter High School, one of the three Catholic schools in the area, Rev. Poynter introduced the public school superintendent as "a voice in the wilderness" (Felton 1972a). Finally, in December 1972, Dayton area Catholic priests signed a statement commending the liberal public school superintendent for his attempt to correct racism in public schools. They said, "Our community needs this kind of leadership" ("41 Area Priests Endorse Carle" 1972).

Some people who strongly supported the desegregation of the Catholic schools did not appreciate the support the priests extended to the public schools. For example, the principal for St. Agnes questioned the sincerity of the priests' endorsement of the public school superintendent. She said these men refused to cope with racism in their own institutions, and she would be more impressed if the priests endorsed an integrated Catholic school system (Schumacher 1973).

In 1976, the buses rolled among the Dayton city schools in the first case of court-ordered desegregation in Ohio. To their credit, the Catholic schools in the Dayton area did not serve as a refuge for white students who wished to avoid the court-ordered desegregation. In 1975 when the desegregation of the students in the Dayton public schools seemed imminent, the Archdiocesan Board of Education in Cincinnati adopted the resolution that "students who are not members of the parish or a parish which feeds students into a high school and who, in the opinion of the principal and the schools' board of education seek admission to avoid desegregation are not to be accepted" (Kinneer 1976).

In 1976 Rev. Poynter sent reminders to all priests and school principals about the admission policy. The result was that there was not a significant transfer gain from Dayton public schools to the Catholic schools. In September 1976 the total enrollment of Dayton area Catholic schools did increase by 325 students to 12,879. This increase came largely from the additional six kindergartens and a second grade in suburban areas unaffected by the desegregation court order. Furthermore, Catholic schools in the Dayton area had nearly 600 empty places at the time. Turning away students did not come easily (Stewart 1976).

Conclusion

Though they shared the same faith, Catholic educators, parents, and clergy in Dayton did not rely heavily on the ideas of religion to discuss the racial integration of their schools. For example, people who opposed consolidating elementary schools talked about the parishioners' property rights. On the other side, administrators who favored racial integration advanced encounter sessions as a means to teach people why they should racially integrate schools. While the encounter sessions built on aspects of traditional faith, they contradicted it as well. The sessions implied that people had to feel the pain of discrimination to recognize and remove it. This view of racial harmony differed from such New Testament passages as the one where St. Paul reminded his readers that people have different gifts and the lowest members should get the greatest care. Where encounter groups recreated the experiences of other people, St. Paul called for reflection and understanding.

References

Allbaugh, Dave. 1968. "Catholic Student Exchange Plan Aimed at Integration," *Dayton Daily News*, 5 May.

Alter, Karl J., Archbishop of Cincinnati. 1968a. Letter to Right Rev. Msgr. James L. Krusling, 18 June.

———. 1968b. Letter to Timothy Nealon, 29 July.

Angela, Sr. Rose. 1968. "Letter," *Dayton Daily News,* 13 June.

Ball, Linda. 1968a. "Catholic Integration Plan Draws Questions," *Dayton Daily News,* 9 May.

————. 1968b. "Bishop Given Petitions Urging Integration," *Dayton Daily News,* 13 May.

————. 1968c. "Catholics Studying Race," *Dayton Daily News,* 29 May.

Barmann, George M. 1968a. "Mixed Reaction Given to Committee Report on Racial Imbalance in Parochial Schools," *Catholic Telegraph,* 16 May.

————. 1968b. "Task Force Begins Study of Dayton Schools," *Catholic Telegraph,* 3 October.

Carton, Wanda. 1968. "Catholic School Exchange Program," *Kettering Oakwood Times,* 17 October.

Cash, Eugene. 1970. "Evaluation of Open Enrollment—Voluntary Exchange." Dayton Area Catholic Schools, Ohio. Unpublished manuscript.

"Catholic Open Enrollment Plan Generating Some Heat." 1968. Editorial, *Dayton Daily News,* 31 May: 22.

"Catholic School Merger Backed." 1969. *Dayton Daily News,* 30 January: 25.

"Catholic School Reforms Rides with Weakened Group." 1969. Editorial, *Dayton Daily News,* 18 April: 22.

"Catholics OK Integration." 1968. *Dayton Daily News,* 26 May.

Christina, Sister. 1968. Letter to Nealon, 15 October.

Cochran, Bud. 1990. Interview with author, 20 March.

Cole, Jerry. 1967. "Racial Balance in Parochial Schools Urged," *Journal Herald,* 17 April.

————. 1968a. "Catholics Overrule Dean," *Journal Herald,* 13 November.

————. 1968b. "Parochial Agency Comes Under Fire," *Journal Herald,* 24 October.

————. 1969. "Bias Muddies School Merger," *Journal Herald,* 11 January: 30.

Connaughton, Msgr. Edward A. 1968. News release, 25 June.

Dansker, Emil. 1968. "Plan Urged," *Dayton Daily News,* 29 June.

Davis, Joseph, SM, et al. 1969. Letter to Task Force, 26 February.

————. 1990. Interview with author, 21 August.

"Dayton Area School Principals Join Task Force Subcommittee." 1968. *Catholic Telegraph,* 21 November: 3.

"Deanery Group Reviews Anti-Bias Program." 1968. *Catholic Telegraph,* 21 November: 11.

De Facto Segregation Committee. 1968. "Racial Segregation in the Dayton Parochial School System." Unpublished manuscript. Dayton, Ohio Parochial Schools.

Donahue, Phil, and Co. 1979. *Donahue: My Own Story.* New York: Simon and Schuster.

Dorenbusch, Rev. Thomas. 1990. Interview with the author, 3 July.

Dreerup, Sr. Mary Ann. 1973. Letter to Bernadin, 1 February.

————. 1990. Interview with author, 7 July.

"Encounters Help Span Gaps." 1972. *Journal Herald,* 2 March.

Felton, John. 1972b. "Area Catholic Schools to Get Their Own Board," *Journal Herald,* 13 October: 1, 16.

————. 1972a. "Friendly Crowd Greets Carle," *Journal Herald,* 20 March.

"41 Area Priests Endorse Dr. Carle." 1972. *Journal Herald,* 29 December.

Goodman, Denise. 1968a. "Liberals Challenge Church," *Journal Herald,* November: 1, 2.

————. 1968b. "Majority Is Satisfied, Alter Says," *Journal Herald,* 12 November: 1, 11.

————. 1968c. "New Catholics Move on Integration Sought," *Journal Herald,* 9 October: 23.

Harris, Henry. 1969. "Negro Parish Raps Catholic Busing," *Dayton Daily News,* 16 April: 69.

Heller, Karen. 1968. "Parishioners Back School Merger Proposal," *Journal Herald,* 19 July: 31.

"Integrating Schools." 1972. *Journal Herald,* 1 March.

"Interim Reports Presented." 1969. *Task Force Bulletin,* May.

Irvine, Bell. 1968. "Letter to the Editor," *Journal Herald,* 7 December.

Kinneer, Larry. 1976. "Catholic Schools Won't Be Busing Haven," *Dayton Daily News,* 23 March: 17.

Kline, Benjamin. 1968a. "Priests Hit Bus Proposal," *Dayton Daily News,* 27 May.

———. 1968b. "School Consolidation for Integration Hit," *Dayton Daily News,* 19 July.

———. 1973. "Area Catholic Schools Near Reckoning Day," *Dayton Daily News,* 12 August: 1C.

"Leader in Catholic School Unity Due." 1968. *Journal Herald,* 25 November: 28.

National Conference of Catholic Bishops. 1973. *To Teach as Jesus Did.* Washington, D.C.: United States Catholic Conference.

———. 1983a. "Discrimination and Christian Conscience." *Pastoral Letters Volume II.* Washington, D.C.: United States Catholic Conference.

———. 1983b. "Protest Against Bigotry." *Pastoral Letters Volume II.* Washington, D.C.: United States Catholic Conference.

———. 1983c. "On Racial Harmony." *Pastoral Letters Volume III.* Washington, D.C.: United States Catholic Conference.

———. 1983d. "Race Relation and Poverty." *Pastoral Letters Volume III.* Washington, D.C.: United States Catholic Conference.

Nealon, Timothy. 1968a. Letter to committee members, 6 September.

———. 1968b. Letter to liberal Catholics, 7 October.

———. 1990. Interview with author, 3 August.

"New Proposals Offered in Dayton School Issue." 1968. *Catholic Telegraph,* 17 October.

"112 Sign Letter Criticizing Advocates of School Proposal." 1968. *Catholic Telegraph,* 12 December.

"Open Enrollment Plan to Be Directed by Nun." 1968. *Catholic Telegraph,* 1 August.

Poynter, Reverend Gail. 1977. "What Position Should Your Diocese Parish Community Take Toward School Desegregation?" Paper presented at the Ohio Catholic Education Association Convention, Cleveland, Ohio. 21 October.

———. 1990. Interview with the author, 6 February.

"Priests' Stand Moral, Sensible." 1972. *Dayton Daily News,* 1 March.

"Programs to Attack Racial Bias Start in Dayton Area Parishes." 1968. *Catholic Telegraph,* 4 July.

"Progress for Catholic Schools." 1968. Editorial. *Dayton Daily News,* 9 May.

Regulinski, Thaddeus. 1968a. Letter to Nealon, 25 October.

———. 1968b. Letter to Chairperson of the Task Force Executive Committee, 9 November.

———. 1990. Interview with author, 9 October.

"School Consolidation Proposed by Educator." 1968. *Catholic Telegraph,* 5 December: 3.

"School Teachers to be Trained in Interracial Harmony." 1972. *Catholic Telegraph,* 28 January.

"75 Students Registered in Open Enrollment Plan." 1968. *Dayton Daily News,* 19 July.

"Sister Christina Slaps Archbishop Rule." 1968. *Dayton Daily News,* 26 September: 29.

Schumacher, Robert. 1973. "Parochial Integration Drags," *Journal Herald,* 5 February: 2, 22.

Stewart, Don. 1976. "Private School Enrollment Spurts," *Dayton Daily News,* 7 November: 1C.

Task Force of Archdiocesan School Board. 1970. "Evaluation of De Facto Segregation Committee Recommendation," Dayton, Ohio.

United States Commission on Civil Rights. 1977. *A Generation Deprived: Los Angeles School Desegregation.* Washington, D.C.: U.S. Government Printing Office.

Vera, Percy. 1990. Interview with author, 25 September.

Chapter Eight
A Private School Sets a Good Example

In 1971 the rector and several parishioners of Christ Episcopal Church founded Center City School to show that racial integration could work in an urban setting. The parishioners hoped to counter the conservative backlash taking place in Dayton school politics. Some years later, a middle-class white woman who described herself and her friends as liberal tried to explain why she and several other people started a private school at the very moment when the liberal board and superintendent of Dayton public schools tried to cause desegregation. She said, "I want you to understand this was not white flight. It was not elitism. We wanted to prove that integrated education could happen in the city, and it could be good education." She added, "There were many of us who lived in Dayton who were concerned about the direction the public schools were taking. We thought we could change things. The sadness that happened with the liberal superintendent, the emergence of the conservative Serving Our Schools party scared us very badly" (Brown 1990).

Although Dayton always had some private schools, they rarely expanded beyond the interests of a few people. Catholic schools were an exception. As explained in chapter three, enrollments in public secondary schools increased dramatically in the 1920s as compulsory education laws expanded to include older children. Further, Dayton was a city of immigrants. Many families wanted their children to learn to be one hundred percent Americans. Public schools were the place for this to happen. Another important reason is that for many years the public schools served specific neighborhoods. As a result, schools served the interests of the people who lived there.

In 1972 there were seven private schools in Dayton besides the many Catholic schools. Of these, four had some sort of religious backing. Three private schools were nonreligious and of these, one offered a college preparatory program. In 1973 Dayton's public schools had nearly 54,000 pupils. In comparison, these seven private schools had small enrollments (Krumm 1973).

First, Dayton Christian Schools was a group of private nondenominational schools founded in 1963 to minister to Christian families who had a desire to teach their children biblical principles. According to a founder of the school, race was never a factor in the administration of the school. The admissions policy held that one member of the family must have had a born-again experience where he or she received Christ as his or her savior. The school began with fourteen students, none of whom were African Americans, but the number of black students grew as the student population expanded. In 1973 the enrollment was 649, and by 1990, 14 percent of the student body was black (Schindler 1990).

Second, Temple Christian School was founded in 1968 as part of Dayton Baptist Temple. The church was started in 1951 by a white minister who came to Dayton from Bible Baptist Seminary in Fort Worth, Texas. It was an independent, fundamentalist, missionary Baptist church. Its congregation grew. In 1952 it bought three acres of land on which to build a basement church. The permanent sanctuary followed in 1958. The pastor took a strong interest in the racial desegregation of the public schools. In 1972 he argued that "It is immoral to force integration." He took this view for two reasons. First, he quoted the Bible to show that black and white people should stay apart. Second, he thought children should go to the schools in their neighborhoods (LaBriola 1972).

Temple Christian profited from desegregation. During the Dayton public schools' first year of busing, 1976–77, the enrollment in Temple Christian School doubled from 245 to 426 students. To people in the school, Temple Christian was not a segregationist school. People in the church and school strongly opposed the intrusions of the state into private lives and institutions. Furthermore, in 1985 the founding pastor said the school had a "few black students" (LaBriola 1985). In 1986 the principal of the school said that parents chose to send their children to Temple Christian for religious reasons. He did not think the students fled segregation, although he admitted that students might have acted differently a decade earlier (Fisher 1986).

Temple Christian endured some controversies as it tried to infuse religious principles throughout the school. In 1978 the school required all staff and faculty to belong to the church. Unfortunately, it made this decision after several teachers who did not belong had signed contracts for the coming year. The principal resigned and some parents removed their children ("Baptist School" 1978).

Dayton's two other religious schools in 1972 were Hillel and Spring Valley academies. Hillel Academy opened in 1961 offering a dual curriculum. One half was Hebrew, involving language and Bible and historical study. The other half included the secular subjects required by the state department of education (Ryckman 1967). Hillel enrolled 165 students in 1973 while Spring Valley Academy enrolled 375. Sponsored by three local Seventh Day Adventist churches, Spring Valley served families associated with a local Seventh Day Adventist hospital (Hamilton 1973).

Of the three nonreligious private schools, the only one that followed a college preparatory curriculum was the Miami Valley School. This school derived from the Marti School founded in 1956 by Dr. Fitz Marti and his wife Gertrude. Begun in their home, the Marti School later moved to a nearby brick building. In 1966 the Marti School was the only non-sectarian private school in Dayton. It changed its name to the Miami Valley School and moved to a new location on farm land in Centerville. This suburb south of Dayton became a popular place for young, white professional families to build homes and raise families. In 1966 the new headmaster claimed Miami Valley was a new school and not a continuation of the Marti School. To combat a reputation of elitism, he stressed that although the Miami Valley School was private and emphasized college preparatory courses, it was open to people from all social classes. The headmaster said, "Some [students] are Negroes, some are Jewish, about 40 percent are from the southern half of Dayton [a section then largely of single-family homes occupied by blue-collar workers], but the majority come from middle-class families" (Leader 1966). In 1973 Miami Valley offered kindergarten to grade twelve with a sliding tuition that ran from $925 per year for kindergarten to $1,950 for grade twelve; about 300 students enrolled.

The two liberal, private schools, Omega and Center City, offered unique curricula that the founders hoped would advance racial integration. Omega Community School offered alternate or open education. Omega was a free school. Students did not have to attend classes. Teachers had to make the class activities attractive enough to the students that they wanted to be there. Proposing the school in 1971, the founders hoped that it could occupy some space in Chaminade high school, then a local Catholic high school for young men. However, as late as July 1972 the organizers did not have a place to meet. Despite these problems, Omega opened in September 1972 in St. Andrew's Episcopal Church with an enrollment of forty-five students and five faculty members. This was the peak. Students left the school until only seventeen remained with four faculty when Omega School closed in 1975. Tuition ranged from $300 to $1,500, depending on the parents' ability to pay (Goldwyn 1972; "Omega School" 1972; Smith 1974). One person associated with the Omega School thought it might have flourished if it had an ambitious and talented headmaster. Center City was fortunate to have the right person to begin the school (Leahy 1990).

Center City Begins

A vital force behind the founding of the Center City School was the rector of Christ Episcopal Church. He was a member of the Dayton public school Board of Education in 1968 when it hired the liberal superintendent to modernize the city schools. He resigned on 19 December 1969 and gave his position to an African American man who had chosen not to run for reelection. He did this to keep a black person on the board. Despite his resignation from the Dayton Board of Education, the rector retained his interest in public schools. On 21 April 1970 the church vestry, the administrative body of Christ Episcopal Church, went on record at the rector's suggestion supporting the then upcoming school tax levy. They sent this endorsement to the school board for publication (Christ Episcopal Church Vestry 1970a).

During the next month's meeting the vestry discussed using Christ Church as a downtown academy for the Dayton public schools. The Dayton schools operated an arts academy, The Living Arts Center, funded by Title III of the Elementary and Secondary

Education Act, in a former factory warehouse near the center of the city. Members of the superintendent's office had met earlier with church officials to consider starting a humanities academy. The vestry formally approved the idea, but financial problems intervened (Price 1969). On 15 September 1970 after the public voted down the third school tax levy, discussion within the vestry turned from having a public school in the church to establishing a private elementary school in the building (Christ Episcopal Church Vestry 1970b).

The rector sought materials for making an application for state funding and information from the National Council of the Episcopal Church on primary schools. He met with a representative of the Kettering Foundation. This foundation did extensive work for private and public schools (as discussed in chapter nine). Miami Valley School had considered using the church as a downtown facility. Instead, it expanded its own campus in Centerville.

On 13 May 1971 at a special meeting of the vestry, the rector introduced a professor from nearby Wright State University to help found a new school in Christ Church. The vestry approved a statement of philosophy and purpose for the proposed day school and filed it with the state Department of Education. The school would be a "Christian school, under church sponsorship and guidance, reflecting the Judeo-Christian tradition and ethic."

However, in a letter the rector sent on 18 June 1971 to the people of Christ Church, he changed the aim of the school. The letter told of a comment he heard after the church underwent a massive rebuilding project. In November 1967 the city manager asked, "Now that you have it, what will you do with it?" The rector went on to answer that question. He said the church was "about to embark on one of the most needed and ambitious undertakings in our hundred years on this spot." The church was going to start a school called Center City School. Its purpose was to "seek ethnic, social, religious, economic, and racial integration and use the city facilities for its civil, recreational, cultural, commercial, natural, and aesthetic resources." In this letter, the rector did not call Center City a Christian school, saying only that the school would "seek to reflect the Judeo-Christian ethic and tradition." He added that the board of directors was "made up almost entirely of members of the parish"

(Price 1971). The congregation did not instantly accept the proposal. Once the school began, however, people took pride in how
well it functioned (Brown 1990).

Around the end of 1971 the rector repeated his statement about
the secular aim of the school in a request for $15,000 from the Epis-
copal Diocesan Council of Southern Ohio. This request stated the
sponsors of the school were "concerned with excellence in education
and related urban issues." In this document, the founders said they
wanted Center City School to be an example for people in public
education. It could be a window showing the city as a place of
mystery, wonder, love of learning, and the meeting of all kinds of
people on the deepest level. They hoped the school would offset
the segregated nature of Dayton and the suburbs. This prevented
children from learning in the kind of world they live in as adults
(Price n.d.).

In his request to diocesan officials, the rector showed how the
private schools would help the city of Dayton. He included a newspaper clipping dated 30 May 1971 announcing that executives of
large corporations did not want to settle in Dayton. They feared the
unsettled nature of the public school system. He added a letter he
had received from the city manager of Dayton. In this letter, the city
manager said that a new private school would help the city because
the failure of tax levies dealt a crippling blow to the city's public
schools. The city manager pointed out two ways the private school
could help. First, it would provide an immediate alternative to the
cadre of young leadership families the manager feared would leave
Dayton. Second, he thought Center City School would advance the
impression that the downtown was still viable.

The editors of the *Dayton Daily News* shared the views of the
city manager. In an editorial, the paper praised the idea as a means
of slowing the misguided politics of the board of education of the
Dayton public schools. The editorial warned the minority faction
on the board, the conservative Serving Our Schools party, that its
efforts to harass and misrepresent mild educational reforms and its
dismissal of desperately needed tax levies would hurt the children of
the working-class people who voted for them. People with money
who voted for the liberal candidates could send their children to
private schools or sneak away to the suburbs. To the credit of Center

City schools, the editorial noted, "this group hopes with scholarships to include the poor ranks" ("SOS Boomerang" 1971).

On 16 June 1971 the board of trustees for Center City School filed articles of incorporation, code of regulation, and bylaws with the State of Ohio. The organization of the school was such that the board of trustees directed the work of four committees. Among these, the development committee raised $27,344 for start-up and scholarship costs. The school charged $500 per year for its kindergarten and $800 for the other four levels. A scholarship committee reviewed the applications of any parent who requested financial aid. The committee allocated money based on the student's need, the available scholarship money, and classroom space. It also considered whether the student's race or social background contributed to the integrated nature of the school. Other committees were the budget and finance committee and the building and grounds committee.

During July 1971 the woman who was to become the headmaster saw an ad in the newspaper asking for applicants for the position of headmaster of the new private school. She applied and went for an interview. Although Center City was to be a Christian school, the woman said during the interview that she would not be the headmaster of a religious school. Nonetheless, the board of trustees hired her. The new headmaster was an instructor at Wright State University near Dayton. She was a published author, and had taught in the Dayton public schools and Hillel Academy (Hyman-Bennett 1990).

The summer of 1971 was a difficult time to begin such an undertaking. There was a telephone strike that made communication difficult. Nevertheless, the new headmaster hired teachers, interviewed prospective students, installed a curriculum, and obtained books and materials (Hyman-Bennett 1990). Everything was in place for the first day of school.

The trustees hoped that 150–180 students would enroll. However, when Center City School opened on 7 September 1971, it had an initial enrollment of thirty-one pupils spread from kindergarten through fourth grade (Polite 1971).

The board hired four teachers and a secretary. The salaries for the teachers totaled $26,400. All four teachers were women; two of them were about forty years old and the other two were twenty-five. One of the teachers was a black woman from the New York City area; the second teacher was Asian and from Hawaii; the third teacher was German but educated in Dayton. The fourth was white and from the Pittsburgh area.

The curriculum of the school was COPE, an acronym for Community Oriented Personalized Education. Instead of grades, the teachers placed the students on the level for which they were prepared. The theme chosen for the first year was Dayton and its people. Kindergarten children learned about their community. They discovered the different kinds of workers that make up a city from the mayor to the water meter reader. Levels one to four pursued the same theme but added to it concern for Dayton's ecology, welfare, cultural opportunities, and business ("Center City School's Curriculum" 1971).

Unlike Omega School, Center City did not follow any radical teaching methods. For example, the headmaster pointed out at the beginning that the school would be informal, but not unstructured. The statement of philosophy sent to the Ohio State Department of Education described the school as ungraded. It was child-oriented, offering self-learning and teacher-directed materials in an open environment. The school expected the teacher to have a central role in instruction. However, it wanted to maintain openness among children, staff, parents, and community.

Parent involvement characterized the first years of the school. The parents had to sign a statement obligating themselves to twenty hours of volunteer work over the course of the year. This was beyond paying tuition. The presence of willing adults made field trips and individual projects possible.

In the early years, the school buzzed with activity. For example, the September 1971 issue of a school newsletter told of setting up a student council that would participate in the running of the school. It described field trips to the downtown library, the YWCA, a movie theater, and a restaurant. The practice of using the downtown as an instructional facility was not unique to Center City. In this regard, teachers followed a guide entitled *Yellow Pages of Learning Resources.* It offered suggestions of how to explore an area and listed questions to inspire a child (Eason 1972).

Signs of success came soon. On 6 January 1972 the Dayton Area Episcopal Council Screening and Review Committee reported favorably on the request to support Center City School. In explaining this action, the committee listed four criteria used to make the decision. First, the Episcopal Committee's report noted that Center City School was a community-wide affair. Proof of this was the heterogeneous makeup of the board of directors. At first, members of Christ Church formed the board. By January the fifteen members included people from different racial, geographic, occupational, and religious backgrounds. Some parents of students sat on the board. Furthermore, the students came from different socioeconomic, racial, religious, and ethnic backgrounds. Scholarships helped here. Second, the report said, highly respected educators in the area endorsed the approach of Center City School. Authors of the report found the headmaster outstanding. They felt she recruited a fine staff. Third, the committee pointed out that Center City School was not a place for children fleeing from the public schools. Instead, they thought the school was a model for public school teachers. Fourth, the report complimented the success with which the Center City board raised money, though 1971 was a poor year for funding in the Dayton area. Support came from a local foundation, three industries, two local newspapers, individuals, organizations, and Christ Church. Consequently, the committee recommended giving Center City School the funds requested.

Center City School quickly obtained accreditation from the State of Ohio. After only two years, on 14 May 1973 the Ohio State Board approved the school. The inspection team praised the school's community relations. It noted the innovative nature of the curriculum. However, the team recommended that the school translate the statements from the philosophy into the course of study. They recommended allotting more time in the day for students to study required subjects.

Translating the philosophy into the course of study was difficult. Center City School was always clarifying its aims. In plans, it was described as a Christian school. When the school opened, it was not religious. In 1971 the rector of Christ Church said to his parishioners that the purpose of the school was to seek social and racial integration to teach the students in a setting similar to the one in which they will live as adults. Yet in 1972 the rector said that racial integration was not the goal of the school.

In January 1972 *Notes and Events*, a local publication from Wright State University, published an interview with the professor of education who had been associated with Center City School since its beginnings. He said that the guiding philosophy of Center City School was racial integration (Richards 1972). This comment elicited a strong response from the rector of Christ Church, who wrote a letter published in the February 1972 issue of *Notes and Events* in which he acknowledged the professor's service to the school. He added that the professor misstated the aim of Center City School. The rector said the guiding philosophy of Center City School was excellence in education and realizing the wholeness of the pupil. He added that racial integration was a limiting interpretation (Price 1972).

Even the desire for Center City to be an inspiring model to public school educators came into question after the school opened. In September 1971 the rector of the school had written the diocesan officials saying Center City would be a window for people in public education to recognize the opportunities available to urban schools. However, in March 1972 the headmaster of Center City School told a newspaper reporter that teachers in big buildings such as public schools would have difficulty doing the things that Center City School's teachers could (Herd 1972).

According to the headmaster, the school offered individual attention for each child administered in a familial setting. In January 1973 in a paper entitled "Present Curriculum and Design," the headmaster said that Center City School was not an institution but a family of seventy people. This meant involving the parents, having students sharing, and encouraging teachers to cooperate. She said that parents, teachers, and pupils considered the school themes successful. Students and teachers used the city as a resource to explore themes. They walked over to the mayor's office, to the library, to nearby banks, to the post office, and to corporate offices. The teachers tried to give each child individual attention. Clubs within the school engaged in sports, cooking, arts and crafts, piano, and quilting. They had a student council and a school store. The school held regular assemblies with student participants. In 1972–73 Center City installed learning stations to enrich the curriculum and encourage independent learning. The headmaster ended the paper noting the school would change as the needs of the people in it change (Hyman 1973).

Although it was small, Center City was soon financially independent. A progress report issued during the 1973–74 school year showed the school had grown to having eighty students, with five full-time teachers and four part-time aides. The income of $77,877 more than matched expenses of $77,200. Since the students came from different racial, cultural, economic, and social backgrounds, the school met its aim of integration. Although the school tried to bring more people to the school from the southern suburbs of Dayton, the headmaster offered two reasons why they did not come to Center City School. First, people had not heard of the school. Second, the name was synonymous with the inner city that they avoided (Richwine 1973).

During its first year of operation, most of the students came from Dayton View, an integrated neighborhood in North Dayton, and from the mostly black West Dayton (Polite 1972). By September 1975 enrollment rose to 110 students. Further, scores on the Metropolitan Achievement Tests were high. Out of seventy-five children tested, forty-five were above grade level in reading and twenty-four were above grade level in math. Most important, the children's rate of learning was fast. Out of fifty-four children tested, sixteen made more than one year's growth in a school year in reading and ten did the same in math. Few children left the program dissatisfied. In 1972 six students left the school. In 1973 eight students left and in 1974 nine students did not return. The reason most frequently given was the family moved from the area. Another mark of success came in the addition of more grades for students to stay in Center City School.

In the 1975–76 school year, an ad hoc committee of parents conducted a survey of pupils attending Center City School to measure the interest in adding more grades. On 17 November 1975 the committee sent a letter to all parents saying the survey showed there was not adequate interest to add more grades. On receiving the letter, the parents changed their minds. By 11 December 1975 several parents said they would be interested. Center City School added a sixth grade and began planning for a middle school.

Center City School Changes

Unfortunately, the 1975–76 year represented a turning point. On 12 May 1975 the headmaster resigned to move to Harrisburg, Pennsylvania, where her husband had taken another position (Brown 1975). After an extensive search, the Center City board of trustees appointed a new headmaster. The new headmaster proved personally unable to work with the teachers or parents, and the trustees dismissed him on 22 November 1976 after less than three months (Center City Board of Trustees 1976c). In his place came a man who had retired from the Dayton public schools as supervising principal of seventeen elementary schools and one middle school. Under his direction, the enrollment at Center City School remained stable at about 110 students. At the same time, the number of minority students increased. Unfortunately, the parents' involvement declined.

The changes in the ratio of white to black were rapid. Photographs taken when Center City School began in 1971 indicate that there were about ten black students and about twenty-four white students. In 1976 out of a total of one hundred and twelve students forty-four were black. In 1978 out of one hundred and twelve students sixty-eight were black, and in 1979 out of ninety-eight students sixty-nine were black. More of these students received scholarships than did the earlier classes.

As the number of black students increased in the school, discussion on the board of trustees turned toward finding ways to have more black parents become members. On 25 May 1976 members asked whether the board should continue to meet at a local country club that had the reputation of being for whites only. The board discussed increasing its size to include more African Americans (Center City Board of Trustees 1976a). In June 1976 the discussion continued over increasing black parents' participation in school governance. This discussion raised the question of the role of the trustees (Center City Board of Trustees 1976b).

When the planning group began the board was selected as a group of professional people with special skills and contacts who could advance the school. As the school became established, the role of the board changed to represent the people sending their children to the school. At least one member thought the new direction for the trustees hurt the school (Morrow 1990).

The changes in the student population also brought changes in the school. For one thing, the number of students receiving scholarships increased, so the financial strains increased. Parents no longer had to pledge volunteer work because both parents often worked during the day. Most important, the parents who began the experimental school left with their children. People who had less of an investment in the idea took their places (Dwight 1990; Brooks 1990).

The leadership changed with the students. The new headmaster was a friendly, congenial man, He was a careful administrator who worked well with teachers and took care of the necessary paperwork. However, he was not the diligent visionary that the first headmaster had been (Dwight 1990; Brooks 1990).

One factor remained constant throughout the existence of Center City School. This was the attention the rector paid to the school and to the children who came. In the morning as the children entered the building to climb the stairs to the classrooms, hc greeted them. He attended assemblies and special performances. He talked and played with the youngsters, and they loved to be near him. His presence was so strong some people thought of him as the school; one parent said when she had to withdraw her child because of financial problems, she cried for days because she felt she was letting down the rector. His high standing in the community advanced the school in many ways. Center City received a considerable amount of positive publicity that was in part due to influence of the rector. Members of the board of trustees helped the school receive media attention because some of them worked for the local newspapers. However, the rector raised funds and provided stability to the school (Brooks 1990; Brown 1990; Dwight 1990; Morrow 1990).

A committee of parents conducted a survey from 1 December to 15 December 1978. It polled former and present members of the school to obtain an objective measure of the changes that had taken place in Center City since the fall of 1971. A total of 271 people received questionnaires. The return rate varied. For example, only seven out of fifty former students returned questionnaires but thirty out of ninety-nine parents returned theirs.

The committee's report stated the strengths of the program to be location, small class size, focus on individualized learning, and loving family atmosphere. The report noted weaknesses as frequent turnover in staff, lack of space, problems hiring qualified teachers, and reduced parental involvement. Some problems were financial, the report concluded. Of the nine former teachers who returned questionnaires, five of them had left Center City School to take better-paying jobs. The survey uncovered a loss of the family atmosphere. Former teachers ranked parental involvement as an important strength of Center City. Then present teachers complained about the lack of parent involvement.

Most important, the survey illustrated ambiguity in the aims of the school. The former teachers and the present teachers who returned questionnaires were unclear about the philosophy of the school. Former teachers felt the philosophy focused on individualization and the family atmosphere. One former teacher stated she never knew there was a philosophy. Then present teachers felt it centered on individualization. Three teachers said the school provided the best possible education. The present teachers also thought part of the philosophy was to bring together children of various backgrounds. According to the survey, parents saw the aim of the school differently than did members of the board of trustees. The current and former parents cited individual educational programs as most important. Both groups of parents saw the racially integrated setting as important to the children. Current and former board members felt Center City served a vital need in the revitalization of the downtown area. No other group mentioned this aim.

In June 1979 the trustees appointed another headmaster to direct Center City Schools. She faced a formidable task. Teachers' salaries and benefits were not easily raised. Space in an urban setting was always difficult to find. Parents could not become involved overnight. The new headmaster tried to emphasize the individualized programs that were the school's strengths.

The emphasis on individualism had always been present in the school. For example, in January 1973 the founding headmaster described all the aspects of the school as tools to enable the child to develop his or her capacities. For example, she said that the purpose of being a family-type school was to offer children an environment where they felt comfortable. Community resources provided a variety of avenues to explore. Individualized and personalized programs allowed each child to work on an appropriate level. In extracurricular events, the aim was to intermingle all children by interest area. Even such cooperative endeavors as a student council developed individual capacities of leadership (Hyman 1973).

The thrust of individualism increased after the founding headmaster left. For example, a brochure produced some time during the middle 1970s said the urban setting provided examples of work in commerce, government, and culture. Taking an apparent slap at the newly desegregated public schools, this brochure said that a mixed classroom is not an exercise in percentages but a realistic urban experience. Yet the aim of the school, said the brochure, was to help a boy or girl become more of an individual.

As individual attention increased in the school, the symbol of the school changed. The original logo of Center City School was a cross with a circle in the middle. Although the horizontal axis was twice the vertical, this looked like a crucifix, calling back the desires of the original founders to have a Christian school. People said the symbol was a crossroads such as the intersection of First Street and Main Street in Dayton near where Christ Episcopal Church stands. The new logo was a circle with an arrow leading to the middle and drawing the name, "Center City School," into it. Like other ads, the new brochure praised the individual attention each child received. Although the pictures in this brochure were of racially integrated students, this fact did not appear in print. Instead the brochure claimed the school "offers not only quality education, but Excellence in education."

Despite the best efforts of the Center City people, the beginning of the 1980s was unkind to their school. Although the school continued to receive favorable notices in the press, these stories were often pleas for help. For example, on 26 November 1980 a publication aimed at boosting activities in the city carried a story about Center City School, saying the school supplied a sense of creative realism. It quoted the new headmaster saying the school was different from other schools because it used the downtown as a laboratory. The story added there were only sixty students in the 1980–81 school year, and tuition was $1,250, with scholarships available. According to the story, the Center City School was moderate, not radical. It quoted the new headmaster saying, "This is not a snob school. It is progressive but not permissive." Furthermore, the new headmaster praised parents for their involvement in school activities, noting 98 percent of them attended all parent-teacher conferences.

The last comment captured the changes in the school. Enrollment had dropped extensively. However, in 1972 or 1973 the founding headmaster of Center City would not have pointed to attendance at parent-teacher conferences as a sign of involvement. In those years, parents were teacher resources, car pool drivers, and aides.

The years from 1970 until 1980 brought dramatic changes to Dayton, as discussed in chapter three. Many factories left the city and the employees followed. Service and sales industries shrank. In the face of these social changes, trustees formed a Center City School in the 80s Committee. At the meetings, this committee tried to decide what Center City had to offer that was truly unique. They found small class size and an urban setting as the important innovations. The major problem was that financial sources of contributions threatened to decline ("CCS in the 80s" 1980a).

On 1 March 1981 Center City School in the 80s Committee discussed options for the future with the board of trustees. The rector presented information on beginning a parochial school in place of Center City. This course of action seemed unreasonable to the board. They did not think it would attract larger numbers of students. The board considered turning Center City into a program for gifted children but decided this would not save the school. The school's original philosophy of operation was not far from the gifted programs being discussed. The trustees did not want Center City School to live on its endowment ("CCS in the 80s" 1980a).

The new headmaster telephoned parents of children in the school to ask if they would come back next year and if they could pay increased tuition. The answers were disheartening (Center City Board of Trustees 1981). Consequently, the headmaster wrote to the parents of the nearly sixty students left in the school. She told them there would be no Center City after June 1981. She said that the school was experiencing declining enrollment and increasing costs. Center City closed with an endowment of nearly $100,000.

The final ceremony for Center City was the annual "Moving

Up" day program. The students were sad. "I don't want it to close," one student complained. "It's my favorite school. I liked the teachers and my friends. I'm going to miss it" (Milton 1981).

Conclusion

The story of Center City may show that pleas for flexibility, for alternate schools, or for tolerance do not explain why people should sacrifice to stay together. Center City School offered a multicultural setting. The diverse student body allowed children to learn in a setting similar to one in which they should work as adults. This implied the best society was an aggregate of highly developed yet tolerant individuals. The flaw in this ideal was that it did not say what held those individuals together.

In Center City School, the glue among the individuals was the emotional attachment among teachers, parents, children and the rector. This was called a family atmosphere. In the curriculum statements this family atmosphere seemed to exist to encourage each child to pursue his or her interests and develop his or her potential talents. The hope was that mature individuals would learn and work well with many different people. Often the headmaster and the teachers modeled this behavior (Dwight 1990).

This hope was in the curriculum guides. An example is a document entitled "Purpose, Philosophy, Characteristics of Children, Objectives Scope and Sequence, Course of Study," written in January 1973. It began by saying the Center City School was an effort to save a dying city, allowing the black, the poor, the concerned to chart their own destiny, to decide their own methods of learning, and to minister to their own needs. The statement of purpose followed, saying "the program will be individualized, yet recognizing the importance of children sharing ideas, discussion and the need for interaction."

Unfortunately, this purpose implies that people stay together until they no longer profit from each other. The rector may have felt that having people in the church increased the chances of their becoming religious. However, affection for religion did not tie these people together. Many families saw the church only as a gracious host. As a result, as more families left the city and moved to the suburbs, interest in Center City School dwindled.

References

"Baptist School." 1978. *Journal Herald,* 3 September.

Brooks, Delores. 1990. Interview with author, 11 October.

Brown, Arlene. 1981. Letter to Parents, 12 March.

Brown, Diane. 1990. Interview with author, 25 July.

Brown, Kathryn. 1975. Letter to Center City School board members, 12 May.

"CCS in the 80s." 1980a. Minutes of committee meeting, 9 February.

------. 1980b. Minutes of committee meeting, 1 March.

Center City Board of Trustees. 1976a. Minutes of meeting, 25 May.

------. 1976b. Minutes of meeting, 2 June.

------. 1976c. Minutes of meeting, 22 November.

------. 1981. Minutes of meeting, 7 April.

"Center City School's Curriculum." 1971. Unpublished brochure.

Christ Episcopal Church Vestry. 1970a. Minutes, 21 May.

------. 1970b. Minutes, 21 April.

Dayton Area Episcopal Council Screening and Review Committees. 1972. "Report on Investigation of Center City School," January.

Dwight, Rose. 1990. Interview with author, 25 September.

Eason, Yla. 1972. "Kids Learn from Yellow Pages" *Dayton Daily News,* 15 October: 4C.

Fisher, Mark. 1986. " Desegregation Plan," *Dayton Daily News,* 7 September.

Goldwyn, Ron. 1972. "Structure—A Dirty Word," *Journal Herald,* 20 July.

Hamilton, Clem. 1973. "All Eight Establishments," *Dayton Daily News,* 7 October.

Herd, David. 1972. "No One Answer Is Education," *Dayton Daily News,* 1 March.

Hyman, Lois. 1971. Newsletter, Center City School, Dayton, Ohio, September.

------. 1973. "Present Curriculum Design and Projection," Center City School, Dayton, Ohio, January.

Hyman-Bennett, Lois. 1990. Interview with author, 29 September.

Krumm, Kathleen. 1973. "Private Schools in Nutshell," *Dayton Daily News,* 29 August.

LaBriola, Carrie. 1972. "Busing and the Clergy," *Journal Herald,* 26 February.

------. 1985. "Pastor Retires," *Dayton Daily News,* 13 September.

Leahy, Peg. 1991. Interview with author, 27 June.

Leader, Julie. 1966. "New Miami Valley School," *Dayton Daily News,* 13 March.

Milton, Karla. 1981. "Center City School Now a Memory," *Dayton Daily News,* n.d., June.

Morrow, Ralph. 1990. Interview with author, 21 September.

Nichols, Jim. 1980. "Center City School," *Downtowner,* 26 November.

"Omega School." 1972. *Dayton Daily News,* 5 May.

Polite, Dennis. 1971. "Center City School Gets Fast Start," *Dayton Daily News,* 9 September.

------. 1972. "Public Private Schools Inrive Together," *Dayton Daily News,* 23 August.

Price, Gordon. 1969. Letter to William Levy, 29 January.

------. 1971. Letter to the people of Christ Church, 18 June.

------. n.d. "Application to Executive Committee of the Episcopal Diocesan Council of Southern Ohio." Center City School, Dayton, Ohio.

------. 1972. Letter. *Notes and Events,* February.

------. 1990. Interview with author, 29 January.

"Private Education Alive and Well in Center of Dayton." *Notes and Events,* January 1972: 2–3.

"Purpose, Philosophy, Characteristics of Children, Objectives, Scope and Sequence Course of Study." 1973. Center City School, January.

Richards, Donald. 1972. *Notes and Events,* January.

Richwine, Anita. 1973. "Downtown School Seeks Students," *Kettering Oakwood Times,* n.d.

Ryckman, Marie. 1967. "Hillel Academy," *Journal Herald,* 24 March.

Schindler, Claude. 1990. Interview with author, 18 July.

Smith, Jay. 1974. "Omega Closed by Disinterest," *Dayton Daily News,* 5 September.

"SOS Is Playing Boomerang Game." 1971. *Dayton Daily News,* 22 June.

Part III

Curriculum, Caring, and Social Reform

Chapter Nine
Curriculum Reforms and Racial Desegregation

In the 1960s, while school districts desegregated their students, curriculum innovators urged public school administrators to adopt models of open education, magnet school organization, or ethnic studies. Federal agencies such as the U.S. Department of Health, Education, and Welfare offered funds from legislative acts such as Title IV of the U.S. Civil Rights Act to support these new programs. Unfortunately, neither open education nor magnet schools suggested reasons for different peoples to work together. Schools could offer multicultural education instead of actual racial integration. Despite any shortfalls of the innovations, the programs did not have a chance to work. Often, school districts adopted parts of the proposals and refused to commit the resources to any orientation. As a result, school districts often began a program of racial desegregation while offering some innovation that contradicted it. While this appeased the school's different constituents, it prevented schools from following a coherent approach.

Experiences in Berkeley, California, illustrate how a popular and innovative curriculum contradicted a successful desegregation program. In January 1958 the NAACP asked the Berkeley, California, board of education to construct a plan to desegregate the schools. The board set up a citizens' committee. In October 1959 the committee suggested hiring more minority teachers and distributing them throughout the system, guarding against black students entering dead end programs, and offering inservice opportunities to teachers to advance interracial understandings. The committee's report did not suggest desegregating Berkeley schools, yet the schools were segregated. Two of the district's elementary schools were more than 90 percent black. More than 95 percent of the students in eight schools were white. One of the junior high schools was three-quarters black. Another was 99 percent white (Kirp 1982, 159).

In May 1962 Berkeley's chapter of CORE asked the board to recognize the segregation in the schools, to commit itself to end it, and to appoint a citizen's committee to produce a desegregation plan. The board agreed. In November 1963 the citizens' committee made its recommendation to shift the buildings' attendance boundaries to promote racial desegregation. In May 1964 the superintendent proposed racial desegregation at all levels of schools. However, the board tried to appease community conservatives by limiting desegregation to the junior high schools. Unsatisfied, the conservatives tried to recall the liberal board and to elect conservative candidates to two vacant seats. Conservative candidates lost by large margins (Kirp 1982, 159–161).

In 1967 a black parents' group, the Committee on Quality Education, asked Berkeley's school board to desegregate the elementary schools. The board made a commitment to eliminate de facto segregation by September 1968. This time the conservatives did not try to unseat the liberal board members. Further, in September 1968, when the desegregation plan began, it went smoothly. As a result, Berkeley, California, became the first city with a population of more than 100,000 to desegregate its schools voluntarily (Kirp 1982, 164–168).

Once integration was in place, though, people began asking for choices among different educational programs. In 1968 a Black Students Union demanded more black studies in the curriculum, new black counselors, and soul food in the cafeteria. A month later, a group called the Brown Berets urged the board to expand its bilingual program to accommodate Latino students. In 1969 a high school arts program blossomed into a school within a school, attracting almost exclusively white students. In addition, an old high school was renamed East Campus to serve alienated white and black students (Kirp 1982, 171).

To make matters worse, the day following the beginning of the desegregation process, the superintendent who had planned it announced his resignation to become the Massachusetts Commissioner of Education. While it is always difficult to assess the contributions one person makes, the superintendent's departure seemed to move the district from racial desegregation. His replacement decided to emphasize student choice over racial integration and accelerated the schools within schools. For example, the new superintendent divided a primary school into three subschools. One part stressed multicultural instruction. A second section followed a traditional approach. The third adopted an individualized teaching model. Other separate programs within schools included an arts program and a Third World cultures program supported in part by a grant from the Ford Foundation (Kirp 1982, 172–174).

Under this new emphasis, some schools achieved racial balance but others did not. One glaring example of resegregation through choice was a school called Black House reserved only for black students. At first, Berkeley's school board hesitated to approve this program. The members agreed to the experiment because they had already approved other programs that appealed to white students. The board hoped Black House offered a form of racial justice. A black board member said the segregated surroundings offered a supportive environment in which black children could learn basic academic skills (Kirp 1982, 175–176).

The drive for separate schools cost a great deal of money, but the federal government defrayed some expenses. For example, in 1971 the U.S. Office of Education awarded the Berkeley schools a $6.1 million Experimental Schools project grant. To win the award, the administration invented schools to satisfy Washington guidelines, calling for different schools in all grade levels. As a result, the federal grant caused the schools to increase the fragmentation in the system (Kirp 1982, 177).

In 1973 the U.S. Office of Civil Rights forbade Berkeley to maintain racial exclusivity in such special interest schools as Black House. Nonetheless, the Experimental Schools continued to divide along racial lines. For example, a black studies program devolved into antiwhite exercises (Kirp 1982, 182–184).

When the Experimental Schools program grant lapsed, new federal monies were not readily available. In the spring of 1975 the Berkeley school district had a $1.5 million deficit that threatened to grow to $2.5 or $3.5 million. To save money, the board reduced personnel, but these cuts hurt the racial integration of the faculty. In 1976 the board issued layoff notices of which 70 percent went to nonwhite staff hired during the preceding few years (Kirp 1982, 188–190).

Despite the financial problems and the attention the superintendent paid to special offerings, the school board never proposed stopping the busing program. Various special interest programs may have helped maintain the possibility of racial integration even if they did not specifically advance it. In 1980 the proportion of whites within the Berkeley system held steady at 45 percent. This was as high as it had been since 1968 (Kirp 1980, 189–192).

Consequently, although the curriculum innovations emphasizing student choice did not reinforce racial desegregation, they may have helped maintain the possibility of integration by preserving people's satisfaction with the schools. During the 1960s and 1970s, other boards of education in cities across the country began to favor open classrooms that depended on changes in the architecture of schools. The aim was to allow for more interdisciplinary activities, self-directed learning, and the use of a variety of media (Cuban 1993, 151). These changes coincided with the civil rights movement. One inspiration for these reforms was the oppression black people faced. For example, to fuel the free school movement, advocates such as Jonathan Kozol and Herbert Kohl wrote about the plight of black children in segregated conditions.

Individualized Education and Racial Integration

Jonathan Kozol and Herbert Kohl roomed together as undergraduates at Harvard University. In 1963, after a year teaching in the Boston public schools, Kozol wrote the best-selling *Death at an Early Age*. His friend Kohl taught in the New York City schools. Finding bright black children facing conditions similar to those in Boston, Kohl wrote the equally popular *Thirty-Six Children*. Like the progressive critics who wrote during the early years of this century, Kozol and Kohl complained about the way schools shaped people to fit into a prejudiced society. They claimed that the children could flourish if freed from adult requirements. However, neither of these individuals nor any similarly-minded romantic critic, such as John Holt or Ivan Illich, diagnosed the cause of the social difficulties. They concentrated on procedures to maximize individual liberation (Welker 1992, 65–74). Furthermore, black and ethnic groups opened community free schools that advanced the free school movement. Consequently, in 1971 there were over 350 free schools outside the system. Within school districts, many administrators adopted models of schools within schools or unique classrooms that featured some open education (Cremin 1974, 73).

It is important to note that the ideas of open education or individualized instruction did not come directly out of the civil rights movement. From 1957 until 1964 the Harvard Teaching Teams Project began the first so-called team teaching school. Conducted by Robert Anderson, this experiment showed that children of different ages and previously assigned to different grade levels could work together profitably. In 1959 Anderson joined John Goodlad to publish these findings in *The Nongraded Elementary School* (Anderson 1994).

The members of the Harvard project decided that school reform depended on the adoption of three organizational components. First, it should be a nongraded approach. Second, it should place children of a variety of ages together into groups that ranged in size from one student alone to twelve together. Third, the teachers should work in teams rather than remain separate and alone in individual classrooms (Anderson 1994).

Although these principles became widely popular, other universities and educational consultants offered different versions of open education. Most important, the federal government and private philanthropies supported this work. For example, between 1965 and 1968 Herbert Klausmeier at the Wisconsin Center for Individualized Schooling created a plan for school improvement with assistance from practitioners at four school districts in Wisconsin. In 1971 Klausmeier began to receive financial assistance from the U.S. Office of Education to set up individualized education nationwide. Soon, nine state agencies began to advocate this version of individualized instruction. In 1974–75 fourteen more state agencies took part. Although federal support ended after the 1974–75 academic year, the Sears Roebuck Foundation began contributing support. With these funds Klausmeier designed and tested materials to train teachers and administrators to individualize education. These materials distinguished Klausmeier's efforts because other proponents of individualized instruction did not offer instructional materials for the children. At any rate, in 1973, to consolidate their efforts, Klausmeier and other educators founded the National Association of Individually Guided Education (Fleury 1993, 216–222).

A third set of projects came from John Goodlad in California. He received a grant from the Institute for Development of Educational Activities (/I/D/E/A/), the educational affiliate of the Charles F. Kettering Foundation, in 1965 to encourage school reform. Goodlad used the money to invite twenty-five superintendents of schools in southern California to form the League of Cooperating Schools. As finally constituted, the league consisted of eighteen schools scattered from Santa Barbara to San Diego. Since the schools varied in size, financial support, and community type, they represented a cross section of the conditions found in most American schools. Originally, Goodlad thought the league schools would model the changes that he had made in the University Elementary School at the University of California at Los Angeles. However, the other school people resisted this notion and the university school dropped from the league (Goodlad 1975, 81–96).

The key idea behind the League of Cooperating Schools was that the individual school building was the key unit of change. If the school was to become a more effective unit, the people in that building would have to do it. No one outside could do it for them. As a result, the League did not try to form a model of proper education. Instead, it offered a description of the processes, the structures, and the personal skills that made reform easy (Goodlad 1975, 96).

The Kettering Foundation took the ideas that Goodlad's League discovered and formed them into a Change Program for Individually Guided Education or IGE. It asked its educational affiliate, /I/D/E/A/, to offer the program without charge to school districts. It spread widely. By 1974, the IGE program influenced about one thousand schools around the country and extended to three dozen other countries (Fleury 1993, 15–16).

The League of Cooperating Schools discovered the ideas that became the IGE process, and it spread the IGE method. When consultants from /I/D/E/A/ entered a school, they brought information about people in different buildings who could help. The consultants suggested the people support each other in a variety of ways. They exchanged newsletters, and they acted as resources for each other (Willis 1974).

Since IGE was a method for carrying out positive change within an educational system, its influence was not the same in all schools. Furthermore, /I/D/E/A/ staff did not suggest that IGE would promote racial integration. This omission may have been intentional. In the 1970s racial desegregation was extremely controversial. If a consultant associated IGE with such things as busing for racial balance, that representative would have alienated many people who otherwise favored school reform (Gies 1994). However, racial desegregation was ever-present. As the consultants traveled to different cities and saw different types of children attending the same school, they were aware of the need to create an environment in which every child could have meaningful interactions with every other kind of child. Consequently, although the words of tolerance and diversity did not appear frequently in their literature, these ideas were in the hearts and minds of the consultants as they sought a way to make it possible for children of all types and ages to be successful in school (Anderson 1994).

/I/D/E/A/ staff drew up a list of thirty-five outcomes to describe conditions they felt should exist in a school capable of providing appropriate learning for students and continuous growth for school staff. Among the thirty-five outcomes, the following examples appeared: First, although the school district had to approve the staff's decision to set up IGE, the focus was on the principal, staff, and students in a building. Second, the entire school had to divide into learning communities. Each community contained a cross section of the teachers and aides who work with at least two age groups of students. Third, each student was assigned an advisor to help the student plan a learning program (Paden 1978, 23–26).

The outcomes suggested that in meetings, the learning community members should select broad educational goals. Further, although each student had a learning program based on specified learning objectives, these programs came from the goals of the learning community. The list of outcomes included requiring that the students could state the objectives and the activities they undertook (Paden 1978, 23–26).

Among the thirty-five outcomes were statements about the responsibility of the teachers and students to gather information about the students' progress systematically. The outcomes added that each student had to accept responsibility for selecting, developing, and pursuing learning objectives. Teachers had to take a similar responsibility for their own development and other teachers in the learning community helped evaluate each other's performance (Paden 1978, 23–26).

According to /I/D/E/A/, schools with these outcomes had positive results. Students appeared to learn more than students in traditional schools. They became self-reliant, and they learned to get along with other people. They did not become behavior problems. Teachers seemed to improve with IGE as well. They engaged in more intellectual activities than did teachers in traditional schools. Teachers also showed more respect for individual integrity and democracy in an IGE setting. The relationships between principals and the teachers grew stronger and more interdependent. Although team meetings and student advising appeared time-consuming, /I/D/E/A/ claimed that implementing IGE did not increase school expenses (Paden 1994).

There was an important omission in the list of outcomes for IGE. The list of outcomes did not mention having students work in groups. Nonetheless, advocates of the IGE system contended that the group was the center of the method. They said the process of school reform opened all the people involved to each other (Paden 1994). The importance of small group work for the IGE system appeared within the following outcome: "A variety of learning activities using different media and modes is used when building learning programs." The word "modes" meant groups of varying size.

In 1971 /I/D/E/A/ produced a film strip and accompanying pamphlet entitled *IGE Learning Modes* to explain the different modes and the benefits they offered. For example, the film strip said that "The small group is used often in Individually Guided Education. Through the small-group situation, many of the higher thinking processes—analysis, synthesis, and evaluation—emerge" (/I/D/E/A/ 1971).

/I/D/E/A/ advertised that four grouping modes worked best. The independent mode had children working alone. Tutorial sessions represented the one-to-one mode. One document called the small-group mode the hub around which most of the IGE program revolves (Bahner et al. 1975). Within the small group mode were task groups that sought to accomplish a specific task, didactic groups that aimed to convey information, discussion groups, and brainstorming and inquiry groups. These groups ranged in size from three students to thirteen. Finally, IGE used a large group mode. IGE advocates said that teachers or administrators could convey information to a large number of people when they were in a large group. Such an organization was useful for movies and guest speakers. However, they warned that traditional schools overused large groups (Bahner et al. 1975).

In addition, /I/D/E/A/ produced materials to teach teachers and administrators to work in small groups because the learning communities would have to function smoothly. Students should learn these same skills. The efforts to teach teachers to use a variety of grouping strategies seemed successful. In 1973 a national study commissioned by /I/D/E/A/ showed that in IGE schools a majority of the teachers used most types of teaching groups. The least popular grouping modes were the brainstorming groups and the Socratic groups (Belden Associates 1973).

Unfortunately, the name "Individually Guided Education" suggested the children worked alone. It did not imply that the program inspired cooperation among children. It did not suggest that the model could serve as an introduction to racial integration. Furthermore, the children who learned within the system felt as if the system was individually oriented. Once in awhile, they may have worked with other children. However, they felt as if they chose their own activities and monitored their own progress. The teachers made the students feel as if they were important individually, not as a group (Westlake 1995).

To some extent, supporters of IGE felt that allowing students the freedom to learn and to set their own objectives prepared the children for racial integration. In this regard, IGE echoed the cries for respect and human dignity that motivated the civil rights movement. IGE methods asked teachers to treat the students as unique individuals. As a result, IGE fit the mood of the times. Further, the name "Individually Guided Education" increased its popularity. Once individualization became part of a national trend, more schools adopted this model to fashion themselves in line with what they saw as the best practice at the time. This was especially important for the residents of disadvantaged or rapidly changing neighborhoods who wanted to assure themselves that they were not harming their children.

In a way, IGE profited because its programs offered an alternative to the central control of individual school buildings. In Dayton, people in different neighborhoods opposed centralized control for different reasons. As explained in chapter four, African Americans in the Inner West section of Dayton sought black control of black schools. When the planning council lost that battle, the residents blamed the liberal school board. To some extent, they supported white conservatives who wanted neighborhood schools. On the other hand, the residents of Dayton View had supported the liberal school administration. However, they condemned the conservative members who followed. Consequently, at different times, residents of both groups wanted to free themselves from the central board. IGE promised that the building administrators, the faculty, parents and students would control the reformation of each particular school building.

However, since IGE encouraged community control, it could reinforce racial segregation or discourage it. In Dayton, Ohio, African American residents who participated in the Model Cities program resisted racial integration, fearing it placed black children in a minority. Teacher inservices about IGE from /I/D/E/A/ were an important aspect of the process of school improvement funded by Model Cities in Dayton. As described in chapter four, a federally funded program in Dayton View, an adjacent neighborhood, helped public and private schools sustain a racially integrated neighborhood. Yet, like Model Cities, the directors of the Dayton View Stabilization Program included Individually Guided Education in their proposals. Consequently, although the two projects in neighboring sections of the city had different outcomes, they used the same educational model of IGE.

After 1975 the number of schools that opted for IGE did not grow and schools that had adopted IGE used the system less. The problem may have been financial. Private philanthropies and state agencies stopped giving funds to networks of schools sharing IGE

(Fleury 1993, 222). At the same time, /I/D/E/A/ began to charge school districts for the services it had previously offered free.

A second reason IGE lost popularity was that people thought it offered activities that were less intellectually challenging than those offered in traditional models of education. IGE schools furthered this perception by evaluating the success of the model on the changes in the students' desire to learn. They ignored the gains the children made in academic learning (Fleury 1993).

IGE may have lost popularity because of bureaucratic tendencies. As with any reform, the superintendent of a district had to accept it. In the zeal to apply it, administrators sometimes ignored the wishes of /I/D/E/A/ staff, and imposed IGE on their faculties. Under these circumstances the method had to fail. At other times, an incoming superintendent could consider the model closely associated with the previous administrators no matter how successful an IGE school was. Unfortunately, many superintendents wanted to be recognized for initiating innovative and successful programs. They did not want to continue the policies of their predecessors (Gies 1994).

The tendency of superintendents to ignore the plans of their predecessors may explain why Dayton schools did not embrace IGE. Since /I/D/E/A/ was a local company, it should have had extensive influence. Beginning in 1969, a newly appointed liberal superintendent sponsored programs of IGE, team teaching, and building reorganization to encourage racial desegregation. During his tenure, Longfellow Middle School in Dayton View turned to IGE. Located on a busy thoroughfare, the school sported a large sign made by the children saying, "This is Longfellow Where We Have Equal Educational Opportunity for All." As a result, thousands of people driving to and from work associated that building with the innovative ideas of a liberal superintendent. After the appointment of a conservative superintendent in 1973, Longfellow remained an IGE school complete with advertising, but the model did not spread to other buildings. During a drive to reduce costs because of shrinking enrollments in the 1980s, the board withdrew the IGE program from Longfellow, removed the signs, and left the sole IGE program in an elementary school in an out of the way section of east Dayton (Caras 1994).

During the 1980s and with a new superintendent, the school board chose another curriculum model to improve schools and enhance racial integration. This was the magnet school concept.

Magnet Schools and Racial Integration

Magnet schools were long a feature of school integration. In 1963 several civil rights groups asked the Los Angeles school board to begin a program of racial desegregation that included magnet schools. Soon politicians offered to incorporate individual choice with racial integration. During the 1976 presidential campaign, the Democratic party's platform called for a variety of mechanisms to cause racial desegregation. One of these was the use of the magnet school concept. In September 1976 the U.S. Congress enacted amendments to the Emergency School Aid Program. They included a provision to begin a new program of offering federal funds to school districts to plan for magnet schools for racial desegregation (Orfield 1978, 157; 276; 432).

Unfortunately, some city school boards, such as Houston, Texas, and Cincinnati, Ohio, accepted magnet schools as the only type of desegregation they would employ. In these cases, the magnet schools may not have improved racial desegregation. Typically, the school boards spent considerable sums of money to offer superior education in these schools located in African American neighborhoods. They may have neglected the other schools. However, white students refused to apply for entrance (Orfield 1978, 325; 405).

In 1983 about 4 percent of the nation's high schools had specialized curricula. This included the magnet schools. Since these institutions offered students opportunities for advanced study, the Carnegie Foundation for the Advancement of Teaching recommended that large urban districts develop magnet schools in the arts or science for gifted and talented students (Boyer 1983, 239).

In Dayton, magnet programs had been popular for some time. Although groups disagreed about their organization, everyone seemed to approve of the idea. The popularity may stem from the fact that, like community control, magnet schools could maintain segregation or advance integration. For example, in 1973 when the U.S. district court seemed ready to order desegregation, the conservative school board proposed several magnet programs as alternatives to compulsory district-wide racial desegregation.

Even when magnet schools encouraged racial desegregation and enhanced instruction, the school administrators might seek to dismantle them. One surprisingly successful magnet program in Dayton was a music magnet that began modestly in 1980. Supported for two years by a federal grant, the program recruited about fifty string and orchestra players from the elementary schools in Dayton. The racial composition of the students roughly matched the racial composition in the district. As these children moved through the grades, new children replaced them in the elementary school. The board of education added a middle school and a high school component as the first group of children matured.

There were only two aspects that made the program a music magnet. First, the children stayed together in the same building to play harder music. Second, local musicians from the Dayton Philharmonic Orchestra gave the children one half hour per week of private instruction in addition to small group or ensemble work. In other regards, the children mixed with the rest of the students in the building. Despite the small change in their programs, the racially integrated students in Dayton's music magnet came to dominate youth orchestras in the area.

However, in November 1986 the Dayton public schools suggested dismantling the music magnet. A Grade Structure Task Force commissioned by the school board released its report on how to improve the Dayton public schools. Since the members of the task force found the per pupil cost of such things as a music magnet program to be high, they recommended turning all high schools into what they called comprehensive schools. This proposal would have eliminated a music magnet program in the district.

In December 1986 Dayton's Grade Structure Task Force held a series of five meetings to tell the public why they decided to dismantle a successful, racially integrated program. A group of about two hundred parents whose children attended the music magnet program attended each meeting. Although the task force estimated the extra cost of the music magnet to be $245,000, parents contended that this figure included normal operating costs that would be spent anyway; the parents held that the only extra cost was for the private lessons. Further, the parents contributed a lesson fee to reduce this expense (*Quarter Notes* 1987). Because of the protest, the school board chose to spread magnets throughout the system (Madison 1987).

In November 1988 the superintendent's office sent questionnaires to randomly selected people listed in the phone book and to parents of children in the schools. In addition, teachers and students in the schools and attenders at various parent–teacher conferences filled out questionnaires. From these responses, the school administration decided what types of magnet schools people wanted. Some magnet themes included programs that already existed in the Dayton schools such as an IGE elementary program, a structured elementary school, and the visual and performing arts sequence. To these themes, the Dayton schools added a Montessori elementary program, a classical and traditional elementary program that utilized the great books, an environmental science program, a computer science theme, an extensive international studies program, and a professional studies sequence (Smith 1989, 9–10).

In 1989, the Dayton public schools applied to the U.S. Office of Education for four million dollars to establish twenty-five magnet schools designed to attract students of different racial, ethnic, social, and economic academic achievement. This decision was in line with the 1975 court order that allowed Dayton public schools to establish magnet schools to prevent racial isolation (Smith 1989, 9).

To ensure a smooth transition to the new system, the grant application charged a Bi-Racial Magnet School Advisory Committee with compiling information that would aid in operating the magnet schools. A director of magnet programs oversaw the process, and a treasurer located monies and maintained records of expenditures. A director of evaluation assured that the racial composition of the student enrollment and of the teaching staff of each magnet school was within 15 percent of the ratio in the district as a whole (Smith 1989, 17–22).

In 1990 the school board applied to the Office of Education for an additional $2 million to expand the magnet school idea into seven elementary schools, two middle schools, and a high school career center. Unfortunately, in May 1991 the superintendent announced that the district would release eighty teachers, many of whom had been hired to strengthen the magnet programs. At the same time, a million-dollar sports program remained untouched because, the superintendent said, urban children needed sports more than suburban children (Harty 1991).

The schools did not cause the financial problem. The county auditor's office miscalculated and received less taxes than expected. This error cost the Dayton schools, a community college, and county health organizations a total of $2.8 million (Flynn 1991).

Despite these problems, surveys showed that Dayton residents continued to support the magnet schools. In 1992 the board of education hired the McKenzie Group from Washington, D.C., to survey the public schools. Although the McKenzie report did not reveal finances, it contended that the magnet schools were costly. With the expiration of the federal grant, the general operating funds would have to support the new schools. However, the survey also found that the residents of Dayton liked magnet schools. Most of the children who attended magnet schools chose them because of the building's academic focus. The McKenzie people found that even parents of children then enrolled in private schools found the magnet school themes attractive. Furthermore, the students in the magnet schools did better on basic skill tests of reading, writing, and mathematics (McKenzie 1992).

However, the McKenzie survey found that most of the magnet programs did not differ from the curricula offered in other non-magnet schools. The McKenzie survey criticized the Dayton schools for failing to measure the achievement of students in the area emphasized by the magnet, though the district had promised to do this on the grant application. The McKenzie group speculated that such special measures might encourage the principals in the magnets to emphasize their buildings' uniqueness (McKenzie 1992).

Dayton public schools did not adopt the special methods of evaluating the magnet schools that the McKenzie group recommended nor did they move to strengthen the magnet themes. When the board decided to have magnet schools, they did not change the building administrators or the faculty. At best, they proposed to add special experts such as the artists who conducted special lessons in the arts magnet. Even after the schools became magnets, the board appointed administrators without any experience or expertise in the magnet area to head the magnet schools.

Most important, the school board adopted principles of management that weakened efforts to establish the magnet schools. In 1992, the Towers Perrin consulting service submitted a management study of the Dayton public schools. Commissioned by Dayton's business community, the study certified the need for increased resources and became a cornerstone in a school tax campaign. At the same time, the Towers Perrin report called for the school buildings to have greater control over resources, programs, and operations. In line with this request, the Dayton superintendent reorganized central office staff, moving curriculum supervisors into an advisory capacity, reducing their number, and increasing the range of their operations. As a result, building administrators took charge of the curriculum development of magnet programs.

The idea of site-based management weakened the magnet themes for three reasons. First, many building principals did not have the training to know what could be done to strengthen the magnet theme. Second, principals worked sixty or more hours per week running the buildings and did not have time to keep up with developments of best practice in curriculum areas. Third, although the principals typically turned to teachers' committees to make curricular suggestions, often the teachers who volunteered for such committees did not have an interest in the magnet themes.

Finally, the board missed an opportunity that came about because of a teachers' strike to use school finances to sharpen the magnet themes. In 1993, after the Dayton schools passed a tax levy, the teachers struck for higher wages. Both parties could have avoided the strike, but personal animosities between the superintendent and the president of the Dayton Education Association overshadowed reasonable negotiations (Belcher 1993). As part of the agreement to end the strike, the board allowed the personnel in the school buildings to submit proposals for funds for educational improvement. In this way, the board ensured that new money did not go for teacher salaries, and it reinforced the previously approved policy to move toward site-based management. For the teachers, the decision allowed them latitude to form planning teams that would try new ideas in their buildings. Although teachers were not paid for such curricular development, they could ask for money to visit other schools, to bring in curricular specialists, or to hire substitutes, allowing extensive faculty meetings.

The problem was that, when the board wrote the guidelines for those proposals, they did not require that the money reinforce the magnet themes. While many proposals that the buildings' planning teams sent to the central office contained some reference to the magnet theme of the building, some did not. For example, the arts magnet high school submitted a proposal to engage in team-building workshops. They did not propose to infuse the arts throughout the curriculum or to use arts activities to strengthen working relationships.

At best, the Dayton school administrators held ambivalent attitudes toward magnet schools for at least two reasons. First, financial concerns loomed large. To some extent, the decision to have magnets may have been a way to cut the costs of all programs. After all, a federal grant was available. However, by spreading magnets throughout as many buildings as possible, the superintendent mollified parents who wanted specialized training for their children while he ensured that no program received more money or attention than any other. Second, anti-intellectualism within the administration played a role. One superintendent displayed a disinterest in academics when he released teachers needed by the magnets during the financial crisis in 1991 but refused to reduce the sports program. Furthermore, that superintendent's successor accused teachers of being too academic, saying that he earned only Cs and Ds in elementary and high school, yet he was successful in life (DeBrosse 1995).

Unfortunately, the administrators' uncertain attitude contributed to the magnet schools' lack of focus. Changes in the music magnet program illustrate this tendency. Until 1989 students in Dayton's music magnet gained a reputation for high musical achievement. Once the citywide magnets began, arts magnets could not admit students based on ability. Instead, the students simply had to complete a previous magnet program, reside within the attendance area, or contribute to racial balance. Consequently, as the programs broadened, inexperienced students joined the music program. To control costs, private music lessons became group lessons. Not surprisingly, the quality of the children's playing declined.

However, simple racism did not cause the administration to weaken magnets while adopting them district-wide. Although three superintendents held office in Dayton between 1984 and 1995, they were all African Americans. Furthermore, during that time, the school board remained racially mixed despite changes that resulted from elections.

Interestingly, in 1986 during the protest against the closing of the music magnet, several parents and several civic leaders argued that special interest schools would attract students from the suburbs (*Quarter Notes* 1987). This did not happen. Despite adopting magnet schools, the Dayton schools continued to lose white students slowly and steadily. In 1986–87, 61.6 percent of the 29,609 students in the Dayton public schools were minority group members. In 1993–94, the number of students dropped to 27,140 and the percentage of minority students rose to 64.6 percent.

The magnet programs could not attract white suburban children into the city for two reasons. First, Dayton's program made all the magnets operate in much the same way as the comprehensive schools had operated before. As a result, they did not offer anything different from the programs the children received in the suburbs. Second, the people in the suburban communities considered the city and its schools dangerous. As a result, they tended not to enter the downtown.

Even if Dayton's magnets had been wonderful, they might not have attracted children from the suburbs. Experiences in other parts of the country showed that magnet schools contributed to desegregation only in those cities where the students had to choose a magnet or attend buildings where their presence enhanced racial balance (Hochschild 1984, 70–72). Unfortunately, the suburban children in Dayton did not have to be part of any desegregation plan.

In other cities, magnet schools presented four general problems. First, the magnets did not involve many children. At most, in some cities, the magnets enrolled 40 percent of the children. In other cities, only 2 percent of the children attended magnet schools. Second, some magnet schools attracted white students while other schools attracted minority students, making it difficult for the magnets themselves to offer racial balance. Third, the magnet schools were expensive. For example, in St. Louis, the cost for magnet schools was roughly double per pupil what the cost was in regular classrooms. However, these were starting expenses and operating costs dropped to normal in subsequent years. Fourth, the magnet schools attracted the best students and teachers in particular areas, causing a decline in the educational opportunities in the other schools (Hochschild 1984, 70–79).

While magnet schools posed many problems, some researchers claim they produced more desegregation than did mandatory plans. For example, Christine Rossell says that magnet schools offer more interracial exposure even when they result in less racial balance. Rossell defines interracial exposure as the percentage of students who are white in an average minority child's school. This measure is a sophisticated statistical calculation involving the number of minorities and the proportion of whites in a school (Rossell 1990, 33–35).

Rossell argues that a desegregation plan that seeks high levels of interracial exposure may tolerate some racial imbalance to allow more minority students to meet more white students. On the other hand, a plan that has racial balance as a goal might try to spread as evenly as possible the few white children in a largely minority district. She says the problem is that such a strategy aggravates white flight (Rossell 1990, 35–39).

Rossell challenges the generally accepted view that county-wide metropolitan desegregation plans are most successful. Looking at the changes in twenty desegregation plans, including Dayton, Ohio, over a period of ten years, she says that county-wide metropolitan desegregation plans had the greatest decline in interracial exposure. On the other hand, the school districts with the least decline in interracial exposure were those districts with voluntary plans and greater minority enrollment. Rossell found the most important determinant of interracial exposure in a district to be the level of such exposure before the desegregation began. Districts with less than 30 percent minority students retained more white students after the plan took effect. Surprisingly, the second most important determinant was the nature of the plan. Mandatory plans caused more white flight than did voluntary plans (Rossell 1990, 192–194).

Rossell found that county-wide and citywide plans suffered from virtually the same loss of white enrollment at the school level. However, county-wide plans appeared more successful because there were more white students in the system than there were in plans restricted to a city. As a result, the total effect in a county-wide plan was less because fewer schools suffered big losses. However, those districts with voluntary magnet plans experienced less white flight than those districts with mandatory plans (Rossell 1990, 194–195).

Rossell argues that magnet schools do not bring about white flight. Most white Americans support the principle of racial integration. They will enroll their children in desegregated schools when they see those schools offering superior resources and innovative curricula (Rossell 1990, 195–203).

Rossell's findings and her conclusions rest upon two things: first, the use of the measure of interracial exposure as the criterion of school desegregation; second, her belief that white people flee mandated segregation. If her measure is unreliable, her conclusions are suspect. Further, if white flight is not as large a problem as she contends, mandatory desegregation plans are best.

Some statistical researchers claim that Rossell's studies are flawed in two ways. In trying to capture racial mixing and white flight, Rossell's interracial exposure measure offers a statement of central tendency. Consequently, interracial exposure may not change even when enrollment shifts dramatically within a school. However, there is no consensus among researchers how to best measure racial integration, as the authors of different studies employ different measures. Some statisticians suggest that Rossell overstates the problem when she assumes white people will flee a desegregation order. At the worst, the loss of students in Boston schools was about 5 percent of the total enrollment. This is far less than Rossell uses in hypothetical examples to justify the use of voluntary measures of desegregation (Fife 1992, 16–25).

Thus, in a comparative study of intervention strategies in the same twenty school districts that Rossell used, Brian Fife comes to the opposite conclusion. According to Fife's calculations the most coercive measures were the most successful. For example, the court applied a high level of coercion to the Dayton schools compared to other cities, and the decrease of segregation was the second largest in the sample. On the other hand, Cincinnati, which is only forty-five miles from Dayton, used a largely voluntary plan with magnets. The plan increased racial segregation in the Cincinnati schools. Interestingly, when Fife used Rossell's interracial exposure measure to decide the success of desegregation plans, he found voluntary methods to be ineffective (Fife 1992, 119–123; 130–131).

While Rossell and Fife disagree about whether magnet schools advance desegregation, their argument is about arrangements of attendance patterns within school districts. They do not discuss how curriculum planning enhances racial segregation. At the risk of overstatement, the magnet school idea could be antithetical to racial integration. That is, magnet schools could encourage people to look upon the institutions as catering to the needs of individuals rather than providing opportunities for all people to learn to live together. To some extent, a third curricular alternative, multicultural education, shares the same flaw.

Multicultural Education and Racial Integration

In the aftermath of urban riots, members of minority groups and their supporters pressured school boards to introduce or expand ethnic studies. Civil rights groups such as the NAACP and the National Urban League called upon educators to use textbooks that accurately portrayed the contributions and the experiences of African Americans. Publishers produced books that met this criterion.

The pressure on local school boards was often intense. For example, in 1967 African American residents and white college students in Dayton greeted the new superintendent with demands for more black history courses in the elementary and high schools. In part, ethnic studies served practical aims. Dayton's Model Cities Demonstration Project offered black children courses in black culture or history to build their sense of ethnic pride.

Frequently, multicultural education was a means to introduce students to information about other groups of people. For example, in 1974 the Ohio Department of Education recognized that many schools lacked texts that wove relevant material about minority groups into the fabric of the book. Consequently, the department offered the guide *Providing K–12 Multi-Cultural Curricular Experiences* as a resource for teachers to use during the period between phasing out the old books and buying the new texts. Unfortunately, the guide was no more than a list of facts about events and famous members of four minority groups listed in chronological order (Ohio Department of Education 1974).

While the Ohio curriculum guide was inane, a black studies program could turn into an antiwhite episode. This happened in Sausalito, a small but diverse school district in California. At most, one thousand students attended the schools during the desegregation controversies. They came from wealthy families from the town of Sausalito, from families on houseboats, from military personnel stationed at nearby forts, and from families in Marin City, which was almost exclusively black. In September 1963 CORE asked the school board to rectify the segregation between Marin City and Sausalito schools. The school board asked the California Commission on Equal Opportunity in Education for help (Kirp 1982, 195–200).

In July 1964 the state commission recommended that the school board create a citizens' advisory committee to decide the appropriate actions. In July 1965 the citizens' committee urged the school board to desegregate the buildings in the ratio of 75 percent white and 25 percent black students. The board agreed and drew up a plan that involved only a few students and took them only short distances. The white residents accepted the plan and kept their children in the schools (Kirp 1982, 201–203).

Trouble began in 1968 when the Sausalito district hired a black-power advocate as a teacher in the upper grade school. The teacher formed a black studies committee and began introducing members of the Black Panther Party from nearby Oakland to his school. In 1969, at the teacher's recommendation, the district hired some Black Panthers as consultants and named another black power advocate as principal of the same school. As the school turned dramatically toward black militancy, white families left the school at an alarming rate (Kirp 1982, 204–205).

Several white parents complained to the county superintendent of reverse racism. He referred them to the Marin County grand jury. In February 1970 the education committee of the Marin County grand jury responded to parents' complaints, accusing the Sausalito school board of supporting deplorable political causes rather than educating the children. The grand jury recommended that the Marin County school superintendent take over control of the Sausalito schools, hire credentialed principals, and eliminate racially biased overtones in the curriculum. While the grand jury could not enforce its recommendations, its conclusions led white parents to form a group called Citizens for Excellence in Integrated Education. The parents campaigned to recall two board members who supported the black separatist administrators, and the board began to bend to the pressure (Kirp 1982, 207).

On 4 May 1970 the board fired the building principal who favored black power. During the meeting, Panthers tried to intimidate them by coming to the room with guard dogs, standing against the walls, and brandishing steel staves. Subsequently, black students boycotted the school in support of the former principal, violence followed, and the district closed the school. During the chaotic events, the superintendent resigned, the two challenged board members lost the recall election, and the three remaining board members resigned. A new board, dominated by the Citizens for Excellence in Integrated Education took control (Kirp 1982, 209–210).

Often, black power advocates said that racial discrimination was an outgrowth of the exploitation required by the capitalist system. Consequently, Black Panther Party members often turned to some form of communism such as Maoism for the answer to racial injustice. Even if such an orientation did not become antiwhite, it would find few advocates among the public schools. Consequently, educators sought to broaden the study. They defined all Americans as members of some ethnic group, and they examined characteristics shared by all ethnic groups. Under this pattern white, Anglo-Saxon Protestants were the dominant group. Other groups included Greek Americans, Polish Americans, and Jewish Americans. Most important, these educators considered racism an outgrowth of a common tendency of groups to reject outsiders.

The aim of ethnic studies or multicultural education was to reduce the chances of children harboring biases against other ethnic groups. Consequently, teachers sought to show how many individuals artificially elevated the habits of their own ethnic groups and minority groups manifested ethnocentrism in efforts to advance their own cultural virtues. Teachers noted how predominant groups disparaged the speech patterns of other groups (Banks 1975, 57–58).

To reduce feelings of superiority among students, teachers in ethnic studies sought to show that groups maintained economic resources or political power irrespective of their ability to contribute to the society. Furthermore, the students learned that ethnic groups did not think of their neighborhoods as culturally deprived just because they were different. Teachers in ethnic studies taught the students that victors wrote history using abstractions such as deprivation to justify the domination (Banks 1975, 64–75).

Rather than teach children to accept the views of the dominant society, teachers designed ethnic studies around decision-making and social action skills. This was to create students who could take affirmative actions to resolve social issues. In this spirit, they sought to equip the students to clarify their own values. One author noted that, in some cultural settings, accepted school values such as obedience to commands from police officers was abnormal. In other settings, virtues such as honesty may be inappropriate. As a result, the process of values clarification became an important aspect of the teaching method (Banks 1975, 28–29; 103–107).

Underlying ethnic studies was the belief that the antidote to racial discrimination was the virtue of tolerance. Unfortunately, it seemed that, in ethnic studies, tolerance superseded any group's values. The result was all views, even religious ones, appeared as equals. The only unifying ideal was an almost aggressive acceptance of diversity that, if accepted, made pluralism impossible. Ironically, in 1974 a group of parents in Charleston, West Virginia, made this criticism while protesting the selection of several new and so-called multiethnic textbooks.

The schools in West Virginia are organized in a county-wide system. Charleston is the state capital and it lies within Kanawha County. In 1974 the Kanawha County school board selected the texts according to state guidelines asking for representation of the viewpoints, the attitudes, the values, and the contributions of different ethnic groups that make up the United States. The texts came from such reputable firms as D.C. Heath Company and Scott-Foresman. A textbook selection committee chose the books from a list approved by the West Virginia Department of Education (Candor 1976).

One school board member and a group of parents complained

that the books threatened belief in God, made patriotism appear foolish, portrayed ethical norms as dependent on the situation, and made slang appear as acceptable as standard English. News of the protest received national attention for several months (Cowan 1975).

The Kanawha County School Board member who criticized the texts stated frequently that the selections in the books advocated a form of relativism that undercut all values. Nonetheless, educators refused to see the Kanawha County textbook controversy as a criticism of multicultural education. The National Education Association held an inquiry while the controversy was taking place. The commission decided that people from Appalachia had their own culture and resisted ideas from the outside. The NEA panel concluded that the West Virginians could profit from more multicultural education. In 1986 Edward B. Jenkinson called the controversy in West Virginia the first schoolbook war. He said the battle spread to other cities around the United States as conservatives tried to censor texts (Jenkinson 1986, 12–14). Several newspaper commentators attributed the protest in West Virginia to the fact that stories by famous African American authors appeared in the textbooks. Evidence to show the presence of racism abounded throughout Kanawha County (Cowan 1975).

While religious fundamentalists resisted multicultural education, many African Americans approved of it. Not surprisingly, in 1977 the Association for Supervision and Curriculum Development (ASCD) called multicultural education a tool to eliminate discrimination with regard to race, sex, class, and handicaps. The ASCD said that its affection for democracy led the organization to commit itself to the process of ensuring that all curriculum materials offered a realistic treatment of cultural pluralism (Grant 1977, 1).

According to the ASCD, multicultural education was the recognition of cultural pluralism. This meant that teachers and students came to prize diversity, develop understandings of cultural patterns, respect individuals of all cultures, and develop productive interactions among people of diverse cultural groups. ASCD urged multicultural programs to show how groups influenced each other to combat the view that groups live in isolation. ASCD predicated its faith in multicultural education on a belief in the strength of diversity. As a result, ASCD called for the deliberate advancement of what it called diversification. This meant that schools had to provide opportunities for students and teachers to encounter different ethnic and cultural groups (Grant 1977, 3–5).

Although the ASCD offered multicultural education as a means to end discrimination, it could appear as a substitute for physical integration. As described in chapter seven, the superintendent of Dayton's Catholic schools used multicultural education to teach children to be tolerant of other groups when he could not reorganize the schools. More important, overzealous application of multicultural education sometimes diverted school people from the democratic goals it was supposed to enhance (Thomas 1981, 13).

M. Donald Thomas, superintendent of schools in Salt Lake City honored by the NAACP for promoting equity in the schools, complained that the concern for cultural pluralism had gone mad. Thomas thought the problems derived from seven tendencies. First, the view that schools should offer separate courses according to ethnic interest such as black studies for black students separated the children rather than brought them together. Second, misinterpretation of federal court decisions about bilingual education led school districts to hire people based on ethnic origin rather than on the teachers' ability to meet the needs of the children. Third, Thomas feared a view of moral relativism pervaded programs of cultural relativism and taught children to accept behavior such as cheating or lying that undercut good human relationships. Fourth, Thomas contended that Christian evangelicals used the arguments of pluralism to reintroduce school prayer and to censor school texts. Fifth, the trend toward mini-courses and real life courses reduced the time for serious educational endeavors. Sixth, Thomas claimed that teachers tried to survey so many ethnic groups that the children received only a cursory view of different practices with little substance. Finally, Thomas thought cultural pluralism encouraged special interest groups to plead for special attention, ignoring the needs of the entire school district (Thomas 1981, 13–18).

While Thomas warned about the excesses of multicultural education, he did not disparage its aims. He agreed that children should know more about diverse cultures. Like multicultural educators, he believed such knowledge would reduce racism. Unfortunately, teaching children about different ethnic groups is the least effective way to reduce prejudice. Although the children know better, their understanding does not influence their behavior (Allport 1958, 451).

Curriculum Aims and Racial Integration

Individualized education, magnet schools, and ethnic studies did not offer an explanation of why different people had to live and work together. These approaches could advance desegregation, but they could support segregation as well. Interestingly, few school people adopted any approach wholeheartedly. Instead, they offered what they considered a sound curriculum. To this, they added some activities for developing human interrelationships. An illustration of such a tendency may be found in the Ohio State Department of Education's 1984 publication, the *Curriculum Guide for Successful Teaching in a Desegregated Setting*.

The director of the Division of Equal Educational Opportunities selected representatives from several school districts in Ohio that had gone through racial desegregation to form a Desegregation Teaching Strategies Task Force. The task force identified the goals, the objectives, the activities, and the settings that led to what the guide called quality instruction (Ohio Department of Education 1984).

The task force divided the lesson outlines into five general areas: assignment practices, counseling needs, discipline needs, security and safety, and special curricular activities. The section on assignment practices discussed the importance of a team approach to placing students in different classrooms and in special programs. The aim in this section was that student placements should derive from objective criteria such as assessment of student needs from cumulative records, standardized tests, and parental interviews. Once placed, the school staff used formal tests and student activities to evaluate the student's progress.

In the section on counseling needs, the task force offered eleven plans designed to help prepare the counseling staff to work with a heterogeneous group of students. These plans recommended assigning less than six hundred elementary students or three hundred secondary students to each counselor. They suggested hiring minority counselors for minority youth.

The aim of the section on discipline and security affirmed the need to establish guidelines on discipline and the importance of publishing them in a handbook. This section called for teachers and administrators to enforce rules equally and consistently. The authors included several suggestions on how to unite the teachers, the parents, and the children's peers together in a consideration of the building's goals.

The section on safety offered suggestions to reduce problems on the buses and on school property. Finally, the section on special curricular activities offered suggestions for a range of activities that included career education and multicultural experiences. For example, as part of multicultural research, students had to complete the last names of famous black Americans when given a series of clues. Another lesson asked the students to define the words "racial" and "ethnic."

Thus, Ohio's *Curriculum Guide for Successful Teaching in a Desegregated Setting* offered practical suggestions that the members of the task force thought would improve school life. Unfortunately, the suggestions were random and their arrangement arbitrary. That is, the curriculum guide did not come from a thoughtful analysis of the social conditions that made desegregation necessary. Instead, the curriculum makers assumed the teachers would have racially mixed classes. Within that context, the curricularists suggested ways to meet the children's needs. They made administrative suggestions. They recommended some student choice or individualization and included multicultural education even if its supporters would not recognize their model in the offerings.

While it appears miseducative, such an eclectic approach served the political situation school people faced. First, the public had ambiguous feelings about racial desegregation. For example, in 1977, during the seventh month of a court-mandated plan for cross-district busing in Dayton, a researcher asked eighty-two black parents and 180 white parents what they felt about busing. In general, these Daytonians agreed that it is beneficial for "children to get to know children of the other major racial groups in the area." White adults disapproved of busing, which would cause meetings among children of different races. On the other hand, black parents approved of busing (Kimble 1980). Other nationwide public opinion polls revealed similar ambivalence (Rossell 1990).

Second, Ohio's curriculum guide for desegregated schools reflected the practical political compromises that went on in any school district. At best, every interest group sought representation in every proposal and their ideas prevailed in proportion to the pressure they could exert. As a result, schools reproduced social interests much more than they changed society. This was true in public and Catholic schools. Things may be different in cases where people set up independent alternate schools. However, the history of Dayton's Center City School shows that the desire to provide individual attention may leave the school people unable to become countercultural forces.

Other educational historians, such as Herbert M. Kliebard, have come to similar conclusions. Kliebard concludes *The Struggle for the American Curriculum* with the observation that no group could clearly win control of the curriculum. Instead, he notes, all the tendencies of our culture, whether good or bad, were represented in the schools. He says the schools had intellectual and anti-intellectual tendencies; they became places of liberation and of restraint; and the schools encouraged social reform while they perpetuated social inequality (Kliebard 1992).

The case of the racial desegregation of Dayton schools suggests that Kliebard is correct. The curricula chosen for the various schools reflected the contradictory aspects of the culture they served. In the African American neighborhood called Inner West, the Individually Guided Education program served segregationist aims. In the adjacent neighborhood of Dayton View, the same program served racial integration. Later, the Dayton city schools offered a system of magnet schools to soften the order to desegregate. Yet, to offset problems of higher costs and charges of elitism, the curriculum within those schools resembled that of other nonmagnet schools. Finally, such programs as multicultural education enabled children to learn about people from different racial groups while they remained in their neighborhood schools. Perhaps schools could work no other way.

References

Allport, Gordon W. *The Nature of Prejudice*. New York: Doubleday & Co.

Anderson, Robert. 1994. Interview with author, 21 September.

Bahner, John, et al. 1975. *The Learning Climate*. Dayton, Ohio: Charles F. Kettering Foundation.

Banks, James. 1975. *Teaching Strategies for Ethnic Studies*. Boston: Allyn and Bacon.

Belcher, Ellen. 1993. "Teachers Strike Didn't Have to Happen," *Dayton Daily News*, 15 April.

Belden Associates. 1973. "Individually Guided Program." A national evaluation conducted for /I/D/E/A/, Dayton, Ohio.

Boyer, Ernest. 1983. *High School*. New York: Harper and Row Publishers.

Candor, Catherine. 1976. "A History of the Kanawha County Textbook Controversy." Ph.D. ED.D. thesis. Virginia Polytechnic Institute and State University.

Caras, Gregory. 1994. Interview with author, 15 June.

Cowan, Paul. 1975. "Holy War in West Virginia," *Village Voice*, 9 December.

Cremin, Lawrence. 1974. "The Free School Movement," *Today's Education*, September–October: 71–74.

Cuban, Larry. 1993. *How Teachers Taught 1890–1990*. New York: Teachers College Press.

DeBrosse, Jim. 1995. "Williams—Living Proof of New Ways," *Dayton Daily News*, 6 April: 6A.

Fife, Brian. 1992. *Desegregation in American Schools*. New York: Praeger.

Fleury, Bernard. 1993. *Whatever Happened to IGE?* Lanham, Maryland: University Press of America.

Flynn, Adianne. 1991. "Auditor Lays Shortfall to Mistake," *Dayton Daily News*, 27 July.

Gies, Frederick. 1994. Interview with author, 29 September.

Goodlad, John. 1975. *Dynamics of Educational Change*. New York: McGraw-Hill.

Grant, Carl A., ed. 1977. *Multicultural Education: Commitments, Issues, and Applications*. Washington, D.C.: Association for Supervision and Curriculum Development.

Harty, Rosemary. 1991. "Cuts in Dayton Schools," *Dayton Daily News*, 22 May.

Hochschild, Jennifer. 1984. *The New American Dilemma*. New Haven: Yale University Press.

/I/D/E/A/ 1971. *IGE Learning Modes*. Dayton, Ohio: Charles F. Kettering Foundation.

Jenkinson, Edward B. 1986. *The Schoolbook Protest Movement*. Bloomington, Ind.: Phi Delta Kappa Educational Foundation.

Kimble, Charles. 1980. "Factors Affecting Adult's Attitudes Toward School Desegregation," *Journal of Social Psychology* 110: 211–218.

Kirp, David. 1982. *Just Schools*. Berkeley: University of California Press.

Kliebard, Herbert M. 1992. *The Struggle for the American Curriculum 1893–1958*. New York: Routledge.

Madison, Nathaniel. 1987. "City Board Splits," *Dayton Daily News*, 16 January.

McKenzie Group. 1992. "Community Survey Results and Findings." Dayton: Dayton Public Schools.

Ohio Department of Education. 1974. *Providing K–12 Multi-Cultural Curricular Experiences*. Columbus, Ohio: Office of Equal Educational Opportunity.

———. 1984. *Curriculum Guide for Successful Teaching in a Desegregated Setting*. Columbus, Ohio: Division of Equal Educational Opportunities.

Orfield, Gary. 1978. *Must We Bus?* Washington, D.C.: Brookings Institution.

Paden, Jon S. 1978. *Reflections for the Future*. Dayton, Ohio: Charles F. Kettering Foundation.

———. 1994. Interview with author, 27 July.

Quarter Notes. 1987. Dayton Public Schools, Winter.

Rossell, Christine. 1990. *The Carrot or the Stick*. Philadelphia: Temple University Press.

Smith, Franklin. 1989. "Application for Federal Assistance." Dayton Public Schools: Superintendent's Office.

Thomas, M. Donald. 1981. *Pluralism Gone Mad*. Bloomington, Ind.: Phi Delta Kappa Educational Foundation.

Towers Perrin. 1992. "Management Study of the Dayton Public Schools," 11 August.

Welker, Robert. 1992. *Teacher as Expert*. Albany: State University of New York Press.

Westlake, Rebecca. 1995. Comment to author, 16 May.

Willis, Charles. 1974. *What We Have Learned about the /I/D/E/A/ Change Program for Individually Guided Education*. Dayton, Ohio: Charles F. Kettering Foundation.

Chapter Ten
The Politics of Caring

As courts and the U.S. Office of Education required school districts to begin racial desegregation, educators constructed special programs to help children who lived with low income families. Using words of helping and caring to justify many expensive educational programs, the educators followed two different directions. One direction was to change the child. The second was to change the system of schools and human service agencies. Although these programs showed limited success, educators said that the failure of a program showed the need for better information and increased financial support.

In the 1960s, after the U.S. Supreme Court declared racial segregation illegal, private schools throughout the South advertised curricula and teaching methods designed for white children. Although some scientists supported the contention that mental abilities followed racial lines, most educators rejected this notion. Nonetheless, educators believed that economically deprived children learned differently than affluent middle-class children. Calling this retardation cultural deprivation or the results of a culture of poverty, educators created special techniques to offset its effects.

The theory of cultural deprivation changed the long-standing American view of poverty. During the nineteenth century, inspirational writers such as Horatio Alger told millions of young children that poverty offered the best preparation for success in adult life. These authors wrote novels and stories telling young people that wealth often spoiled rich children while adversity enabled poor children to develop habits of industry and trustworthiness. The messages from these novels appeared in such school texts as the McGuffey readers well into the twentieth century. Further, artists capitalized on the popular distrust of wealth. For example, F. Scott Fitzgerald contrasted a formerly lower-class hero, Gatsby, to rich people who were too self-centered to recognize virtue in other people. However, by the 1960s, the popular view of poverty changed.

In 1959 anthropologist Oscar Lewis noted similarities in family structure, interpersonal relations, time orientations, value systems, and spending patterns among people in lower-class settlements in London, Glasgow, Paris, Harlem, and Mexico City. By 1961 he offered an extensive description of the personality traits formed by what he called the culture of poverty. These included a disregard for savings, a lack of respect for privacy, a tendency to use violence in the training of children, an acceptance of early initiations into sex and consensual marriages, a disposition toward authoritarianism, and a present-time orientation with little ability to defer gratification (Lewis 1961, xxvi).

Lewis recognized that some traits of the culture of poverty extended into the middle class, but the same actions differed in each level. Drinking among the middle classes was a social amenity, but among the poor, alcohol hid failure. Lewis decided that the differences derived from lower-class people's efforts to solve the problems their poverty caused. Unable to obtain credit from banks, they organized informal credit devices or borrowed from local money lenders at high interest. Unable to afford doctors, they came to distrust hospitals and relied on home remedies (Lewis 1961, xxvii).

Lewis based his conclusions on his many book-length studies in which he allowed the often eloquent subjects of his study to reveal themselves. In this sense he was more a novelist than a social scientist, asking his readers to admire the strengths his characters portrayed. To show the strength of the human spirit, Lewis separated the fact of poverty from the culture of poverty. He felt that the East European Jew or the members of lower castes in India could be destitute without being part of the culture of poverty. He believed that people created a culture of poverty when they lacked a sense of religious or social identity. For him, the culture of poverty showed that people existing at the margins of society were not pathological. Consequently, Lewis estimated there were only about six or ten million people living in the culture of poverty in the United States. Other authors who followed Lewis's idea of people forming separate cultures within lower-class enclaves did not restrict the meaning of the phrase.

In 1962 Herbert Gans described life among the white ethnic residents of the West End of Boston before urban renewal destroyed the neighborhood. Gans found a coherent culture reminiscent of a country village in this urban area. In 1965 Jack Weller applied Gans's ideas to the people in Whitesville, West Virginia, where he was a minister in a United Presbyterian Church. According to Weller, the culture of Appalachia emphasized an unwillingness to accept help, a sense of fatalism, a desire for action, and close ties to a small group. He added that these cultural traits appeared whenever people existed in an environment that limited or defeated them (Weller 1965, 5–45).

The writers who applied the catchy term, a culture of poverty, to any person suffering from economic deprivation did so for good reasons. They wanted to inspire affluent people to seek an end to poverty. In the process, though, they made poor people appear sick. For example, although Michael Harrington led President John Kennedy to launch a war on poverty, he did it by popularizing the view that poverty's restrictions warped poor people. In 1962 Harrington estimated that forty to fifty million Americans lived in poverty. Ironically, for at least three reasons, the people who enjoyed a high standard of living could not see them. First, poor people lived in places that middle-class people never entered. Second, clothes were inexpensive, so they dressed like the more affluent. Third, poor people lacked a voice. Political parties did not represent their interests. Trade unions did not stand up for their rights. Lobbies did not campaign for their legislative program (Harrington 1962, 9–13).

During the 1930s, Americans created a welfare state to reduce the mass impoverishment of the depression. Unfortunately, Harrington said, all welfare programs, including social security, helped the poor least of all. To him, the greatest tragedy was that their environment and values prevented economically deprived people from taking advantage of the opportunities schools provided. Harrington contended that poverty was self-perpetuating. Crammed into unhealthy slums, the poor sickened more than members of other social classes. As a result, they could not hold steady jobs. Unable to afford better housing or food or medical attention, they seemed destined to spiral ever downward. The result was a psychology of the poor which led to more homes without fathers and a fear of authority that contributed to more failure (Harrington 1962, 16–23).

Although Harrington used the same term, culture of poverty, as Oscar Lewis, he meant it as a way to describe the way poverty defeated people. As a result, Harrington rejected the idea that poverty prepared a child for success, and he lacked the scientific caution of Oscar Lewis. Harrington had a cause. He told well fed, optimistic Americans that it was intolerable for unnecessary poverty to twist the spirits and maim the bodies of millions of people (Harrington 1962, 24).

Harrington noted that many types of people suffered from poverty. However, he said that African Americans comprised 25 percent of the invisible poor. Consequently, any policy of social regeneration that excluded blacks would exclude other impoverished groups such as Appalachians and the aged. He concluded that the ultimate solution to poverty was racial and social integration (Harrington 1962, 81).

While Harrington used the term, "culture of poverty," as a rhetorical device, Frank Riessman used the term in 1962 to delineate educational strategies to meet the needs of these children. Although the title of his book was *The Culturally Deprived Child*, Riessman said that he disliked the term "culturally deprived." It implied the children lacked a culture, but Riessman thought these children had their own culture with several positive characteristics. He accepted the term because it was popular, and he frequently reversed it to the "deprived culture."

Riessman believed that a cultural approach revealed to teachers the motives of students who appeared unwilling to learn. For example, he discounted the view that the culture of the deprived discredited education. He thought that deprived people stressed the importance of vocational training to rise out of the slums. Teachers did not recognize this orientation as one that appreciated education, because the people did not value learning for its own sake. In this regard, Riessman believed that teachers had to understand their students, not love them. He complained about guidance counselors who honestly deplored discrimination yet wanted to protect the students who came to them for help. These counselors advised lower-class black students not to pursue professional training because of the trauma that might result from the difficulty of obtaining suitable employment. Riessman said counselors should have inspired the black youth to try to break the discrimination. This would have given the children of the deprived culture the respect they wanted (Riessman 1962, 1–24).

Riessman asserted that economically deprived children learned through the physical manipulation of objects. He advised teachers to use role playing to teach history or to use games of shopping to teach arithmetic. He told teachers to counter the anti-intellectualism of the deprived culture by showing the practical applications of abstract ideas. Schools should hire more male teachers and combat the polite feminism of the school, he thought. If male teachers and masculine literature stressed vigor and courage, deprived people would admire the school (Riessman 1962, 25–34).

At best, Riessman was guilty of over-sociologizing. That is, he drew educational conclusions too readily from sociological theories. At worst, Riessman disregarded whether his assumptions about children who came from lower-class homes were true or not. He attended more to the practical suggestions teachers might follow. Despite these shortcomings, other educators imitated him. Most important, the U.S. Congress supported their efforts.

Cultural Deprivation Theory Justifies
Compensatory Education

In 1964 the U.S. Congress opened the War on Poverty. The Job Corps offered vocational training and employment. The Community Action Program offered money to help low-income people to fight poverty themselves. VISTA recruited college students to work with low-income people in the United States. To direct these efforts, the Congress gave the Office of Economic Opportunity (OEO) emergency powers (Zigler and Muenchow 1992, 2).

By midyear, the OEO had a surplus of $26 million in its Community Action Programs. Cities were unwilling to accept these funds because the programs it sponsored seemed to encourage financial mismanagement, popular discontent, and Communist infiltration. Faced with this problem, the director, Sargent Shriver, asked his family pediatrician and other advisors to think about a program to help poor children. They devised a proposal to improve children's physical health through such things as immunizations and neurological examinations. The proposal sought to offer success experiences enabling the children to supplant the patterns of failure they had established. An important innovation included the parents of the children so they could feel the benefits of success along with their children (Zigler and Muenchow 1992, 7–20).

The initial proposal for Head Start did not call the children culturally deprived. Several members of the Planning Committee wanted to include that term in the proposal. Other members felt the term was a misnomer. In the spirit of compromise, the committee wrote the proposal emphasizing the diverse patterns that characterized the children's behavior (Zigler and Muenchow 1992, 20–21).

President Lyndon Johnson heartily approved of Head Start. In the summer of 1965 he allocated almost $90 million to serve over half a million children in a national summer Head Start program. To begin the 1965 summer program, Mrs. Johnson held a White House tea in which she announced Head Start would reach out to children whose low-income homes had damaged their cognitive systems. Although some participants cringed at the excessive hopes politicians put on Head Start, the exaggerated claims advanced the program. Before the summer program even began, the president said he budgeted $150 million for a year-round program (Zigler and Muenchow 1992, 22–24).

Federal money came from other sources as well. In 1965 the Elementary and Secondary Education Act, Public Law 89-10, helped school districts to improve their educational programs. These included preschool programs that met the special needs of educationally deprived children. The act extended funds to educational centers, universities, and state departments of education to conduct research and to improve elementary and secondary education. The effect was startling. Federal funds supporting elementary and secondary education rose in one year from $890,685,000 to $2,408,209,000. Much of the money went to help children who came from the culture of poverty (Bailey and Mosher 1968, vii–viii).

In drafting the guidelines for the appropriation of monies, officials in the Office of Education emphasized educational services and discouraged construction of school facilities. They estimated these projects would involve 5.4 million children around the country and would cost about $200 per child. Consequently, they designed project application forms that emphasized support for educationally disadvantaged children and discouraged federal monies going into any school district's general funds (Bailey and Mosher 1968, 114–123).

In the first year of operation, the Elementary and Secondary Education Act directed $987.6 million to the education of educationally deprived children. Of this, $11 million went to the education of handicapped children. Fifty-two percent of this money was for instruction and two-thirds of that was for remedial reading and language arts instruction. About 3,600 new school libraries opened. Nearly $75 million went for such special projects as reducing dropping out of school and improving remedial reading (Bailey and Mosher 1968, 114–123).

Helping and Power

Critics such as William Ryan noticed that efforts to help low-income people seemed to reinforce the position of the people who extended the aid. In schools in Boston, Massachusetts, and New Haven, Connecticut, Ryan found the folklore of cultural deprivation forestalled questions about recruitment of teachers, achievement of racial integration, or school governance. Ryan said that educationists advocated Head Start, smaller classes, teaching machines, or Swahili to change the child, yet they resisted such suggestions to change the system as opening decision-making to community lay people (Ryan 1971, 34–35).

While Ryan described how the educators' intentions to help the children justified their access to power and federal money, his description is simplistic. Despite Ryan's criticism, the idea of cultural deprivation could advance the racial integration of schools. An example is the work of Martin Deutsch, a professor of early childhood, who thought that low-income children learned differently than affluent children. Deutsch believed that racial integration of schools was essential to the creation of a democratic social order. Further, he warned school people not to group the students of similar abilities together. This would result in racially segregated classrooms within a racially integrated building. Instead, he recommended the school use the notion of cultural disadvantage to find ways to educate diverse groups (Deutsch 1967, 281–294).

In Dayton, at times, cultural deprivation theory advanced the racial integration of schools. To prepare for cross-district busing, Dayton public schools sponsored programs in interethnic sensitivity for administrators and faculty. In hopes of improving interpersonal relations, the session coordinators taught the participants that children coming from disadvantaged homes think differently than children coming from advantaged circumstances. As the building administrators and faculty learned the reasons for the apparent rebelliousness of disadvantaged children, they could become more tolerant and better able to offer constructive lesson plans.

In part, of course, Ryan is correct. The idea of cultural deprivation could reinforce the authority of an established bureaucracy. However, citizen groups outside education could use the rationale of cultural deprivation to undercut the authority of the established school board. In the Dayton Model Cities Demonstration Project described in chapter four, different groups used the idea of cultural disadvantage to reinforce their own power.

Model Cities in Dayton began as a traditional urban project. Later, it became a black separatist program. In 1967 Dayton's city administration set up a Special Committee on Urban Renewal (SCOUR). The committee applied for a Model Cities grant to improve the quality of life of the residents of Dayton's Inner West section. SCOUR's 1967 application said that compensatory education services should extend from preschool through upper secondary level. These programs would make up for nonsupportive homes, deprived environments, and prevailing disinterest in school success. The premise of the 1967 application was that there was something wrong with the homes and the neighborhoods in which the children lived. While SCOUR added that racial discrimination compounded these problems, they expressed confidence that intervention strategies could overcome these flaws (Special Committee on Urban Renewal 1967).

After the U.S. Department of Housing and Urban Development approved Dayton's 1967 application, a group of African Americans complained that the city administration overlooked the wishes of the people living in the target area. They demanded that the residents on the Model Cities planning council decide how to spend the federal money coming to the project. Ironically, the activists and the members of the planning council had only narrow ties to the community themselves. Yet they called their administration a form of community control. Most important, these activists said they should have authority because the residents suffered from cultural deprivation.

In 1969 the black activists wrote the Model Cities comprehensive plan attributing the educational problems found in the Inner West area to discrimination. They saw discrimination even in equal treatment. For example, the 1969 Model Cities comprehensive plan acknowledged that the Dayton Board of Education spread its budget evenly among the schools throughout the city. The activists thought this was unfair because the children in the Model Cities neighborhood had special needs and problems. Consequently, an equal portion was not enough to enable these children to achieve at the same level as students from other homes.

Furthermore, in 1969 the black separatists argued the residents of Inner West Dayton suffered three types of educational discrimination. First, the residents played no role in policy-making or administrative decisions. For example, the comprehensive plan asserted that none of the seven members of Dayton's Board of Education school board lived in Inner West Dayton. Further, Model Cities planning council members concluded that the forbidding facts of the school board's organizational structure and operation discouraged community involvement. Second, the 1969 Model Cities plan argued that schools delivered inadequate services to Inner West Dayton. The proof was the low achievement of students, the high number who drop out, and the few students going on to college. Third, the 1969 Model Cities plan contended that Inner West residents could not use those city services that existed. That is, the 1969 comprehensive plan asserted that since the school board did not communicate or share power with the parents, the parents felt alienated and, in turn, the children did not identify with the goals of the schools.

In the 1969 Model Cities comprehensive plan, the black activists exaggerated the failings of the city school board to justify their own desire for power. First, the school board did not ignore African Americans. Consistently since 1954, at least one black person was an elected member of the board. Although none of the seven mem-

bers of the school board lived in the Inner West section in 1969, one
member lived nearby on the west side of Dayton. Further, in 1969
the new superintendent tried to remedy past problems by hiring
African American administrators and introducing black studies and
ethnic sensitivity programs into the schools. The Model Cities comprehensive plan did not mention these improvements. They wanted
to give the planning council a reason to control the area schools.
They wanted to control the finances of the schools in the Model
Cities area. They wanted to select staff, principals, and teachers for
the schools. Consequently, Model Cities black activists argued that
children in slum schools needed schools run by community residents and staffed by African American teachers and administrators.
They argued that the children had to see black people as powerful
and as role models. In this way, the black activists added, the deprived children would see that schools were for black children and
for white children.

While the planning council made such an agreement with the
city commission, Dayton's school board never agreed to give the
Model Cities planning council the power to control schools in its
area (Goodman 1969). However, the point is that, despite Ryan's
assertion that the concept of cultural deprivation reinforced the institutions as they existed, any group seeking power and authority
could use the idea to its advantage.

Compensatory Education Fails

No matter how it was applied, the idea of cultural deprivation reinforced the American belief that schools could solve the problems of
poverty. In this case, it was short lived. Although the federal support of educational programs for educational disadvantaged youth
began in 1964, almost immediately studies began to question the
policy. Among these critical studies, the report on *Equality of
Educational Opportunity* that appeared in July 1966 was the most
prestigious.

Directed by James Coleman, *Equality of Educational Opportunity* made a plea for the racial integration of schools. The report
noted that most American students attended segregated schools. Yet
minority group students had larger classes, fewer books, and poorer
facilities and programs. The teachers of Negro students had poorer

preparation than did teachers of white students. Most important, the so-called Coleman report found that the educational progress of a poorly prepared minority student improved in a racially integrated setting. Moreover, such racial integration did not hinder the performance of well-prepared white students (Bailey and Mosher 1968, 142–159).

On the other hand, this report raised questions about the ability of any school to influence the academic achievement of students. Buried in the middle of the summary was the following statement: "The first finding is that schools are remarkably similar in the way they relate to the achievement of their pupils when the socioeconomic background of the students is taken into account" (Coleman 1966, 21). Although the meaning of this finding was not immediately clear to uninformed readers, it implied that schools could not compensate for children's home lives. As a result, it threatened the established American belief that improved educational equality would result in more evenly distributed educational achievement.

During the 1966–67 academic year, the Carnegie Corporation supported a seminar for members of the Harvard University faculty to discuss the Coleman report's findings. Some papers presented in the seminar questioned whether programs to improve schools would improve the students' achievement. These papers noted that no matter what was done to make schools better for poor children, the social backgrounds of students who came from middle-class, educationally oriented families enabled them to outstrip students who came from deprived backgrounds. Consequently, two participants suggested that the federal government launch long-term research projects to decide the direction of national, state, and local educational policy (Mosteller and Moynihan 1972).

Unfortunately, the federal government had little experience directing educational research or any other type of study. Until the launching of Sputnik in 1957, the federal government offered only modest support for research in science. In 1950 the National Science Foundation received $3.5 million. By 1966 this budget had grown to $480 million. Furthermore, President Kennedy established the Office of Science and Technology to coordinate science activities throughout the government. This model of federal control of research and development for science was the one that influenced planning for the federal control of educational research (Sproull et al. 1978, 13–16).

However, education and science were different. Unlike science, education did not have a strong knowledge base, for two important reasons. First, people who conducted research in education did not talk with school teachers, and when the researchers were open, teachers ignored the studies. Second, schools responded to many different constituencies that would try to direct the research. As a result, important research questions often went unanswered. These problems were less severe among scientific institutions so they could build a base of studies to direct practical affairs. Nonetheless, in 1964 the U.S. Office of Education set up centers for research in education. It established laboratories to apply the research findings. Finally, it created an information center to distribute the results (Sproull et al. 1978, 16–18).

The federal government sought to organize educational research as it tried to increase the influence of planning in all programs. In 1965 the U.S. Bureau of the Budget required every federal agency to establish a central office for program analysis, planning, and budgeting. The Office of Economic Opportunity (OEO), which controlled Head Start, complied early by establishing an Office of Research, Planning, Programs, and Evaluation. In 1968 the new evaluation division of OEO proposed a nationwide study of the Head Start program (Zigler and Muenchow 1992, 60–61).

The results of the first study of Head Start cast more doubt on the power of education to solve social ills. Ohio University and the Westinghouse Learning Corporation joined to conduct a study of 1,980 Head Start children and compare them to 1,983 children in the control group. The children were in first, second, or third grade. They took a variety of standardized achievement tests and three attitudinal measures. Completed in less than a year, the study concluded that Head Start did not produce widespread cognitive and affective gains. As a result, the report could not describe the benefits of Head Start as satisfactory (Zigler and Muenchow 1992, 64–72).

While some researchers complained about inadequacies in the studies showing the failure of educational programs, other researchers accepted the reports on face value. In 1969 Arthur Jensen argued in the *Harvard Educational Review* that genetics predisposed students to levels of intelligence and scholastic achievement. He began his article with the following sentence: "Compensatory education has been tried and apparently has failed" (Jensen 1969).

The controversy over the value of compensatory education offered President Richard Nixon a way to solve one of his own political problems. Throughout 1969 President Nixon vetoed several bills calling for increased appropriations to education. National education groups resisted these vetoes and used them to criticize the administration. To relieve this ill will and create a distinctive educational policy, Nixon chose to emphasize research. On 3 March 1970 Nixon proposed the creation of a National Institute of Education. He said the federal government should not simply spend money on education, but should find out which programs offer the most return for the investment. This would be the job of the Institute (Sproull et al. 1978, 33–34).

By the time Nixon made his speech, compensatory education had become big business. Attracted by funds from the Elementary and Secondary Education Act, corporations and entrepreneurs produced a wide range of materials to help disadvantaged children. These materials assumed that deficits in the children's background caused school failure. For example, curriculum specialists prepared materials to expose the children to sights, objects, and sounds not found in the low-income, urban neighborhoods. Books and lessons included material about minorities and urban life. These texts emphasized the relevance of school for urban children. With programmed learning machines, children learned individually and avoided the shame of public failure (Rees 1968, 100–107).

Beyond producing materials for children, businesses published materials to prepare teachers to work in the inner city. For example, in 1969 Science Research Associates, a subsidiary of IBM, published an "Inner City Simulation Laboratory" designed by a professor from Ohio State University. The assumption behind the kit was that teachers became frustrated when they did not understand the ways the background of the disadvantaged children set up school failure. The package containing the kit reinforced this message. It had a large picture of a surly looking black ten-year-old male sitting at a classroom desk about to launch a paper airplane.

The "Inner City Simulation Laboratory" kit consisted of a series of movies, a data book, and replicas of student permanent records complete with pictures of the children. These records described a fictitious city school where almost all the children were members of low-income minority families, many of whom received public assistance. Instructions enclosed in the kit asked prospective teachers to do several things: construct sociograms of the interactions in the classroom, describe alternatives for helping children with language problems, decide the children's apparent self-image, and predict their resulting expectations of the school. The incidents with the students revealed problems with aggressiveness, inability to defer gratification, and concrete rather than abstract orientations. The kit suggested that parents exacerbated the problems because they resorted to violence in disciplining the children, showed no interest in school, or lived away from the children. According to the laboratory kit, these conditions made the teaching different in inner city schools than it was in affluent suburbs (Cruickshank 1969).

In developing special materials for inner city schools, curricularists followed widely accepted views about the early socialization of children and school failure. These explanations fell into four categories. One type of explanation was that the authoritarianism of parents coupled with their early withdrawal from supervision caused children to reject all adult authority. A second category held that the early experiences of African American children caused them to feel distrust of other people and the children carried this distrust to their schools. A third opinion was that African Americans developed child-rearing practices during slavery that discouraged personal achievement, and they carried these practices on to the present. The fourth category was the viewpoint that African Americans tended to have matriarchal families. Lacking a father figure, male children became impulsive and immaturely dependent. The result was school problems. Although many researchers subscribed to one or more of these views, there was little evidence that these characteristics appeared among children of poverty more than among affluent children. Nor was there proof that differences in personality caused school failure (Katz 1969).

In 1966 Scott Cummings distributed questionnaires to sixth-grade and twelfth-grade students and sixth-grade and high school teachers in five metropolitan areas in Connecticut: Bridgeport, Hartford, New Haven, Stamford, and Waterbury. Cummings found some support for three interpretations to explain school failure. That is, family socialization experiences did seem to exert some influence on the development of children's cognitive skills but much less than proponents of cultural deprivation theory suggested. Cummings also found that teachers unfairly categorized the children's academic skills, as proponents of the self-fulfilling prophecy would expect. However, he could not find that this negative labeling hurt the children's cognitive development. Finally, Cummings found that tracking and ability grouping reinforced social class and racial distinctions as Marxists contended. College preparatory classes appeared more often in schools with mostly white enrollments, and black students taking vocational courses felt their teachers and counselors treated them unfairly. Although all three interpretations appeared partially correct, intervention programs based on any interpretation could enjoy only limited success (Cummings 1977).

In the 1980s President Ronald Reagan's administration tried to repeal Title I of the Elementary and Secondary Education Act. The administration aimed to consolidate categorical programs such as funds for educationally disadvantaged children. In 1982 Reagan's budget proposal merged forty-four school programs into two packages totaling $4.4 billion. States would have used the funds for any authorized activities that they chose (Salomone 1986, 176). While the Congress approved a less radical measure, federal support for the education of culturally deprived children dwindled. For example, in the 1982 budget, the Reagan administration cut the proposed increases for Head Start from $125 million to $13 million. The administration reorganized Head Start, seeking to reduce the length of time children stayed in programs while increasing the number of children who attended (Zigler and Muenchow 1992, 191–199).

By 1988 projects such as Head Start regained popularity because of studies done in the late 1970s with small groups of children in more expensive and longer-lasting Head Start type programs. These children from low-income families achieved more academic success, were more likely to hold jobs as adults, and less likely to become delinquent or pregnant as adolescents than their counterparts without such preschool preparation. In the middle 1980s, studies of Head

Start programs showed similar results (Zigler and Muenchow 1992, 204–205).

Institutional Change as Compensatory Education

Though appropriations for project Head Start increased after Reagan left the presidency, educators turned to programs that sought changes in the institutions rather than alter the experiences of the children. Private philanthropies offered support. Instead of assuming the children should change, educators set out to reform businesses, schools, and social work agencies. They adopted the name, "children at risk," to suggest that contemporary helping service ignored the children.

This approach avoided the problem of trying to show that children failed because of their backgrounds, but it suffered from two similar problems. First, it was an article of faith that children faced unfriendly social structures. For example, the idea of a self-fulfilling prophecy popularized by the movie *My Fair Lady* and the play *Pygmalion* suggested that teachers caused children to fail by thinking of them as inept. However, studies such as those done by Paul Willis in 1977 found that children's peer groups in low-income areas discouraged academic success. Willis noted in a main case study and five comparative studies that as a result of a complex process, working-class children in England affirmed their own counter-culture and rebelled against schools and counselors. Despite the best efforts of people to help, the children became laborers like their parents (Willis 1977).

Second, the projects depended on the help of the people who directed the supposedly faulty institutions. Consequently, the people who profited from the system had to change such complex institutions as schools to serve social justice. While reform could serve the leaders' self interest, it could threaten other important goals such as academic achievement. Not surprisingly, as the proposed changes threatened the existing structures, imperiled groups tried to shift the project's direction. As a result, over time, the directors compromised with their critics, lost sight of the original goals, and set themselves up to fail. At least, this is what happened in Dayton.

In 1987 the Anne E. Casey Foundation in Greenwich, Connecticut, offered the city of Dayton and nine other American cities $20,000 each to develop proposals to respond to the needs of at-risk youth. The Casey Foundation named these programs "New Futures." The name signified that the Casey Foundation rejected the view that academic failure, dropping out, and teen pregnancy happened because children had low aptitudes, poor characters, or inadequate home lives. New Futures believed that the problems arose because community institutions failed to do what they could to equip children with the expectations, opportunities, and supports to become responsible and successful adults. The Casey Foundation wanted the cities to develop plans to enlist the leaders of local institutions in creating environments infused with the view that all young people were able and entitled to succeed (*New Futures* 1988, 1–5).

Dayton accepted the challenge and won the grant. On 4 March 1988 the Casey Foundation awarded Dayton ten million dollars to fund its proposal to reduce academic failure, teen pregnancy, and youth unemployment. Four other cities received similar awards. They included Lawrence, Massachusetts; Little Rock, Arkansas; Pittsburgh, Pennsylvania; and Savannah, Georgia (*New Futures* 1988, 2–3).

From local sources, the Dayton initiative raised another $10 million in matching funds for the five-year undertaking. Dayton's New Futures initiative enlisted eighteen business managers, local government and school officials, agency executives, and union leaders to serve on the Collaborative to act as a board of directors. The Collaborative chose the director of the Miami Valley Regional Planning Commission to become the chief staff person. She had directed the proposal-writing team and had extensive experience working with different groups in the Dayton area (Stenning 1994, 3–5).

New Futures wanted to build on the tradition of cooperation that existed among Dayton's human service agencies. Since 1974 the Miami Valley Regional Planning Commission had staffed a coalition of human service planning and funding organizations called the Partnership. In 1987 the partnership added an advisory board of community leaders called Dayton Area Council on Youth to address issues related to at-risk children throughout Montgomery County. New Futures hoped to bring these coalitions together, use the talents of local leadership, and reform institutions (*New Futures* 1988, 48–50).

Unlike the New Futures projects in other cities, Dayton's plan concentrated on the school district. The reason was simple. The superintendent of schools enjoyed the support and approval of business and community leaders. Further, in 1986 the superintendent issued a "Call for Excellence," listing reforms that New Futures sought. These included improving general academic performance, raising school attendance, encouraging school-based management, and involving the business community in the schools. As a result, it seemed reasonable to select intervention strategies focused on schools as delivery sites (*New Futures* 1988, 48–50).

The middle schools invited the most reform. In 1987–88 Dayton restructured the middle schools, leaving only seventh- and eighth-graders in the same building. Within the middle school buildings, teachers formed clusters or groups. Each cluster worked with a set of 150 students. Consequently, the Collaborative selected two of Dayton's middle schools whose principals sympathized with the aims of the project. Dayton public schools helped by offering to make several adjustments within those buildings (*New Futures* 1988, 85–90).

During the summer of 1988, before the project started, the district collected information about each student enrolled in the pilot schools to prepare individual learning plans. The school district obtained permission from the state department of education to offer extra tutoring supported by the Disadvantaged Pupil Program Fund. The district extended the school day in both buildings to 4:30 P.M. from Mondays to Thursdays to allow time to work with the children. Further, the district assigned a full time nurse to each target middle school. As a result, the Collaborative hoped to display progress within the five-year period of the grant (*New Futures* 1988, 85–90).

Dayton's New Futures Collaborative selected four major interventions as targets. These were to prevent dropping out of school and to enhance academic performance, to set up a case management system, to begin an employment program, and to prevent teenage pregnancies.

To achieve the first intervention, preventing dropouts and enhancing academic performance, the New Futures program tried several things. It offered $15,000 for instructional materials to each cluster. New Futures extended opportunities to teachers for training to introduce new methods of instruction. The collaborative offered to pay for release time allowing teachers to design curricula appropriate to special needs of the students. New Futures paid teachers or community associates to stay after school to conduct academic enrichment activities with the children. New Futures suggested giving rewards such as pizza to pupils who showed success (Stenning 1994, 7–8).

The key to the Dayton New Futures initiative was the second intervention, the case management system. The program hired twenty-five community associates to serve as case managers, and assigned them to the two target middle schools. Two or three community associates joined each cluster of teachers within the two middle schools and served as an advocate for about fifty students (Stenning 1994, 8–9).

While in the school, the community associates were subject to the direct authority of the principal. Community associates introduced the child to appropriate human service professionals that would enhance the student's natural support system of family, friends, and church. In turn, these support systems would reduce barriers to academic achievement or employment. In this way, the Dayton planners envisioned the community associates as catalysts for changing the way youth services operated. The community associates sent the information they discovered about weaknesses in service delivery to the New Futures Collaborative. The board used that information in making decisions about staffing, funding, and organization of relevant services (*New Futures* 1988, 50–51).

To design their strategy to improve youth employment, the New Futures Collaborative consulted two studies of Dayton schools done by outside consulting firms. From the recommendations these consultants made, the Collaborative chose three objectives to add to the extended day program offered in the two middle schools. First, they decided to show the youth the connection between education and a successful career. Second, they emphasized academic remediation as part of career training. Third, they supported college mentoring activities designed to introduce the students to college campuses and available scholarships (Stenning 1994, 26–29).

The Collaborative selected three methods to reduce teen pregnancies. First, they hoped the students would build more successful futures because of the restructured middle schools. Second, they introduced a program of human growth and development that emphasized abstinence and the responsibility of males to postpone sexual activities. Finally, they wanted to expand health services through school nurses (Stenning 1994, 29).

In the middle schools, New Futures charged the school nurses, the community associates, and home economics teachers to set up a Peer Education Program. The idea was to have selected students give accurate health information to other students. Since Dayton did not have a comprehensive human development curriculum, the New Futures' sex education program was an innovation. However, there had been a public outcry against explicit sexual education in the schools. As a result, New Futures adopted an approach that required people to avoid discussing methods of birth control or disease prevention unless students asked specific questions. Despite this limitation, New Futures' sexual education advanced collaboration among different agencies. These programs included the Dayton Boys/Girls Club, Teen Connection, Planned Parenthood, Womenline, the Urban League, and the Combined Health District. Although the school programs emphasized sexual abstinence, New Futures convinced two health agencies in west Dayton to offer contraceptive services to teenagers (Stenning 1994, 30–31; 39).

Although the Collaborative selected four sensible interventions and chose simple ways to achieve them, small problems caused major difficulties. For example, teachers found it difficult to obtain any of the money promised for classroom materials. Many teachers ignored New Futures' offers to hire consultants or to pay for professional advancement. Furthermore, New Futures was unable to give positive reinforcement to the students who needed it. Those students who could have benefited from the extended day refused to come during the extra hours. The cluster teams gave the awards or trips to pizza parlors to students who showed excellent achievement, not to those who made improvements (Stenning 1994, 14–16).

Some teachers may not have taken advantage of New Futures because they felt it devalued traditional academic activities and insulted them. The preliminary evaluations of the schools by the Casey Foundation said that the children faced such severe social problems as parental neglect and drug abuse. The implication was that education could not go on within the buildings until the social problems disappeared. New Futures appeared to discredit academics when the community associates took over a science laboratory in a target middle school. Those offices were air conditioned, but classrooms were not (Harty 1990). Further, teachers must have blamed New Futures when they lost programs built over years. For example, in a target middle school, New Futures threatened to displace a surprisingly popular string music program, but a supervisor and parents rallied to the teacher's defense.

However, these unwise decisions were not consistent with the policies of the Collaborative. A building principal may have made them. Unfortunately, decisions such as turning laboratories into offices could escape the Collaborative because the New Futures had an unusual division of labor. Unlike other programs in other cities, Dayton's New Futures program created an organization called Community Connections to oversee the case management services. Community Connections had its own system of authority that included supervisors in the school buildings and lead community associates. The separation was so complete that the Collaborative contracted the case management duties from Community Connections (Stenning 1994, 19–20).

The benefit of this division of labor was that Community Connections devoted full-time attention to day to day problems while the Collaborative focused on administrative policies. Unfortunately, the Collaborative lost sight of details in the program's operation. The Collaborative hoped that they would remain in touch with everyday matters because the membership included school officials and the directors of the agencies. This may not have been enough.

At the end of the first year, two groups evaluated Dayton's New Futures. One group was an outside consulting firm designated by the Casey Foundation. The other group consisted of Dayton school people and New Futures representatives. Both groups found that the Dayton community knew little about the New Futures initiative. In part, the lack of publicity derived from the conservative nature of the Dayton plans. Most important, unlike New Futures in the other cities, Dayton's Collaborative did not use the planning period to alert the public to an impending youth crisis. It did not garner support for a redirection of schools and other institutions (Stenning 1994, 33–35).

The outside evaluators noticed a serious problem regarding the case management system. Dayton's New Futures expected the community associates to accomplish three things: to bring together the assessments made by other social agency professionals and teachers, to enhance communication among different agencies, and to make recommendations to change procedures if necessary. The community associates did not serve these functions. While they referred children to other agencies, they could not cooperate with other professionals. For example, teachers accepted the information about the children that community associates provided during cluster meetings. Neither the social workers nor the school personnel would cooperate with the case managers as professionals. Many teachers thought New Futures should hire more teachers and teacher aides, not community associates (Stenning 1994, 23–25; 35–36; 85).

To some extent the Casey Foundation caused friction. In their documents, they referred to the community associates as the "eyes and ears of the Collaborative." The Foundation meant that the community associates brought back information about the students that the Collaborative needed to make policy decisions. However, personnel in the schools and other agencies thought the community associates spied on them (Stenning 1994, 52).

Despite the problems, the first-year evaluation praised the community associates for developing strong and positive relationships with the children they served. The community associates had approximately fifty children apiece. They had met over 85 percent of the parents and mailed every parent information about the program (Stenning 1994, 38–39).

In fairness, community associates who spent their time with children might have been unable to provide the basis for new levels of cooperation among human service agencies. For example, a community associate once told prospective teachers at the University of Dayton about a child who fell asleep in class. The child lived with his grandmother who could not tell time. Not knowing when the child should go to the bus stop, she sent him several hours early. While problems like this are easy to solve, the community associates had to visit the homes, win the confidence of the caregivers, and discover the difficulties. Not only does this take time, but information from hundreds of cases like this does not imply anything except that every child needs an advocate.

Nonetheless, in the second year, 1989–90, New Futures took steps to improve. First, the group responsible for the case management system, Community Connections, selected a new director who promised to clarify the role of community associates and to justify their qualifications for the roles they played. Second, the Collaborative assigned a specific group to collect information about the students in a systematic way, hoping to improve decision-making at all levels. Third, the Collaborative secured specific agreements with cooperating agencies, listing the desired goals and detailing the expected cooperation (Stenning 1994, 50–54).

Unfortunately, Community Connections made an ill-advised decision. To save money, the agency hired only twelve new community associates instead of the expected twenty-five. This cut made it difficult for community associates to follow their students into high schools and remain in the middle school as well. The community associates had to travel among schools, work in different settings, and establish relationships with teachers and school personnel who were unfamiliar with New Futures (Stenning 1994, 50–53).

The evaluation of the second year was disappointing. To the good, the clusters within the pilot middle schools offered more academic enrichment activities and improved guidance despite staff complaints about overwork. However, the two pilot Dayton middle schools resisted the innovations New Futures promised. Neither the comprehensive health curriculum nor the youth employment program existed. Furthermore, despite many hours of specific training, the community associates lacked skills needed for their jobs (Stenning 1994, 48–64).

It seemed that after two years, New Futures could not show measurable success. Dayton school administrators said that grades, attendance, and test scores in the two pilot middle schools remained unchanged. The special programs after school that New Futures sponsored attracted only 25 percent of the students. Critics said New Futures was drifting without a strong plan. The lack of definite results frustrated the leaders on the Collaborative (Harty 1990).

During the third year, 1990–91, the superintendent of the Dayton schools asked to expand the case management system to all intermediate and secondary schools and to such agencies as the juvenile court. He offered to assign 140 Dayton public school staff to become community associates. Although the New Futures program set up a committee to consider these increases, none of them took place (Stenning 1994, 65–67).

Second, the Collaborative decided to initiate a pilot program to find ways the different social agencies could work together. The Collaborative selected the chronic absenteeism of students as the focus. Since students who were absent often had health problems, suffered from family difficulties, or engaged in drug abuse, the members believed this could involve the work of many agencies. However, the pilot project differed from the original case management model in that it was smaller and more intense. It included only 210 students in the eighth grade. Six community associates would work with them and follow them into high school (Stenning 1994, 68–69).

Third, the Collaborative hired a public relations firm to learn how people perceived New Futures. The consultants interviewed students, parents, teachers, community associates, human service workers, business executives, community leaders, and news reporters. Students and parents thought New Futures was the community associates. Teachers saw the New Futures initiative as insulting their own efforts. Human service personnel felt used and believed that New Futures employees did not solicit their suggestions. Business leaders predicted failure because the goals were set too high. The public relations experts thought these findings showed clearly that New Futures needed a better communication strategy (Stenning 1994, 70–72).

As a result, in February 1991 the leaders of the Casey Foundation, New Futures, Community Connections, and directors of the appropriate human service agencies met for two days. They tried to define the integrated service system Dayton needed. At those meetings, the members agreed upon an interagency team model. The members of the team included the school building's advisor for Community Connections, the community associate responsible for the particular child, Dayton school staff, and representatives of appropriate human service agencies. They required each participating agency to provide appropriate service quickly. If problems appeared, the team informed the Collaborative (Stenning 1994, 74–75).

On 18 April 1991 Dayton's New Futures submitted a second-phase plan to the Casey Foundation that outlined the changes the Collaborative made. While the Casey Foundation approved of the pilot project focusing on chronically absent youth and the inter-agency agreements, they found the plan to be modest. That is, the Foundation staff complained that the cooperating agencies, including the Dayton schools, did not change policies to participate in the interagency agreement. Nor did the plan ask Dayton businesses to go very far in offering such things as increased employment opportunities for the youth (Stenning 1994, 82–83).

Although the Casey Foundation approved the second-phase plan, the midpoint assessment of Dayton's New Futures was disappointing. The evaluators noted that, in the first year, the community associates spent their time offering direct services to children and could not organize the work of various agencies. The evaluators acknowledged that, in the second year, the Collaborative tried to clarify the role of the community associates, but confused the issue. Evaluators thought the most important task lying before the community associates was to organize the information they had gathered about specific cases. As it was, the community associates had records of what they did, but they could not give a summary of numbers of encounters, referrals, and outcomes. The lack of organized information deterred evaluations of their efforts or decisions about appropriate policies (Stenning 1994, 85–87).

Conditions worsened in 1991–92. As the fourth year of the program began, a new superintendent took office in the Dayton schools. Although he had been the deputy superintendent when the Dayton schools applied for the New Futures program, he characterized New Futures as misguided and as having no impact on the children at one of his first board meetings in 1991. As a result, he added that he would not accept grants to help at-risk youth in the future. The new superintendent said New Futures ignored the elementary children, where the best opportunity for change existed (Stenning 1994, 88–90).

Even if the new superintendent's views were true, they were unfair. One explanation for his remarks was that he wanted to garner support among teachers who disliked New Futures. In choosing the new superintendent, the school board denied the application of an assistant superintendent strongly favored by the teachers. To lessen the teachers' antipathy, the new superintendent may have tried to attack an initiative they disliked. A second possibility is the superintendent faced pressure to reduce school costs, and he may have criticized New Futures to avoid contributing to the program. Third, the superintendent may simply have wanted to shape the program to reflect his administration instead of his predecessor's.

While the superintendent's intentions were not clear, the results were evident. The superintendent's criticisms signaled a withdrawal of school support for New Futures. In May 1991 the administration of Dayton public schools had agreed to support the Chronic Absenteeism program and had assigned personnel to work on the intervention teams. In September 1991 after the new superintendent took office, the Chronic Absenteeism project began in earnest. Almost immediately, the Dayton public schools questioned the purpose of the separate project and its relationship to other aims such as boosting the children's scores on standardized tests. By January 1992 the schools had not provided alternate educational opportunities for the truants as promised. This was a major problem because the school staff did not want the chronically absent children returned to their classrooms. Since the school administration refused to spend the extra money it had promised, the chronic absenteeism project ended (Stenning 1994, 92–93).

By the fifth year, community associates no longer worked with specific children but served on intervention teams for the entire school. Instead of concentrating on middle school children and following them into high schools, they worked in elementary, middle, and high schools. Since the Casey Foundation was about to end its funding, the Collaborative decided in December 1992 to stop offering any direct services. As a result, all community associates and their supervisors lost their jobs. In May 1993 New Futures employed only five people. New Futures gave the equipment used by community associates to the Dayton schools. In September 1993 the Collaborative changed the name to the Youth and Family Collaborative for the Greater Dayton Area (Stenning 1994, 98–110).

After five years and twenty million dollars, New Futures could not show it had increased graduation rates, improved employment or college admissions, or reduced teenage pregnancies (Belcher 1993). On the other hand, New Futures established a wellness center, enhanced interagency cooperation, and accumulated a wealth of information about the students in Dayton's schools (Stenning 1994, 104–113). In addition, New Futures prepared computer files tracing the progress of each child enrolled in grades six through twelve in the Dayton schools over the five years of the initiative. Some news was good. Course failure rates improved dramatically among high school students and generally among intermediate students. Out of school suspension rates at both intermediate and high school level dropped, while they remained steady at the elementary school level. The annual dropout rate improved dramatically at the high school level though they worsened at the intermediate level (Metis Associates 1994).

Unfortunately, a great deal of the information gathered by New Futures was distressing. For example, average daily attendance at all levels declined. The reading scores for intermediate school students improved, but the scores among elementary and high school students worsened. Graduation rates were low. The children enrolled in eighth grade in the first year of New Futures should have graduated by the end of the fifth year. Only 31 percent of those children graduated on time. Nineteen percent transferred out of the system and 21 percent remained in the system. The rest had been expelled, officially dropped out, or disappeared (Metis Associates 1994). By comparison, in surrounding communities, the graduation rates were much higher. In Oakwood, a wealthy community next to Dayton, 97 percent of the students graduated in four years. Furthermore, in most of the other communities near Dayton, 80 to 90 percent of the students graduated in four years (Fisher 1990).

The New Futures information gave some evidence of continuing white flight. While enrollments increased in elementary and intermediate schools, fewer students enrolled in the high schools. Far fewer white students went on to the secondary schools than black students. Interestingly, of all students, black students showed more potential for graduation than did white students (Metis Associates 1994).

Other findings raised alarm. For example, despite sex education programs advocating abstinence, 53 percent of Dayton's secondary students reported having sex. Of the sexually active children, 32 percent said they did not use birth control, and almost 9 percent of the young women became pregnant (Metis Associates 1994).

In 1994 Dayton's New Futures published a report to the community entitled *Their Future Is in Our Hands.* It showed there were too many children in Montgomery County living in poverty or not living with two parents. It noted that too many teenage women were having babies. The report pleaded for citizens and governmental agencies to work harder to reduce these problems. It concluded, "We have no choice."

Conclusion

In trying to solve social problems caused by segregation and poverty, educators said they faced a social crisis. However, the words of helping and caring justified programs that ran short periods and cost millions of dollars. At the end, the programs showed little success. The failures justified more expenditures.

However, something has to be done to help troubled youth. Schools are reasonable institutions to offer such help to low-income children. The problem is that educators only created new organizations under their control. Interestingly, many groups imitated this strategy. In the 1960s, African American activists in West Dayton used the fear of riots and the notion of cultural deficit to gain community control of the schools. In the 1980s community and business leaders used a similar argument to change the operations of established human services.

Neither Dayton's Model Cities program nor Dayton's New Futures initiative called for the racial desegregation of schools in Montgomery County. However, efforts to help disadvantaged social classes can also support increased efforts to promote genuine racial integration. Such philanthropic endeavors can involve people from several walks of life. In most institutional settings, though, the idea of caring seems to justify someone being in control and someone being served. Most important, compensatory education seems to justify the continued separation of racial and social groups.

References

Bailey, Stephen K., and Edith K. Mosher. 1968. *ESEA: The Office of Education Administers a Law.* Syracuse, N.Y.: Syracuse University Press.

Belcher, Ellen. 1993. "A Look Back at New Futures," *Dayton Daily News,* 23 May.

City of Dayton. 1969. *Model Cities Project Application.* Model Cities Special Projects File, American History Research Center, Wright State University.

Coleman, James. 1966. *Equality of Educational Opportunity.* Washington, D.C.: U.S. Department of Health, Education, and Welfare.

Cruickshank, Donald. 1969. *Inner City Simulation Laboratory.* Chicago, Ill.: Science Research Associates.

Cummings, Scott. 1977. *Black Children in Northern Schools.* San Francisco: R&E Research Associates.

Deutsch, Martin. 1967. "Dimensions of the School's Role in the Problems of Integration." In Martin Deutsch and Associates, *The Disadvantaged Child.* New York: Basic Books, 281–294.

Fisher, Mark. 1990. "1 in 4 Pupils in County Dropping Out," *Dayton Daily News,* 1 April.

Gans, Herbert. 1962. *Urban Villagers.* New York: Free Press.

Goodman, Denise. 1969. "Cash Could Revive Model Cities," *Journal Herald,* 28 May.

Harrington, Michael. 1962. *The Other America.* Baltimore: Penguin Books.

Harty, Rosemary. 1990. "What's Missing Here?" *Dayton Daily News,* 6 May, 1A, 8A, 9A.

Jensen, Arthur. 1969. "How Much Can We Boost IQ and Scholastic Achievement?" *Harvard Educational Review* 39 (Winter): 3–123.

Katz, Irwin. 1969. "A Critique of Personality Approaches to Negro Performance," *Journal of Social Issues* (Summer): 13–27.

Lewis, Oscar. 1961. *The Children of Sanchez.* New York: Random House.

Metis Associates. 1994. *Dayton New Futures Initiative: The Five-Year Report.* Dayton, Ohio: New Futures.

Mosteller, Frederick, and Patrick Moynihan, eds. 1972. *On Equality of Educational Opportunity.* New York: Random House.

New Futures: Plans for Assisting At-Risk Youth in Five Cities. 1988. Staff report. Washington, D.C.: Center for the Study of Social Policy.

Rees, Helen. 1968. *Deprivation and Compensatory Education.* New York: Houghton Mifflin Co.

Riessman, Frank. 1962. *The Culturally Deprived Child.* New York: Harper.

Ryan, William. 1971. *Blaming the Victim.* New York: Pantheon Books.

Salomone, Rosemary. 1986. *Equal Education under the Law.* New York: St. Martin's Press.

Special Committee on Urban Renewal. 1967. *A Model Cities Plan for Dayton.* Dayton, Ohio, Miami Valley Regional Planning Commission Library.

Sproull, Lee, et al. 1978. *Organizing an Anarchy.* Chicago: University of Chicago Press.

Stenning, Ronald. 1994. *Their Future Is in Our Hands.* Dayton, Ohio: New Futures.

Weller, Jack. 1966. *Yesterday's People.* Lexington: University of Kentucky Press.

Willis, Paul. 1977. *Learning To Labor.* New York: Columbia University Press.

Zigler, Edward, and Susan Muenchow. 1992. *Head Start.* New York: Basic Books.

Chapter Eleven
Schools and Social Reform

In 1954 the NAACP won in its fight against the racial segregation of schools. However, subsequent efforts to remove racial segregation from education revealed the complexity of modern society. A variety of people came forward to remove different forms of racial separation. In response, many other people tried to defend values and institutions threatened by social change. They held many different viewpoints, and they sought goals ranging from self-aggrandizement to the advancement of social values. Furthermore, people at any one level, such as in local districts, could not act alone. Their desires were subject to influences from authorities at other levels, such as state or local agencies. Despite the variety of actors, they tended to focus on ways to engineer racial integration or to protect the institutions they held dear. They did not think deeply about why different peoples should live together.

In 1954 the courtroom battle focused on such narrow questions as the meaning of previous court decisions and whether separate facilities could be equal. The U.S. Supreme Court justices did not base their decision on ideas of social justice. When southern politicians formed what they called massive resistance, they disregarded the moral implications of racial segregation. They contended that states had the right to select laws governing the conduct of its citizens. Consequently, after the widely publicized controversy in Little Rock, Arkansas, people argued over the respective roles of the federal courts, the federal administration, and state governments. They did not directly discuss the need for racial integration.

For nearly a decade, racial integration remained an idea rather than a reality. Then, in 1963, outraged by events in Birmingham,

Alabama, the public called for Congress to pass the Civil Rights Act. This gave the Department of Health, Education, and Welfare the power to force school districts throughout the South to desegregate racially without going through lengthy court battles.

For a short time it seemed that federal bureaucrats could engineer the racial integration of local school districts. Public sentiment changed, however, and conservatives learned that public protests could prevent desegregation. In 1965 HEW turned its attention to northern school districts such as Chicago. Almost instantly, in the resulting controversies, HEW lost the power it had. The public resistance to busing peaked in 1974 as masses of white people in South Boston tried to keep buses from taking children to buildings in Roxbury. Further, a public movement to draft an amendment to the Constitution forbidding cross-district busing for racial balance gained enough strength to become credible. It died in 1974 when the Supreme Court decided that white suburban children around Detroit did not have to attend urban schools to end segregation.

Nonetheless, public protests against cross-district busing continued in two forms. First, white people and middle-class people left the cities and moved to suburban communities. Second, the remaining urban residents voted against school taxes in hopes that school administrators would be unable to pay for transportation for racial balance. The effect of these two acts was tragic. They left urban schools with students from lower social classes who typically required more attention than did students from more affluent homes. Moreover, the voters rejected proposed school taxes, depriving the schools of the money to pay for the education the students needed.

It is important to note that the debates about racial integration were not struggles of good against evil. People on both sides acted out of a variety of motives, and unexpected consequences often resulted from the different reforms.

For example, some people sought school desegregation for reasons other than social justice. In the 1960s and 1970s, school desegregation offered many opportunities for personal gain. Once they resigned themselves to the inevitability of desegregation, some educators in southern states used it to replace black teachers and administrators with white counterparts. Many school administrators found reorganization for racial balance to be a way they could reduce expenses without facing criticism. Most important, many citizens, educational consultants, and civil rights activists found they could apply for federal grants to support an amazing range of programs and to pay large salaries.

Furthermore, racism and ignorance were not the only reasons people resisted school desegregation. It was true that racial politics opened avenues for individuals to pursue personal grievances or satisfy desires for power. However, some conservatives imitated the appeals for freedom and personal liberty that motivated the drive for racial integration. After 1954 liberals contended that the Supreme Court said that black children had a right to attend racially integrated schools. Conservatives reversed this argument and contended that children had the right to go to schools in the neighborhoods where they lived. Neither of these rights existed. In 1974 the Supreme Court decided that black children deserved protection from discriminatory policies. However, the justices accepted some segregated schools. Similarly, in 1973 the Court held that repairing the results of prior discrimination was more important than preserving neighborhood schools. Nonetheless, people used these nonexistent rights to justify the creation of complicated and sophisticated schemes of school reorganization.

Since the controversies over the racial desegregation of schools were complicated, it appeared to be an impossible goal. This was not true. A case study can illustrate the complicated paths people followed as they pursued racial integration. Most important, such a study may reveal a pattern suggesting what can or should be done in future efforts. Dayton, Ohio offers a complex picture recalling events that took place in many other northern cities.

Racial Integration in Dayton

In 1913 Dayton was one of the first cities to adopt the city manager form of government, which tried to organize public administration in the manner businesses operated. School administration followed a similar pattern. Introduced by business leaders, this model promised to take politics out of city and school affairs. An organization like the All Dayton Committee selected candidates for city commission and the school board. These candidates ran at large promising to serve the interests of the entire city, not just a small constituency.

Other cities across the country imitated Dayton because this model promised many advantages.

Unfortunately, the segregation and low incomes endured by African Americans represented a failure of the progressive model. The 1954 U.S. Supreme Court decision encouraged some of Dayton's residents to pursue racial integration. Changes took place in hiring practices in many businesses. Civil rights activists pushed for racial integration in downtown stores and entertainment centers. However, progress was slow until 1966. A brief riot showed that Dayton's progressive form of city and school administration had neglected the African Americans in a section of West Dayton. To correct this oversight, people in different neighborhoods began to renew their own communities. They received federal assistance in these efforts and turned away from the progressive ideal of centralized, expert planning. Building up public distrust of any ethic that offered to bring people together, activists sought local resident control of the projects.

In some ways, the idea of community control was similar to the concept of states' rights southern politicians used in the 1950s to resist the federal courts. As a result, community control could reinforce segregation. This was the case in Dayton's Model Cities Demonstration Project where African American activists sought black control of black schools. However, community control could also justify racial integration. In the Dayton View Stabilization Project, the members of the community committed themselves to racial integration. They sought to make their neighborhood the keystone in a national movement to revitalize racially integrated urban centers.

The Model Cities program and the Dayton View Stabilization Project ended in 1975. However, they left an important mark on city governance. Dayton's city administration turned these programs and other Model Cities projects throughout the city into a system of seven priority boards. Designed to function as decentralized city agencies, the priority boards offered neighborhood residents the chance to decide what programs the city would offer within their area. As a result, Dayton earned national recognition as a model for citizen participation. Unfortunately, a survey of city residents in 1994 showed that only a third of Dayton's residents could identify their priority board (Bischoff 1995).

The drive for racial integration extended into the suburbs where few black people lived. In 1968 Dayton adopted a fair housing ordinance. Unfortunately, these laws proved to be unenforceable. Subsequently, in 1972 the Miami Valley Regional Planning Commission (MVRPC) offered the first of several nationally recognized plans to encourage low-income housing dispersal. These plans won the approval of the conservative federal administration, which saw the racial integration of neighborhoods as preferable to school busing for racial balance. Ironically, the MVRPC programs failed for lack of federal administrative support.

Dayton's public school board tried to desegregate its schools. However, this effort lasted only from 1967 until 1972. It hired a superintendent who worked to dismantle the segregation the former superintendent and school boards had imposed. He hired black administrators, racially desegregated the faculty, and encouraged the introduction of studies such as black history. He set up middle school programs and introduced innovative educational programs. To garner public support, he pointed to the continual pressure he received from the U.S. Department of Health, Education, and Welfare. Nonetheless, he generated local opposition. Two individuals who disliked the direction that the school board took applied to the All Dayton Committee (ADC) to become candidates for the school board. When the ADC rejected them, the individuals formed their own political party and selected candidates.

This populist party, Serving Our Schools (SOS), promised to return the schools to what its members called the ideals of common people. Dayton's SOS was often confused with the moderate Save Our Schools movement. Middle-class and professional people in southern states formed Save Our Schools organizations to resist segregationists who wanted to close public schools rather than racially integrate them. However, Dayton's SOS was not a moderate group. Its members accused business and professional people of spending lavishly to impose racial desegregation and innovative instruction on other people's children. In this way, Dayton's SOS party campaigned against school taxes and educational improvements. Although complaints about liberal policies filled the SOS campaigns, SOS members said they favored neighborhood schools and some form of basic instruction.

In December 1971 the liberal board admitted that it had caused racial segregation. The board asked the superintendent to desegregate the city schools. It asked the Ohio Department of Education to join Dayton city schools with those of the surrounding suburbs to make a metropolitan school district. Less than a month later, a school board dominated by conservative SOS members rescinded those decisions. More important, HEW stopped requiring local districts such as Dayton to racially desegregate. As a result, the liberals on Dayton's school board and the local NAACP turned to the courts to force the conservatives to desegregate the schools. The liberal superintendent opened his files to the NAACP lawyers to help them prove the board had acted wrongly (Dimond 1985, 127).

In 1976 the U.S. district court ordered Dayton public schools to begin a program of district-wide desegregation. Despite the NAACP's appeals, the federal courts refused to order a metropolitan busing plan for Dayton. As a result, although city schools had the most successful cross district busing program up to that time, it did not include most of the white children in the metropolitan area. Finally, throughout the 1970s and 1980s, area factories closed and manufacturing and service jobs moved elsewhere. Consequently, the population of the metropolitan area declined and more white children attended suburban schools.

During the five school board campaigns held from 1971 until 1979, liberals sought to reinforce racial desegregation in spite of the resistance from the SOS party. They formed political parties such as Independent Citizens for Good Schools and Citizens for Better Schools, collected funds, and campaigned against the SOS. They chose bland nonideological names to appear objective and uncommitted. On the other hand, SOS members accused the liberals of being the party of busing. Although the SOS claimed to express the will of the people, in 1969 and again in 1971 liberals polled more votes than the conservatives. The liberals lost those school board elections because of the way the votes were split. In 1973 seven votes made the difference.

Trying to be politic, the liberal candidates for school board did not ask voters to recognize the need for racial integration. When the liberals had to justify the racial integration of schools, they pointed to some outside agency such as the courts. They said that Dayton should integrate its schools because that was the law. Surprisingly, liberal clergy in Dayton would not bear witness to the need for racial integration. They even refused the embattled liberal superintendent's direct request to do so in 1971. Instead, during school board elections, the liberal clergy set up debates and distributed objective-looking comparisons of the various candidates for the school board. On the other hand, conservative clergy used the Bible to justify continued segregation. When the U.S. district court ordered the public schools to desegregate, liberal religious leaders did not celebrate the truth of the decision. They encouraged people to obey a lawful order.

Although the conservative SOS party dominated Dayton school affairs for a decade, the party created its own downfall by campaigning against school tax levies. Financial problems forced Dayton schools to close in 1971 and a tax levy passed in November of that year. In 1980 financial problems caused SOS members to lose their campaign for the school board. The legacy of conservative resistance to school taxes remained in Dayton. It was not until June 1983 that Dayton voters approved another school tax levy by the narrow margin of 154 votes out of 37,042 votes cast. The levy passed because voters in former SOS strongholds on the east side of Dayton narrowly approved the levy for the first time since 1971. These voters had opposed taxes because they disliked busing for racial balance (Brown and Ancona 1983).

In 1973 SOS fulfilled a campaign promise to remove the liberal superintendent. The death of an SOS school board member threatened to reduce the party to minority status. Fortunately for SOS, a local judge appointed the former superintendent to fill the vacancy. The former superintendent voted with SOS to replace the liberal superintendent with an individual more supportive of the SOS party.

However, in most other ways, the SOS members could not bend Dayton's public schools to their will. SOS board members had to preserve the middle schools, an innovative arts program, and Individually Guided Education that they vowed to dismantle. They kept these programs to convince the U.S. district court that they would save any program that encouraged racial desegregation. Further, they administered the cross-district busing program they fought against after losing the suit to desegregate the schools.

As white and middle-class black people left the city in large numbers, the number of students in Dayton's public schools dropped. However, the schools served increasing percentages of lower-class black and white families. Educators tried to help these children in two ways. First, they sought to correct the supposed retardation of children caused by poverty. Second, they tried to change the structure of schools and businesses to make them accessible to lower-class children.

In the 1960s and 1970s educators argued that lower-class children failed in schools because they suffered from cultural deprivation. School people accepted extensive support from the federal government to develop materials and programs designed to compensate for this problem. Following this national trend, sponsors of Dayton's Model Cities Demonstration Project contended in 1969 that African American school children in West Dayton suffered cultural deprivation. The program proposal said that the residents of the area had to control their own schools to correct this deprivation. In addition, they needed extra money not available to other schools in the city. Consequently, members of the Model Cities planning council argued that the black schools in West Dayton should remain segregated. In such surroundings, teachers could tailor the curricula to fit the unique needs of the children. These arguments did not stop the federal courts from ordering racial desegregation. However, African American residents of West Dayton may have believed the pleas for continued school segregation because they refused to support liberal candidates for the school board.

Despite the millions of dollars the Model Cities Demonstration Project received, evidence of success was limited. By 1975 the Model Cities educational component had introduced several innovative programs and some individuals claimed these programs helped them. Unfortunately, Congress did not accept these reports as evidence of success and stopped the funding. Further, the federal government sought to reclaim funds misspent by the Model Cities planning council.

In the 1980s, with the help of private philanthropies and business corporations, educators sought to construct programs changing the schools. These structural improvements were supposed to encourage economically deprived children to succeed. In 1987 the

Casey Foundation offered to fund a New Futures program for the children said to be at risk. This program promised to be different from earlier efforts that sought to change the nature of the culturally deprived child. Dayton's New Futures tried to open schools and work places to children of poverty. Case managers worked hard to contact other welfare agencies and orchestrate efforts to help each child. Unfortunately, although New Futures consumed twenty million dollars in five years, it could not show success.

Most important, advocates of the Model Cities Demonstration Project and New Futures used the programs' failure to ask for increased study and effort. It is not clear why compensatory education or at-risk programs failed. To some extent, they set out to accomplish too much and claimed simplistic measures would offer great benefits. In part, they never had a fair chance to prove their value. Sometimes, the programs suffered unfair evaluations. Other times, they lost essential support. For example, although observers called Dayton's Model Cities Demonstration Project the most successful in the nation, it ended when the national mood turned against federal support of urban renewal.

Some critics argued that the programs failed because the concept of cultural deprivation and the idea of at-risk children reinforced elitist views of education. In each case, the student was the client and the teacher or the community associate was the professional who knew what the children needed. Although some commentators thought such elitism prevented lower-class people from controlling their own schools, this was not true. Any group could use these ideas to gain control. In 1969 black activists used the argument of cultural deprivation to try to take control of the schools in Dayton's Model Cities neighborhood away from the central school board.

On the other hand, Dayton's New Futures suggested that schools might help lower-class children if each child had an advocate to minister to his or her needs. However, the children might rebel against the pressure to conform to the schools' ideals of success. For example, in 1977 Paul Willis found that working-class children created their own culture to resist school people's efforts to help them.

In the 1980s researchers such as James Coleman contended that there was something about the sense of shared purpose or social capital enjoyed by Catholic schools that enabled them to serve minority and disadvantaged children better than public schools did. That is, he found that, in Catholic schools, such youth had lower dropout rates, higher scores on standardized tests, and greater chances to go to college or succeed in the work force. Unfortunately, if the Catholic schools accepted many non-Catholic children, this would weaken the close relationships among the children's parents that made the schools successful. At any rate, in Dayton and in other cities, Catholic schools were not open to disadvantaged youth. Despite aid from diocesan officials, the tuition was high in urban Catholic schools where disadvantaged children lived. On the other hand, suburban Catholic schools used their own parish funds to make tuition considerably lower than it was among their urban counterparts.

Religious leaders faced a difficult situation in Dayton in the 1960s. Since the progressive city administration had neglected African Americans, people considered ideals that promised to unite all people as disguises for racial discrimination. Thus, instead of democracy, people sought some sort of pluralism that encouraged every group to tolerate other different groups.

Despite the popular distrust for universal ethics, religious organizations had the means to point out why people from different races should live together. Throughout the 1950s and 1960s, national organizations of most religious denominations drafted statements condemning racial segregation on religious grounds. However, local pastors seemed unable to bring these ideals to their faithful. Researchers noted this problem in the controversy in Little Rock, Arkansas, in 1956. However, the greater irony was that, to some extent, religious thought seemed to justify continued segregation. For example, the U.S. Catholic bishops called for prudence in ending racial segregation. They seemed to think that, as religious feelings increased among all people, the artificial barriers between peoples would disappear. Unfortunately, this made religious leaders appear tolerant of racial prejudice.

There are two reasons why religious leaders might have thought that personal religious conversion was the best antidote to race prejudice. First, mainstream denominational schools faced the same problems of white flight, loss of financial support, and resegregation that public schools faced when they tried to desegregate. In the face of these threats, church leaders retreated, believing that the spread of religion would hasten racial integration. Second, religious faith changed segregationist academies. Often begun to maintain racial segregation, these schools soon enrolled some African Americans who adopted the value frame of the school people. Usually, African Americans remained in the minority in such schools. Nonetheless, religious principles overshadowed racism to some extent.

However, religious schools and public schools do more than share the same communities. In this regard, the Dayton case shows the extent to which Catholic schools and public schools were interconnected. Although these school systems lacked formal ties, the same people participated in controversies in two or more settings. For example, many teachers in the Catholic St. Agnes Elementary School became actively involved in liberal public school board members' political campaigns. After St. Agnes School closed, they joined the public schools. The chairperson of the Ad Hoc De Facto Segregation Committee that tried to hasten the racial integration of Catholic schools taught English in a Dayton public school. Further, members of Christ Episcopal Church founded Center City School in downtown Dayton to show public school people that racially integrated urban education worked.

Most important, in Dayton, the people in Catholic schools used the same ways of thinking about racial desegregation that people in public schools employed. As a result, the religious people ignored the traditional language that could have deepened the debates about racial integration. Three examples illustrated this tendency. First, administrators in both public and Catholic schools looked at racial segregation in therapeutic terms. That is, they saw the resistance to desegregation as stemming from white people's unwillingness to consider the problems African Americans and economically deprived people faced. As a result, they looked to some interethnic sensitivity sessions as a solution. Administrators in Dayton's public and in Dayton's Catholic schools came to hold this view strongly.

Unfortunately, the interethnic sensitivity sessions did not inexorably prove the necessity of racial or social integration. The sessions could suggest that people had to live apart because every ethnic group had its biases against other groups. A person could come out of the sensitivity sessions thinking that there were too many obstacles preventing the reconciliation of differences. More important, the sensitivity sessions contradicted the religious reasons for racial integration. The format of the sessions implied that people could best know each other when each person knew what other people experienced. Traditionally, religion taught people to love each other because God loved them all.

Second, administrators in both systems sought to appeal to some legislative or popular body to justify the need for racial desegregation. As a result, administrators in both systems set up broad-based commissions to study the problems of racial segregation and to suggest solutions. These commissions did not propose anything new or surprising. At times, the commissions legitimated what was obvious and diffused the responsibility for the choices. At other times, the commissions made it possible for administrators to avoid acting because administrators were not bound to enact a commission's recommendations. However, the commissions made public and Catholic schools appear responsive to their constituents. As a result, dissenters often amassed public criticism to show that the commission expressed an unpopular view.

The third way public and Catholic schools were interconnected was that participants in the controversies made them contests of rights. That is, in Dayton, liberal Catholics quoted documents from the U.S. Civil Rights Commission to explain that black children had a right to a racially integrated education. In this manner, they repeated liberal arguments for the racial desegregation of public schools. On the other hand, conservative Catholics complained that parents had a right to send their children to the parish school they helped build. In this way, the conservative Catholics recalled conservative arguments to preserve neighborhood public schools. Of course, as with public schools, neither of these rights existed in the U.S. Constitution or in the Catholic Church's canon law.

White families may have left Dayton to avoid cross-district busing for racial balance. However, suburban schools near Dayton lost students because the local economy had slackened, causing many people to leave the area. Further, Catholic schools supported the public schools and refused to accept transfers fleeing racial integration. Nonetheless, Catholic schools experienced some growth, but it was in the suburbs unaffected by the court order. This took place because, in Dayton as in other cities, throughout the 1960s and 1970s many newly affluent Catholics were among the white people who left the cities.

Conclusion

Like religious leaders, school people rarely called for racial integration. Instead, they tended to portray themselves as driven by courts, by public opinion, or by the need to solve a crisis. When they did act, they tried to adopt programs that reflected a combination of all the different points of view in the community. Unfortunately, these eclectic proposals did not do justice to any of the views they included.

Educators offered curriculum proposals such as individualized education and magnet schools to advance racial integration. These proposals tried to enhance the interests of the abilities of individual students in buildings that underwent desegregation. Unfortunately, they were not designed to reinforce the racial integration of students. Consequently, these programs could be used in segregated settings. On the other hand, ethnic studies programs offered to counter racism and thereby make racial integration possible. However, these courses could undercut ideals that would bring people together by teaching children that human values served the interests of particular ethnic or social groups.

Nonetheless, the situation was not hopeless. Solutions to the problems of racial segregation existed in metropolitan reorganization, educational parks, or dispersal of low-income housing. However, these proposals could succeed only when people from different racial and social groups wanted to live and work together. Lacking the agreement to pursue this goal, reform efforts became a tangle of contradictory initiatives and resistances. In part, the problem was that people did not want to think about blending their concern for individual freedoms with necessary social obligations. Instead, they talked of legal requirements, pedagogical preferences, or racism. Even religious leaders and educators abandoned theological references when they supported the racial desegregation of schools. As a result, calls for racial integration sounded like pleas for people to sacrifice their individual opportunities and extend aid to less fortunate people.

This was bound to cause problems, because sacrifice often hurts everyone.

In Dayton, Ohio, people forgot that personal freedoms flourished in the midst of social obligations and benefits. Such ideas were available in religion and in philosophy. Most important, these ideas could have become the center of an educational politics that put community and commitment to living and growing together at the center. This could have provided the basis for a perspective that valued racial integration and avoided the dangers of excessive compulsion.

Unfortunately, after forty years of trying to racially desegregate schools, the Dayton area remained a segregated community. The students in the city schools came from African American or lower-income families. The students in suburban schools were mostly from white or professional families. Furthermore, the divisions between the races and the social classes had important educational consequences. In 1995 the *Cleveland Plain Dealer* rated the standardized test scores from 600 Ohio school districts. Oakwood, an almost exclusively white suburban community adjacent to Dayton, ranked sixth in the state. On the other hand, Dayton city schools, where over 60 percent of the students were black, ranked number 596 ("Study" 1995).

References

Bischoff, Laura. 1995. "Some Leery of Turner's Meetings," *Dayton Daily News,* 8 September: 1B.

Brown, Maureen, and Paula Ancona. 1983. "School Levy Squeaks Past," *Dayton Daily News,* 8 June.

Dimond, Paul. 1985. *Beyond Busing.* Ann Arbor: University of Michigan Press.

"Study: Income, Parents Keys to Success." 1995. *Dayton Daily News,* 21 August.

Index

Ad Hoc De Facto Segregation Committee, 218–219, 226–227, 331
advisory committees, 4, 43–44, 95, 102–103, 191–193, 274, 332
African Americans abandon desegregation:
in Dayton, 127–128, 169–170, 174
in Oakland, 35–36
oppose NAACP, 34
All Dayton Committee, 105
Alter, Archbishop Karl, 207, 216, 223–225
Anderson, Robert, 265
Association for Supervision and Curriculum Development, 285
at-risk, 306–318, 329

Battelle Memorial Institute, 119
Berkeley, California, 261–264
bilingual education, 33
Bills, Robert, 56–59
Birmingham, Alabama, 50–51, 322
black power:
in Berkeley, 262–263
in Dayton, 118–119, 299–300
in general, 34
in Sausalito, California, 282–283
black teacher plight, 10–13
Blum, Virgil, 70
Boston, Massachusetts, 17–21, 322
Brinkman v Gilligan. See Dayton suit
Brown, H. Rap, 93
Brown v Board of Education, 3
busing:
in Boston, Massachusetts, 20–21
constitutional amendment against, 17, 38, 41
in Dayton, 132, 160–163, 189–195, 200–203
suburban reactions, 160–162, 322
successes, 194–195, 326

Campbell, Ernest Q., 49–50
Campbell, Ronald, 106
Casey Foundation, 306–318
Catholic officials:
attitude toward racism, xvi, 59–61, 210–211
in Boston, 53
in Chicago, 63, 64
in New Orleans, 61–63
Catholic schools:
attitudes toward, 70
in Boston, 21
budgets in inner cities, 71
in Chicago, 63–67
in Dayton, 207–237
minority students and integration, 59–70, 72, 73
tuition in, 70–71
Catholic schools and public schools:
support desegregation, 235–236
white flight, 59, 73–74, 236–237
Center City School, 244–257, 331
Central High, Little Rock, 5–7
Chicago, Illinois:
migration of Catholics, 67
public schools, 13–15
Christian schools. *See* private schools
Cincinnati, Ohio, 272, 280
citizen coalitions:
in Dayton, 129, 131–132, 134, 192
in Oakland, 35
in San Francisco, 31
in St. Louis, 42
in Wilmington, 26
Citizen's Committee, 81. *See also* All Dayton Committee
Citizens for Better Schools, 166–177, 326
city manager model, xiii, 80–81, 109

clergy:
  in Boston, 53
  in Dayton, 91, 143, 157–158, 167–
    168, 192, 3327, 330
  in Detroit, 54
  in Little Rock, 49–50, 330
  in Wilmington, 54
Coleman, James:
  Catholic school effectiveness, 72–73,
    329–330
  criticism of compensatory education,
    300–301
  on white flight, 22
community control, 113–153, 324–325
compensatory education:
  evaluation of, 300–306
Connaughton, Monsignor Edward A.,
    208, 217, 222
conservative-liberal split, 105–110
consolidation of Catholic elementary
  schools:
  in Pennsylvania, 227–228
  reaction of various groups, 214–216
  recommendation, 212
  as result of declining enrollments,
    234–235
  task force study, 217, 222–231
Crain, Robert, 73
cultural deprivation theory:
  and compensatory education, 295–
    297, 329
  origins, 291–295
  and power, 298–300, 328–329
Cummings, Scott, 304–305
curriculum:
  and compensatory education, 303–306
  in private schools, 248– 257
  and racial integration, 261–289

Daley, Richard, 15
Davis, Brother Joseph, 224–226
Dayton Board of Education:
  admission of guilt, 102, 326
  attitude of voters, 171–172
  commitment to desegregation, 94–95
  resolutions to desegregate, 103–104
  reverse resolutions, 158–159
Dayton Board of Education v Brinkman.
    See Dayton suit
Dayton Christian Schools, 201, 242
Dayton Human Relations Council, 143
Dayton Metropolitan Housing
    Authority, 143

Dayton New Futures, 307–318
Dayton, Ohio:
  location and population, 79–80
  pattern of segregation, 80
  reasons for selecting, xii-xiii
  reform of municipal government, 80–
    81
Dayton schools:
  centralized administration, 83–84
  early efforts to integrate, 87–91
  early segregation, 84–87
  high schools, expansion of, 85–86
Dayton suit:
  appeals court, 187, 188, 197–198
  injunctive relief, 199–200
  U.S. District Court, 182–187, 189–
    190, 196–197
  U.S. Supreme Court, 188, 195–196,
    198–199
Dayton View Stabilization Project, 128–
    142, 324
Declaration of Constitutional Principles,
    5
De Facto Segregation Committee:
  evaluation of, 222–230
  report, 208–212
desegregation:
  Catholic parents opinions, 211
  reasons for, 322–323
Detroit, Michigan, 37–40, 322
Deutsch, Martin, 297
Dimond, Paul, 203
Donahue, Phil, 214, 220
Dunbar school, 86–87, 89

East Texas, 11–13
Economic Opportunity Act, 114
Eisenhower, Dwight, 7
elected officials:
  contributions, XVI
  effect of reform, 323–324
  pursue peace, 193
Elementary and Secondary Education
    Act, 296–297
encounter group training, 231–234,
    331–332
Essex, Martin W., 107, 200
ethnic studies. See multicultural education
ethnic ties:
  in Boston, 19
  in San Francisco, 32–33
Evans v Buchanan, 24

faculty desegregation:
    beginnings in Dayton, 88–90
    success in Dayton, 98–99
fair housing laws, 143–144
Faubus, Orval, 6
federal government and cities, 21, 113
Federal Housing Authority, 82, 142,144
federally subsidized housing:
    projects in WWII, 82
    racial integration and, 144
    types of residents, 146
Fife, Brian, 280–281
Finger, John, 190–191
FORCE, 118–119, 215
Foster, Gordon, 189
Foster, Marcus, 36
Fox, Willard, 106–107
freedom of choice:
    in Berkeley, 263–264
    in Dayton, 99–100, 158, 183
    in Greensboro, 9
    in Little Rock, 5
    in Nashville, 27
    for teachers, 98
French, Dr. Robert:
    on board of education, 164–165, 168,
        170
    and desegregation, 88–90
    end of superintendency, 94

Gans, Herbert, 293
Geringer, Dan, 135
Glatt, Charles, 172–173
Gleason, Ralph, 60
Gordon, William, 188–189
grade per school per year, 27
Greeley, Andrew, 68–70
Green v County School Board of
        New Kent County:
    influence on Milliken v Bradley, 39–40
    and open enrollment, 3
Greensboro, North Carolina, 8–10
Groff, Josephine, 170

Harrington, Michael, 293–294
Harvard Teaching Teams Project, 265
Head Start:
    and cultural deprivation theory, 296–
        297
    in Dayton, 126
    research about, 302–303
Hillel Academy, 201, 243
Hills v Gautraux, 41

Hodges, Luther, 8
Houston, Texas, 272
Hughey, U.A., 108, 168

/I/D/E/A/:
    and individualized instruction, 266–272
    in Model Cities, 126–127
Independent Citizens for Good Schools,
        107–108, 326
individualized education:
    in Berkeley, 263–264
    in Center City School, 244–257
    with racial integration, 264–272
Individually Guided Education:
    in Dayton, 270
    in Longfellow, 137–138
    origins, 265–272
Inner City Simulation Laboratory, 303–
        304
interethnic sensitivity. See encounter
        group training

Jackson, Mississippi, 57
Johnson, Lyndon:
    black teachers, promise to, 11
    in Chicago, 15
    and Head Start, 296
    and model cities, 115
Jones, Nathaniel R., 181

Kanawha County, West Virginia, 284–
        287
Kettering Foundation,135. See also
        /I/D/E/A/
Keyes v School District No. 1:
    effect on bilingual education, 33
    effect in Dayton, 187, 197
    in neighborhood schools, 19
    segregation without state law, 4
King, Martin Luther Jr.:
    reasons for desegregation, xvi
    summer of 1963, 50–52
Klausmeier, Herbert, 265–266
Kliebard, Herbert M., 289
Kohl, Herbert, 264
Kozol, Jonathan, 264

Lau v Nichols, 33
League of Cooperating Schools, 266
Lewis, Oscar, 292–293
Little Rock, Arkansas, 5–8, 321
Longfellow Elementary School, 136–137,
        271

low income housing dispersal. *See* Miami
    Valley Regional Planning Com-
    mission

magnet schools:
    in Dayton, 183–187, 272–279
    general problems, 278–279
    and racial integration, 272–281
    in St. Louis, 44–45
Marshall Kaplan, Gans, and Kahn
    Inc.,121–122
Marshall, Thurgood, 3
Massive Resistance, 4–5
Mayor's Ad Hoc Riot Study Committee,
    92–93
McCarthy, Reverend Edward A., 213–
    214, 222–223
McGee, James, 169
McGovern, George, 17
McIntosh, W.S., 91–92
McLin C.J. Jr, 92, 108, 117
Memphis, Tennessee, 57–58
Metropolitan Churches United:
    and busing, 192
    and desegregation, 158
    in school board campaigns, 167–168
metropolitan desegregation plan:
    NAACP requests, 181–182
    recommended in Dayton, 103–104,
        185, 189–190
    school board requests, 157–158
Miami Valley Regional Planning Com-
    mission (MVRPC), xvii, 144–
    148, 325
middle schools:
    in Dayton, 101–102
    for desegregation, 99, 184
    with at-risk, 308–313
Milliken v Bradley:
    effect on Delaware, 25
    in general, 37–41
minority language program, 184–187
Model Cities:
    city wide, 148–152
    cultural deprivation theory and power,
        298–300, 328
    in Dayton, 115–128, 150–153, 324,
        328
    in eleven cities, 121–122
monitor desegregation:
    advisory committee in St. Louis, 43
    citizens advisory board in Dayton,
        191–192

Montgomery County Fair Housing Cen-
    ter, 148
Morgan v Hennigan, 18
multicultural education:
    aim, 283–284
    in Berkeley, 263–264
    and racial integration, 281–287
Multiple Motivation, 133–135, 138–140

NAACP:
    aims of, xiv, 3, 321
    in Chicago, 13–14
    in Dayton, 108–109, 181
    in Delaware, 24
    in Detroit, 37, 39, 40
    displays interest in Dayton, 160
    effect on black teachers, 10–11
    in Little Rock, 6
    in North Carolina, 9
    in Oakland, 34, 35
    in San Francisco, 31, 32
    in St. Louis, 44, 45
    sued HEW, 16
Nashville, Tennessee, 27–30
National Institute of Education, 303
National Teachers Exam, 10–11
neighborhood schools:
    in Boston, 19
    defense of, 161–162, 332
    similar among Catholics, 229
Nevin, David, 56–59
New Futures. *See* Dayton New Futures
New Orleans, 61–63
newspapers:
    and catholic schools, 213, 215
    and desegregation, 104–105, 161–162
    and encounter groups, 232
    and superintendent, 165–166
    and parties, 175–176
    and private schools, 246–247
Niles, Curtis, 207–208
Nixon, Richard:
    and desegregation, 17
    creates National Institute of Educa-
        tion, 303
    and model cities, 148, 150

Oakland, California, 34–37
Ohio, state of:
    compulsory school attendance, 86
    legally segregated schools, 84
Ohio State Department of Education:
    closing schools, 107

and ethnic studies, 287–289
recommendation for Dayton, 102
open enrollment in Chicago Catholic
  Schools, 64–67
open enrollment in public schools. *See*
  freedom of choice
Open Enrollment Voluntary Exchange,
  220–222
open and fair housing, 142–148
Orfield, Gary, 59

Patterson, John H., 80–81
Pettigrew, Thomas:
  on clergy, 49–50
  on white flight, 22
Phillips, Chief Judge:
  Dayton board guilt, 197–198
  remands decision, 187–188
Powell, Adam Clayton, 14
Poynter, Reverend Gail A., 231–234
private schools:
  and desegregation in Dayton, 201
  in Dayton, 241–244
  effect on public schools, 59
  in Nashville, 29
  survey of, 55–59
  tuition grants for, 9
  See also Center City School

quotas:
  in Chicago Catholic Schools, 66
  for housing, 131–132

Racial Imbalance Act, 17–18
Reagan, Ronald, 305
resegregation:
  Academy of Our Lady, 65–67
  in Dayton, 95, 97
resident control:
  in city wide Model Cities, 149
  in Model Cities, 118
  problems with, 122–123
Riessman, Frank, 294–295
rights, human, xv, 3, 332
riots:
  among students, 96–97
  in Dayton, 91–94, 116, 117, 120, 129
  in Detroit, 37–38
Riot Study Committee, Mayors Ad Hoc,
  92–93
Romney, George, 145
Rossell, Christine, 73, 279–280

Rubin, Judge Carl:
  dismiss complaint, 196
  first opinion, 182–183
Rummel, Archbishop Joseph, 62–63
Ryan, William, 297

San Francisco, California, 30–33
Sausalito, California, 282–283
Save Our Schools movement, 325
school board elections in Dayton, 105–
  108, 157–177, 326–327
Schuster, Rev. James F., 227–228
segregated parishes:
  in Chicago, 63
  in New Orleans, 61
Serving Our Schools (SOS), 105–106,
  175–177, 325–327
Sisters of Notre Dame, 65, 135, 215
site-based management, 276
Southern Christian Leadership Conference, 51, 52
Spring Valley Academy, 243
St. Agnes Elementary School, 135–137
St. Leo Community School, 71
St. Louis, Missouri, 41–46
St. Thomas Community School, 71–72
student transfers:
  in Dayton, 195
  in Nashville, 29–30
superintendents:
  in Chicago, 14–15
  in Dayton, 97–98, 105–107, 157–
    160, 162–166, 313–316, 325,
    327
  in Greensboro, 9
  and IGE, 271–272
  and magnet schools, 277
  in St. Louis, 42–43
suspension of students, 42–43
Swann v Charlotte-Mecklenburg:
  approve ratios, 3
  effect in Dayton, 187, 197
  effect on Nashville, 28

tax levies:
  in Dayton, 105–108, 195
  in Detroit, 38
teacher unions, xvii, 12, 26, 98–99, 168–
  169
Temple Christian School, 201, 242
Thomas, M. Donald, 286
Thurmond, Strom, 5

U.S. Civil Rights Act:
  title IV, 16–17
  title VI, 13
U.S. Commission on Civil Rights:
  race relations in Dayton, 93
  support of citizens, 74
  on white flight, 23
U.S. Department of Health, Education,
    and Welfare:
  effect on black teachers, 11
  pressure in Dayton, 95–96, 109
  role of, 13–17, 322
U.S. Division of Equal Opportunity, 96
U.S. Housing and Community Develop-
    ment Act, 147

U.S. Housing and Urban Development
    Act, 144

Whalen, Charles W.,162
white flight:
  in Boston, 21
  in Catholic schools, 64–69, 234–235,
    330–331
  controversy about causes, 22–24
  in Dayton, 201–202
Wilmington, Delaware, 24–27
Wine, Joe, 130–140
Wisconsin Center for Individualized
    Schooling, 265–266

Riley